EARLY ENGLISH STAGES

1300 to 1660

Volume Two 1576 to 1660, Part I

EARLY ENGLISH STAGES 1300 to 1660
By
Glynne Wickham

Volume One 1300 to 1576

Volume Two 1576 to 1660, Part I

Volume Two 1576 to 1660, Part II

Volume Three Plays and their Makers to 1576

Volume Four Requiem and an Epilogue

EARLY ENGLISH STAGES

1300 to 1660

Volume Two 1576 to 1660, Part I

by

GLYNNE WICKHAM

London and New York

First published 1963 by Routledge & Kegan Paul Ltd
and Columbia University Press

This edition first published 2002
by Routledge
11 New Fetter Lane, London EC4P 4EE

Routledge is an imprint of the Taylor & Francis Group

© 1963, 2002 Glynne Wickham

Typeset by RefineCatch Limited, Bungay, Suffolk
Printed and bound in Great Britain by
TJI Digital, Padstow, Cornwall

British Library Cataloguing in Publication Data
A catalogue record for this book is available from the British Library

ISBN 0–415–19782–1 (set)
ISBN 0–415–19784–8 (volume 2, part I)

Publisher's note
The publisher has gone to great lengths to ensure the quality of this reprint
but points out that some imperfections in the original book may be apparent.

Inigo Jones' Backcloth for the first scene, *Luminalia* (1638). (See Notes to Illustrations, p. 379.)

EARLY
ENGLISH
STAGES

1300 to 1660

Volume Two 1576 to 1660, Part I

by
GLYNNE WICKHAM
Head of the Department of Drama, University of Bristol

Routledge and Kegan Paul
LONDON

TO
MY WIFE

PREFACE

IN Volume One I have tried to collect together a wide variety of source material relating to stage practice in the Middle Ages. The governing factor in the choice of this material was the idea that what is seen in the theatre matters at least as much to an audience as what is heard: in other words, that records of spectacle are at least as worthy the attention of historians as literary texts. As a result of this attempt to give equal weight to the visual and aural elements of dramatic art and to regard audiences as individual human beings, it became clear that our early drama could not be regarded as a self-conscious, self-contained art form. Many varied pursuits and pastimes of everyday life contributed much more to stage practice in the Middle Ages than anything deliberately formulated by theorists or critics of the time as indigenous or proper to the medium.

Colour symbolism in stage costume, for example, was not, as we might think, the bright invention of some designer or producer, but was taken over from both the ecclesiastical iconography of mosaic, fresco, stained glass and statuary and from the conventions of Heraldry: as an identification device long familiar to society at large, it was therefore a good one for identifying characters in a play. Or again, music in stage directions concerning action involving God or angels is there not for emotive effect or 'atmosphere', as we might think, but because music *was* harmony and so was heaven. Music was heaven and heaven was music—as everyone knew who had ever read Augustine or Boethius, and as others who could not read had come to know by word of mouth from those who could. * It is even harder for us to realize how directly audiences of the Middle Ages associated the characters in their biblical and moral plays with the here and now. Herod, Abraham, Peace or Lechery were assumed to have come, as it were, from their homes, to be among the audience, as visible, as tangible, as real, in short, as human as any individual in that audience, speaking their language, conducting their social and political affairs along identical lines, and thus ironing out time past and time future into an immediate present equated with eternity. Above all, we must learn to

* See John Stevens, 'Music in Mediaeval Drama', in *Proceedings of the Musical Association*, 84th Session, 1957/58.

recognize that the audiences for this theatre possessed the capacity to accept mimetic action on two levels simultaneously. Where 'actor' and 'character' were inevitably fused within the same person, they nevertheless remained distinguished from one another for the beholders as 'the person representing' and 'the person represented'. This dual concept of the actor at work on the stage is about as far removed as can be imagined from the modern ideal of equating the character with the acting of it so closely as to simulate actuality of feeling and behaviour down to the smallest detail. This double image, not the photographic reproduction of the seemingness of things, was their stage realism. Always, contemporary philosophy dictated the inner meaning of the things said or done and made explicit in the drama; contemporary practice in real life dictated the form in which it was expressed on the stage. The forms existed to express the meaning and not as ends in themselves. Plot, character and language were framed and handled to compel attention, and attention was focused on the meaning which, in its turn, had immediate significance and relevance both for the individual spectator and for the society of which the individuals were members.

Armed with this source material, it is possible in this second volume of *Early English Stages* to trace the progress of this tradition through the sixteenth and seventeenth centuries, assuming that its basically emblematic stage-conventions will survive until changes in philosophical thought and in real life practice have become large enough to make those conventions meaningless to their audiences. Revolutionary changes in religious and political thought on the one hand, and in social behaviour on the other, characterize the sixteenth century in England. It is thus natural to anticipate some reflection of them in theatre practice both on the stage and in the auditorium. By far the most important of these three changes is that in religious thought, characterized by the Reformation and, specifically, by the transference of the headship of the Church of England from the Pope to the sovereign.* The sovereign's assumption of ultimate authority in doctrinal matters automatically translated the subject matter of a predominantly religious drama into a political issue. State censorship becomes inevitable, and the very concept of drama as a means by which to mirror the cosmos in art is itself threatened: by 1660 this concept is virtually dead.

The concept of independent nationhood, developed at the expense of internationalism, marks the second change in the thinking

---

* See *EES*, i, Ch. IV and Appendix D.

of sixteenth century society that finds expression in the theatre. It is reflected most acutely in the formulation of dramatic theory differing widely from country to country, but common to all in one respect: a gradual exposure of divergence between the characteristics of life as lived in a country and the traditional stage conventions employed to depict it in the theatre. Devices evolved through an approach to art which sought to make eternity live in the present came to seem inadequate for the full depiction of the particular national and individual moment. Where England and the English are concerned, Ben Jonson crystallizes this sentiment in his Prologue to *Every Man In His Humour*.

> Though neede make many *Poets*, and some such
> As art, and nature have not betterd much;
> Yet ours, for want, hath not so lov'd the stage,
> As he dare serve th'ill customes of the age:
> Or purchase your delight at such a rate,
> As, for it, he himselfe must justly hate.
> To make a child, now swadled, to proceede
> Man, and then shoote up, in one beard, and weede,
> Past threescore yeeres: or, with three rustie swords,
> And helpe of some few foot-and-halfe-foote words,
> Fight over *Yorke*, and *Lancasters* long jarres:
> And in the tyring-house bring wounds, to scarres.
> He rather prayes, you will be pleas'd to see
> One such, to day, as other playes should be.
> Where neither *Chorus* wafts you ore the seas;
> Nor creaking throne comes downe, the boyes to please;
> Nor nimble squibbe is seene, to make afear'd
> The gentlewomen; nor roul'd bullet heard
> To say, it thunders; nor tempestuous drumme
> Rumbles, to tell you when the storme doth come;
> But deedes, and language, such as men doe use.*

The peculiar bibliographical circumstances surrounding this famous Prologue only serve to confirm my contention. The play was first performed at the Globe in 1598 (Shakespeare being one of the actors) and printed in Quarto in 1601. The Prologue does not accompany this edition of the play, but appears in the Folio of 1616. The supposition that it was added for some comparatively late revival of the play is substantiated by Jonson's most recent editors on the grounds that 'it implies a security of conviction in dramatic theory which it is very doubtful whether Jonson had in 1598 or even in 1601 attained.'†

* *Works*, iii, p. 303.
† See *Works*, i, pp. 333 *et seq.*

The third major change relates to social behaviour, and affects the auditorium of theatres more sharply than the stage. The mediaeval concept of an hierarchical society where position and privilege is geared by a kind of slide rule to responsibility and service is threatened in the sixteenth century by the new power of monetary wealth.* The increasing distinction of classes in society brought about by the power of money to work changes in the hierarchy of feudal degree brings with it a corresponding increase in the outward display of social status and privilege. This is reflected in the theatre by the splitting of the audience into broad social strata governed by conditions of admission (prices and entrée) and with it a divorce between sophisticated and popular taste. Whether one compares the range of admission prices at the Private Theatres with those prevailing in the Public Theatres, or whether one compares the hissing of John Fletcher's *The Faithful Shepherdess* off the stage of the Globe in 1609 with its successful revival at Court in 1634, the moral is the same.

My prime purpose therefore in this volume is to exploit the new material collected in Volume I by applying the conclusions that can be derived from it to the factual material concerning the theatre in the period 1576–1660 that is already available in print, as well as to such new material as I have happened to find.

Broadly speaking, Book I of this volume is devoted to an assessment of the nature of the drama and theatre which the sixteenth century inherited from the mediaeval past, and provides an account of how this tradition stood up to the assaults of religious, political and social changes of the sixteenth century. This has seemed to me an indispensable preliminary to any fresh attempt to determine the physical appearance of Elizabethan and Jacobean theatres and the nature of the performances given in them: for whether it is Shakespeare's plays, or the Globe Theatre, or Richard Burbage's acting which happens to be of special interest to each of us, all of them are as much the product of a reaction against the established past as they are signposts to a future which had still to be defined. They all take their particular place, but only as single items within a religious, political, social and aesthetic upheaval of revolutionary proportions. If then we want to view them accurately, we must try to set them within an historical context which is far wider than is generally allowed in most of the existing studies of special aspects of the subject: for that context, to borrow a phrase from the Tournament, is nothing short of the Pas d'Armes of cosmic drama in England.

* See L. C. Knights, *Drama and Society in the Age of Jonson*, 1937.

Book II of this volume (together with the whole of the final volume now in preparation) concerns theatre buildings and performances given in them. Space in this present volume allows an examination of changes in aesthetic taste during the sixteenth and seventeenth centuries, and permits a detailed investigation of conditions of play production both in London and in the provinces from the building of The Theater in 1576 until its demolition in 1598.

*   *   *

An inevitable price to be paid for dividing an essentially homogeneous subject into three separate volumes by arbitrary date lines is to seem to split it into self-contained and independent parts corresponding to the periods of historical time prescribed by the date lines. In this instance, however, where Volume I is subtitled *1300–1576*, Volume II *1576–1660 (part 1)* and Volume III *1576–1660 (part 2)*, the date lines of division should not be interpreted as hard and fast in every detail. In the first volume I have tried to depict the growth of English theatrical tradition up to the chosen date line, 1576, and to point out how far beyond 1576 that tradition was likely to stretch. In this second volume, while primarily concerned with what is new on our own side of the date line, I am necessarily interested also in whatever roots these novel elements had already put down on the far side of the date line. As a result some subjects come in for separate treatment in both volumes, yet are not treated as a whole in either. For example, the Tudor Interlude. I have argued in Volume I that the Interlude is the crucible in which a predominantly amateur and religious drama came to be translated into a predominantly professional and secular one: moral and scriptural Interludes of the sixteenth century look back towards the mediaeval past. Scholarly, farcical, neo-classical Interludes however, look forward to a different future, forecasting regular tragedy and comedy. They cannot therefore be ignored in Volume II. They merit discussion in both volumes, but from a different standpoint and with different aspects accented in each. Thus I have deliberately excluded from the first volume any serious discussion of humanism, of the Reformation, of the Renaissance, or of the interaction of one upon the other, all of which govern the growth and the form of the Tudor Interlude, since each of these forces impels a breach with the mediaeval past rather than its perpetuation into the future: these aspects of the subject can be handled more appropriately within the present volume.

In dividing the material in this way and ignoring the dateline as between one volume and the next from time to time, my object has been to preserve a consistency of approach to the subject as a whole which, despite division by date line, in fact reflects faithfully the essential duality of the old and the new in theatrical thought and deed that runs across the datelines in both directions.

If choice of the year 1576 to serve as a date line marking the close of Volume I and the start of this Volume requires justification, it is this. In the year 1574 the Earl of Leicester's players were granted a royal Patent to perform regularly on weekdays as well as on public holidays in London: and in 1576 a member of that company of players, James Burbage, erected a building principally, if not exclusively, to enable these players to exploit the financial advantages of this Patent to their fullest extent. Before that time English drama had been an occasional affair, having its inspiration in religious devotion or social recreation: after that time financial reward tends to take precedence over both. Thus the year 1576 conveniently marks a watershed between what may reasonably be called 'a public service theatre' and what thereafter may with equal fairness be described as 'a commercial theatre.' The days of the former are not fully numbered until a Commonwealth under a Lord Protector replaces hereditary monarchy in England: nor does a commercial theatre come to reign supreme and unrivalled until the Restoration of that monarchy: but the transition between the two is accurately pinpointed in the building of 'The Theater' in 1576. Thus if the first drama in these islands that can be described as English was one of worship, and if its successor was one of social recreation, then the third and last that must be included within the title 'Early English Stages' is the strictly commercial theatre which mirrors in its beginnings the rise of capitalism in English society and which, despite the occasional protests of peasants, poets, philosophers and pedants during the next three hundred years, has stayed with us ever since. Only in quite recent times has there been any marked revival of that amateur dramatic life in the nation at large which was so widespread in Tudor England until the excommunication of Queen Elizabeth I in 1570, and the threat of foreign invasion, caused it to be suppressed.

The date line dividing Volume II from Volume III, 1597/98 is again chosen arbitrarily for convenience, but it too takes its justification from the nature of the subject. It could be argued that 1604/05 would be a better date for division, since choice of it would separate the open stages of the Elizabethan era from the proscenium-arched stages which Inigo Jones introduced into Jacobean England in that year, and which were destined to eclipse their predecessors in general favour under Charles I and Charles II.

This change, however, was one initiated in Court circles at the instigation of aristocratic and academic enthusiasts: it had no bearing upon popular taste and, at least to start with, no bearing on popular practice in the public theatres. A change of far greater consequence to the professional stage, at least in my opinion, was the order issued by Elizabeth's Privy Council in 1597 for the suppression of *all* the London Playhouses, an Order which in the event was not enforced: for I see this Order as marking the end of a period of uneasy experiment during which professional acting companies were seeking to secure a livelihood for themselves at the expense of amateur groups, and the start of a period in which all theatrical activity was strictly regulated by royal licence. Inigo Jones' work for the Court Masks was merely one feature of this activity and derived directly from these changed conditions. Detailed study of theatre building and play production thus divides itself between this volume and its sequel by the date line 1597/98. This volume concludes with a study of the Swan, built in 1596, but does not extend to include the building of the first Globe which opened its doors to the public in 1599.

GLYNNE WICKHAM

Department of Drama
University of Bristol

ACKNOWLEDGEMENTS

AT a time when it is becoming increasingly difficult for anyone in academic life with administrative responsibilities to keep up with even a respectable fraction of those developments in research and shifts of opinion in criticism which affect his own subject, an author's debt to other scholars who send him off-prints of their own articles or loan him their own gleanings is necessarily great. I am particularly indebted on this account to Professor F. P. Wilson for the loan of his own transcript of the Accounts of the Office of Works in the period 1578 to 1642 (to be published as an Appendix to Volume III), and to Mr. D. S. Bland for a copy of his transcript of Guildhall MS. 4160, an account of the Combat at Barriers at the Inns of Court, 1616. N. D. Shergold and J. E. Varey have similarly kept me abreast of their own remarkable work in respect of the public stage in Spain during the sixteenth and seventeenth centuries: although the fruits of their work will figure more prominently in Volume III than in this, I think this is the proper place to acknowledge their assistance, since without it I should undoubtedly have found it much harder to determine how to divide the material relating to other subjects besides the Spanish between these two volumes.

I wish to thank the Librarian of the Society of Antiquaries for permission to consult the Fairholt Collection in the Society's Library and to photograph many items in it for inclusion among the illustrations to this volume and its sequel. My thanks are also due to the Town Clerk of Exeter for permission to photograph the ancient Guildhall, to the National Portrait Gallery, the Huntington Library, the H. M. de Young Museum in San Francisco and the Bibliothèque Nationale, Paris, for allowing me to photograph paintings, engravings and prints in their possession.

In preparing the text for the printer I am again deeply indebted to Mrs. Dora Pym both in point of criticism and of correction. Finally, I should like to thank my colleague, Miss Marion Jones, for spotting errors in the proofs which had escaped my attention, and Mr. Allan Bullock, Lecturer in Italian in the University of Bristol for his help in preparing the translation of the long extract from the *Diario* of G. Pavoni which is printed in Appendix H.

CONTENTS

LIST OF ILLUSTRATIONS

FIGURES

xix

LIST OF ILLUSTRATIONS

PLATES

LIST OF ILLUSTRATIONS

xxi

ABBREVIATIONS, CUE-TITLES, SYMBOLS, ETC.

Arches of Triumph	Stephen Harrison, *The arches of triumph erected in honour of K. James I at his maiesties entrance and passage through his honourable citty of London 15. March 1603. invented and published by S. Harrison and graven by W. Kip*, London, 1604, fol.
Bowers' Dekker	The Dramatic Works of Thomas Dekker, ed. Fredson Bowers, 4 vols., 1953–61.
Bullen's Middleton	The Works of Thomas Middleton, ed. A. H. Bullen, 8 vols., 1885–86.
CM	Enid Welsford, *The Court Masque*, Cambridge, 1927.
Davenant	*The Dramatic Works of Sir William Davenant with Prefatory Memoir and Notes*, ed. J. Maidment and W. H. Logan, 5 vols., 1872–74.
EES	G. Wickham, *Early English Stages, 1300–1660*, Vol. I (1300–1576), 1958.
ES	E. K. Chambers, *The Elizabethan Stage*, 4 vols., Oxford, 1923.
English Drama	W. C. Hazlitt, *The English Drama and Stage under the Tudor and Stuart Princes, 1543–1642*, printed for the Roxburghe Library, 1869.
EDC	J. T. Murray, *English Dramatic Companies, 1558–1642*, 2 vols., London, 1910.
EP	R. Withington, *English Pageantry, An Historical Outline*, 2 vols., Harvard, 1918–20.
Fishmongers Pageant	J. G. Nichols, *The Fishmongers Pageant on Lord Mayor's Day 1616 devised by Anthony Munday* (ed. Nichols), London, 1844, fol.
Govt. Reg.	V. C. Gildersleeve, *Government Regulation of the Elizabethan Drama*, N.Y., 1908. Reprint, 1961.
Henslowe's Diary	W. W. Greg, *Henslowe's Diary*, ed. with commentary in two vols.: i. Text ii. Commentary, 1904–08.
Henslowe Papers	W. W. Greg, *Henslowe Papers*, being documents supplementary to *his* Diary, 1907
HEP	T. Warton, *A History of English Poetry* (a full reprint —text and notes—of ed. London, 1778–81), London, 1840.

J & CS	G. E. Bentley, *The Jacobean and Caroline Stage*, 5 vols., 1941–56.
Machyn's Diary	*The Diary of Henry Machyn, citizen and Merchant-Taylor of London, 1550–1563*, ed. J. G. Nichols for Camden Society, Vol. XLII, 1848.
MSC I, II, III & V	*Collections, Volume I*, ed. by W. W. Greg for the Malone Society, 1909–11.
	Collections, Volume II, ed. by W. W. Greg for the Malone Society in three parts, 1913, 1923 and 1931. References given under *MSC II* are to the 1931 composite volume, "Blackfriars Records" (p. 1) to "Dramatic Records: The Lord Chamberlain's Office" (p. 321 *et seq*).
	Collections, Volume III, ed. by D. J. Gordon and J. Robertson for the Malone Society, 1954.
	Collections, Volume V, ed. by F. P. Wilson for the Malone Society, 1959 (1960).
Med. Stage	E. K. Chambers, *The Mediaeval Stage*, 2 vols., 1903.
Lucas' Webster	*The Complete Works of John Webster*, ed. F. L. Lucas, 4 vols., 1927.
Origines Italiennes	H. Leclerc, *Les Origines italiennes de l'architecture théâtrale moderne*, Paris, 1946.
PJI	J. Nichols, *The Progresses, Processions and Magnificent Festivities of King James the First*, 4 vols., London, 1828.
PQE	J. Nichols, *The Progresses and Public Processions of Queen Elizabeth*, 3 vols., London, 1st ed. 1788–1804. Unless the page number is definitively clear, references are given to the signature and not to the page.
R.O. (E & M)	A. Feuillerat, "Documents relating to the Revels at Court in the Time of King Edward VI and Queen Mary" (The Loseley MSS.) in *Materialen zur kunde des alteren Englischen Dramas*, ed. W. Bang, vol. XLIV, Louvain, 1914.
R.O. (Eliz.)	A. Feuillerat, "Documents relating to the Office of the Revels in the Time of Queen Elizabeth", in *Materialen zur kunde des alteren Englischen Dramas*, ed. W. Bang, vol. XXI, Louvain, 1908.
Scenes and Machines	L. B. Campbell, *Scenes and Machines on the English Stage during the Renaissance: a classical revival*, 1923. Reprint, 1961.
Survey	John Stow, *The Survey of London*, ed. C. L. Kingsford, 2 vols., 1908.
Works	*The Dramatic Works of Thomas Heywood now first collected with illustrative notes and a memoir of the author*, 5 vols., London, 1874.
Works	Ben Jonson, *Complete Works*, ed. C. Herford and P. Simpson, 10 vols., 1925–52.

BOOK ONE

Regulating the Theatre

I

NEW STAGES FOR OLD

WHEN obliged to condense into a manageable narrative the mass of source material that survives from Elizabethan, Jacobean and Caroline England concerning the stage, together with the volumes of critical works written subsequently about it—or rather to distil from all this material the quintessence of what happened and why—it is probably wise to start with some simple statement of belief, before attempting to argue any particular viewpoint in its full context of detailed evidence, lest this detail should distort or overwhelm the main gist.

The theme of the first volume then, with all detail stripped away, was that the stagecraft of Shakespeare's theatre represented a climax to centuries of mediaeval experiments rather than a new beginning of Renaissance inspiration. These experiments, as I viewed them, originated in a theatre that drew its vitality from religious worship, but came slowly to be matched by a theatre provided wholly for social recreation. By Elizabethan times, the distinctive qualities of the theatre of social recreation—professional actors, performances at times other than Calendar Festivals, compact plays for relatively small casts—were becoming predominant, while the qualities of the theatre of worship were losing ground as a result of official censorship. A consequent reappraisal of all dramatic values and theatre practice, as I argued then, was likely to have had to take place during Elizabeth's reign and after. By no other reasoning could I explain to myself the known fact that the proscenium arched stage, with its painted perspectives, should have been introduced into England less than ten years after the building of the first Globe theatre, and the still more extraordinary fact that this new style of theatre had apparently won sufficient approval to doom the Globe style of theatre to less than a hundred years of active life.

These changes have proved as difficult for historians to explain as they appear startling and drastic in the context of their own time. However, I would like to beg the reader's indulgence and ask him to accept the following explanation, temporarily without question, and then to test it against the evidence offered in later chapters of this book. My argument, stated in its simplest terms, is that a stage of mediaeval invention, employed for indoor and outdoor performances alike, religious and secular, was transmitted from the fifteenth century to the sixteenth and from the first of the Tudor sovereigns to the last. James Burbage's 'Theater' of 1576 and the other Public Playhouses imitated from it were novel in giving permanency to both a stage and an auditorium which had previously been built as required and dismantled immediately after use, a stage and auditorium where place had been represented in terms of symbols or emblems. Neither before nor after this changeover from occasional to permanent structures was the representation of place on the stage governed by notions of verisimilitude or photographic reproductions of actual landscape. By contrast, the proscenium arched stage designed by Inigo Jones in 1605 for Jonson's *Mask of Blackness* clearly sought to express place in a landscape painter's terms of reference.

'First, for the *Scene*, was drawne a 𝕷𝖆𝖓𝖉𝖙𝖘𝖈𝖍𝖆𝖕, consisting of small woods, and here and there a void place fill'd with huntings; which falling, an artificiall sea was seene to shoote forth, as if it flowed to the land, raysed with waves, which seemed to move, and in some places the billow to breake, as imitating that orderly disorder, which is common in nature.'[1]

All Jones' experiments from this time forward are intimately related to providing the dramatic narrative of the author with scenic background conceived as landscape. Furthermore, the public playhouses built in Charles II's England conform with this new, landscape-artist's technique of stage picture and not with the earlier stage picture of representation by symbol.

I believe this to have been the salient difference between the Globe style of playhouse and that of the Jacobean and Caroline Court Mask. Viewed from this standpoint, Shakespeare's Globe and all other playhouses resembling it in architectural design are theatres which provide permanent homes for a stagecraft based on representation by formal symbols: the theatre of the Stuart Court Mask and the Restoration public playhouse has rejected this form of representation and is groping its way, however fitfully, towards the naturalism of actuality. From the Globe one can look backwards over the centuries and, in the *sepulchrum* of the liturgical *quem quaeritis* and in the *sedes* of later ceremonies, trace the beginnings of its stage conventions; but one cannot look forward. Its stage conventions do not develop: they are superseded. From the theatre of *The Mask of Blackness* one can look forward over the next three centuries to fully changeable scenery, to actuality for scenic background photographed by the ciné-camera, and nowadays transmitted instantaneously by the miracle of television; but one cannot look back. Its stage conventions do develop; but they have no English antecedents.

Anyone who cares to reflect upon this viewpoint for more than a

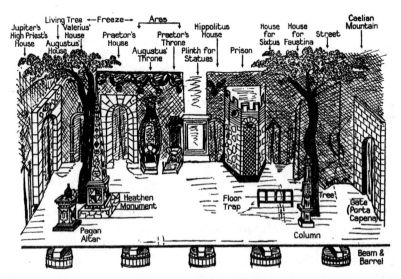

Fig. 1. Diagrammatic outline of the stage-setting for the play of St Lawrence, Cologne, 1581. The stage is made of planks nailed to wooden beams raised on barrels. Curtains hang in the arches that represent 'houses'. The thrones are backed with damask cloth and velvet. The monuments are marbled. The audience faces the stage.

moment or so will perceive that a change in attitude to scenic representation as fundamental as this must have consequences for other related elements in drama, not least to speech and language. Poetry is an artificial language, a strictly formalized manner of speech. On the stage its artifice is in constant danger of exposure. It is not without significance therefore that prose tends to replace poetry as the normal language of the theatre within the sixty-year period (1605–1665): for this is only another aspect of the changing attitude to scenic representation. In 'heroic tragedy' Davenant and Dryden tried to protract the life of that poetic stage-language which they had inherited from Beaumont and Fletcher,

Shakespeare, Marlowe and the anonymous authors of the Miracle Cycles, by linking it to the new landscape-conventions of stage-craft. Buckingham's *The Rehearsal* gives us a contemporary record of how indigestible audiences found the mixture. Dryden's own desertion of the form in 1677 merely acknowledges as accomplished fact what, in 1618, Jonson had forecast, in the light of his experiences in working on Court Masks with 'Inigo, Marquess Wouldbe', would ultimately follow.

> 'Pack w(i)th your pedling Poetry to the Stage,
> This is the money-gett, Mechanick Age!'[2]

The 'stage' that Jonson speaks of here is the public theatre of his own time where the conventions for representing place in terms of symbols, whatever their shortcomings, at least still serve the poet and do not invite the audience to place a rational viewing of the physical scene as a barrier between the poet's image and their own sensibility to it. This I believe to be the essence of the change both in theatrical and dramatic forms in England during the period 1576–1660 to the detailed study of which this present volume is devoted.

I have simplified the nature of the change to the barest bone in order that it may be recognized. When, however, one comes to consider the detail, the flesh and tissue as it were upon the skeleton, the actual processes of change appear to have been very slow and so gradual as to seem at times self-contradictory. For instance, when John Webb designed the settings for Davenant's *The Siege of Rhodes* in 1656, he inscribed the word 'Rhodes' in bold letters in a 'compartment' cresting the proscenium arch; the purpose was thereby to label the perspective landscapes on the stage in front of which the action and dialogue passes, and thus enable the audience to identify the scene. Yet is this practice so very different from the 'scriptures' with which Lydgate labelled his Pageant theatres of 1432, or from those which Jonson and Dekker affixed to their triumphal arches for James I's Coronation in 1603?* Or again, if the new techniques of scenic representation employed in Court Masks between 1605 and 1613 were so startlingly different and better than the old ones, why when the first Globe theatre was destroyed by fire in 1612, was it not rebuilt to the new pattern instead of being virtually a replica of itself, albeit 'fairer than before'? More remarkable still, when the Fortune Theatre was burnt down in 1621 (three years after the building of Inigo Jones' Banqueting

---

* See *EES*, i, pp. 82–83 and 102–103, and Plates XII, No. 15 and XVII, No. 22.

Hall in Whitehall) that too was rebuilt to resemble its former self
and not the new-style theatre of the Masks. Why? These examples,
and many others which we shall encounter later, lead me to suppose
that the actual paraphernalia of stage settings, the techniques of
construction and so on, were not subject at the time to nearly such
drastic changes in physical appearance as the words 'Apron Stage'
and 'Proscenium Arch' have come to suggest to us. We have come
to regard the stage of the typical Elizabethan public playhouse as
an open one, essentially free of scenic clutter, the stage of the
Stuart Mask as a closed one, essentially complicated by a maze of

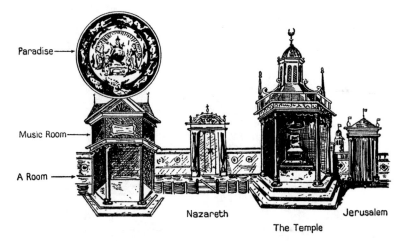

Fig. 2. Diagrammatic outline of 'mansions' or 'houses' for the Passion Play,
Valenciennes, 1547, simplified from the illumination in B.N. MS. Français,
12, 536. The music room, or 'place for the sileté' as it is labelled in the
'compartment' below Paradise, should be compared with the trumpeter's
position in De Witt's sketch of the Swan Theatre (Plate VIII, No. 11).

scenic machinery and landscape painting. We have come in consequence to contrast the two, almost as opposites in appearance,
and certainly with far greater definition than I think we have
evidence to warrant.

I am myself going to argue in subsequent chapters of this
volume and its sequel that a Jacobean playgoer who had attended
Samuel Daniel's Mask at Court in 1604, *The Vision of the Twelve
Goddesses*, who had seen Jonson's and Jones' *The Mask of Blackness*
at Court in 1605 and who had attended several plays both at Court
and in the public playhouses between 1604 and 1606, would not
have been aware of many material differences between the stage
conventions that met his gaze on these several occasions. Even

7

twenty years later, as Charles I succeeded to his father's throne, and when Inigo Jones' experiments in scene-changing were well advanced, I doubt whether this same theatregoer would have remarked much more by way of difference between the old style of theatre and the new than that the 'houses' (*sedes, domus, aedes*) which had been familiar to his father and grandfather as well as to him were now strictly organized according to the optical rules of

FIG. 3. Diagrammatic outline of a stage setting for a Mask by Inigo Jones. Scenic units of the 'mansion' type are here arranged to accord with the optical principles of a landscape in receding perspective. The design, among those in the Duke of Devonshire's Collection at Chatsworth House, corresponds in many respects to the stage directions for the first scene of Thomas Carew's *Cœlum Britannicum* (1634).

perspective instead of being loosely spread about, either round the floor of the hall or, in the public theatres, towards the back of the stage. Whether situated to suit the actors' convenience or arranged in relation to the 'vanishing point' of the designer's drawing board, the scenic objects in question continue to be thought of as 'houses', 'devices'. (Cf. Fig. 3 with Fig. 2, and the Frontispiece with Fig. 1.)

In short, I am going to argue that the so-called 'mansion staging' or *décor simultané* of the Middle Ages was imported intact into the first permanent theatres of Elizabethan London; that it survived in the public theatres with some modifications occasioned by increasingly adroit use of the tiring-house wall (its doors, its recesses, its

8

windows) until these theatres were closed in 1642; that it served
the indoor plays and masks of Elizabeth's Court, and that it was
reorganized rather than banished from Court in the landscape
formalism of Inigo Jones' experiments beneath and behind the proscenium arch. I am thus asking the reader to accept a paradox. On
the one hand we must try to visualize the stage-craft of the period
1576–1660 and beyond as essentially homogeneous—traditional,
emblematic techniques of mediaeval invention undergoing various
slow modifications. These changes were caused in part by the
empirical reasons of practical convenience and in part by a desire
among the more sophisticated members of society to formalize both
dramatic structure and its accompanying scenic background in a
manner more rational than had been deemed necessary before. On
the other hand we must try to recognize that the differences in
stage-craft which characterize the extreme limits of this same
period 1576–1660 represent a radical change in the balance of
power in the theatre between the architect-painter-machinist and
the poet-dramatist. The slow, piecemeal nature of the changes in
stage conventions, so my argument goes, served to conceal the
emerging pre-eminence of what Dekker called 'dumb poesie'—or
'stage design' in our vocabulary—over what he termed 'speaking
pictures'—or the dialogue, plot, theme and characters of the
dramatist as we would call it. This emblematic language of
Dekker's itself provides a vital clue to the nature of the change.
Jonson recognized what was happening; that 'which by a specious
fyne/ Terme of ye Architects is called Designe' he says, 'in ye
practised truth Destruction is/ Of any Art, . . .'[3]—but his was a
lone voice that fell on deaf ears among courtiers fascinated by the
novelty of Jones' changing pictures and dazzled by the spectacle of
the Queen and her family as active participants in the centre of
these pictures. These pictures, because more formal in concept and
design, were still far removed from those images of actuality which
flicker before us on our television screens, as the reader may quickly
judge for himself by visiting the little Court Theatre at Drotning-
holm in Sweden, or by glancing at the Frontispiece to this volume
and at Figure 3 on the previous page. Yet, somehow or other, both
the landscape settings of the Masks and the photographic realism
of television must be erased from our minds if we wish to resume
contact with the Elizabethan theatre and its methods. We must
contrive to forget these images of actuality which have, for so long
now, invited audiences to accept things seen and heard on stage or
screen at their face value. Instead we must try to substitute a
vision of actors and dramatists working in a theatre that was as

acutely alive to the phenomena of actuality as we are, but which preferred to devote its energies to interpreting these phenomena as emblems of the spiritual realities behind them. Secular the Elizabethan theatre undoubtedly became as a result of state censorship: but the emblematic form of dramatic art which it presented to its audiences was recognizable still as a legacy from the theatre of worship that had developed in the Middle Ages. With government of the universe at the centre, rather than the figure of some film-star or a popular 'personality', this drama was richer in texture than our own—as proportionately richer as the drama of Periclean Athens than that of Augustan Rome. Expressed at its simplest, what we are about to discuss in this volume in terms of the advent of the proscenium-arched, landscape stage, is the battle for pre-eminence in the English theatre between the emblem and the image: and no more graphic emblem could be found to figure this than the substitution of women for boy-actor impersonators of women in the presenting of female roles on the stage. Only if we are ready to accept a play with the houselights at full can we say that we are genuinely in touch with Elizabethan concepts of play-production.

If this change is to be my principal concern, it is to be coupled with another one of scarcely less importance, the relation of the particular pattern of change in England to that followed in other European countries. In Italy it occurred earlier and was both swifter and more drastic. In Spain too the change occurs, but so slowly as hardly to be discernible except by comparing conditions at the extreme time limits of the period of change. In France it comes jerkily, in sudden fits and starts. Only in the Low Countries does the change in its timing appear to have something in common with that in England. There, as late as 1637, we can see in the Amsterdam *Schouwburg* a theatre built by a man thoroughly acquainted with Italy and its scenic landscape theatre, Jacob van Campen.[4] Yet this man preferred to base his design on the traditional stages of the Chambers of Rhetoric just as the builders of the second Globe theatre and the second Fortune in London had chosen, some years earlier, to copy their fire-wrecked wooden O's instead of Inigo Jones' novel landscape stage for Masks at Whitehall. Why then was the pattern of change among European countries not uniform? It is my belief that if we give this irregularity the study it deserves we may well get nearer to an accurate understanding of what happened in England than we should otherwise do if we confined our attention to a narrower, strictly national historical context. As I trust I have demonstrated adequately in

Volume I, an international religious drama common in all essentials to the whole of Europe in the thirteenth and fourteenth centuries was challenged in the fifteenth century, and maybe earlier, by a drama of courtly leisure and social recreation. This latter sort of drama was much more closely geared to national temperament and manners, because the product of individual Courts, than was the religious stage which had taken its genesis from, and continued to be governed by, a single Catholic Church. The English historian Edward Hall, for example, reporting on a Court Disguising in 1512, notes the presence in this secular entertainment of certain novel features: being of recognizably foreign origin they are worth reporting as such—"after the manner of Italy".* More important features of a similarly distinct, national kind characterize the French farce or the English Interlude with sufficient clarity for historians of dramatic literature to discuss them as specific and identifiable dramatic genres. Moreover, it was this drama of Courtly 'Revels' rather than the drama of religious Festivals that stood to gain most from the general reawakening of interest in the precedents of classical drama as interpreted and propagated by humanist patrons during the late fifteenth and early sixteenth centuries. What results therefore is a uniform pressure towards change in dramatic themes, structure and accompanying stage conventions in all European Court 'Revels' deriving from neo-classical studies and experiments. On the other hand this same pressure towards change loses much of its seeming uniformity as it becomes flavoured with the fast emerging differences of a specifically national character between one country and the next. When these differences of national temperament and manners become sufficiently pronounced to split into warring factions the uniform religious life and government shared by all Europe for over a thousand years, then indeed it becomes idle even to seek for uniformity of progress in the development of recreational drama in Court or academic circles. Had this theatre been anywhere a fully regular and professional theatre when these storm clouds broke over Europe, things might have been different, but it was not: it was at best the partner and rival of the more ancient religious stage. In these circumstances, the speed and nature of the change between one country and another in their various theatres of courtly leisure is inevitably interrupted and dislocated by the varied changes in the status of the religious stage. As religion becomes intertwined first with national politics and then with international causes, so the theatre everywhere becomes a subject of political controversy. In Italy, France

* See *EES*, i, p. 218.

and Spain, fear lest the religious stage should provide Protestant factions within the nation with an object of easy ridicule provokes swift and firm action: in Spain, Church and State ally with one another through the Inquisition to reform it: in Italy and France they agree to suppress it. In Protestant countries the theatre's roots in, and enduring links with Catholicism present a challenge, not to say a threat, of so disturbing an order as to demand the imposition of a similarly rigorous censorship and a curfew for very different reasons. It is these religious pressures on the theatre together with their varying consequences in different countries which so jolt and disrupt the ordinary sequence of change between one country and another during the sixteenth century: to posterity it thus appears that no coherent pattern of change of international application is remotely discernible. And yet I think that there is a pattern and that this pattern is discernible to us, or can become so, if we make the effort to view the theatre of the sixteenth century as a reflection of the life and times of which it was a part and not simply as itself or, more narrowly still, in terms of the life and works of any particular individual. It is beyond the scope of this volume to attempt to depict this pattern in any detail, but I do hope to indicate its probable outline and thereby to point a way to further investigation which it would be profitable for others to undertake. My own immediate interest is the impact of international changes in religious thinking and associated politics upon the English theatre. To do this adequately, I deem it necessary as a first priority to submit the words Renaissance and Reformation to scrutiny lest in using them as labels we oversimplify and confuse the very issues we are trying to disentangle and to clarify. The next priority will be to examine in detail the forms of censorship and control which both central and local government officials felt obliged to impose upon dramatists, actors and those charged with maintaining discipline among audiences as a consequence of changes in religious government and doctrine. Then, and only then, as I believe, is it likely that conclusions will emerge that can suffice to explain both how James Burbage came to build his 'Theater' in 1576, and not before or after, and the actual changes in stage practice that took place in this country between 1576 and the building of theatres in Dorset Gardens and Lincoln's Inn Fields in the first years of Charles II's reign.

II

REFORMATION AND
RENAISSANCE

ALMOST any aspect of the Elizabethan and Jacobean stage, if
looked at within the narrow limits of Shakespeare's lifetime,
appears *ad hoc*, expedient, arbitrary. Shakespeare's 'wooden O'
can possess for us the reality of a stage and auditorium, arena-
shaped and built of wood, and yet seem to lack both predecessor
and successor. Boy actors can strut upon these stages of our mind's
eye as the creators of Juliet, Viola or Cleopatra; yet we are hard
put to recognize their prototypes in Miracle Cycle or Morality
Play, and can hardly forget that boys were soon to be eclipsed by
women in the theatres of the Restoration. Some of the playwrights
and actors who worked in this 'wooden O' we acknowledge to
have been men of sufficient influence and affluence to endow a
College of God's Gift at Dulwich or to buy a home on the scale of
New Place at Stratford from their earnings; others warrant description as murderers, bankrupts or alcoholics: bracketed together they stand before us as a race as far apart from their
anonymous predecessors as they lack parallel in subsequent centuries. Perhaps only the words Puritan and Courtier or Cavalier,
which for us figure largely in all studies of the subject, link this
theatre and its actors, its playwrights, its plays and its audiences to
a definite past and a recognizable future: for these words, in their
turn, have affinities with 'Reformation' and 'Renaissance', words
which by extension have come respectively to suggest a divorce
from an undesirable past and a movement into a desirable future.

Both words have been bandied about for several hundred years,
gaining a clarity of definition with the passage of time, but drifting
proportionately further away from the events which they are supposed to describe. 'Reformation' has come to be associated exclusively with ecclesiastical history, 'Renaissance' with the exodus
from the 'monkish darkness' of mediaeval scholasticism. The effect

has been twofold: on the one hand to make the sixteenth century appear to have been a time of far more sharply defined change in England, especially in the Church and in scholarship, than it in fact was, and, on the other, to obscure the detail of those actual changes, which, in aspects of life other than the Church and scholarship, truly characterize the sixteenth century. The theatre is a case in point. 'Mystery' and 'Morality' plays are assumed to have been replaced by 'comedy and 'tragedy', permanent theatres and perspective scenery to have replaced pageant-waggons, inn-yards and 'mansions'. Reformation and Renaissance are taken to have intervened between the primitive naïveté of the mediaeval stage and the dramatic splendours of post-Armada enlightenment.

In one sense of course this is true; for the Miracle and Morality plays which had formed the standard fare of theatre-goers in the fifteenth century, together with their accompanying waggons and mansions, are conspicuous by absence in the late seventeenth century. Yet in another sense it is untrue: for, as modern scholarship has been revealing steadily, much of the old was absorbed into the new, and in some respects changed in name only. If then we are perplexed today by the fact that historians have tended to represent these changes as being so much more radical than they actually were, we may explain it by their having taken them to be the natural consequences of the Reformation and the Renaissance: for both words have come to be associated with something the Victorians called Progress, and to imply both radical change and change for the better at that. Comparatively little thought has been given to the idea that one consequence of the Reformation may have been to put a brake on some aspects of the Renaissance and vice-versa. It would seem however from the evidence of the plays written at the time, and from that of documents concerning their performance, that ideas of Renaissance inspiration were in constant conflict with those of religious reform, while the aspirations of ecclesiastical reformers were perpetually obstructed by the support offered to the theatre by antiquarian apologists in high academic and social circles. The time has come therefore to start a new survey of theatrical practice in the sixteenth and seventeenth centuries by submitting both Reformation and Renaissance *as words* to scrutiny and, in more precise language, to try to discover what actual changes these blanket-labels have served to shroud. *

* C. S. Lewis introduces his volume on the sixteenth century in the *Oxford History of English Literature* (Vol. III) with a very long and useful discussion of this question; but as the drama is excluded from this volume, it is not in his brief to consider the consequences of his own findings to the theatre.

1 *Reformation*

Where the theatre is concerned, the most convenient starting point is Henry VIII's break with Rome and his subsequent assumption of supreme authority over the English Church: this we can both date precisely and associate with a precise change in theatre practice affecting actors and audiences. This event is pinpointed in the alterations made by the town clerk of Chester in 1532 to the document used annually for advertising the local Cycle of Miracle Plays.* The phrase 'and that every person disturbing the same plays in any manner or wise to be accursed by the authority of the Pope Clement's Bulls unto such time as he or they be absolved thereof' is neatly scored through: so too is the phrase 'not only upon pain of cursing by the authority of the said Pope Clement's Bulls, but also', which refers to the assembling of the audience.

These changes simply take note of the fact that the Pope is no longer deemed to possess any authority over the conduct of the actors or the audience. From thenceforth such matters lay solely with the monarch or his deputy on the spot, the mayor. But could the matter rest there? We have seen that in fact it did not; that the Banns and Proclamations for the Chester plays were altered again and again within the next sixty years, and that the alterations correspond closely to changes in the government of the country's religious life. We have seen moreover that the condition of the religious stage in Chester between 1570 and 1600 was paralleled in York, Wakefield, Coventry and Lincoln.† In short we are confronted with a gradual introduction of State Censorship, operated by the Court of High Commission for the North on behalf of the Privy Council in London acting for the sovereign; and this as a direct consequence of the Reformation.

If we want to know why this severe curtailing of free speech descended on 'merrie England' at the hands of 'good Queen Bess', we need only look at a succession of Acts of Parliament passed between 1543 and 1598 which survive on the Statute Book for our inspection.‡ The earliest of them suggests that Henry VIII had good reason to ponder the startlingly widespread effects of adding the words *fidei defensor* to his titles, not least in the theatre: from 1531 onwards, thanks to the work of Archbishop Cranmer and Lord Chancellor Cromwell, dramatic performances, public and private, had become a hotbed of political controversy. The Act of 1543 is

* See *EES*, i, pp. 342, 343.
† *Ibid.*, i, pp. 114 *et seq.*
‡ For details of the Acts see Ch. II, pp. 63, 67–69, 73, 75 and 80.

seemingly an inoffensive measure, since what it sets out to control is simply 'interpretacions of Scripture': but the qualification attached, 'contrarye to the doctryne set forth or to be set forth by the Kinges Majestie' is less innocuous.[1] This clause automatically links doctrinal argument with politics, since the arbiter is the sovereign.

We must try to remember here that the individuals involved in this controversy were members of a society in which the spoken word still counted for much more than the printed word. It was this fact that made the stage so troublesome to politicians. Edward VI and Elizabeth I found it necessary to equip the occupants of pulpits with a *Book of Homilies* to serve in lieu of original sermons lest preachers in doubt on points of doctrine should inadvertently wander into heresy and risk a prosecution on that account.[2] And if the pulpit served as a focus of opinion, so did the stage, since both attracted large assemblies of people most of whom were illiterate and ready to give themselves emotionally to the rhetorical declarations of accomplished orators.[3] When on to the nationwide division of opinion on the religious issue was grafted the emotionally inflammatory question of the succession to the throne, or, looked at the other way round, when the choice of sovereign had come to be inextricably linked with the form of religion to be practised in the country, preaching from stage or pulpit could quickly lead to breaches of the peace. Successive governments therefore between 1543 and 1603, whether Protestant under Henry VIII and Edward VI, Catholic under Mary, or of Protestant reaction under Elizabeth, found themselves obliged to bridle the theatre lest it serve to unseat them.

Tudor governments found their predicament in this respect further aggravated by two specifically theatrical factors inherited from the stagecraft of the Middle Ages—the acute proximity of the audience to the actors and the convention of direct address. * When audiences had been trained over many generations to regard themselves as actively engaged in the stage action rather than as passive onlookers outside it, and when actors had been schooled in the techniques of communicating with those audiences through such devices as the soliloquy, the aside and the rhetorical question, it is clear that the physical conditions of performance came much nearer to resembling those of a modern public meeting than anything made familiar to us by 'method' actors segregated from their audience by orchestra pit, front of house curtain and proscenium arch. And since these conditions of performance frame the pre-

---

* See *EES*, i, pp. 59 *et seq.*, and 249 *et seq.*

16

sentation of subject matter that was essentially topical, however formal the disguise of parable and allegory, the fears which Tudor governments professed towards the theatre can at least be appreciated by us as well grounded. Even stage costume was not without its dangers. Thus a play of Protestant polemic, for example, offers the following guidance to the producer concerning the actors' wardrobe.

'Lete Idolatry be decked lyke an olde wytche, Sodomy lyke a monke of all sectes, Ambycyon lyke a byshop, Covetousnesse lyke a pharyse or spyrituall lawer, false doctryne, lyke a popysh doctour, and hypocresy lyke a graye fryre.'[4]

The recurrent use of the word 'lyke' in this quotation provides us with the key to the problem as a whole: for everything about this drama was two-faced—a seeming exterior masking hidden truth.* Any play or acting is by its very nature pretence: this was admitted much more frankly in Tudor England than it is nowadays, and, in consequence, it was more natural for spectators to assume that what they saw and heard was an emblem in which truth was to be divined than that text, acting, costume and setting represented an exact copy or image of the actual world as most of us tend to assume today when watching a film or a television play.

Control, in terms of Tudor plays therefore, if it was to be effective, had to be of two kinds: censorship of the text and policing of the auditorium. The measures actually taken will be treated in detail in the course of the ensuing chapters: here it can suffice to single out only the most obvious and far reaching. There is first the deliberate suppression of the existing religious stage: this was virtually accomplished by 1590. Secondly there is the gradual extension of the powers of the Revels Office to include those of a Licensing Authority, whose permission had to be obtained before any play could be either performed or printed. These measures sufficed in themselves to kill the amateur theatre of the craft-guilds, leaving the government only the more tractable professional companies to handle. The most important single measure employed to discipline the professional companies was the regulation of the patronage on which rested their authority to act at all. Under Elizabeth I, James I and Charles I, the companies were brought progressively more tightly under the control of the Royal Family. It is no exaggeration to say that, by 1642, when Civil War started, acting in England was permitted by Royal prerogative or not at all. Since actors, however, could not make a living as

---

* The word derives from the Latin *quasi* and *ad modum* as used in the rubrics of liturgical plays. See Plate IV, Nos. 4 and 5.

professionals exclusively from performances at Court, they had to have liberty to perform to public audiences both in London and the Provinces. There, as one might expect, the Royal prerogative was exercised through the magistrates and mayors who represented the sovereign in town and country. An acting company had only to present the license received from the Master of the Revels to the Mayor of the town visited to safeguard the latter from inadvertently permitting heretical or seditious subject matter to inflame or incense the citizens under his care: but he usually took the precaution of having a 'private view' in his Guildhall before approving public exhibition. * In this of course he was only perpetuating his traditional jurisdiction, as the person responsible for keeping the King's Peace, over the place of performance.

With both dramatist and actors thus securely muzzled, governments could afford to pass on responsibility for discipline in the auditorium to the acting companies themselves. Dangerous buildings or unruly behaviour among the spectators could be dealt with under the normal provisions of law for the maintenance of the peace. Frequent breaches of the peace, by reflecting on the company's conduct of its affairs, would quickly brand its leader as *persona non grata* to the magistrates and thus impinge directly on the company's livelihood, since the magistrates could be expected to exercise their jurisdiction against the company by refusing its members a suitable place in the town in which to perform their plays.†

The effectiveness of these restrictive measures can best be seen by comparing the theatrical conditions prevailing in England in the sixteen-sixties with those that had prevailed before Henry VIII's break with Rome. Under Charles II drama in England had come to mean two theatres depending for their existence upon Royal Letters Patent, and functioning in London only, instead of a natural activity permitted to and pursued by the sovereign's subjects in every city, town and village in the realm. It is true that the two Patent Theatres of the sixteen-sixties gave regular performances by professional actors on workdays and holidays, winter and summer, whereas the drama of the fifteen-twenties was usually occasional, more often amateur than professional, and limited to Calendar holidays: but this does not affect the major issue demonstrated in this comparison. Drama as a popular art form, despite Shakespeare, despite the spectacular Court Masks, despite the building of London's first permanent theatres, was in fact dying

* See *EES*, i, pp. 269 *et seq.*
† See Ch. IV, pp. 106 and 142–148 below.

fast during the Elizabethan and Jacobean era. The texts of plays written before and after the boundaries of these dates show that a drama of cosmic scope and content had dwindled within little more than a hundred years into one of coterie appeal: drama, in its subject matter, had been effectively divorced from religion. Thus cut off from its *fons et origo*, it has drifted ever since whither the winds of commerce have cared to blow it. Its ultimate degradation is to be seen in the television play sponsored by an advertiser. However splendid a person the advertiser may be, it remains a fact that the drama he sponsors is no longer an art to be served, but has become a means to further a strictly commercial end, the increased sales of the product advertised.

Regrettable as it may seem to us, there can be little doubt that the Reformation was directly responsible for the imposition of State censorship upon the English theatre, for the suppression of the religious stage under the aegis of this censorship and, indirectly, for obliging the theatre in its struggle for very survival to espouse a form of patronage which could only serve to divorce it from popular support, and thereby sap its native vigour.

2 Renaissance

The Tudor Interlude is the most obvious single indication of a similarly direct external influence upon the growth of English drama, but of academic, neo-classical origin. The initiative here was taken by schoolmasters, choirmasters, university dons and their pupils. Plays by the ancient Latin and Greek dramatists were revived and presented both in the schools and colleges and before the sovereign and his court. Terence's *Phormio* was presented before Henry VIII by the boys of St. Paul's School in 1528, and it was on Plautus' *Miles Gloriosus* that Nicholas Udall based his own *Ralph Roister Doister*. Moreover, these performances were justified as encouraging a good Latinity and a mastery of oratorical delivery.

Nor can there be any doubt that these performances encouraged an interest in genre and in formal qualities of play-construction for which there was no precedent in England. Where in the fifteenth century, Lydgate can describe literary narratives as comedies and tragedies, by the seventeenth century comedy and tragedy as distinguishing terms are strictly applied to plays. The line linking the 1528 performance of the *Phormio* via performances of Aristophanes' *Pax* at Trinity College, Cambridge in 1546, Euripides' *Iocasta* at Gray's Inn in 1566 to Jonson's *Catiline* and Milton's

Samson Agonistes, is as clear and direct a product of the Renaissance in England as the censorship is an outcome of the Reformation. So, too, are the settings prepared by Inigo Jones and his pupils for masks and plays between 1605 and 1640. Yet if it can be said that Elizabeth I was as ready to watch Plautus' *Aulularia* at Cambridge in 1564, James Calfhill's Latin play *Progne* at Oxford in 1566, Dekker's *Old Fortunatus* in 1590, or Shakespeare's *Twelfth Night* in 1601, it should be remembered that the majority of her subjects were not. Shakespeare thought it necessary to make radical alterations to Plautus' *Menaechmi* before presenting it to a popular audience: Jonson was obliged to change all the Italian names of his first version of *Every Man In His Humour* into English ones to keep the play in public favour: and Fletcher's *The Faithful Shepherdess*, a Pastoral based on Guarini's *Pastor Fido*, was hissed off the stage of the Globe in 1609. And while critics like Puttenham, Sydney, Gager and Jonson finally won support for the doctrines of Aristotle and Horace as represented by Vives, Scaliger, Castelvetro, and other sixteenth-century Italian interpreters, English drama conforming to such patterns in the sixteenth century was written for small audiences of courtiers and intellectuals, or for readers only.

Thus, while both Reformation and Renaissance can legitimately be regarded as having each affected the development of English drama in an independent and recognizable manner, the measure of these respective effects differed markedly, since it is as much in terms of audiences as of plays that these effects have to be measured. The Reformation, as a movement involving change, received popular support and was held in check by the power vested in the minority—the government and the Court: the Renaissance, also considered as a pressure implying change, was championed by a powerful minority but failed to find much popular support. Where the theatre was concerned, therefore, the shade of religious and political opinion represented by the audience during the sixteenth century was always likely to affect the repertoire of the plays presented at least as profoundly as any academic arguments about their artistic merit.

3 *Renaissance versus Reformation*

Attention has so far been directed only to the implications for the theatre of Reformation and Renaissance considered as separate agents; and, if the full story of the fate of the English theatre in the sixteenth and seventeenth centuries were as straightforward as the preceding narrative, it would not present the problem to historians that it has done. Unfortunately this is but a small part of the story, since the direct pressures of the religious and political and academic issues are underscored by the indirect and contrapuntal pressures of these three in conflict with each other. The late E. M. W. Tillyard posed the question whether the widely held belief in the existence of a Renaissance in England was grounded on fact or fiction, * while Professor Lewis, in anatomizing the nature of English humanism, has gone so far as to expose the very idea of a *renasanta* as a myth of humanist invention. There are clear signs of something novel having entered English life very early in the sixteenth century, if not even earlier: a new vitality is made manifest to posterity in Henry VII's Chapel at Westminster, in Hampton Court, in Tudor madrigals, or in the writings of such men as Sir Thomas More and the schoolmaster authors of the early Interludes. Yet before the century had reached the half-way mark, most expressions of this newly awakened spirit seem to have come to a standstill, or at least to have encountered a sharp reaction to their forward progress. Even so, there is still the phenomenon of Spenser, Sydney, Shakespeare and a host of other artistic giants to be accounted for before the century is out. If this is the Renaissance, then it is a fitful and hesitant affair.

A question which seems to me to be at least worth asking is whether this clearly recognizable brake upon the advance of Renaissance thinking in England during the middle years of the sixteenth century was caused by the intervention of the Reformation? In other words, did the alignment of loyalties behind Henry VIII and his reformist ministers in Church and State occasion a corresponding realignment of views about humanist philosophy in general and Italian expressions of it in particular? If we extend our vision of the sixteenth century sufficiently to set it between the fifteenth century and the seventeenth, then the evidence of literature and art would suggest that the fifteenth century's fearful preoccupation with death and Judgement Day had been replaced in the seventeenth century by that surging confidence in man's potential achievement signalized by the founding of the Royal Society. Yet, on the other hand, in Cromwell, Milton and Bunyan the seventeenth century appears just as clearly to perpetuate a view of life recognizably mediaeval, at its best highly moral and at its worst grimly ascetic. Dr. Tillyard, taking his stand squarely in the sixteenth century, appeared to sense this same ambivalence there.

* *The English Renaissance: fact or fiction?*, 1952.

'It is, then, on balance', he writes, 'no fiction that the conception of man's position changed from the Middle Ages to the Renaissance. The Elizabethan conception was neither that of the *Dies Irae* nor of another hymn: the one shouted by Swinburne into the shocked ears of the Victorian middle classes:

"Glory to Man in the highest! For Man is the master of things!"

It was aware of both these incompatibles and to its glory succeeded in combining a measure of each.'[5]

This precarious balance is perhaps nowhere mirrored in sharper focus than in the Elizabethan theatre: for there we may see a bitter conflict raging between those for the one part who, having successfully suppressed the religious stage, were bent on suppressing its popular successor, and those, for the other part, who had found in dramatic entertainment an ideal instrument for expressing their own exuberant concern with the excitement of being alive. As Jacobean and Caroline times succeed the age of Elizabeth, so the battle between the supporters and the opponents of dramatic art crystallizes more sharply as one between Puritan and Cavalier. Perhaps it is the open conflict of the Civil War which has made this division of viewpoint seem particular to the seventeenth century. * Is it, however, any more real in kind than it was to such ascetically minded men as Robert Grosseteste, John of Salisbury or Thomas de Cobham in the thirteenth and fourteenth centuries?

> (Th)ey forsakë (th)at (th)ey toke—
> God and herë crystendam—
> (Th)at make swyche pleyys to any man
> As myrácles and bourdys [i.e. buffoonery],
> Or tournamentys of grete prys.
> (Th)ese are (th)e pompes (th)at (th)ou forsoke
> Fryst whan (th)ou (th)y crystendam toke.[6]

So wrote Robert Mannyng of Brunne in 1303. A century later an anonymous Wyclifite author complains that,

'myraclis pleyng . . . makith to se veyne si(gh)tis of de(s)gyse, aray of men and wymmen by yvil continaunse, eyther stiryng othere to letcherie and of debatis.'[7]

---

* Actual events in the period 1642–1656 such as the closure of the London theatres by the Parliamentary side or Cromwell's choice of Inigo Jones' Banqueting Hall in Whitehall as the setting for Charles I's execution are sufficiently striking in themselves to explain the confining of historical vision to the narrow limits of this period. It is nevertheless misleading to follow this example, since the context is itself artificial, being both too late and too narrow.

What weight such views carried at the time is beside the point: the fact that the viewpoint existed in the Middle Ages is what counts, since this supplies a basis for the steady development of a fundamental division of opinion which Renaissance and Reformation thinking served to crystallize in the sixteenth century—a division in society between those who aggressively welcomed the potentialities of life to be tasted through the senses and those who sought to subdue the senses. And if in the seventeenth century the bitterness of this controversy is exacerbated by Civil War, the outcome of the war by no means resolves it. Late in the eighteenth century the theatre is still the subject of the same debate as it was in the fourteenth century.

'Most of the present stage entertainments sap the foundation of all religion, as they naturally tend to efface all traces of piety and seriousness out of the minds of men; but . . . they are peculiarly hurtful to a trading city, giving a wrong turn to youth especially, gay, trifling, and directly opposite to the spirit of industry and close application to business.'[8]

The author is John Wesley, the date 1764 and the occasion a letter to the Mayor and Corporation of Bristol opposing the proposal to build the Theatre Royal.*

The essence of this conflict as it appeared to Shakespeare and his contemporaries was seized on by the master satirist, Ben Jonson, exemplified in the contradictory attitudes and actions of Zeal-of-the-land-Busy, the Puritan of *Bartholomew Fair*, and provided the classic type of stage hypocrite for others to copy and expand. Zeal-of-the-land-Busy is described by another character, the gamester Tom Quarlous, as

'A notable hypocriticall vermine . . . One that stands upon his face, more then his faith, at all times; Ever in seditious motion, and reproving for vaine-glory: . . . derides all *Antiquity*; defies any other *Learning*, then *Inspiration*; . . . a fellow of a most arrogant, and invincible dulnesse.'[9]

Approaching the booths of the fairground, Busy instructs his companions in how to comport themselves.

'. . . let not your eyes be drawne aside with vanity, nor your eare with noyses . . . Look not toward them, harken not: the place is *Smithfield*, or the field of Smiths, the Grove of Hobbi-horses and

---

* This is the same Theatre Royal as stands today in King Street. Despite the well organized opposition, it was built by private subscription and opened in 1766.

trinkets, the wares are the wares of divels. And the whole *Fayre* is the shop of *Satan*! . . .' etc.[10]

Then, sniffing the scent of roast pork wafting from the pig-woman's booth, he promptly proceeds to advise his friends to enter, on the grounds that

'Wee scape so much of the other vanities, by our earely entring.'[11]

Just such vanities are the stalls of fairground knick-knacks.

'The afflicted Saints', he says, '. . . are troubled, very much troubled, exceedingly troubled, with the opening of the merchan-dize of *Babylon* againe, & the peeping of *Popery* upon the stals, here, here in the high places. . . . A shop of reliques!'[12]

There is a curiously confused but very important equation between Catholicism and pleasure evident in this and other similar passages, which it is essential that Protestants like myself should try to un-derstand. Busy's indignation rises to such a pitch that he upsets a stall and thereby occasions a breach of the peace. For this he is put in the stocks. Asked while there by a constable who he is, he replies,

'One that rejoyceth in his affliction, and sitteth here to prophesie the destruction of *Fayres* and *May-games*, *Wakes*, and *Whitson-ales*, and doth sigh and groane for the reformation, of these abuses.'[13]

How soon this 'prophecy' was to be fulfilled! Busy provides his reason.

'. . . it is my calling, . . . an extraordinary calling, and done for my better standing, my surer standing, hereafter.'[14]

Who is this man, one is bound to ask? A contemporary of Marlowe, Drake, Sydney and Inigo Jones, or the disciple of St. Jerome, Grosseteste and Bromyard? That he is not a Catholic is very clear.

'Thou art the seate of the Beast, O *Smithfield*, and I will leave thee! Idolatry peepeth out on every side of thee.'[15]

This is a Calvinist voice, the harshest voice of the Reformation. It rings out again in Busy's retort to someone who has just quoted Horace, but this time as an illiterate voice.

'Friend, I will leave to communicate my spirit with you, if I heare any more of those superstitious reliques, those lists of Latin, the very rags of *Rome*, and patches of *Poperie*.'[16]

This brings us very near to the heart of the matter. Catholicism and the Latin language, at least among men of such limited mental calibre as Busy, are identified with one another: * the classical Renaissance with the Papacy and Anti-Christ. Here, it seems to me, is one important reason behind the hesitance of the English Renaissance. The adventurous pursuit of the Hellenic spirit led by Italians in the Latin tongue, in which quest Henry VII and Henry VIII were so actively engaged, received a sudden and sharp rebuff in 1531, as a result of Henry's differences with Rome. It was possibly not so much Henry VIII's action in assuming authority over the English Church as the Papal counter-action of excommunicating Henry which challenged every individual Englishman and put to him the question, 'How may I combine an interest in things Italian with loyalty to my sovereign?' The majority who, in C. S. Lewis' words, were used to regarding their duty as 'doing what they were told', chose to resolve the dilemma either by turning their backs on Rome and on all things associated with Rome, including neo-classicism, or else by acting as cautious apologists for the new humanism.

It would be pleasant to think that the academic world rose above this controversy. The evidence, alas, is directly to the contrary; for the new learning, where study of the Bible and the Liturgy was concerned, became a two-horned beast with Greek and Latin claiming respective rather than conjoined adherents. The two languages which, studied together, formed the basis of the new enlightenment, came instead to align themselves under the pressure of religious controversy with one or other of the rival factions. Those advocating the study of Greek became suspected of heresy by Catholics, while those who championed Latin at the expense of Greek came to be regarded by Protestants as reactionary and, by inference, as Papists. In 1556, for example, Sir Thomas Pope, founder of Trinity College, Oxford, wrote,

'My lord Cardinalls grace [Cardinal Pole] has had the overseeinge of my statutes. He muche lykes well, that I have therein ordered the Latin tongue to be redde to my schollers. But he advyses me to order the Greeke to be more taught there than I have provyded. This purpose I well lyke: but I fear *the tymes will not bear it now.* I remember when I was a young scholler at Eton (About the year 1520) the Greeke tonge was growing apace; the studie of which is now alate much decaid.'[17]

* During the Commonwealth, Latin, which till then had survived as the language of the law courts, was abolished in favour of English. Latin however replaced English again shortly after the Restoration.

Three years earlier the author of the Catholic play, *Respublica*, had stigmatized a Protestant clerk through the mouth of Avarice as,

'Sir John Lack Latin, my friend.'[18]

In this way men of genuine learning took to wasting their time by diverting their abilities into the sterile pursuit of metaphysical polemic. This dilution of true Renaissance studies in England (paralleled curiously in our own times by the effects of Marxist theory on the arts in Russia) combined in point of time with the effects of the dissolution of the monasteries upon English education. It is impossible to escape the conclusion that this event of the late fifteen-thirties put the sharpest of all brakes upon the progress of the Renaissance in England: for its effects were felt simultaneously all over the country. In the schools and universities it led to what Roger Ascham termed *ruinam et interitum* (the ruin and extinction) of the school curriculum, to the abrogation of University Degrees as antichristian, and to an horrific climax in the stripping of Duke Humphrey's library at Oxford of all its books and MSS.[19] While Oxford and Cambridge, however, had other means of redress because of their continuing contacts with foreign centres of learning, smaller provincial centres had none once the monasteries had disappeared. Thomas Warton, in his *History of English Poetry*, while in one breath describing the monasteries as 'nurseries of illiterate indolence' was nevertheless fair-minded and far-sighted enough to add with the next that by their abolition 'many towns and their adjacent villages were utterly deprived of their only means of instruction.' When we come to consider the fate of the provincial theatre in the sixteenth century, as opposed to that of the dramatic spectacles in London, this must be reckoned as a factor of outstanding consequence; for, to quote Warton once again, 'provincial ignorance . . . became universal.'[20] If the traditional religious plays were once to be suppressed, where could authors be found to replace them? It was not until the last decades of the century that masters in the newly-established free grammar schools could claim to possess the necessary learning and authority to fill the gap.

A fortuitous coincidence, the publication in 1534 of Polydore Vergil's *Anglica Historia* (which was destined to have a profound effect on that most English of all dramatic genres of the sixteenth century—the history or chronicle play) added fuel to these academic fires. Polydore was merely one of many Italians who, encouraged by Henry VII, had found enough work and lived long enough in England to be regarded as a naturalized Englishman.

He came to Court in 1502, was employed in the collecting of Peter's Pence and was installed as archdeacon of Wells Cathedral in 1508. As an author he had an established reputation from the publication of the *De Inventoribus Rerum* and several minor works before he was commissioned by the first two Tudor sovereigns to write an official History of England. Despite the fact that in the nature of this commission Vergil was bound, if judged by any objective standards, to work as a Tudor apologist, he made a notable contribution to the writing of English history. Yet at the moment of the publication of the *Anglica Historia*, this very virtue was regarded by many as an outrage, not to say a crime. Vergil's error lay in having tried to separate historical fact from sentimental fiction. Many of the most cherished of English beliefs were quietly scored through by his pen. British descent from Trojan Brutus, the prowess of Arthur, last king of the Britons, Merlin and his prophecies of an *Arturius redivivus* in the Tudor dynasty were exposed as fraudulent impostures.* Both Henry VIII and his father may well have been prepared to accept this as a necessary price for the appraisal of their dynasty and its aspirations in the humanist form that would alone command respect in other European Courts.† At any rate, Vergil enjoyed sufficient royal favour to stay in England for another twenty years before returning to Italy for good. However, popular sentiment and patriotism, insulted in this way, rounded in fury on the scurrilous Italian offender—the viper harboured for so long by a trusting Court and country. Professor Greenlaw has neatly summed up the repercussions in the phrase 'the battle of the books', a battle still being fought out as the sixteenth century passed into the seventeenth.[21] Chapman can publish his translation of *The Iliad* with Jonson's approval, but Dekker still thinks of London as *Troia-Nova Triumphans*.‡ The historian William Camden, Jonson's tutor at Westminster—

> 'most reverend head, to whom I owe
> All that I am in arts, all that I know.'[22]

—can still say

'For mine owne part, let Brutus be taken for the father and founder of the British nation: I will not be of contrarie minde.'[23]

* See *EES*, i, pp. 73 *et seq.*

† The 2nd edition of the *Anglica Historia* was published in 1546 and the 3rd in 1555. The 1st edition treated of events up to 1509. Events between 1509 and 1537 were not treated until the 3rd edition: by that time Mary Tudor was on the throne.

‡ See *EES*, i, p. 88, n. 54.

This bears eloquent witness to the length of the battle if not to its initial fury. John Bale however gives us a taste of that in his play *Kyng Johan* written within a few years of the publication of the *Anglica Historia*. In his attempts to justify Henry VIII's break with Rome, Bale found in King John's struggle with the Papacy a convenient prophecy of things to come, but was much embarrassed by Polydore Vergil's realistic and harsh assessment of John. His remedy was simple: a rhetorical question to his audience.

> 'What though Polydorus reporteth him very ill
> At the suggestions of the maliciouse clergy?
> Think you a Roman with the Romans cannot lie?'[24]

Not only in plays and literature, but in the other arts also the immediate effect of the Reformation is a sudden ostracism of Italian example and a consequent reversion to the most solidly traditional English precedent to hand. Only in the leading schools and the two universities was the humanist activity of the early part of the century able to proceed with any freedom: but there, as I have already indicated, it did so in isolated seclusion, fostered by individual enterprise and in an atmosphere very different from that prevailing in the well patronized, well organized and well subsidized *Accademii* of the Italian Principalities.[25] This largely accounts, where Italian precept is concerned, for the flying start that poetry derived from Petrarch and Ariosto had on the other arts during the latter part of the sixteenth century. In English architecture the mid century reversion is to the perpendicular style, inset with occasional Italianate decorative motifs surviving from the earlier period: in painting it is to Flemish portraiture, and the result is measurable when a miniature by Nicholas Hillyarde is compared with a fresco by Michaelangelo: in the theatre it is to the native Miracle Cycle and Morality Play. The reversion is away from the neo-classical basilica, from landscape painting and statuary, from Italian reconstruction of Latin plays and theatres. Bale counters his hated 'popetly plays' by writing what almost amounts to a Protestant Miracle Cycle, *God's Promises*.[26] The old Morality Play was similarly adapted to Protestant purposes in a stream of anti-Catholic polemical Interludes in which the matter debated counted with audiences for far more than the form in which it was cast. The vitality of this subject matter, a positive contribution of the Reformation to English drama, can scarcely be stressed too strongly; for it gave to English drama of the time a relevance to daily life among all ranks of society which Italian comedy and tragedy, self-consciously imitating archaic models of academic appeal, failed to attain.*

The point at issue then may be summed up as follows. The humanist attitudes introduced into England by thinkers, scholars and artists in the reign of Henry VII pass from a basis of assumption to one of question. During the reign of his son, as problems of religious reform become dominant in English life, the values of a pre-Christian Roman society, deemed at first to be unquestionably worthy of imitation, come later to be balanced against those of a

Fig. 4. Diagrammatic outline of the Gatehouse, Stanway House, Gloucestershire, c. 1593.

Christian society seeking to liberate its conscience and its religious rituals from Roman dominance. Latin, accordingly, becomes a language to be revered as the foundation stone of sound education and at the same time abominated as 'the rags of Rome'. And since all aspects of this question were directly subject to the tides of political thinking in the period 1530–1580, it is hardly surprising that contradiction rather than clarity should colour all artistic reflections of English life at the time. Enthusiasm for the precepts of

* A list of editions of Interludes is supplied by T. W. Craik in *The Tudor Interlude*, pp. 142–149.

foreign antiquity is everywhere matched by a reliance upon modern, national achievement.

In our drama, then, it is to be expected that by the close of the sixteenth century those novel trends of thought which marked the reign of Henry VII and the first half of his son's should be still apparent yet strongly tempered by continuing reliance upon earlier precedents. Marlowe illustrates the point succinctly. Within his short life he achieved in *Dr. Faustus, Edward II* and *Dido, Queen of Carthage* three plays based respectively on religious, historical and classical source material. This Janus-like position, looking forward with the humanists and, at the same time, backwards to the achievements of the native past, may be observed in remarkable de-. tail within one of these same plays, *Edward II*. In a cast list of genuine historical figures there exists one person of great importance to the plot who has no factual precedent in the chronicles of Edward's reign; he is the professional torturer, Lightborn, equipped with fatal, red-hot spit, who dominates the grisly scenes in Berkeley Castle. He may, however, be compared with another Lightborn in another and an earlier English play, the Chester Cycle. This earlier Lightborn, as a follower of Lucifer the angel, is sent to Hell for his 'foule pryde', and there becomes *secundus Demon*. In that environment his normal equipment would naturally include a sharp-pronged fork and a red-hot spit. I do not want to argue that Marlowe cribbed this idea directly from the Chester Cycle; but simply as a parallel it is striking enough to support my contention that even those Elizabethan poets schooled in neo-classical literature had by no means rejected the traditional dramatic fabric of the religious stage. We may conclude then, with a fair claim to accuracy, that Italian neo-classical example made heavy inroads upon the English drama, both in point of subject matter and of its treatment, but that the Reformation served to temper the pace of its progress and thus to preserve a marked degree of continuity in English dramatic structure. The result is that Elizabethan and Jacobean plays, however noticeable the influence of Seneca, Plautus, Terence and Horace, mirror their origins in mediaeval religious plays with equal clarity.

4 *Reformation versus Renaissance*

This strange conflict between the rival claims of the Reformation and the classical Renaissance upon Englishmen in the mid sixteenth century can conveniently be observed in action in the debate sur-

rounding Polydore Vergil's *Anglica Historia* already instanced. *
Both in the commissioning of it by Henry VII and Henry VIII and
in the style in which it is written, this work is a product of the
humanist attitude to history. Yet the date of publication, 1534,
brought both author and book into conflict with English national-
ism as exemplified in the Reformation: for an Italian, intimately
associated with the Papacy, had dared in this book to debunk
cherished popular beliefs. Yet despite the storm that this provoked,
and despite the concerted efforts of patriots to refute his arguments, Vergil nevertheless influenced most of his detractors profoundly in the manner of their own writing. While contradicting or
refraining from accepting many of his views and reverting to
tradition instead, they chose to adopt much of both his purpose and
method in their own Chronicles. Hall and Holinshed, whose narratives were drawn upon so frequently for the plots of Elizabethan
history plays are among the most notable. 'As far as prose style is
concerned', writes Denys Hay in a recent study of Vergil's work,[27]
'it is scarcely an exaggeration to trace ultimately to his pen the
bulk of the English narratives of fifteenth century history written
in the sixteenth. Hall . . . translates Vergil and in this way the
latinity of Vergil entered the English canon.' In other words,
despite the rising tide of Reformation prejudice against latin as a
language, English historical writing comes to possess a distinctly
latin flavour. Mr. Hay stresses a still more striking procedural
debt.

'From Vergil Hall derived three fundamental notions: history is the
record of the past in a form designed to perpetuate fame and glory
—it is "memory by litterature"; it must nevertheless be based on a
critical use of sources; it must have an argument . . . The dominant
motif which Hall attributed to the reigns of fifteenth-century
English kings became, in didactic poetry and the theatre, the life-
blood of every historical personality and situation: the concrete was
turned into a conflict of personalities . . . an inscrutable God or a
malevolent chance could occasionally be invoked by the Elizabethan poet, but essentially he saw the past in terms of human
character in its relations with an absolute justice.'[28]

In this instance however I think a good case can be made for arguing that the conflict of Reformation and Renaissance attitudes was
working in the reverse direction: for whereas few students of
English literature or drama would deny that the Elizabethan poets

* See pp. 26–28 above.

31

looked at the past in this way, many would dispute with Mr. Hay the degree of their debt to Vergil in this. Sermons, Miracle plays and the Pageants of the Royal Entries had for generations represented Biblical history in this way and could have given Vergil as good a lesson on this subject when he first came to England, as any he bequeathed to the Elizabethans in his own writing.* Before Vergil took up residence in England, the authors of the pageants prepared for Henry VII's Entry into York, Worcester, Hereford and Bristol during his Progress of 1486 use ancient and modern history in precisely this way.

Yet, at the end of the sixteenth century, if Shakespeare can still write a play about the Trojan war, assuming that most members of his audience will both recognize the Trojans as their ancestors and the Greeks as their enemies and regard these Trojan ancestors as beset by enemies resembling the deadly sins of the suppressed Morality Play, we must admit in the division of the play into formal Acts and Scenes, in the special language in which much of it is phrased and in many of the arguments advanced by Greeks and Trojans alike, a consciousness of humanist precept unimaginable in the popular drama of early Tudor times. The attitude adopted to plays and playmaking by Sydney, Jonson, Fletcher or Heywood and made explicit in their critical essays reveals the nature of the debt to humanist theory and example which in Shakespeare's work remains a notable paradox. The classical Renaissance is thus a reality in England since things Italian, more especially ideas of Latin and Greek origin, were clearly seized in welcoming embrace by the first two Tudor sovereigns: but Henry VIII's rejection of the authority of the Pope in England and the consequent alignment of forces on the continent behind the two protagonists translated the issue from a domestic dispute into a national and even international cause. The emotion generated enveloped all artistic expressions of national life and thought, and resulted in a temporary rejection of things Italian because of their affinities with Rome and the Papacy. The English position for the remainder of the century takes the form of a nation attempting to unite itself behind a Protestant sovereign. The Marian reaction and the excommunication of Elizabeth illustrate the nature and scale of the threat to this unity, and explain the frosting of the green shoots of neo-classicism put up in the Tudor spring. Artistically the nation sustains itself from its roots until the death of Mary Queen of Scots and the defeat of the Spanish Armada have brought security from without and a re-

* See *EES*, i, pp. 71–81. On the nature of the latinity professed by the humanists in England see *O.H.E.L.*, iii, Ch. 1.

laxation of tension from within. A thaw in the 'cold war' with everything Italian follows quickly on these events: but it is a thaw hedged about with reservations and provisos. Complete capitulation to Italian standpoints is impossible since the norm has become Protestant English. The Italian alternative must fit in where it can or be rejected where it cannot. In the theatre, even the most ardent of neo-classical enthusiasts, Ben Jonson, adopts this stand. In the Prologue to *Every Man Out of His Humour* (1600) he entertains his audience to this critique of the Italian cult of the unities.

> 'CORDATUS: If those lawes you speake of, had beene delivered us, *ab initio,* and in their present vertue and perfection, there had beene some reason of obeying their powers: but 'tis extant, that that which we call *Comœdia,* was at first nothing but a simple, and continued *Song,* sung by one only person, till SUSARIO invented a second, after him EPICHARMUS a third; PHORMUS, and CHIONIDES devised to have foure Actors, with a *Prologue* and *Chorus*; to which CRATINUS (long after) added a fift, and sixt; EUPOLIS more; ARISTOPHANES more than they: every man in the dignitie of his spirit and judgment, supplyed something. And (though that in him this kinde of *Poeme* appeared absolute, and fully perfected) yet how is the face of it chang'd since, in MENANDER, PHILEMON, CECILIUS, PLAUTUS, and the rest; who have utterly excluded the *Chorus,* altered the property of the persons, their names, and natures, and augmented it with all liberty, according to the elegancie and disposition of those times, wherein they wrote? I see not then, but we should enjoy the same licence, or free power, to illustrate and heighten our invention as they did; and not bee tyed to those strict and regular formes, which the nicenesse of a few (who are nothing but forme) would thrust upon us.'[29]

Only a zealous neo-classicist would have dared to introduce a passage of this sort into a stage play for a popular audience; but the use made of it, the particular point argued, is that of an English nationalist who is not going to be tied by foreign rules which muzzle his native genius.

As a signpost within this context, Ben Jonson is an especially important figure, for he represents not only the extreme scholarly standpoint, but also that of Catholic recusancy. It is the standpoint argued sixty years later by Dryden for the benefit of Charles II and the intelligentsia returned from exile at Catholic, classical Versailles; it is the position which, in his *Essay of Dramatic Poesy,* he particularizes first in the dispute on the superiority of modern dramatists over the ancient ones and secondly in the militant championing of native English drama against the French. This plea is one which we must expect to find argued (or indeed simply assumed) with far greater emphasis by those with less pretension to scholarship and by those with deeper Protestant persuasions.

Pride in native achievement is common to both parties, but agreement is fractured when the nature of this achievement is extended to include tradition: for Protestants must by definition query, at the least, the value of any tradition of Catholic inspiration. Jonson may take over the 'type' characters derived from Italian interpretations of Plautus, Terence and Horace, together with the 'Virtues' and 'Vices' of the traditional English Morality play, graft them on to the manners of his own London, and arrive at a new comedy of Humours:[30] but Protestants of Calvinist persuasion may with equal justification regard all English plays as derived from Catholicism and therefore to be shunned. In *Bartholomew Fair*, Zeal-of-the-Land-Busy voices this opinion in tones which have echoed and re-echoed from the pulpits of Non-conformity ever since. At the Fair, Busy tries to break up a puppet play of Hero and Leander.

'I wil remove *Dagon* there, I say, [*i.e. the puppet theatre*], that *Idoll*, that heathenish *Idoll*, that remaines (as I may say) a beame . . . in the eye of the brethren.'

The puppeteer protests,

'Sir, I present nothing, but what is licens'd by authority . . . I have the Master of the *Revell's* hand for't, Sir' [*i.e. the signed licence*].

Busy's retort is contemptuous of all authority other than that of his own bigotry: he is ready to act as an *agent provocateur* to enforce that!

'The Master of the *Rebells* hand, thou hast; *Satan's*! hold thy peace, thy scurrility, shut up thy mouth, thy profession is damnable, and in pleading for it, thou dost plead for *Baal*. I have long opened my mouth wide, and gaped, I have gaped as the oyster for the tide, after thy destruction: but cannot compasse it by sute, or dispute; so that I looke for a bickering, ere long, and then a battell.'[31]

The battle was in fact not long in coming, and in the wake of it the theatre was silenced for nearly twenty years. The theatre that was readmitted to England with the Restoration was a classical theatre where symmetry ruled in place of emblem. The cause espoused by the Tudor humanists had triumphed; but the price paid to the Reformers had been the withdrawal of popular support.

5 *The Subject Matter of English Drama*

The argument that I have tried thus far to present may be summarized as follows:

1 A vigorous Renaissance occurs in England at the close of the wars of the Roses lasting through the first forty to fifty years of Tudor rule.

2 Reformation of the English Church involves an automatic and inseparable reformation of the English religious stage.

3 This Reformation comes into conflict with all aspects of the preceding Renaissance which were directly traceable to Italian (more specifically Latin and Roman) sources.

4 This conflict is resolved in the ultimate triumph of the classical Renaissance, but only on terms acceptable to both British nationalist sentiment and established Protestant opinion.

If these contentions be admitted, there follow two inescapable conclusions. The first is that these four factors could suffice in themselves to make English drama written after 1530 distinctly different from that written in European countries where these factors are not observable in similar conjunction: the second is that this distinct national pattern of development takes its shape from the particular ebbing and flowing of the conflict between Reformation and Renaissance ideals as dictated by English domestic and foreign policy.

As I have already suggested at the end of Volume I, the process of copying the individual dramatic components of the macrocosmic cyclic Miracles in terms of the little world of man had started in the fifteenth century if not earlier.* From the standpoint of dramatic structure, the Fall, the Passion and the Judgement are the basic nuclei of the archetypal pattern: the microcosmic copies take the respective forms of the Fall of Princes, the martyrdom of Saints and the path to personal Salvation prescribed by the Morality Play. We are here of course in a world where neither Renaissance nor Reformation pressures have begun to make themselves felt. Both however are to be observed in the emergence of convenient and artistic shape; but, in recognizing this, it is important not to overlook the fact that the survival of the archetypal Miracle Cycles as a popular dramatic entertainment through most of the sixteenth century served to suggest the desirability of linking the newly tailored microscosmic parts into a similarly co-ordinated whole and thereby

---

* See *EES*, i, pp. 315 *et seq.*

preserved something of the epic quality of the original model. This process has very evidently been achieved when Shakespeare reaches the height of his powers: and it results, at his hand, in a drama still patently religious in scope and tone, if wholly concerned in its cast lists and dialogue, whether in chronicle play, in comedy or in tragedy, with human beings sketched from every walk of life in Elizabethan society.

The reader is of course at liberty to link such thought processes at a conscious level as loosely or as closely as he cares to the actual labours of dramatic composition in the sixteenth century: but, as material on which dramatists could base their preparatory thinking for such composition at the time, it was clearly available to any educated person, and it does serve to explain why the history play as a genre is English and without contemporary parallel in France or Italy. It serves to explain further why English comedy and tragedy of the time should bear in its form so much closer a resemblance to the history play than to Latin comedy or tragedy, since the traditional emphasis upon narrative and debate was never rejected in favour of situation. To me it seems clear therefore that while the Reformation causes the Miracle Cycle and the Morality to be suppressed, it paradoxically enforces the survival of the forms. Because they are English they are preferable to the papistical Italian alternatives and thus come to be grafted to the new and less contentious subject matter of romance, of classical mythology and of national history. From the Miracle Cycles the new plays received their structural form, a consecution of scenes: from the Moralities they took their thematic *exemplum*, salvation and damnation discussed in a national context rather than in that of universalized mankind.

For instance, in Shakespeare's *King John* (more properly *The Life and Death of King John*), just as in Bale's *Kyng Johan*, scene follows upon scene with the same disregard for unity of place as does play upon play within the Miracle Cycles; the relationship between John, Arthur and Philip of France in Shakespeare's play reflects that between Elizabeth, Mary Queen of Scots and Philip of Spain with the same didactic topicality as the cast list of a Morality play reflects the spectator's own struggle with incarnate vice and virtue for personal salvation, or as Bale's play reflects Henry VIII's struggle with the Pope. These principles also lie behind the construction of plays described by their authors as comedies and tragedies, even when classical precept is being taken seriously. In Lyly's comedy *Endymion* myth replaces scriptural or national history as subject matter; but despite the masquerade of mythological characters—Tellus, Cynthia, Endymion and so on—the play is even more directly topical than *King John* in that it is Elizabeth's personal relations with Mary Queen of Scots and the Earl of Leicester, rather than the government of her country, which lies at the heart of the play under the traditional outer garments of parable and allegory. In *Gorboduc*, a tragedy (performed in 1562 and subsequently printed in 1565) which is reputed to be the first in English written in the classical manner, government once again provides the theme:—specifically, the consequences to subjects if the monarch fails to provide the kingdom with an heir.

Despite the suppression of the religious stage therefore, and despite the growing powers of the licensing authorities in Elizabethan England, there is ample evidence to prove that plays continued to reflect the didactic function inherited from the Morality Play, Saint Play and Miracle Cycle of the mediaeval past. In the theatre, however, the grip that a play takes upon the imagination and emotions of its audiences depends as much upon what is seen as upon what is heard: actor, costume and setting combine to contribute as much if not more of the total experience of the play in action as the author's written text. And we should remember that where the Elizabethan censorship of subject matter may have made the theatre doctrinally inoffensive to Zeal-of-the-Land-Busy and his like, it had neither suppressed the stagecraft associated by tradition with the Catholic ritual out of which it had developed, nor reformed the public appetite for the glamour of this ritual. Busy equates the theatre with Dagon and Baal, that is to say with idolatry: as a profession he holds it to be profane.

'I say, it is prophane, as being the Page of *Pride*, and the waiting woman of *vanity*.'[32]

It is on exactly these grounds that stained glass in churches was broken, that frescoes were white-washed over, that vestments and other ornaments of Catholic ritual were abolished. Vestments are the most interesting item in the present context, in that they illustrate better than anything else the continuity of stage convention on either side of the Reformation. Before the Reformation vestments had been used as costumes for the Miracle Cycles, a practice which, in its turn, was a legacy from the earliest liturgical plays. Here, as an example, is an extract in translation from the Latin stage directions in a fourteenth century prompt-book: Philip de Mézières' *Festum Praesentationis Beatae Mariae*.

'The two angels, Gabriel and Raphael, shall be dressed in white amices, with stoles about their necks, forming crosses on their breasts. They shall wear birettas, tightly fitted above their ears, which shall be triangular or quadrangular in shape, not too wide, with two cloth strips in the back, just as in a bishop's mitre. . . . The two angels shall have wings, and shall carry red staffs in their right hands.'[33]

At the Reformation, the commissioners appointed by the government to simplify and anglicize church ceremonies disposed of many vestments by gift or sale. In 1560 the Church of Holy Trinity, Chester disposed of most of its church-furnishings. 'Church goods delivered to Mr. hardware, Maior', included 'the best cope and the vestment & appurtenances.'[34] The inventory also discloses that 'Mr. Rafe goodman receved a vestment of satayn' while 'Will'm leche re(ceve)d a vestment & 2 tunacles of blew velvet w(hi)ch we sould to him for 40^s.' Among the interested recipients of a further sale ten years later were actors.

'Sould to Thomas Shevyntons sonne the belman & Tho' dychers sonne 3 course vestments & a course stremer to make players garments . . . viij s.'[35]

At Chelmsford the churchwardens hired out complete wardrobes of costumes for as much as £2 19s. 0d. a time to groups of actors in the region from 1562 onwards.[36] In 1574 the wardrobe was sold outright for £6 12s. 4d. We get some idea of the nature of this 'players gere' from Worcester where a cathedral inventory of 1576 includes

'A gowne of freres gyrdles. A woman's gowne. A K(ing)s cloke of Tysshew. A Jerkyn and a payer of breches. A lytill cloke of tysshew. A gowne of silk. A Jerkyn of greene, 2 cappes, and the devils apparell.'[37]

As the sixteenth century passed into the seventeenth, Elizabethan doublets and cloaks, and even Roman-style helmets and greaves, displaced birettas, copes and albs on the stage; but the richness of the new apparel testified to its ancestry, and the actors who wore it could with reason be described as 'pages of pride' and 'waiting women of vanity'.

What had happened in the matter of stage costume happened also in respect of scenic equipment. A monument, tomb or sepulchre had been required in the very first play of all, in the Easter *quem quaeritis* introit of the three Maries and the angel: it was needed for Lazarus and for Christ in Miracle plays and Saint plays:*

* See *EES*, i, p. 167.

Henslowe could still find enough use for it to buy two in 1598.*
Robert Greene demands one for his romantic Chronicle *King James
the Fourth*. The play opens with this stage direction:

Music playing within, enter ASTER OBERON, *King of Fairies; and* Antics, *who
dance about a tomb placed conveniently on the stage; out of the which suddenly
starts up, as they dance,* BOHAN, . . . etc.

And it is probably with this device in mind that some fifteen years
later Shakespeare penned this:

> CLEOPATRA: How now! Is he dead?
> DIOMEDES: His death's upon him, but not dead.
>   Look out o' the other side your monument:[38]

When then, in the structure of plays, in costume and in setting,
Elizabethan and Jacobean Londoners could still spy the prototypes
beneath the veneer of change, how could it be said that the religious
stage, this offensive, three-dimensional enactment of Catholic
'idolatry', had been exorcised from the land? This is the essence
of Busy's complaint, and of all those others who, but for the personal intervention of the monarchy, would have succeeded in closing the theatres some forty years before the Civil War did it for
them. Busy of course represents Puritanism at the level of Elizabethan tradesmen—he is described as having started life in
Banbury as a baker—and his way is that of the demagogue. The
more he thunders abuse at the object of his dislike the funnier he is
to intelligent people and the more ineffective his railing becomes.
More subtle is the way of David Rogers, author of the *Breviary of
Chester* and prototype of many subsequent puritan opponents of the
arts and humanities, who employs the smoke screen of 'modern
enlightenment' to bring the old religious stage into disrepute.†
This method is far more dangerous, since it flatters those to whom
it is addressed and lays an axe to the roots of the offensive tradition.
Rogers and his like represent the past as 'the tyme of Ignorance
wherein we did straye', while 'the fyne witt, at this day aboun-
dinge', so they say, 'at that day and that age had verye small
beinge'. When the Dean of York sets about suppressing the Creed
Play, it is on the grounds that though 'plawsible' years ago, 'and
wold now also of the ignorant sort be well liked, yet now in the
happie time of the gospell, I know the learned will mislike it.'‡
   Progress is with us: a new myth is launched. If the arts are to

* *Ibid.*, i, p. 247.
† See *EES*, i, p. 372; also p. 135.
‡ See *EES*, i, p. 114.

survive this attack, the riposte must be in terms of pre-Christian theory, in terms of neo-classicism, in terms of anything that can escape the stigma of mediaeval Catholic parentage. By the mid seventeenth century the study of Greek and Roman literature, direct inspiration from the Bible, and 'modern' philosophies based on the observed contemporary phenomena of natural science and the power of money form the new data from which the riposte is made. Milton, Dryden, Bunyan, Inigo Jones, Wren, Locke and Hobbes are the sort of men that make it: *All for Love* replaces *Antony and Cleopatra,* and a domed basilica is substituted for the mediaeval vaulting of St. Paul's Cathedral. Congreve's Mrs. Marwood can think of nothing ruder than Gothic, Pope, nothing more sweetly barbarous than native woodnotes wild. Dryden states in his *Essay of Dramatic Poesy* that where he 'admires' Jonson, he 'loves' Shakespeare; but this does not alter the fact that, to make Shakespeare's plays acceptable to the audiences of his own day, Dryden himself initiates that process of adapting the texts to rid them of 'rudeness' in form and content, and thereby establishes a practice which with Rymer's support, was to become standard throughout the eighteenth century and for much of the nineteenth. This knowledge seems to me to speak more eloquently than any other in support of the contention that traditional, mediaeval and pre-Reformation values of dramaturgy took precedence in the Elizabethan theatre over 'modern', neo-classical values of Italian inspiration. In theatre architecture too, whatever we may surmise about the exact visual appearance of Shakespeare's 'wooden O', by the time that stage performances are made legitimate again after the Civil War and Commonwealth, the buildings (two of them in London alone) have become Italian in appearance both inside and out: the plays, having lost all contact with the macrocosmic archetype of the Miracle Cycles, have also lost any sense of need to attempt to mirror the microcosmos. Fragments of it suffice, and only coteries attend. Drama and religion, having lived in holy matrimony for some five hundred years, are given a decree of divorce *nisi* at the Reformation, which, under the pressures of the Renaissance, is made absolute shortly after the Restoration.

In directing attention to the damage done to English drama in the name of progress and enlightenment during the latter half of the sixteenth century and increasingly through the seventeenth at the expense of the mediaeval past, I am aware that I have largely left out of account those positive forces that nevertheless stimulated the 'University Wits' and many other Elizabethans into creating between them the most remarkable range of plays the world had seen since Athenian democracy was at its prime. Perhaps the easiest way of redressing the balance is simply to reverse the emphasis on some of the points already made, allowing the positive instead of the negative side to speak for itself.

First, then, if the Reformation occasioned the suppression of a healthy religious stage, it thereby created a vacuum that had to be filled quickly if the theatre was to survive; and this in turn gave the young men coming to maturity in the fifteen-seventies and fifteen eighties an unexampled market for new plays. Secondly, and scarcely less important, the spate of anti-Catholic and anti-Protestant plays written between 1530 and 1560 developed techniques of argument and debate in dramatic form much more swiftly than might otherwise have happened. Moreover, the topicality of this debate kept English drama in much closer touch with life as lived in the country as a whole and at all levels of society than its major rival of Italian, academic origin. Thus 'conflict', which had first been developed dramatically in the physical combats of the Tournament and the figurative battles between Vices and Virtues of the Morality play, came to acquire a centre-stage position in the art of the sixteenth century English playwright. This particular English development was in turn to provide Peele, Greene, Marlowe and their successors with an instrument that enabled them to take full advantage of the opportunity offered to them by the suppression of the existing canon of dramatic texts to supply actors with a stock of new plays. The following extract from Greene's *King James the Fourth* may illustrate the point.

KING OF SCOTS	Now I am free from sight of common eye,
	Where to myself I may disclose the grief
	That hath too great a part in mine affects.
ATEUKIN (*aside*)	And now is my time by wiles and words to rise,
	Greater than those that think themselves more wise.
KING OF SCOTS	And first, fond king, thy honour doth engrave
	Upon thy brows the drift of thy disgrace.
	Thy new-vow'd love, in sight of God and men,
	Links thee to Dorothea during life;
	For who more fair and virtuous than thy wife?
	Deceitful murderer of a quiet mind,
	Fond love, vile lust, that thus misleads us men,
	To vow our faiths, and fall to sin again!
	But kings stoop not to every common thought;
	Ida is fair and wise, fit for a king;
	And for fair Ida will I hazard life,
	Venture my kingdom, country, and my crown:
	Such fire hath love to burn a kingdom down.

In this short passage from Act I, scene i, we are introduced not only to the conflict that is perplexing the hero between the ethics of a marriage arranged for political ends and those of heart's desire, but we are shown how this conflict is likely to be exploited by the villain. We can thus jump ahead to Act II, scene ii, and encounter this passage without surprise.

ATEUKIN Hear me, O king! 'tis Dorothea's death
      Must do you good.
KING OF SCOTS What, murder of my queen?
      Yet to enjoy my love, what is my queen?
      O, but my vow and promise to my queen!
      Ay, but my hope to gain a fairer queen:
      With how contrarious thoughts am I withdrawn!

Hero and villain are here contrasted as sharply as the Challenger and Defender of any Tournament, while at the same time the familiar ethical debate of a Morality play is presented in soliloquy as 'contrarious thoughts'.

To this centrifugal concept of conflict in dramatic structure Elizabethan dramatists brought their own refined sense of poetic values, acquired through classical studies of Renaissance inspiration in the schools and universities: for there, at least, from Henry VII's time onwards, the classics had come to stay. Lyly with his ornamental style, Marlowe with his mighty line, and others with an equally personal contribution (all fostered under humanist direction in the classroom), were thus enabled to bring a freshness of approach to their exciting task of supplying the theatre with a new canon of play texts. In addition, they had the good fortune to be presented with both this opportunity and this challenge at a moment in national history when life itself—the source from which the subject matter of the new plays had to be drawn—was at its most challenging and vivid. The Reformation, whatever its causes and consequences in realms of theology, had long since ceased to be a simple dispute between Martin Luther or Henry VIII and the Pope: it had become an international cause with England in the van and with nothing less than the future of Europe and the New World at stake. Just as Greek drama of the fifth century B.C. reflected the moment of grandeur when the city state of Athens accepted and met the challenge from the Persian Empire, so now a time of destiny had arrived for England, a moment that even the nation's crassest sheep could hardly fail to notice, let alone its ablest poets. These poets had inherited from the Miracle Cycles a great architectural pattern of composition designed to demonstrate the nature of the universe to man, together with the pioneer attempts to copy at

least the several components of this pattern in terms of the microcosmos. For anyone with spirit enough to take the risk, the time
was ripe for an attempt to weld these components together; the
self-confidence born of national victory provided the motive force
to make the attempt: and, in this post-Armada climate, while the
archetypal, macrocosmic pattern still survived in the memory of
eye-witnesses, it was in fact made. If Marlowe's *Dr. Faustus* is the
last avowedly religious play to have been produced on the Tudor
stage, it forecasts *Measure for Measure* or *The Duchess of Malfi* with
as much clarity as it reflects its own *exemplum* in the traditional
Miracle Cycle and Morality Play. From Everyman, Mankind and
Humanum Genus, Dr. Faustus, with his good and evil angel, is
patently descended. What links him and his devilish machinations
to Bosola, Duke Ferdinand and his brother Cardinal is a change of
attitude to both the nature and quality of individual man in his
relation to society; Renaissance thought.

The decadence which is generally deemed to have entered into
late Jacobean and Caroline drama springs, in my opinion, as much
from specifically theatrical causes as from any serious shortage or
weakening of literary ability. Webster we must remember, together with Shakespeare, Jonson, Dekker and many others, wrote
their plays despite the censorship. What they had to contend with
however was complicated for their successors by other restrictive
practices relating to the right to act and the right to perform.
Perhaps the most inhibiting factor of all upon the writing of plays
was the growing interest in stage spectacle of the landscape artists:
for this provided a threat to all the emblematic conventions which
had governed dramatic art up to that time.

6 Theatre Practice

I have already suggested that while the Reformation affected the
theatre directly by the transfer of ultimate authority over audience
behaviour from the Pope to the sovereign, and secondly by the imposition of State censorship of plays, nevertheless the banishment
of subject matter of religious and Catholic inspiration from the
stage did not carry with it any automatic prohibition of the stage
craft that had accompanied it. * I have suggested furthermore that
the Renaissance affected the theatre directly by focusing attention
on questions of propriety and form—notably in point of genre,
decorum and symmetry. There are however at least three other

* See pp. 37–39 above.

factors of importance—affecting theatre building, the status of actors, and the tastes of audiences alike—all of which can be attributed to the curious mixture of Reformation and Renaissance pressures working upon one another in Tudor England.

The first is a new outlook towards the occasions on which it was appropriate for dramatic performances to be given. The suppression of the religious stage could not help but loosen the old ties between dramatic entertainments and the Red Letter days of the ecclesiastical Calendar, and open the way to a regular and professional theatre. The second was the fate of Pageantry: for Pageantry not only escaped the stigma attaching to the religious stage, but positively advanced itself in usefulness as an instrument of historical primitivism and national self-aggrandizement. The third factor was the Tudor doctrine of absolutism. The resulting tendency to make national life conform to a pattern set by a central administrative authority in London did not by-pass the theatre.

The importance to Elizabethan drama of the change-over from occasional to regular theatre-going cannot be too strongly emphasized. Performances during the first half of the sixteenth century were regulated directly by appropriate Calendar holidays and thus indirectly by the Church to whose Festivals the holidays were linked. Performances during the latter part of the century came to be permitted within the working week and inside the working hours of the day at that. Climate, the seasons and a respect for Church Festivals (including the observance of Lent and Sunday) continued to play some part in the regulation of theatrical performances: but, by the accession of James I, it was the administrators of the central government who had assumed entire responsibility for prescribing the time and place of English dramatic entertainment.* The impact of this change was immediate and urgent in two directions at least. It affected actors by encouraging the development of companies who, in giving their whole time to acting, must necessarily become regarded as professionals. By contrast, the occasional performers of an earlier time who had given satisfaction in their day came now to be regarded as amateurs. Moreover, professional and amateur status came to be associated, within the nation if not abroad, with London and the Provinces respectively. This difference in status should not be taken to imply that the London professional was potentially a better actor than the provincial amateur whom he largely superseded: but it does mean that the professional was exposed to audiences far more frequently, and that he was thereby enabled to acquire a more far-

* See Ch. III, pp. 90–93 below.

reaching and more assured technique in character portrayal. This becomes important when we consider the second implication of the change over from occasional to regular performances, the need for a permanent base, coupled with that for a rapid increase in the supply of plays. The demand for new plays swiftly extended the range of both characters and situations treated on the stage. The supply of them, together with the increased frequency of performances, could only result in making audiences more critical. Here, the professional actor, by virtue of almost daily contact with audiences, was technically much better equipped than the amateur to deal with a swiftly varying repertory: it was a situation that spelt eclipse for the nationwide amateur theatre, and substantially assisted those whose prime anxiety it was to discredit the old religious drama in terms of 'modern progress'.

The amateur religious theatre had flourished on an expanding drama of religious didacticism provided *locally* by those educated men whom the Church had appointed to watch over the spiritual welfare of everyone domiciled in that locality. Forbidden to perform this repertory of plays, the provincial amateurs had no other and were forced to content themselves with the offerings of professional visitors and the processional pageantry associated with the principal agricultural festivals. *

That Pageantry did survive the Reformation is itself a factor of major consequence. Whether in the form of St. George's Day Ridings, Midsummer Watches or shows associated with the annual installation of a new Mayor, mediaeval conventions of stage-craft found in this Pageantry a channel for self-preservation. The invention of gunpowder late in the fifteenth century had changed the *raison d'être* of Tournaments, but it had not killed them.† If tilting and jousting could no longer be regarded as a training exercise for war, they still remained fashionable forms of exercise for the body and a vehicle for the allegorical disguise of place and person. They preserved their aristocratic exclusiveness and, as a means of flattering patrician self-esteem both in equestrian skill and chivalric conduct, gained in elaboration and prestige from the humanist attitude to Princes and to display. The Elizabethan 'accession tilts' became one of the most spectacular social events of the age, and the joust at Barriers in association with the Mask acquired a new lease of life at Prince Henry's hands at the Jacobean Court: Shakespeare, Burbage, Jonson and Inigo Jones were all concerned, in one way or another, with the preparation of this dramatic Pageantry.

* See Table A, pp. 174–175 below.
† See *EES*, i, pp. 18 and 43–44.

Royal Entries, for similar reasons, developed under the Tudors, attracting the ablest dramatists, painters and artificers of the day to decorate them. Moreover, they became very much more frequent with the institution in London of an annual Lord Mayor's show.* In the fifteenth century Pageantry had battened on history and romance literature in addition to scriptural subject matter. Thus, whatever ground it stood to lose as a result of the Reformation was likely to be more than compensated for by the dual stimulus it received from Renaissance study of classical mythology and from the popular interest in national history awakened by the accession and rule of the House of Tudor. Shakespeare illustrates the point. In the first scene of *Henry VIII*, Buckingham discusses with Norfolk the young king's meeting with Francis I at the Field of the Cloth of Gold. He regrets that owing to ill-health, he was unable to be present.

> 'Then you lost,' replies Norfolk,
> 'The view of earthly glory: men might say,
> Till this time, pomp was single, but now married
> To one above itself.'

In other plays, while Shakespeare did not or could not use scenes from religious drama, he finds it profitable to present upon his stage no less than three Tournaments, and a great variety of other Pageantry.[40]

One of the reasons for the long life of traditional Pageantry and for its survival into a time when it could bequeath its conventions to a regular theatre was the outward and visible prestige which it could give to the Tudor dynasty in the eyes of its own subjects and of foreign visitors. To some extent this exploitation at national level of the popular taste for spectacular display acted as a palliative to the incursions made by the increase in the personal power of the sovereign and his immediate advisers upon the jealously guarded ceremonies of local civic pride. In London, from 1551 onwards the journey made annually by the new Lord Mayor from the City to Whitehall in procession by street and river, and back again to Guildhall, was celebrated by Londoners on a scale hitherto regarded as appropriate to the reception of royal visitors. Similarly in Chester and some other provincial cities much of the stage spectacle formerly associated with local religious plays was transferred to annual civic ceremonies.

Henry VIII's break with Rome translated religious plays into

* The Lord Mayor's Shows were inaugurated in 1535 by the Mercers' Company.[39]

46

political issues and resulted in the central administration interfering with local theatre practice all over the country on an unprecedented scale. In their attempt to impose a uniform pattern of life and thought upon the country, successive Tudor administrations had to decide not only what was and was not suitable for subjects to hear uttered on stages, but when and where such utterances should be permitted, and who might safely be allowed to utter them. Such

FIG. 5. Thetys' sea-chariot: designed and constructed by Garret Christmas for Dekker's *London's Tempe*, the Lord Mayor's Show, London, 1629: from a sketch by Abram Booth.

questions must ultimately resolve themselves into terms of licences and permits: and in the present context this means a regularizing of control over the persons of actors and audiences at least as rigorous as any control or censorship of the texts. As the men on the spot, mayors and magistrates were the persons responsible for ensuring that the King's Peace was kept in the local area under their control. That this jurisdiction could apply to theatrical performances is clear from mayoral edicts dating from 1418 onwards,* and probably earlier. However, as the country divided itself on the

* See *EES*, i, p. 203.

religious question after 1531, the loyalty and discretion of mayors and magistrates came to be regarded as inadequate safeguards for the central government's interest. By 1575 the time is ripe for a show-down with the old order of things, and Sir John Savage, as Mayor of Chester, is summoned to London, imprisoned in the Tower, and obliged to account for his conduct in permitting the Miracle Cycle to proceed despite an injunction to the contrary from the Diocesan Court of High Commission for the North.* This date is significant; for only a year earlier, Queen Elizabeth had granted Letters Patent to the Earl of Leicester's company of actors to perform regularly on weekdays in London, despite the known wishes of the City Fathers to the contrary.

A year later James Burbage builds the *Theater*, the first permanent public playhouse in London. In choosing to place it in Shoreditch, outside the City limits, he also happened to place it outside the jurisdiction of the City Fathers. All the theatres built in London during the next forty years were similarly sited outside the City limits, or in 'Liberties' within the city, in pockets of land (usually land which had passed into the control of the Crown) over which the City had no magisterial control.

Discussing this question as long ago as 1894, T. F. Ordish wrote in his still useful book, *Early London Theatres*,

'Alike in London and the provinces, the companies of players under the licenses of their patrons enjoyed the privilege of public playing. But it was a privilege in the exercise of which the local powers were found to be at variance with the class under whose patronage the drama flourished. Around the stage we see the strife between the old order and the new, and the stage was identified with the old. It is not to be doubted that a good deal of idleness and frivolity, and even vice, hung about the stage, which in its constitution under licenses and privileges of courtiers was a part of feudalism; and when players holding such licenses claimed the right to set up their stages within the city of London, it was discovered that those responsible for the good order and well-being of the city not only resented the intrusion, but asserted their rights, and forbade the stage within the limits of their jurisdiction. It is quite possible that this strife over public stage-playing hastened the development of the Puritan spirit in London.'[41]

It is curious that this idea should not have been enquired into and developed more seriously by subsequent historians, since parallels with this cleavage between the old and the new order in Tudor

* Elizabeth was excommunicated in 1570.

society, associated by Ordish with support for and opposition to the stage in Elizabethan London, have been remarked on often enough where royal favour and prerogative were concerned in Stuart times. Certainly the London theatres would have been closed down in the fifteen-nineties had it not been for Queen Elizabeth's personal intervention in the dispute,—an interest translated after 1603 by James I and his family into direct support for actors, dramatists and designers alike. Hardly less significant is the fact that no permanent theatres came to be built in the Provinces. Touring companies of professional actors based on London visited those cities that had previously enjoyed a lively drama of their own making; but they gave their performances in the town hall, in a church, or other building temporarily allocated to them, and regular amateur dramatics dwindled into non-existence, except at the Universities, the Inns of Court and at some schools.

The link between the licensed theatre buildings and the censored texts is the acting companies. The latter had been obliged to enjoy noble patronage in order to ply their profession from the days when, as minstrel troupes, they had sought to avoid being stigmatized by the Church as rogues and vagabonds: * but the number of companies permitted to operate in the late sixteenth century and early seventeenth becomes notably smaller. The State, in other words, proved a harder task master than the Church had ever done to the acting fraternity; the instrument used against them continued to be the Vagrancy Acts.† Even more remarkable is the steady concentration of this patronage and control, under Stuart rule, into the gift of the Royal Family. How far this was due to Tudor absolutism, to administrative exigency, or to the pressure of Renaissance theory concerning a Prince's part in patronage of the Arts is hard to distinguish. Doubtless all three played some part. What, however, gave a degree of inevitability to all these administrative changes in theatre practice was the creation within the Royal Household in 1545 of a new executive authority, the Revels Office. ‡ Whatever Henry VIII's motives may have been in creating it, by 1573 it is clear that such Household dignitaries as the Secretary, the Privy Seal and the Lord Chamberlain were actively interested in the conduct of its affairs. It is often fancied that, because the word 'Revels' is so closely associated with the leisure recreation of courtiers, the 'Office' was exclusively concerned with the conduct of Court pastimes. Certainly the association was both

---

* See *EES*, i, pp. 179–190 *and 262 et seq.*
† See pp. 104–110 and 335–336 below.
‡ See *EES*, i, pp. 275–279.

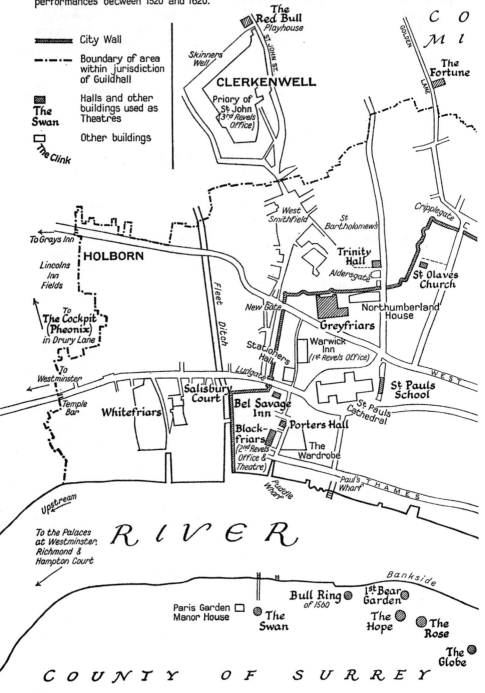

Map showing buildings used as Theatres or intimately connected with dramatic performances between 1520 and 1620.

THE CITY OF

City Wall

Boundary of area within jurisdiction of Guildhall

The Swan — Halls and other buildings used as Theatres

The Clink — Other buildings

C O M I

The Red Bull Playhouse

Skinners Well

ST. JOHN ST.

GOLDEN LANE

The Fortune

CLERKENWELL

Priory of St John (3rd Revels Office)

Cripplegate

To Grays Inn

HOLBORN

Lincolns Inn Fields

West Smithfield

St Bartholomews

Trinity Hall

St Olaves Church

Aldersgate

To The Cockpit (Pheonix) in Drury Lane

Fleet Ditch

New Gate

Northumberland House

Greyfriars

WEST

To Westminster

Stationers Hall

Warwick Inn (1st Revels Office)

Temple Bar

Ludgate

St Pauls School

Whitefriars

Salisbury Court

Bel Savage Inn

St Pauls Cathedral

Black-friars (2nd Revels Office & Theatre)

Porters Hall

The Wardrobe

Puddle Wharf

Paul's Wharf

THAMES

Upstream

To the Palaces at Westminster, Richmond & Hampton Court

R I V E R

Bankside

Bull Ring of 1560

1st Bear Garden

Paris Garden Manor House

The Swan

The Hope

The Rose

The Globe

C O U N T Y   O F   S U R R E Y

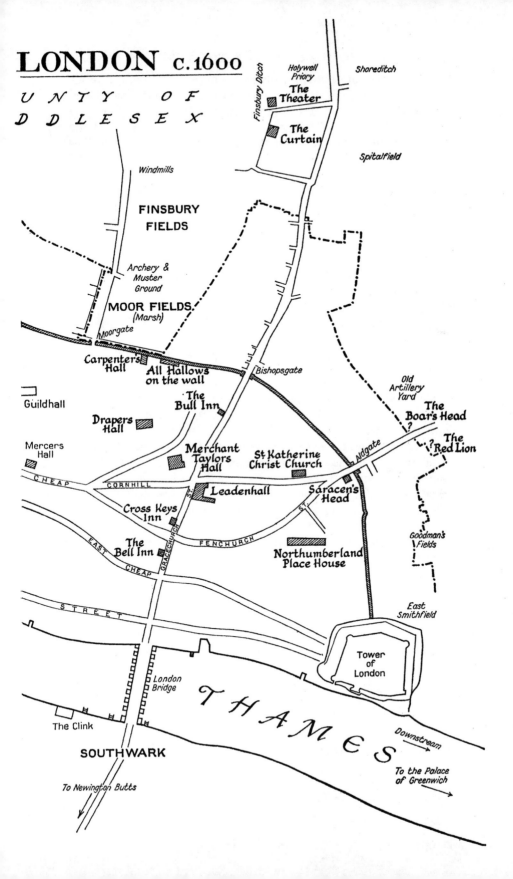

LONDON c.1600

U N T Y O F
D D L E S E X

Holywell Priory

Shoreditch

The Theater

The Curtain

Finsbury Ditch

Spitalfield

Windmills

FINSBURY FIELDS

Archery & Muster Ground

MOOR FIELDS
(Marsh)

Moorgate

Old Artillery Yard

Carpenter's Hall

All Hallows on the wall

Bishopsgate

The Boar's Head
?

Guildhall

The Bull Inn

Aldgate

? **The Red Lion**

Drapers Hall

Mercers Hall

Merchant Taylors Hall

St Katherine Christ Church

CHEAP

CORNHILL

Leadenhall

Saracen's Head

Goodman's Fields

Cross Keys Inn

FENCHURCH

EAST

The Bell Inn

GRACECHURCH

Northumberland Place House

East Smithfield

CHEAP

S T R E E T

Tower of London

London Bridge

T H A M E S

The Clink

SOUTHWARK

Downstream

To the Palace of Greenwich

To Newington Butts

close and important, but it was by no means exclusive of the public theatres, once they had come into existence. In fact, aided and abetted by the Stationers' Company, the whole machinery of State Censorship and control was operated through the Master of the Revels, working directly under the Lord Chamberlain. Nevertheless, there can be little doubt that this concentration of power in the hands of the Revels Office, acting as the agent of sovereign and court, allowed the Court's growing interest in Renaissance theories concerning the symmetrical perspective scene to develop at the expense of both play and player. In the first place stage spectacle became an object of interest in its own right for dramatists who were denied by the censorship so much subject matter which had hitherto in itself served to hold the attention of their audiences. Secondly, the pursuit of scenic verisimilitude opened to question the validity of using boy actors in female roles, the propriety of a multiple setting and, ultimately, the very convention of the emblematic play itself.

The Revels Office, therefore, if it endowed the English theatre in the early seventeenth century with a status that can properly be described as professional, served at the same time, through its licensing power, to let this professionalism develop in the interest of the Court and at the expense of popular support. It is hardly the fault of the dramatists of the period if, in writing to please the more limited audience upon whose favour they depended, their plays strike us as less virile and interesting than those which had been written for both Court and populace with little regard for private status or fashionable taste. Nor did the protection which Revels Office licences afforded to actors against the penalties of the Vagrancy Acts escape attention.

'Players may not be called rogues:' John Coke sarcastically observes in 1615, 'For they bee chiefe ornaments of his Majesties Revells.'[42]

7 Conclusion

I have tried in this chapter to cut away the accretions, associations and overtones which, with the passage of time, have grown up around the words Reformation and Renaissance; I have tried to open to view once again what meaning the changes, implicit in these words, had for Englishmen in the sixteenth and early seventeenth centuries; and, where the theatre is concerned, I have tried to show how the two movements acted and reacted upon one another, often resulting in something different from what might have been expected as a consequence of either the one or the other considered singly. It is a mistake, as it seems to me, to think of the Reformation as simply a rather distant event in ecclesiastical history; for immediately the sovereign takes into his own hands authority for the interpretation of religious doctrine on his subjects' behalf, doctrine and politics become inextricably mixed. Similarly, it is a mistake to equate the Renaissance with academic reaction towards classical learning and artistic precept. A reaction in this direction undoubtedly occurred, but being Italian inspired it could not escape association in England with Rome, the Papacy and Catholicism. If the English Reformation (not forgetting its equivalent in Germany and other countries) was greeted on the continent by a Counter-Reformation, it could well be said that the Italian Renaissance, after an initial friendly welcome into England, was subsequently challenged by a Counter-Renaissance.

In the theatre the result was change, but change that was neither uniform in tempo nor constant in direction. The reason is that the pressure governing the changes was rarely either Reformation or Renaissance *tout simple*. Rather was it usually a subtle mixture of the two in concert, occasioning major differences between the English theatre of the period and the theatres of continental countries. Broadly speaking the theatre in England steadily loses ground as a national art form of wide popular appeal as it gains in professional proficiency. Expressed in other words, the theatre of social recreation, which had reached maturity long after the more widespread theatre of Catholic worship, conquered and banished its rival from national life. Fundamental to this change was State censorship and control, itself a product of both the Reformation and the Renaissance.

III

STATE CONTROL OF BRITISH
DRAMA, 1530–1642

---

1 Control before the Reformation

THE attempts to control plays, players and theatres which
became steadily more frequent and methodical from 1530
onwards were in themselves not the particular inventions of Henry
VIII and his ministers: dramatic performances had excited sufficient opposition to provoke sporadic legislative action from the
start. Whatever the nature of the performance, whether quasi-
dramatic as with Tournaments and ministrel troupes or fully
dramatic as with Miracle Plays and Disguisings, one feature of the
action taken against them repeats itself often enough to warrant
attention. It is simply the very reasonable desire of society, as represented by its governments down the centuries, to prevent
breaches of the peace and the dangers to the community consequent
upon hot tempers and ensuing bloodshed.

I have already treated at length in Volume I the measures taken
to bring Tournaments under control. The effect of these measures
was to transform Tournaments from the bloody battle schools
which were routine in the eleventh century into the artistic forms
of bodily exercise and equestrian prowess still popular in the sixteenth and seventeenth centuries. The means adopted to obtain
this effect was to bring Tournaments under the exclusive control of
the sovereign. His will in these matters was enforced through the
Kings of Arms and Heralds holding authority under the Earl
Marshal, one of the three highest officers of the Royal Household.*
The legislative action taken in the early fifteenth century against
Mumming (which is also treated in detail in Volume I) stemmed
from the same cause; a determination to prevent civic disturbances
at Festival times when, under the cover of disguises and spurred on

* See *EES*, i, pp. 13–19.

by plentiful supplies of wine, damage to private property and even treasonable activities could be practised with small risk of detection. The effect was to translate a former popular folk activity into the sophisticated Disguisings and, subsequently, Masks reserved for the comparative few who were privileged by birth or wealth to attend them.*

Where the religious stage is concerned we may trace an identical pattern of liberty to experiment and develop on a popular basis coupled with, or rather, followed closely by, inhibitions against abuses thought likely to cause trouble. The history of the Feast of Fools provides the most notable example, but the constant disciplining, at least in England, of first the liturgical plays and then miracle cycles, popular moralities and related saint plays argues the same story. The following entry in the Register of John de Trillek, Bishop of Hereford (1344–1361) illustrates the point.

1348. (Between October 6th and November 21st)
'Whereas many of the plays performed in churches contain evil jesting forbidden by the Apostle at any time, and especially unbecoming in the house of the Lord, and further, the devotions of the faithful are disturbed by these exhibitions, the bishop desires to root them out of the diocese, and formally forbids them in the church of L . . ., where they have been frequent, under penalty of excommunication.'[1]

The 'church of L . . .' is more likely to have been that at either Ludlow or Ledbury than the Priory of Leominster, all three of which were among the larger centres of population in the diocese.

It is, however, significant that the imposing of discipline upon the religious stage in this country came to involve a divided authority. As I have argued in Volume I, once religious plays came to be performed on ground that was not consecrated, and which consequently lay outside the jurisdiction of ecclesiastical authority, the *King's Peace* came to be involved as well as the *Peace of God*. The edicts against abuses in the Feast of Fools were of ecclesiastical inspiration and origin since it was the fabric and possessions of churches together with the conduct of their congregations which were affected by these abuses: but the miracle plays and their like impinged upon public conduct in streets, market squares and other places where any riotous behaviour and subsequent harm to persons and property became at once the concern of the town or city. The divided nature of the authority in such cases before 1530 is made

* See *EES*, i, pp. 202–204.

clear in the Pre-Reformation Banns and Proclamation read annually in Chester. The Church takes its part by invoking papal authority, the city by invoking the king's. Spectators who attend performances in seemly manner are rewarded with forty-five days of pardon against their time in Purgatory: those responsible for any disorder are made liable to fine or imprisonment.* The Abbot administers the Pope's interest and the Mayor the King's. Responsibility for discipline over the performers was similarly divided, laymen being the concern of the Mayor's Court, churchmen that of the ecclesiastical Court, as may be seen from other records surviving from Lincoln, Beverley and Coventry.

This is an arrangement which presumably worked well enough so long as the text of the play was not in dispute. The first hint that we get of trouble brewing on this account again comes from Chester. In 1529, as has long been on record, a play of King Robert of Sicily was presented. Sir Edmund Chambers reports this as a fact but refrains from comment; and subsequent historians have been content to follow his lead. However, if, for once, we take J. P. Collier at face value, there is much more to be said about this play.

First, there exists in the Bodleian an ancient romance entitled

'Here is of Kynge Robert of Ciclye,
Hou pride dude him beguile'2

The story, very briefly summarized, tells of a king who denies that God's power is greater than his own. While asleep he is translated by an angel into a court fool and made to accompany the angel, who has usurped the king's own shape, to Rome. King Robert, when properly humbled by this experience, is restored to his own shape and throne.

If, for the present, we associate this romance with the Chester play of 1529 it is immediately apparent that performance of a play with such a plot at a time when Henry VIII was himself engaged in bitter controversy with the Pope over Katherine of Aragon's divorce, could easily give offence. Collier, in making this association between the poem and the play, supports the contention with a letter from someone in Chester on behalf of the Corporation 'destroyed in part by damp, so that it bears no name or date' to an unknown nobleman at Court.

'Our moste humble duetye to your right honorable Lordshypp premysed, we holde it convenyent and proppre to infourme your

* See *EES*, i, Appendix D; also pp. 121, *et seq.*

good Lordshyppe of a play, which som of the companyes of this Cittye of Chester, at theyr costes and charges, are makynge redy, for that your good Lordshyppe maye see wether the same be in any wyse unfyttynge for them, as honest menne and duetyfull subjectes of his Majestye. The sayde playe is not newe at thys tyme, but hath bin bifore shewen, evyn as longe agoe as the reygne of his highnes most gratious father of blyssyd memorye, and yt was penned by a godly clerke, merely for delectacion, and the teachynge of the people to love & feare God in his Majestye, and all those that bee in auctoryte. It is callyd Kynge Robart of Cicylye, the whiche was warned by an Aungell whiche went to Rome, and shewyd Kyng Robart all the powre of God, and what thynge yt was to be a pore man; and thanne, after sondrye wanderynges, ledde hym backe agayne to his kingdome of Cicylye, where he lyved and raygned many yeres.

Thys muche we thought it mete to shewe to your right honorable Lordshyppe, for that your good Lordsh(y)ppe myght knowe the holle of theyr entent that goe aboute to playe this playe on Saynt Peter's day nexte ensewing; and yf your good Lordshyppe shold holde the same unfytte or unwyse at thys tyme, thanne theis pore artifycers will of our knowlege staye the same and . . .' *3

Before dismissing this letter as a forgery—and the convenient lack of names or date makes one suspicious—I think one should recollect that the Town Clerk of Chester, a mere three years later was singularly prompt in scoring out the references to papal control over the audience in the Banns of the Chester Cycle: for Collier's letter is not out of keeping with Newhall's action in 1532, a fact which was unknown to Collier when he quoted this letter. It should also be remembered when evaluating the authenticity of the Collier letter, that the Chester play of The Assumption had, for reasons unknown, already been suppressed several years earlier.†

The point at issue is that any one of these events in Chester, or all of them together, illustrate the sort of difficulty that was arising around the year 1530 from the divided authority over the religious stage in England: it was certain to be aggravated immediately the ecclesiastical authority was called in question by the sovereign. By

---

* Cf. Shakespeare, *MND* III, i. bottom: 'There are things in this comedy of Pyramus and Thisby that will never please. First, Pyramus must draw a sword to kill himself, which the ladies cannot abide . . .' etc.

† The play of The Assumption seems to have been performed last in 1515. On Newhall see *EES. i*, p. 136, especially n.27

1531 Henry VIII, in substituting his own authority for that of the Pope in England, automatically brought control of the religious stage, or at least the control of its auditoriums, as firmly into his own hands as his predecessors had already done with Tournaments, Mummings, Disguisings and troupes of professional minstrel-actors. Nevertheless, this *de jure* change is one which is much more easily conceived in theory than carried into practice: and in fact it took a full hundred years to bring the theatre in this, its most highly self-conscious form, under firm, final and exclusive State control.

To make clear the nature of the problem confronting Tudor governments, and in order to be fair to them, I must now risk a platitude about the nature of dramatic art. The word 'control', which is to occupy so much space in this and ensuing chapters, will inevitably create confusion for the reader until he is himself aware of what precisely had to be controlled: it was not a mere matter of controlling play scripts. A play, fully realized, involves an author, a company of actors, and people congregated together to watch it. To be grouped with the author are the notaries who copied out the parts and the printers who might choose to make a permanent record of it more generally available. With the actors there are the decorators, musical accompanists and technicians to be considered. The spectators are the most complex group of all, since any consideration of them involves a host of subsidiary questions that are properly in the province of the social historian—frequency of performances, accessibility, class, monetary or other distinctions, tastes. Last but by no means least, if drama is an art it can also be a means of livelihood; and once it has become so—as by 1530 it had for many in England—everything that one may say about author, actors or spectators has to be viewed in a context of box-office receipts, of production overheads and personal status in the community as measured by financial reward. In the mid twentieth century all this is familiar enough to appear trite when set out in print as it is here: but when we turn our eyes back into the mid sixteenth century we must remember that most of this had still to be learnt, not to say discovered, by everyone interested in the theatre.

For example, when we talk about the religious stage are we discussing amateur actors, professionals, or both? If amateur, should they not have liberty to use their leisure as they wish without interference? When we discuss the action taken against the theatre by London's Lord Mayor and Aldermen under Elizabeth I what, specifically, is their legislation aimed at promoting or forbidding? Are they afraid of large unruly assemblies of people and of consequent epidemics in time of plague? Are they worried by absenteeism among apprentices and craftsmen as a result of theatrical performances given on weekday afternoons? Has one section of the community any right or justification for forbidding actors, whose talent suffices to earn them substantial rewards, from exercising that talent? What if this action should result in depriving them of this means of livelihood? Should actors, aided and abetted by bright-witted authors, be permitted to inflame public opinion? Is the moral problem implicit here affected at all by the fact that the country is threatened by a foreign invasion or the threat of civil war? These, as it seems to me, are the sort of problems that were provoked by political and social circumstances in the sixteenth century, by the Reformation and the Renaissance in England; problems which, if always lurking beneath appearances, were focused with alarming suddenness and urgency for the first time as issues to which immediate answers had to be found. Not only, therefore, were both sides in the ensuing disputes faced with problems which were in themselves new, but the circumstances of the time forbade the lengthy discussion of fine philosophical points or the procrastination and delay in action which the greater leisure of a more settled time might have allowed. Many, then, of the legislative actions and counter actions that we are to survey and which may seem to us impetuous, bigoted or perverse ought properly to be considered in the light of the times, and interpreted as the posssible consequences of the haste that often attends upon a particular emergency. Such conditions of general national emergency follow swiftly upon Henry VIII's divorce proceedings. In 1531 he assumes the headship of the English Church:* on the 11th July, 1533 he is excommunicated for his pains, and between 1535 and 1539 he dissolves the monasteries with consequences as far reaching for education in England as for the Church. If one reflects for a moment on the furore created by Edward VIII's decision to marry Mrs. Simpson, one is provided with some sort of yardstick to measure both the cleavage in national sentiment which Henry's actions provoked and the bitterness of the passions with which those in favour and those against regarded one another. I think too it is necessary to stress, in contrast to our own more docile times, the violent nature of personal redress that one aggrieved person was likely in those days to have taken upon his adversary. Not only were swords worn and freely used, but a code of honour in which revenge figured so largely as a moral duty had

---

* Confirmed by Act of Parliament in January 1534/35.

the natural effect of swiftly enlarging an affray between individuals into a vendetta between factions. Marlowe for instance was killed in a duel, and Ben Jonson narrowly escaped execution for stabbing Gabriel Spencer to death. I consider these factors basic to all legislative action taken against quasi-dramatic and fully dramatic performances prior to 1530, and still the basic factors governing such action as was taken, at least initially, after 1530.

2 Legislative Action, 1531–1547

Beyond the slender evidence from Chester already quoted and the condign punishment meted out by Cardinal Wolsey to author and actors of a Court play in 1527 cited in Volume I, I see no reason to think that there was any serious desire in government circles before 1531 to interfere with an author's liberty to write what he pleased or an actor's liberty to perform it. Books certainly could not be printed without the sovereign's assent, *cum privilegio regali*; but the evidence of books being suppressed for giving offence is of the slenderest.* Plays and other dramatic entertainments, being the work of 'makers', were not regarded as literature and accordingly only found their way into print in exceptional circumstances. At Court, the procedure regarding dramatic entertainments had been standardized in the Household Order Books, plays and disguisings or masks being selected by the Lord Chamberlain in terms of their suitability to the occasion and readiness for performance.† The actors were adequately disciplined, as adults by the noble patron in whose household they were servants and, as boys, by the choirmasters or schoolmasters who wrote and rehearsed their plays. In the provinces new plays for popular audiences were rare since both the infrequency of performance and the complexity of the organization involved in preparing a performance made traditional texts suffice, occasional redaction of them serving as an adequate concession to novelty. In more sophisticated provincial households travelling professional companies brought a wider variety of plays, but their texts had already received the sanction of the Court or of noble patrons. In all this the tradition of commissioning dramatic entertainments to celebrate particular events or occasions in itself served to keep the risk of controversy to a minimum while at the same time keeping the entertainments closely linked with people, events and life. Whether the entertainment takes the form of a play celebrating the services

* See Ch. IV, pp. 125–126 below.
† See *EES*, i, pp. 275 *et seq.*

of a patron saint like that of St. Thomas at Canterbury or a Disguising of ladies from a rocky brown country and lords from a wooded green one, like that for the marriage of Prince Arthur and Katherine of Aragon, the principle is the same.[4]

In this well regulated climate, it is hardly surprising that the trouble-spots which were so to perplex Henry VIII and his successors in regard to the theatre were not recognized and prepared for in advance although, to our eyes, they had been emerging into view from Henry VII's accession onwards. Professional actors by then were well enough established and organized to want in due course of time a permanent home and a larger share of public support than occasional performances on isolated holidays allowed. The religious stage with its apocryphal stories of the Virgin's life and its representations of the miraculous doings of fabled saints and martyrs was already challenging rationally minded humanists to question their instructional validity. As H. C. Gardiner has pointed out, many Catholics were not only aware of the unhealthy comic and superstitious accretions to the religious stage, but anxious to suppress them before they could be turned to ridicule, especially in Italy and France.[5] Thus the possibility, not to say the probability, of serious division of opinion in Church circles controlling the religious stage was already on the horizon before Henry VIII made himself, rather than the Pope, the ultimate arbiter of its future in England.* To that extent his action may be said to have aggravated rather than precipitated a situation which could only lead to a system of licences and censorship if the religious stage was to be regulated in a manner intelligible to performers, audiences and magistrates alike. In Spain just such an instrument of censorship lay to the hand of ecclesiastical authority in the form of the Inquisition, reorganized and placed under the leadership of Torquemada in 1486. This fact may well account for both the long life of the religious stage in Spain and the ease with which a dramatist like Calderon in the seventeenth century can combine the writing of sacred plays with secular ones: in England, despite the galaxy of dramatic talent that flowered in the lifetime of Lope da Vega (1562–1635) and Calderon (1600–1681) no play of consequence devoted to an avowedly religious subject was written for public performance by professional actors after Marlowe's *Dr. Faustus* (1588).†

---

* The hint of trouble in Chester in 1529 already instanced and the fact that in 1518, both in Ipswich and New Romney, performances of the Corpus Christi Play and the Passion respectively were questioned supports this view.[6]

† An exception is Milton's *Samson Agonistes* which remained unperformed

Like the Spanish, English drama, confronted with the pressures of the Reformation and the Renaissance could not escape the imposition of some form of censorship; but, unlike Spain, England had no previous knowledge or experience, when the moment of crisis arrived in 1531, of how to operate it. A comic comment on the situation is provided by Roger Ascham in a passage from *The Schoolmaster*, published in 1568.

'Yea, the Lord Maior of London, being but a Ciuill officer, is commonlie, for his tyme, more diligent in punishing sinne, the bent enemie against God and good order, than all the bloodie Inquisitors in Italie be in seauen yeare.'[7]

Almost everything about censorship had to be learnt and its efficiency tested by trial and error. The following list provides, on the evidence known to me, a strictly factual account of the action taken towards controlling the stage in England between 1531 and 1547.

> 1532. William Newhall, Town Clerk of Chester, either on instructions from the Corporation or through it on behalf of higher authority, deletes from the Proclamation of the Miracle Cycle all reference to Papal control over the audience.

> 1531. Ipswich: 'Corpus Xi play for ever taken away. Corpus Xi play laide aside for ever by order.'[8]

> 1537. Cambridge: Bishop Gardiner, in his capacity of Chancellor of the University, protests that the performance of Kirchmayer's anti-Catholic *Pammachius* at Christ's College is 'soo pestiferous as were intolerable'.[9]

> c. 1535– York: Letter from Henry VIII to a Justice of the Peace.
> 1540. 'Whereas we understand by certain report the late evil and seditious rising in our ancient city of York, at the acting of a religious interlude of St. Thomas the Apostle, made in the same city on the 23rd August now last past; and whereas we have been credibly informed that the said rising was owing to the seditious conduct of certain papists who took part in preparing for the said interlude, we will and require you that from henceforward ye do your utmost to prevent and hinder any such commotion

---

during his lifetime. The titles of some lost plays recorded in Henslowe's diary suggest that some Old Testament stories were passed for stage performance by the Revels Office in late Elizabethan and early in Jacobean times. *The Virgin Martyr* (Dekker and Massinger, 1618) bears a closer resemblance to films like *Ben Hur* or *Quo Vadis* than to genuinely religious plays.

in future, and for this ye have my warrant for apprehend-
ing and putting in prison any papists who shall, in performing interludes which are founded on any portion of
the Old or New Testament, say or make use of any
language which may tend to excite those who are be-
holding the same to any breach of the peace.'[10]

1540.   Linlithgow, Scotland: Letter from Sir William Eure,
Lord Warden of the Marches toward Scotland, to Lord
Thomas Cromwell, concerning a conversation he had
had with Thomas Bellendyn who had been an eye-
witness to the performance of Sir David Lyndsay's *Ane
Satyre of the Thre Estatis*, recently given before King
James V of Scotland at Linlithgow.

'. . . after the saide enterluyde fynished the King of
Scotts dide call upon the busshop of Glascoe, being
Chauncellor, and diverse other bussops, exorting thaym
to reforme their facions and maners of lyving'.[11]

1542.   London: Bishop Bonner issued an injunction forbidding
the performance of all 'common plays, games and interludes' in chapels and churches.[12]

1543.   London: Act of Parliament 'for the advancement of true
religion and for the abolishment of the contrary.' (See
pp. 15–16 above).[13]

1545.   London: City Proclamation reinforcing the Act of Parliament of 1543. (See Appendix B, pp. 327–328 below.)

This list, sketchy though it is, suffices to illustrate several important points. First, one can deduce from it something of the
machinery devised to meet the crisis as well as glean something of
the nature of that crisis. The crisis is patently occasioned by the religious stage—text, actors and audience. In the attempt to keep the
crisis under control the guiding hand is the sovereign's, working
through his personally appointed Crown servants, his agents in
municipal and magisterial government and finally through the voice
of the people as represented in Parliament. By Proclamation and
letter the sovereign's personal interest is openly declared: hardly
less important in effect are the hints dropped in private conversation with powerful officials.* Municipal, magisterial and parliamentary action are logical sequels.

Two other points which merit comment emerge from study of
the list. It is noticeable that the machinery of control has the mark

* Note that Henry IV rids himself of Richard II this way in Shakespeare's
Richard II, as does Mortimer of Edward II in Marlowe's play.

of improvisation upon it. Perhaps therefore the creation of an Office of Revels in the year 1545, staffed by a Master, Yeoman and Clerk is of greater significance than has generally been assumed. The subsequent use made of the Revels Office as an instrument of Censorship is at least too important to be overlooked in the present context. The second point of interest is the apparent lack of official concern with the actual banning of traditional plays. Any initiative in this direction seems to have been exercised by a particularly zealous local authority (ecclesiastical or municipal) rather than by the central government. H. C. Gardiner supplies a possible reason for this in saying that these plays 'contained few references to the Pope, the destruction of whose influence in England was ostensibly the great objective in Cromwell's and Cranmer's campaign, as it certainly was in Henry's; other doctrinal matter contained in them was not yet offensive to the official creed'[14] To this I would add a further suggestion: that the Church controlled the texts of the religious stage and that, as yet, the Archbishops of Canterbury and York were neither prepared to delegate their authority in the matter to the State nor to show their hand so openly as to risk the popular animosity and resentment which might follow the establishment of Courts analogous to the Spanish Inquisition. This is not to say that the heads of the Anglican Communion were altogether disinterested in the State's action against the religious stage or that they took no part in furthering the State's objective. In fact there is evidence that Cranmer as Archbishop of Canterbury took an active interest in official policy, but that his own hand was carefully gloved. Just as in removing a nail or screw long rusted into place with age, the application of a little oil will ease the task, so Cranmer seems to have decided that the people must be taught to question the validity of their traditional plays before being required to abandon them. The method adopted to attain this end was one frequently used by the Church before—quietly to adapt customary usage to a new end. Example had been given for the method chosen by the German Protestants: provision of a complementary religious stage of Protestant rather than Catholic subject matter. Men will do many things for adequate reward; and, where it was obviously impossible to persuade the cumbersome theatrical organization of the provincial trade guilds to substitute new Protestant plays for the cherished traditional Cycles, it was a comparatively simple matter to commission small companies of professional actors to earn a livelihood by touring them. The surviving evidence of such procedures is again scanty, but there is enough to prove their employment beyond all question.[15] The following quotation from Bale's *Kyng Johan* illustrates the method.

> *Sedition* (to Clergy and Civil order).
> 'Sit down on your knees, and ye shall have absolution
> *A pena et culpa*, with a thousand days of pardon.
> Here is first a bone of the blessed Trinity,
> A dram of the turd of sweet Saint Barnaby.
> Here is a feather of good Saint Michael's wing,
> A tooth of Saint Twyde, a piece of David's harp string,
> The good blood of Hales, and our blessed Lady's milk;
> A louse of Saint Francis in this same crimson silk.
> A scab of Saint Job, a nail of Adam's toe,
> A maggot of Moses, with a fart of Saint Fandigo.
> ... (a further eight lines to the same effect, concluding) ...
> *In nomine Domini Pape, amen!*[16]

The fun to be derived from witnessing such shocking ribaldry is obvious enough: and many there must have been, particularly among those with grievances of any sort against the clergy, who in the mirth of the moment readily accepted the invitation to question the 'popetly plays' as well. Others were doubtless scandalized: and herein lay a cue to danger which in all probability neither Cranmer, Cromwell, Henry VIII himself, nor anyone else who colluded in these schemes to discredit the old drama, anticipated when they launched them. Incensed by the scurrility of the texts or by the ribald reactions of individual spectators to them, the more conservative minded members of audiences retaliated with physical violence. Unruly conduct in 'the auditorium', as we have seen, had always been regarded with apprehension by those responsible for law and order, and had directly occasioned all preceding legislation against the theatre. The letters I have cited from Henry VIII to magistrates in Suffolk and York show clearly enough that it was the risk of riot and rebellion that was most feared now. The only difference in this instance was the direct involvement of the stage with national politics. One legacy therefore of Henry VIII to his son was the inevitability of imposing a more rigorous censorship upon the drama than had ever existed before. If the young Edward VI and Protector Somerset needed any prompting to this end, they received pointed occasion in Kett's rebellion of 1549 when, as Holinshed puts it in his *Chronicle* 'the wicked contrivers of this unhappie rebellion tooke occasion by the assembling of such members of people as reported thither [to Wymondham, a village outside Norwich] to see that plaie, to enter further into their wicked enterprizes'.[17] We do not know what this play was, but I think we may safely assume that it was similar in style and content to that of St. Thomas the Apostle which in York, c. 1540, had sparked off an uprising and occasioned the letter from Henry VIII to the Justices of the Peace quoted on page 62. (See Plates II and III.)

The Censorship, 1547–1558

That the Kett rebellion was triggered off by the performance of a play was a probable consequence of Edward's lack of foresight in repealing his father's Act of 1543 within a few weeks of his accession. Where Henry VIII's Act had permitted the performance of all religious plays provided that they did not presume to 'interpret the scriptures', Edward's repeal of it opened the flood-gates to Protestant polemics of every kind, notably to criticism of the Mass and the Eucharist. That advantage was promptly taken of this liberty there can be no doubt, if only from the shocked comments of Catholics who equated such licence with blasphemy.* Unfortunately for them such blasphemy could no longer be isolated as an ecclesiastical affair since it was perpetrated with the approval of the government of the realm. Objection to it, therefore, at once assumed the guise of treason, since no redress could be hoped for without a change of government. With the drama thus hopelessly entangled in the web of national and international politics, everyone associated with the stage came to find themselves within perilously close range of the gibbet and the block. The first execution of which record survives took place in 1540, when an interlude-player called Spencer, who had formerly been a priest, was burned to death at Salisbury for 'matter concerning the sacrament of the altar'. In London the keeper of the Carpenter's Hall had been arrested 'for procuring an interlude to be openly played, wherein priests were railed on and called knaves'.[19] In such an atmosphere therefore, one may expect efforts to control the stage to take two forms: first, restrictions imposed by the central government to safeguard its own interests and, secondly, what one may term 'local interference', prompted by a very human desire among clerics and laymen in charge of small communities to steer clear of the more perilous side of the law. In respect of the former, Edward's methods follow those of his father—Proclamations, Acts of Parliament, instructions to mayors, magistrates and justices of the peace: but they include new and important points of substance. There is the

* The Venetian ambassador is sufficiently struck by this state of affairs to comment in a letter about these plays.[18]

Proclamation of 1549 inhibiting the performance of *all* plays for two months. In 1551 the Privy Council demand that their licence shall be obtained before any professional troupe of actors perform a play even in the house of their patron. In 1551 another Proclamation obliges printers to obtain leave to publish play texts as well as authors and actors to perform them. I quote here only those extracts from the documents which directly concern us.

Proclamation. 6th August, 1549

'For asmuche as a greate number of those that be common Plaiers of Enterludes and Plaies, as well within the citie of London, as els where within the realme, do for the moste part plaie suche Interludes as contain matter tendyng to sedicion and contempnyng of sundery good orders and lawes, where upon are growen, and daily are like to growe and ensue, muche disquiet, division, tumultes, and uproares in this realme; the Kynges Maiestie ... straightly chargeth and commaundeth al and every his Maiesties subjectes ... that from the ix daie of this present moneth of August untill the feast of all Sainctes nexte commyng, thei ne any of them, openly or secretly plaie in the English tongue any kynde of Interlude, Plaie, Dialogue or other matter set furthe in forme of Plaie in any place publique or private within this realme, upon pain that whosoever shall plaie in Englishe any such Play, Interlude, or other matter, shall suffre imprisonment, and further punishment at the pleasure of his Maiestie.'[20]

The Act of Uniformity, 1549

Section III

'And it is ordeyned and enacted by thauctoritie above saide, that yf any p(er)son or p(er)sons whatsoev(er) after the saide feaste of Penthecoste next com(m)ynge, shall in anye enterludes playes songes rymes, or by other open Wordes, declare or speake anye thinge in the derogac(i)on depravinge or dyspisinge of the same booke *i.e. The Book of Common Prayer* or of anye thinge therin conteyned or any parte thereof ... That then ...'

Penalties: first offence, a fine of £10: second offence, a fine of £20: third offence, forfeiture of goods and imprisonment for life.[21]

SECOND PROCLAMATION of Edward VI relating (among other matters) to dramatic performances. April 28, 1551. (The long s 'ʃ' is altered throughout to the modern short 's').

A Proclamacion set furth by the Kynges Maiestie, with the aduise of his Highnes moste honorable counsail, for the reformacion of Vagabondes, tellers of newes, sowers of sedicious rumours, *players*, and printers without licence & diuers other disordred persons, the .xxviii. day of Aprill in the .v. yere of his highnes most prosperous reigne. . . . . . .

And furthermore, his maiestie straightly chargeth and co(m)-maundeth, that no man be so hardy either to deuise any tale, rumor or talke, touching his maiestie, his Counsail, Magistrates, Justices, officers, or ministers, nor hearing any shche tale, rumor or talke, to tel, reporte, or speake, the same agayne to any other person or persons, then to either one of his counsayl, or to a Justice of peace, and then withall to shew also, of whome he had the same, to thintent that the same person, from whome the tale or rumor commeth, may be punished for the deuising of it, if he deuised it, or for the telling of it to any other person, then by this proclamation is appointed.

And forbicause diuers Printers, Bokeselers, and Plaiers of Enterludes, without consideracion or regarde to the quiet of the realme, do print, sel, and play whatsoeuer any light and phantastical hed listeth to inuent and deuise, whereby many inconueniences hath, and dayly doth arise and follow, amonge the kinges maiesties louyng and faithful subiectes: His highnes therfore straightly chargeth and commaundeth that fromhencefurth, no printer or other person do print nor sel, within this Realme or any other his maiesties dominions any matter in thenglish to(n)g(ue), nor they nor any other perso(n), do sel or otherwise dispose abrode any mattre, printed in any forreyn dominion in thenglishe tongue, onles the same be firste allowed by his maiestie, or his priuie counsayl in writing signed with his maiesties most gratious hand or the handes of sixe of his sayd priuie counsayl, vpon payne of Imprisonment without bayle or mayne price, and further fine at his maiesties pleasor. Nor that any common players or other persons, vpon like paines, to play in thenglish tong, any maner Enterlude, play or mattre, without they haue special licence to shew for the same in writing vnder his maiesties signe, or signed by vi of his highnes priuie counsaill: willing & straightly charging & commaunding al Justices, Mayors, Shirifes, Bailifes, Constables, & other officers and ministers, diligently to enquire for, and serche out al maner offendors within the limites and compasse of their commissions, and specially al suche as shal offende against any poinctes or braunches expressely set furthe in this proclamation, and to punishe the same without remission: Willing lykewise, and also strayghtely charging and commaunding al his good, true, louing and faythefull Subiectes to be aiding, helping, and assisting to all and euery officer in thexecution of their charges, as they tender the fauor of his Maiestie, and the preseruation of the commonwealthe, as they will aunswer to his Maiestie for the contrary at their vttermost perill.

God saue the King.

RICHARDUS GRAFTON
typographus Regius
excudebat

M. D. LI.

Cum priuilegio ad imprimendum solum.[22]

A number of Minutes were made by the Court of Aldermen in London inhibiting plays and players during Edward's reign which followed directly upon the legislation introduced by the central government.*

An act of ecclesiastical government of nation-wide application and consequence to the theatre, remains to be considered: in 1548 the Feast of Corpus Christi was suppressed in England. An immediate consequence of this decision was to disestablish many ancient religious plays from the public holiday with which they had been associated for generations.

'Fforasmoche as there was before thys tyme' reads the Great Black Book of Hereford under December 10th 1548 (fol. 27), 'dyvers corporac(i)ons of Artiffycers, craftes and occupac(i)ons in the sayd Cytey who were bound by the grauntt of ther corporacions yerlye to bryng fforthe and sett forewards dyv(e)rs pageaunttes of Ancy(e)ntt historyes in the p(ro)cessyon in the sayd cytey upon the Day and Ffeastt of Corpus Xri which nowe ys & are omytted and surseassed. . . .'

The entry goes on to say in great detail how they are now to divert their funds to the upkeep and maintenance of the city. The importance of this change lies in the obvious difficulties which would confront anyone trying in future to link plays thus disestablished to some other festival: and, in places where plays were not directly associated with the celebrations attending this particular

---

* Some of these are quoted in Ch. V, pp. 191–196 below. See Chambers *ES*, iv., pp. 261–2 and *MSC II*, pp. 285 *et seq.*

Feast Day, no-one could argue the case for perpetuating performances with the old self-confidence born of tradition when many
towns had already abandoned theirs.

The story of stage censorship in Mary's reign proceeds along
much the same lines, but with important differences of emphasis.
First among these is the deliberate revival of the Miracle Cycles in
places where they had already been condemned, including London
itself.

> 'The sam(e) day [7th June, 1557] begane a stage-play
> at the (Grey)frers of the passyon of Cryst.'[23]

In the same year a performance of a play about the life of St. Olave
was given in St. Olave's Church in Silver Street.[24] (See map on
pp. 50–51.) This clearly argues that the leaders of the Catholic
Church in England had by no means come to regard the religious
stage, as exemplified in the Miracle Cycles, either as effete and
lacking all popular support or as having passed out of clerical control
into the exclusive hands of municipal authority. Secondly, Interludes
of religious polemic with a Catholic bias, if not positively encouraged,
were at least admitted under written licence. Of these only *Respublica* has survived to give us any idea of what form the riposte took.
At a first glance the dialogue might be mistaken for that of a
Protestant play, as also the cast list: yet one character in the latter,
'OPPRESSION, *alias* REFORMATION', bespeaks the contrary. On closer
inspection the dialogue too is notably different in being free of that
obscenity which characterizes most of the Protestant plays. The
satire, however, is no less withering, and the following passage
provides a good sample of it. Avarice, 'the Vice of the Play', is
plotting with his friends, Insolence, Adulation, and Oppression,
how they may obtain Offices in the government of the Lady
Respublica.

Insolence.	Let us then have new names, each man, without delay.
Avar.	Else will some of you make hanging stuff one day.
Oppr.	Thou must new christen us.
Insol.	First, what shall my name be?
Avar.	Faith, sir! your name shall be Mounsire Authority.
Oppr.	And, for me, what is your determination?
Avar.	Marry, sir! ye shall be called Reformation.

After some debate it is agreed that Adulation shall be called
Honesty, while Avarice claims for himself the name of Policy. All
four then try to memorize their new names, experiencing some
difficulty in doing so.

70

Avar.	Policy! Reformation! Authority!
Adul.	Hypocrisy! Defamation! and Authority!
Avar.	Hypocrisy? ha! Hypocrisy? ye dull ass!
Adul.	Thou named'st Hypocrisy even now, by the Mass!
Avar.	Policy, I said; Policy! knave, Policy! Now say as I said.
Adul.	Policy, knave! Policy!
Avar.	And what callest thou him here?
Adul.	Defamation!
Avar.	I told thee he should be called Reformation!
Adul.	Very well!
Avar.	What is he now?
Adul.	Deformation!
Avar.	Was ever the like ass born, in all the nations? . . . Come on! ye shall learn to sol-fa Reformation! Sing on now: *Re*
Adul.	*Re* . . . . . .
Avar.	*Refor* . . . . . .
Adul.	*Reformation.*
Avar.	Policy, Reformation, Authority.

The point thus made verbally is immediately repeated in visual terms, for Avarice then instructs his companions to go and change their clothes for garments more appropriate to their new selves.[25]

The presence of Mary with her consort, Philip II of Spain, upon the English throne could not by itself assure Catholics of a monopoly in plays of this sort: Protestant Interludes were at least attempted. In February 1556, the Lord Lieutenant of Essex is instructed to stop a play of which the Privy Council has heard rumours, and to report on it to the Council.[26] Henry Machyn reports in his Diary that a play about the Eucharist was to be presented in Islington on December 10th, 1557, but that it was stopped before it could begin. It would seem certain that the man Machyn calls 'Ruffe, a Skott', who was either the author of the play or one of the players, was the same 'Ser John Ruffe, prest, a Skott' who on the 20th of December was condemned as a heretic, and burned alive at the stake two days later.[27] It must at least be recognized, however shocking such incidents seem to us, that Mary had given due warning at the start of her reign of the attitude her government would adopt towards such plays and players. In 1553 she issued a Proclamation. It is dated 18th August and is so worded as to leave no room for doubt.

'. . . Her highnes therfore strayghtly chargeth and commaundeth all and every her sayde subiectes . . . that none of them presume from henceforth to preache . . . or to interprete or teache any

71

scriptures, or any maner poyntes of doctryne concernynge religion. Neyther also to prynte any bookes, matter, ballet, ryme, interlude, processe or treatyse, nor to playe any interlude, except they haue her graces speciall licence in writynge for the same, upon payne to incurre her highnesse indignation and displeasure.'

The cause of this interdict is made equally explicit.

'. . . forasmuche also as it is well knowen, that sedition and false rumours haue bene nouryshed and maynteyned in this realme . . .

by . . . playinge of Interludes and pryntynge false fonde bookes . . . concernynge doctryne in matters now in question and controuersye . . .'[28]

'Indignation and displeasure', as we have seen, could mean an indictment for heresy with attendant penalties: it could also mean an inhibition against further playing and the cancellation of permission to perform at all. This latter action was taken in 1556 against a company of players who 'named themsellfs to be the servaunts unto Sr Frauncis Leek' and who had been reported to the Privy Council as a danger to the peace of the realm. The Lord President of the North, the Earl of Shrewsbury, is instructed to suppress the company, the charge being that they had

'wandered abowt the North partes, and represented certaine playes and enterludes, conteyning very naughty and seditious matter touching the King and Quene's Ma[ts] and the state of the realme, and to the slaunder of Christe's true and Catholik religion, contrary to all good ordre, and to the manifest contempt of Allmighty God, and daungerous example of others.'

The consequences are twofold:

(1) All Justices of the Peace in the area are to be instructed that

'they doo in no wyse suffer any playes, enterludes, songues, or any suche lyke pastymes whereby the people may any wayes be steryd to disordre'.

(2) The Lord President is himself instructed to write to Sir Francis Leek

'willing him to cause the said players that name themsellfs his servaunts to be sought for, and sent forthw[th] unto you to be farther examined . . .' and 'that he suffer not any of his servaunts hereafter to goo abowte the countrie, and use any playes, songs, or enterludes, as he will aunswer for the contrary.'[29]

The examination demanded in this instance, together with the report that the Lord Lieutenant of Essex was required to provide in 1556, are worthy of further comment: for this would appear to mark the start of a system of censorship of play texts by licence. The purpose of these examinations is made clearer by three further actions of the Privy Council in 1557. In June the Lord Mayor of London is instructed to arrest a group of players and to prohibit all performances in future 'except the same be first seen and allowed.'[30] Also in June, players are arrested in Canterbury by the Mayor and their 'lewd play-book' sent by him to the Privy Council.[31] In September it is the Council itself that is asking the Lord Mayor of London to arrest the actors and to seize the book of another 'lewd' play, *Sacke full of Newes*, and to forward the book for examination. On inspection, this play proved inoffensive and the actors were released.[32] However, immediately afterwards *all* actors are directed by the Privy Council, through the Lord Mayor, that they may henceforth only act in London between November and March (the Feasts of All Saints and Shrovetide) * and that the plays acted must have received the prior consent of the Bishop of London sitting in Ecclesiastical Court (The Ordinary).[33]

The authority of the Ordinary in such matters is not a Marian invention. The first Act of Parliament against the drama, Henry VIII's Act of 1543, makes the Ordinary, together with two Justices of the Peace of the shire where the Ordinary sits, responsible for deciding whether there has been any infringement of the Act.[34] Mary's order of 1557 therefore only reinforces his authority. I think, however, that we may be permitted to deduce from this, first, that the selection of Bishops to fulfil this function derived from the Church's authority over the religious stage prior to the Reformation; and, secondly, that once confirmed in this position by the State, they were possessed of the necessary authority to suppress the religious stage altogether. If this hypothesis is accepted, then it at once becomes possible to explain why, in Elizabethan times, it is the Bishops, Deans and Archdeacons, who call in the prompt books of the Miracle Cycles and Moralities, and either censor them, as at Wakefield, or confiscate them, as at York.[35]

My own impression is that the censorship of the period 1531–1558 was essentially one devised to safeguard civil order. Breaches of the peace, major or minor, were the constant motive in legislation against the stage: and in this legislation we must interpret

* I.e. during the winter months when outdoor performances were unlikely to draw the large crowds normal in summer. Indoor performances automatically restricted the number of patrons.

such words as 'naughty' or 'lewd' to denote, not childish or vulgar, or obscene, but *wicked* in the sense of dangerous, treasonable or seditious, and *disgraceful* in the sense of profane or blasphemous. It follows that plays proved themselves to be 'wicked' and 'disgraceful', initially at least, by the effects they had on their audiences in performance rather than because of the nature of the text. Only after some two decades of performances of polemical plays did it seem advisable or necessary to try to divine in advance which plays were likely to provoke public demonstrations. This is surely the purpose of the words 'neyther . . . to print any . . . interlude . . . nor to playe any interlude, except they haue her graces special licence for the same' in Mary's Proclamation of 1553 already quoted. Categorical, however, as this wording may have been in expressing the government's intention, it clearly failed in London as well as in more distant provincial cities to carry much weight with either the players or the magistrates. I do not think we need assume deliberate defiance on the part of either as the exclusive reason for the breaches of the Proclamation, occasioning arrest and reprimand, which I have instanced: rather would it seem that, as yet, the government had not possessed itself of adequate executive power to carry its wishes into effect, or, supposing that it possessed the power, that it had not yet devised sufficiently well organized machinery to make that power effective. It is ironical therefore that Mary's efforts to remedy this state of affairs should have succeeded to the point of equipping her Protestant sister with administrative machinery capable of suppressing altogether those same religious plays which she had attempted to revive.

One last word on the censorship prior to Elizabeth's accession in 1558 and her famous Proclamation of 16th May 1559 forbidding all performances without licence. There is little or no evidence of any wish on the part of the Government or of the Church to suppress the theatre *per se*. Breaches of the peace resulting from theatrical performances, as I have said, provided the root cause of government action against the theatre; it was the religious nature of the subject matter of most English plays of the time which, by becoming politically as well as doctrinally contentious as a result of the Reformation, provoked argument, inflamed tempers and occasioned these breaches of the peace. The polemical interludes were, by definition, more contentious than the Miracle Cycles. Thus, although the start of the censorship can be traced to interference with the wording of the Banns and Proclamation of the Chester Cycle, Cycles there and elsewhere survive the first thirty years of state censorship in sporadic performances along with the academic drama of neo-classical inspiration. It is a different spirit, in the latter part of the sixteenth century, which gives the *coup de grâce* to the great Cycles, and launches an all-out attack on the theatre itself, whether religious or secular subject matter be treated on its stages.

The Censorship under Elizabeth I.

Apart from the changes directly attributable to a reversion to Protestant government, Elizabeth's attitude to the stage during the first decade of her reign does not appear to have differed much from that of her sister, her brother or her father. In the years 1558–1571, her government adopted the machinery of censorship and control bequeathed to it by its Marian predecessor without seeing fit to institute any novel measures of its own devising. An exception is the Proclamation of May 1559 which banned the performance of all plays without prior licence. Yet this, in effect, only extended to performances of plays the measures which Mary had taken against the printing of them six years earlier. In both instances the grounds for action are the same. Mary's Proclamation concerns 'doctrine in matters now in question and controuersye, touchinge the hyghe poyntes and misteries of christen religion': Elizabeth's Proclamation seeks to control plays which 'are not convenient in any good ordred Christian Common weale to be suffred', and follows up the section of the Act of Uniformity (promulgated a week earlier) forbidding discussion on the stage of 'anything in the derogation, depraving or despising of the same book [of Common Prayer], or of anything therein contained . . .'. Similar action was taken against printed plays a month later, and a Patent issued setting up the High Commission for ecclesiastical causes with jurisdiction in all these matters.[36]

The phrasing of the Proclamation of 1559 admits explicitly that the religious controversies in question were now officially recognized as issues of national politics*; for the magistrates charged with the enforcement of it are warned not to license plays 'wherin either matters of religion or of the gouvernaunce of the estate of the common weale shalbe handled or treated.' The explanation given is that these are 'no meete matters to be wrytten or treated upon, but by menne of aucthoritie, learning and wisedome, nor to be handled before any audience, but of grave and discreete persons.' The powers given by this Proclamation to the Mayor 'or other chiefe officers' in cities and towns corporate, and to the Lord

---

* This also applies to the wording of the Injunctions of June 1559.

Lieutenants or two Justices of the Peace in the shires, form the basis of the censorship of all drama and of control of all playing places in England throughout Elizabeth's reign. That they did not suffice to meet the situation, however, is made clear by the government's subsequent actions.

Both in terms of accumulated experience and more adequate administrative machinery Elizabeth's government was better equipped than any of its predecessors to cope with such a problem as stage censorship. Yet when this government shows itself so embarrassed by the problem as to seek still more sweeping powers of control, posterity must assume that factors not hitherto encountered occasioned this embarrassment. Government action during the thirty-three years between 1570 and the end of the reign includes the reorganization of the Revels Offices with the establishment of its Master as an official licenser of plays and playhouses, the setting up of a censorship commission on which the Revels Office, the Church and the City of London were all directly represented, action against the stage in Poor Law regulations, Star Chamber orders for the registration of all plays appearing in print and even an Order in Council authorizing the demolition of all theatres in and about London. Faced with this knowledge we must either assume that Elizabethan governments were far less capable of executing their wishes than those of Mary, Edward VI, and Henry VIII—and as I have suggested, with better administered machinery, this would hardly seem likely—or else endeavour to find out what new problems confronted Elizabethan governments in their relations with the theatre to provoke such aggressive action against it.

If I am correct in putting this complexion upon the pace and order of the development of stage censorship, the nature and quality differentiating the regulations of the period 1530–1570 from that which followed it in the reigns of Elizabeth and James I becomes reasonably clear. The early censorship was expedient in nature and experimental in quality: breach or defiance of it was regular, since doubt still existed concerning the necessity of censorship. During the later period no one questioned the need for censorship (at least there is no record of protest or query) and defiance of it was exceptional, but the question of who should possess the right to exercise it loomed very large. Up until the fifteen-sixties tradition and the improvisations of the early Tudors had given Church officials, magistrates in town and country and the sovereign's private advisers almost equal rights in interfering with stage performances as occasion demanded and local circumstance suggested. Any attempt therefore to organize the censorship along more systematic and efficient lines was certain to provoke conflict among the interested parties and to deflect attention from the nature of the subject matter censored and the activities proscribed towards the power-politics of exercising the right to license. In such a situation we should not expect Catholics, Puritans, or others with vested interests in the subject matter of the drama, to align themselves consistently with any one of the rival factions seeking to dominate the censorship, but rather with that body which appeared to possess most authority at the time. Similarly, we should expect those people who sought to earn their living by providing public audiences with dramatic performances to seek to turn these divisions among their would-be controllers to their own advantage.

A hint of the trouble that overtook Elizabethan governments is provided in a letter which Edmund Grindal, as Bishop of London, sent to the Privy Council in February, 1564.

'Mr. Calfhill this mornynge shewed me your letter to him, wherin ye wishe some politike orders to be devised agaynste Infection. I thinke it verie necessarie, and wille doo myne endevour bothe by exhortation, and otherwise. I was readye to crave your helpe for that purpose afore, as one nott vnmyndefulle of the parishe.

By searche I doo perceive, thatt ther is no one thinge off late is more lyke to have renewed this contagion, then the practise off an idle sorte off people, which have ben infamouse in all goode common weales: I meane these Histriones, common playours; who now daylye, butt speciallye on holydayes, sett vp bylles, whervnto the youthe resorteth excessively, & ther taketh infection: besydes that goddes worde by theyr impure mowthes is prophaned, and turned into scoffes; for remedie wheroff in my jugement ye shulde do verie well to be a meane, that a proclamation wer sette furthe to inhibitte all playes for one whole yeare (and iff itt wer for ever, it wer nott amisse) within the Cittie, or 3. myles compasse, vpon paynes aswell to the playours, as to the owners off the howses, wher they play theyr lewde enterludes.'*

This letter should serve to remind us of the many Protestants who had exiled themselves in Germany and Switzerland during the Marian persecution, and of the influx of Lutheran and Calvinist doctrine which accompanied the return of these men into England at Elizabeth's accession. Grindal's parenthesis—'and iff itt wer for ever, it wer nott amisse'—is mild compared to the views of

* Given, with sources, in *ES*, iv, pp. 266–7.

Puritans about the stage proclaimed and published between the fifteen-seventies and 1642.

Another clue to the nature of the trouble is offered in Sir Thomas Benger's conduct of the affairs of the Revels office. This was not only ineffectual enough to provoke Lord Burghley into calling for reports from Benger's subordinates about the working methods used in the office, but to admit of one of these subordinates, the Clerk, Thomas Blagrave, taking over as acting Master from that time (1572/3) until Benger's death four years later.

The third fact to be remarked is the startling change in the status of at least one of the professional acting companies in London at this time. In 1574 the Earl of Leicester's Company received a Patent under the Great Seal to perform regularly in London on weekdays; and within two years of being accorded this privilege, the company equipped itself with a permanent playing place for these performances, the Theater, in Shoreditch.

At first glance the sequences of events listed above appear to be quite independent of one another. Closer scrutiny, however, while it may not alter the unrelatedness of the actual events cited, at least suggests a relationship between them significant enough to have provided Elizabethan governments with grounds for serious anxiety about the future of the theatre. If we take Grindal's letter to be symptomatic of a rising tide of Puritan opposition to the continuance of dramatic performances, and if we take the status accorded by the Privy Council to the Earl of Leicester's Company of actors to indicate that the Court did not share the Puritans' hostility to the stage, we at least find ourselves confronted with a situation that is different in kind from any which we have encountered in tracing the progress of the censorship in earlier years, but potentially just as dangerous. Instead of the State seeking to control the Catholic religious stage, men of extreme Protestant persuasion are now pressing the State to ban all plays. It is, moreover, a situation which of itself would give Lord Burghley good grounds for reorganizing the Revels office.

Puritan hostility to the theatre has been made so familiar and discussed so often by apologists of the drama that we may perhaps be misled into thinking that Puritan sentiment was alone to blame for the stormy history of the stage in Shakespeare's lifetime. In fairness, I think we must admit that the addiction of the Court to dramatic entertainment together with the stubbornness (not to say tyranny) of its supporters may have played just as large a part in the exacerbating of feeling on the subject which provoked the need for stricter measures of control. The evidence which survives for our examination certainly reveals that Puritan agitation against the theatre was sufficiently vociferous for the government both to acknowledge it and to go some distance to meet it: but the same evidence reveals with equal clarity that between 1570 and 1642 the Court took very good care in conceding points to extreme Protestant sentiment in the Church, in Parliament and in the City of London, to ensure that the control asked for and granted should in fact be exercised by itself through its own nominees. Since most of the documents which form the corpus of this evidence have been transcribed and printed in full by Miss Gildersleeve, Sir Edmund Chambers and Professor Bentley and are now readily available for consultation, I can myself afford to be fairly brief in my examination of them here.

The censorship to which Shakespeare was subject during his lifetime seems to me to have passed through four distinct phases, each lasting approximately one decade. In the first, covering the fifteen-seventies, the government set the pace by finally suppressing the religious stage, partly by its various attempts to control the itinerant acting companies in the provinces, and partly through its endeavours to place dramatic performances in London securely under the aegis of the Master of the Revels as the official representing the wishes of the Privy Council in general and the Lord Chamberlain in particular. The second phase, covering the fifteen-eighties, is dominated by the vigorous reaction of the City of London, aided by the Church, against the Court's steady accretion of licensing power, and culminates in the establishment of a licensing commission on which City, Church and Crown were equally represented. The fifteen-nineties mark the virtual elimination of the Church from active control of the drama, leaving a precarious balance between City and Crown and inviting a final duel for the ultimate authority. In the last phase, covering the first decade of James I's reign, the Crown vested itself with autocratic control of plays and players, leaving to the cities and shires only a limited authority over the actual places of playing within their local jurisdiction. This action eliminated all effective opposition to the drama among the populace at large. What the Court could not foresee was that popular resentment, on this count as on many others, might become so violent and so well organized that it took recourse to reversing the position by overthrowing the authority of the Crown itself with armed rebellion.

It is helpful to bear this general picture of the trend of events in mind when considering the year-by-year evidence of legislation controlling the stage which, because of the quantity of detail, can easily seem so incoherent as to amount to no more than an erratic sequence of whimsical, spiteful and otherwise personally motivated actions. In fact, the fifteen-seventies mark the most determined and sustained efforts made by any Tudor government up to that time to deal firmly with all aspects of theatrical performances—plays, play-makers, times and places of performance, audiences and actors. There can be little doubt that these measures were triggered off by the long expected, but long delayed, excommunication of the Queen in February, 1570.

The first of many measures to regularize the position of actors in Elizabethan society was 'An Acte for the punishement of Vacabondes and for Releif of the Poore & Impotent'—an Act first put on the Statute Book on June 29th 1572 and subsequently amended in 1576, in 1584–85, and again in 1597–8.[37] It was the actor's traditionally nomadic habit of life, governed by his need to find audiences, which brought his profession under the terms of the Poor Law legislation rather than his being necessarily either poor or a vagabond. Furthermore, the specific purpose of the Act, as far as actors were concerned, was to give magistrates power to deal with tramps and felons who, being 'of no fixed address' and lacking any 'recognized employment', passed themselves off as actors when arrested as vagabonds. No actor who could prove himself the servant of 'any Baron of this Realm or . . . any other honorable Personage of greater Degree' had anything to fear from this Act. His security rested in the respectability of his patron, and it was the joint responsibility of both to ensure that the plays in the com-pany's repertoire were properly licensed for performance. A lapse in this respect on the part of the actors automatically brought trouble upon the patron who stood to forfeit his right to maintain actors among his Household servants.

If this Act of nationwide application was inhibitive in tone, the Patent given to the Earl of Leicester's company two years later (1574) was permissive. In the progress of the censorship its significance was twofold. In the first place it stated, in respect of a single acting company, everything which in the Act had been left unstated (and therefore ambiguous) concerning any legitimate act-ing company's rights to perform plays. In the second place, it prescribed the Master of the Revels as the person to whom plays should be submitted for licensing. It is notable that an attempt three months earlier by the Privy Council to establish similar con-trol of playing places (at least in London) through its own nominee had been rejected by the Lord Mayor and Aldermen.[38] Another attempt was made to achieve this objective when the

Master of the Revels position was fortified in 1581 (seven years later) by the award of another Patent.[39] This Patent confirmed Edmund Tilney as Master, in which capacity he had been acting since 1578, and authorized him to license all

'plaies, plaiers and playmakers, together with their playing places, to order and reforme, auctorise and put downe, as shalbe thought meete or unmeete unto himselfe or his said deputie in that behalfe.'[40]

The government, however, in seeking to secure full control over the theatre ran into the age old difficulties occasioned by the need, where drama is concerned, to control an auditorium as well as a script and performers. If the State was in the process of taking over from the Church the responsibility for deciding what subject matter should or should not be presented on the stage, and who should perform it, municipal authorities remained as keen under the new regime as they had been under the old to preserve their time-honoured right to control the physical conditions of performance. In London, where the struggle for ultimate control of the stage between 1573 and 1603 was toughest, this was the City's strongest weapon: for every attempt by the government to impose its will on property within the jurisdiction of the City Council could be deemed an infringement of civic liberties and could be consequently repulsed with ease. This point can be illustrated readily by reverting for a moment to the events of 1574 cited above. When the Privy Council sought to nominate a certain Mr. Holmes to have 'appointment of places for playes and enterludes within this citie' the Lord Mayor and Aldermen declined to accept a suggestion which infringed on rights 'extending to the hart of our liberties'.[41] This incident occurred in March. In the same month the Lord Mayor had forbidden certain players to perform in the city (Leicester's company, quite possibly, included) as we learn from a Privy Council Minute requiring him 'to advertise their Lordships what causes he hath to restraine plaies, to thintent their Lordships may the better aunswer suche as desyre to have libertye for the same', an action which was promptly followed by the granting of the Patent to Leicester's Company.[42] What strikes me as important about this sequence of incidents is that where the Lord Mayor successfully defends his own right to control playing places within his jurisdiction he does not so much as challenge the Patent granting Leicester's company the right to perform in London.

In the mid seventies then—immediately prior, that is, to the building of the Theater—I think we may fairly say that the Crown had established its right of control over acting companies, and that City Councils both in London and the Provinces could, if they so wished, deny these same companies a place in which to perform. Neither party had as yet achieved supremacy over the other in the matter of licensing texts. The Crown had obliged all companies to obtain a licence before any play could be performed, but as yet had to rely upon the civic authorities to administer this order. Considerable ambiguity therefore still remained concerning the actual licensing of plays, the clarifying of which was in no way assisted by the Church's lingering interest in the matter. In the North of England, at this time, Crown and Church combine against the City Fathers to suppress the last of the Miracle Cycles and popular Moralities.* In London Church and City combine against the Crown in attempts to suppress the public performance of the new secular plays. York, Wakefield, Chester and Coventry lose their Cyclic dramas: in London, increasingly frequent epidemics of plague are interpreted as signs of God's vengeance for the 'withdrawinge of the Queenes Maiesties subiectes from dyvyne service on Sonndaies and hollydayes', to the 'inordynate hauntyinge of great multitudes of people . . . to playes, enterludes, and shewes'.

Confronted with this uncertainty (the product of the will to control without effective executive power to enforce), Crown, Church and City all base their official pronouncements on those grounds which establish best their respective claims to supremacy. With the Church, a traditional authority to censor is now reinforced by right of 'this happie time of the gospel' (as opposed to times of 'ancient ignorance'). When the City of London issues an Act of Common Council in December 1574 enacting that 'henceforthe no playe . . . shalbe openlye played or shewed within the liberties of the Cittie . . . which shall not be firste perused and Allowed . . . by suche persons as by the Lorde Maior and Courte of Aldermen for the tyme beinge shalbe appoynted . . .', it is the owners of the property in the City on or in which plays are performed—Tavernkeepers, Innkeepers and others—who are held responsible, and penalised for any infringement.† The Crown acts through both its statutory control over the acting companies and its own private instrument, the Office of Revels.

Thus by recourse to rough and ready generalization, it is possible to discern a fairly distinct picture of the state of stage censor-

* The immediate cause for stern measures in that region was undoubtedly the Northern Rebellion of 1569 followed by the Queen's excommunication.[43]

† See Ch. V., pp. 195–196 below.

ship at the half way point in Elizabeth's reign. The successful suppression of the religious stage, together with the translation of occasional performances by professional acting companies into a regular, weekday, business concern, had served between them to emphasize two traditional features of control of the stage and to leave a disputed void in place of a third. As stated at the start of this chapter, control of theatre means control of play, actors and audience. By the fifteen-eighties public attention had come to be focused on the control which civic authorities had traditionally exercised over auditoriums in and about the City of London; similar attention was being directed to the Crown's powers over the composition of acting companies by the growing economic strength of these companies derived from weekday playing. At the same time, the suppression of the religious stage had established both Crown and civic authority as the partners of a Reformed Church which, prior to that Reform, had exercised a virtual monopoly in the licensing of play texts.

At this point two major external pressures begin to influence the London scene, the growing interest in Renaissance thinking and the rising tide of Puritan feeling. The former, repressed for nearly fifty years as a result of religious controversy, was now surging towards freedom in all the Arts, encouraged and financed by courtly patrons; the latter, hostile to exuberance of any sort and especially to the supposedly frivolous extravagance of plays, was rapidly increasing its following among the monied trading classes. Neither Court nor City could remain unaffected by these historical and international pressures of the time, both of which added a new incentive to the quest for ultimate control over the theatre. Puritan feeling goaded the city into striving to profit from the Church's waning interest in its right to license plays in order to achieve the ultimate suppression of plays and play-acting. Courtiers, inspired by Renaissance ideals, sought to strengthen the Crown's position with a view to protecting its own enjoyment and privileges. Documents surviving from the eighties and nineties bear eloquent witness to these new overtones, and distinguish this phase of the struggle for control from all its predecessors. Acrimonious, however, as these new pressures were to make the struggle, it might well have been both briefer and more bellicose but for the alarming increase in outbreaks of plague on the one hand and of violence in and about the theatre buildings on the other. These two grim spectres haunted both parties to the quarrel, and tempered the most headstrong councils in both camps with a degree of restraint bred from reflection and common sense.

The Puritan onslaught upon the theatre appears to have been launched in the seventies in a series of translations from the writings of continental Protestants, in original pamphlets, in tracts and sermons and in books.*

'Great then is the errour of the magistrate' writes Geoffrey Fenton in 1574, 'to geve sufferance to these players . . . How often is the maieste of God offended in those twoo or three howres that those playes endure, both by wicked wordes, and blasphemye, impudent jestures . . .' etc., etc.[44]

The year 1577 saw the publication of John Northbrooke's *A Treatise wherein Dicing, Dauncing, Vaine playes, or Enterluds . . . commonly used on the Sabboth day are reproued by the Authoritie of the word of God and auntient writers.* A second edition followed in 1579, the year in which Stephen Gosson printed his famous *The Schoole of Abuse, Containing a pleasaunt invective against Poets, Pipers, Plaiers, Iesters and such like Caterpillers of a Commonwelth.*[45] This literature and the spate of far more virulent attacks which followed it paved the way for action by the City Council in London. In 1582 the Lord Mayor writes to the Master of the Company of Ironmongers as follows:

'These shalbe straightlie to charge and command you, that forwithe uppon the receit hereof you call before you all the freemen of your said companie, and give to everie one of them straightlie charge and commandement that they or anie of them do at annye time hereafter suffer any of ther sarvants, apprentices, journemen, or children, to repare to goe to annye playes, peices, or enterludes, either within the cittie or suburbs thereof, or to annye place witheout the same, uppon payne of everie servant so offendinge, or master so sufferinge, to be punyshed at the dyscretion of me and my brethren. Fayle you not hereof, as you will answer the contrarie at your perill.
Geven at the Guildhall, the iij daie of Aprill, 1582.

Sebright (Town Clerk)'.[46]

Either shortly before this or shortly after (the latter is more probable) the Corporation took its most vigorous action to date in deciding to ban all performances of plays in the city and to petition the Privy Council for similar action in the suburbs. The language of this edict is as significant as its substance.

'For as much as the playing of Enterludes, & the resort to the same

---

* It could of course be justified at that time as a gesture of loyalty to the excommunicated Queen.

are very daungerous for the infection of the plague, whereby infinite burdens and losses to the Citty may increase, and are very hurtfull in corruption of youth with incontinence & lewdnes, and also great wasting both of the time and thrift of many poore people and great prouoking of the wrath of God the ground of all plagues, great withdrawing of the people from publique prayer & from the seruice of God; and daily cryed out against by the graue and earnest admonitions of the preachers of the word of God; Therefore be it ordered that all such Enterludes in publique places, and the resort to the same shall wholy be prohibited as ungodly, and humble sute be made to the Lords that lyke prohibition be in places neere unto the Cittie.'[47]

Until the present century, this Edict was thought to have been issued in 1575 and to have been directly responsible for the decision taken by the actors to build their theatres, in 1576 and after, outside the city walls. Modern dating of the Edict in 1582 or thereabouts obliges us to reconsider the reasons for building The Theater and The Curtain in Shoreditch; and this question is discussed in Chapter V.[48] It concerns us more nearly at the moment to remark that, with the date advanced from 1575 to 1582, this Edict follows almost as promptly upon the Crown Patent giving the Master of the Revels authority to license plays, players and playhouses, as the City Edict of 1574 follows upon the granting of the Patent to Leicester's Company with its reference to the licensing powers of the Revels Office. This may only be coincidence; but to me it suggests move and counter-move in the dispute for control of the censorship.

A year later fate placed a trump card in the hands of the City. In 1583 an accident occurred, on Sunday, January 13th, when part of the auditorium for bear-baiting, in Paris Garden on the South Bank, collapsed, killing some spectators and injuring more. The Lord Mayor wrote next day to Lord Burghley attributing the disaster to 'the hande of god for suche abuse of the sabboth daie', and was given, in reply, an assurance that the matter would be discussed by the Privy Council: in the meantime he had a free hand 'to make a generall prohibition within everie warde of that Citie and liberties, that no person . . . shold on the Saboth daie resort to any such profane assemblies or pastimes.'[49] This victory for the City was followed up in the summer of 1584 by a request to the Privy Council to pull down the Theater and The Curtain which, very surprisingly, was granted. For reasons which we can only surmise—probably through the intervention of the Lord

Chamberlain on behalf of his own company of players who performed at The Theater—the order was not carried out. Performances, however, were inhibited frequently and for long periods
during this and the next decade as a result of epidemics of the
plague; for in an effort to keep this scourge under control, Court
and City acted as one in condemning public assemblies whenever
the number of deaths ascribed to plague began to rise sharply.

Another factor indirectly aggravating public feeling about
theatres was the lack of those 'front of house' amenities which we
now take for granted: reserved seats, tickets, and audiences who,
in their occupancy of seats, generally respect the sentiments of
their neighbours. In the playhouses of Elizabethan London it was
more usual to stand than to sit, and a riot in the auditorium, if not
routine, occurred often enough to cause anxiety to officials whose
job was to prevent breaches of the peace.[50] These two circumstances, plagues and the rowdiness of crowds in holiday mood,
played directly into the hands of the theatre's enemies and were
used constantly to bolster otherwise flimsy moral and political
arguments for its suppression. The government's reliance upon the
city and county magistrates in controlling both plague and breaches
of the peace thus inevitably weakened its position in defending the
theatre against religious bigotry and commercial greed. On the
other hand, the government could and did rely on two other circumstances which favoured the Court's interest and which the
City could not plead. The first was the need to prepare performances for the Queen's entertainment and the second was the fact
that the leading acting companies enjoyed the licence to act as
personal servants of powerful noblemen whom it did not pay the
city to offend. The Privy Council thus argued that without the
opportunity to perform plays to public audiences the standard of
acting and presentation would be inadequate to furnish the
seasonal revels at Court. In November, 1581, the Lord Mayor and
Aldermen were instructed to lift the ban on plays imposed in July;
and, as this letter illustrates the Privy Council's interest in the
plague, in breaches of the peace, and in the quality of the Queen's
entertainment, it is worth quoting in full.

'After our hartie commendations. Whereas for auoyding the increase of infection within your citie this last somer yow receaued
order from vs for the restrainte of plaies vntill Mighelmas last.
For that (thankes be to god) the sicknesse is very well seised and
not likely in this time of the yeare to increase; Tendering the
releife of theis poore men the players and their redinesse with

conuenient matters for her highnes solace this next Christmas, which cannot be without their vsuall exercise therein; We haue therefore thought good to requier yowe forethwith to suffer them to vse such plaies in such sort and vsuall places as hath ben heretofore accustomed, hauing carefull regard for continuance of such quiet orders in the playeng places as tofore yowe haue had. And thus we bidd yowe hartelie farewell from the Courte at Whitehall this xviij⁰ of Nouember 1581.

Your Louing frendes,

Edward Lincoln	Thomas Sussex	Amb. Warwick
Robert Leycester	H. Hunsdon	James Croft
Christopher Hatton		

To our very Louing frendes the Lord Maiour, mr. Sariant Flete-wood Recorder, and the Aldermen of the Cittie of London'.[51]

With both sides thus using every means open to them in jockey-ing for control of the stage during the fifteen-eighties it is not surprising that a stalemate resulted, and that in 1589 a Commission should have been set up giving both City and Court equal rights with the Church in censorship and control. The immediate cause of this novel action by the Privy Council was almost certainly the Martin Marprelate controversy, a Puritan attack on the Estab-lished Church in which the theatres had sided with the govern-ment: but, in doing this, 'the players [took] upon themselves to handle in their plaies certen matters of Divinytie and of State unfitt to be suffred',—the very matters which Elizabeth's Proclamation of 1559 had forbidden. In consequence, by Star Chamber decree, the Archbishop of Canterbury,

'is desired that some fytt persone well learned in Divinity be appointed by him to joyne with the Master of the Revells and one other to be nominated by the Lord Mayour, and they joyntly with some spede to viewe and consider of suche comedyes and tragedyes as are and shalbe publickly played by the companies of players in and aboute the Cyttie of London, and they to geve allowance of suche as they shall thincke meete to be plaied and to forbydd the rest,'[52]

This Decree unquestionably rescinds the authoritarian powers vested by the Patent of 1581 in the Master of the Revels, Edward Tilney, over 'all and every plaier or plaiers with their playmakers, either belonginge to any noble man or otherwise' by requiring the Master to join 'with two others [the nominees of the Archbishop of Canterbury and the Lord Mayor] . . . to call before them the severall companies of players (whose servauntes soever they be) and to require them . . . to delyver unto them their bookes, that they maye consider of the matters of their comedyes and tragedyes, and thereupon to stryke oute or reforme suche partes and matters as they shall fynd unfytt and undecent to be handled in playes, bothe for Divinitie and State . . .'

No evidence survives to tell us how this partnership worked in practice. We have no reason to think it could have been a happy or easy one to operate. What we do know is that the Master rapidly developed his own powers into a profitable business concern. Henslowe's papers reveal that he was paying Tilney in 1592 for licensing plays at his own Rose Theatre, in 1596 for licensing both the Rose Theatre itself and the plays performed in it and, by 1600, for licensing the Fortune Theatre.[53] It is to be doubted whether Tilney would have wanted to share the proceeds of these and similar licences with the Archbishop of Canterbury and the Lord Mayor of London. The surmise that he quickly dispensed with their services on the licensing commission, or that they quickly lost interest only to regret it too late, is strengthened by the correspondence which passed between the three in 1592. The upshot of this, very briefly, is as follows. The Lord Mayor attempted to come to terms with Tilney, but failing to obtain satisfaction appealed to Archbishop Whitgift for help. Whitgift promised to discuss the matter with Tilney and suggested trying whether money could persuade where words could not. The Lord Mayor thanked the Archbishop for his help and promptly acted upon it. On March 18th he sent two Aldermen to see Tilney, presumably to discover how big a bribe was necessary for him to accede to their wishes. I say 'presumably' because on March 22nd, the Lord Mayor wrote to the Merchant Taylors Company asking them to consider 'the paymente of one Anuytie to one Mr. Tylney' in order that 'playes might be abandoned out of this citie.' The Company did as they were asked in considering the matter; but they decided that while ready to oblige in any other way they could not do so with cash. *[54]

The most reasonable hypothesis therefore is that Tilney had already stolen a march on his partners in the licensing commission by being the recipient of a substantial cash income from licensing plays under his Patent of 1581; that he refused to abandon this source of income without at least equivalent remuneration; and

* The Merchant Taylors' business sense was sound enough to recognize the danger of a 'precedent' of this kind; and so, apparently was that of the Mercers Company!

that the figure at which he chose to reckon the income proved much too large for either the Church or the City to be willing to part with. This hypothesis at least enjoys the advantage of explaining why the bribe talked of takes the form of an annuity and not a single lump payment. It has the further advantage of explaining why both City and Church seem to have abandoned the struggle to obtain control of the censorship. The City, it is true, made one last attempt to abolish the theatre, but that is not the same thing; and that attempt was made in any case, not through the commission, but on the more familiar grounds of jurisdiction over playing places. On the evidence surviving from the nineties, the commission became a dead-letter after 1592 and the Master of the Revels emerged triumphant as the undisputed licenser of the English stage, responsible to the Lord Chamberlain alone. The effects of this victory were perhaps nowhere more significant than upon the future of the company of actors, licensed as the Lord Chamberlain's Men, whose leading player was Richard Burbage and whose most promising playmaker was William Shakespeare.

It is hard for us to appreciate imaginatively just how bleak the future must have seemed to anybody depending for his livelihood upon theatrical performances in 1592 and shortly afterwards. The great, corporate, dramatic enterprises of the religious stage which had served to make drama in England a truly national art, had finally disappeared; and although it was the contentious nature of religious subject matter rather than acting *per se* which had occasioned their suppression, drama as an art could not but suffer in popular esteem from the methods used to suppress religious plays. Something of which sovereign and government appeared to disapprove strongly enough to penalize on occasion by fine, imprisonment and even death, could hardly continue to be regarded in so hierarchical a society as Tudor England as a joyous, healthy and honest pastime or pursuit. In the capital the theatre was under constant attack from merchants who disliked their apprentices taking time off to patronize it, by Protestants who equated the stage of their own day with that of ancient Rome as viewed by the early Christians, and by responsible administrators whose duty it was to safeguard citizens from the perils of disease and riot. And to cap it all, the sovereign on whose interest and support the theatrical profession could alone base its hopes of survival, was an old woman without an heir whose death was near and whose deposition was being discussed. At any moment the stage could find itself at the centre of a political battleground as bitter and as bloody as the religious battlefield from which it had so narrowly escaped. The precise part played by Shakespeare's *Richard II* in the Essex Rebellion of 1601 will perhaps never be known; but it was against this political and theatrical background of doubt and despondency that James VI of Scotland was greeted into London's streets with a pageant welcome prepared by Jonson, Dekker and Middleton, in which Edward Alleyn was one of the principal spokesmen, and Stephen Harrison the prime deviser of spectacle at a cost of £784.[55]

The Final Phase: 1603–1666

The fiercely disputed tussle for control of the theatre ceases astonishingly and abruptly with James I's accession. The story remaining to be outlined is one of violent extremes, and can be briefly told. At one end it is marked by a sweeping victory for the Court which lasted forty years: at the other end by a victory just as sweeping for the opponents of the stage and far more lasting in its effects.

Within three or four years of his Coronation James had virtually appropriated into his own hands control of players, plays, playmakers and theatres. In May 1603, the actors known as the Lord Chamberlain's Company, including Shakespeare and Burbage, were translated by Royal Patent into members of the Royal Household with the rank of Grooms of the Chamber and with the title of The King's Men. Sometime between then and February 1604 the Admiral's company and the Earl of Worcester's Company were transferred, by similar process of Royal Patents, into the Households of Prince Henry and Queen Anne respectively. Thus, almost at a single stroke, the leading actors of the day were snatched out of the hands of their enemies into the sanctuary of the sovereign's personal protection, or that of his family. The Patents, by specifying the places in which the Royal companies were authorized to perform in London—the King's men 'w(i)thin theire usual housse called the Globe', Prince Henry's Men at the Fortune and the Queen's Men at the Curtain—served also to protect the players in their performances and their property. Provision was also made in the Patents to guarantee the companies the right to perform in provincial cities.[56]

Lest London, Middlesex, or Surrey magistrates should be in any doubt on the point, the Privy Council wrote to them on April 9th 1604, Lent being over, requiring them to,

'Permitt and suffer the three Companies of Plaiers to the King, Queene, and Prince publicklie to Exercise ther Plaies in ther severall and usuall howses.[57] In July, 1604, the Elizabethan 'Acte for Punishmente of Rogues, Vagabondes and Sturdie Beggars' was revised by Parliament yet again and this time the privilege formerly accorded to 'any Baron of this Realme, or any other honourable Personage of greater Degree' to license a company of players to travel in his name was summarily withdrawn.* The effect of this Act could only be to deprive the provinces of their remaining local acting companies and to strengthen still further the three Royal London Companies by handing over to them the unopposed right to tour the provincial circuits previously open to competition.

The Companies of boy-actors were similarly brought under Court control. The Children of the Chapel were relicensed as the Children of the Queen's Revels in 1604. The St. Paul's boys' Company was reorganized in 1607/8 and known thereafter as the Children of the King's Revels. In the same year James I allowed his second son, Charles, Duke of Albany (later Charles I) to take over Queen Elizabeth I's former players who, since 1603, had been working under the patronage of the Duke of Lennox in the provinces. In 1611 he allowed another Company to be licensed under the patronage of his daughter, Princess Elizabeth.[58]

Court control of the affairs of the stage, thus secured, was administered through the Lord Chamberlain and his executives in the Revels Office. Elizabeth's last Master of the Revels, Edmund Tilney, did not die until 1610; but Sir George Buck, who had been promised the reversion of the post in 1597, became active 'in the office at James' accession. From 1606 onwards he started licensing plays for printing as well as for acting, a practice which was taken over by his successors and turned to considerable financial profit. It was through the Master that the Royal Companies were informed that on account of plague, Lent, or other hindrance they must discontinue their performances: but the Master was here acting on the orders of the Lord Chamberlain who was in turn communicating to him the wishes of the Privy Council.[59] It is one of the most striking features of the evidence we are surveying that James I's accession brings to an almost complete halt the long succession of pleas and protests to the Council about the theatre from the Lord Mayor of London and his Council, from provincial magistrates and from the Church (as represented by the Archbishops of Canterbury and York and the Bishop of London), which had characterized the previous seventy years: and it is difficult to resist the conclusion that this startling change was primarily due to

* See p. 80 above: also Ch. IV, pp. 105–6 and below.

James' swift, thorough and autocratic actions outlined above. Their efficacy may be judged from a letter of Lord Strafford's describing a meeting of the Privy Council in 1637 when the Lord Chamberlain (Lord Pembroke and Montgomery), Archbishop Laud and King Charles I were all present.*

'Upon a little abatement of the plague, even in the first week of Lent, the players set up their bills, and began to play in the Blackfryars and other houses. But my Lord of Canterbury quickly reduced them to a better order; for at the next meeting of the Council his Grace complained of it to the King, declared the solemnity of Lent, the unfitness of that liberty to be given, both in respect to the time and the sickness, which was not extinguished in the City, concluding that if his Majesty did not command him to the contrary he would lay them by the heels if they played again. My Lord Chamberlain [Pembroke and Montgomery] stood up and said that my Lord's Grace and he served one God and one King; that he hoped his Grace would not meddle in his place no more than he did in his; that the players were under his command. My Lord's Grace replied that what he had spoken in no way touched upon his place, etc., still concluding as he had done before, which he did with some solemnity reiterate once or twice. So the King put an end to the business by commanding my Lord Chamberlain that they should play no more.'[60]

This letter serves to illustrate both how closely the theatre was still linked to affairs of Church and State (in the eyes of the government, if not in subject matter) and how peremptorily a question, which would have occupied much time, ink and paper in Tudor days, could be handled in the years immediately preceding the Civil War. Yet, at the same time, it raises another large question. What had become of opposition to the stage—in London in particular and in the country at large?

Besides the three companies of players licensed by Patent in 1603–4, several others came into being between 1610 and 1630. Some of these were genuinely independent companies, Prince Charles' (the Duke of Albany's) Company being the first; others were redistributions or fusions of previous companies. Only one was specifically based upon a provincial city as opposed to London, *Her Majesty's Servants of her Royal Chamber at Bristol*, which was granted its Patent on July 17th, 1615. All were royal companies;

* Strafford Letters, II, 56; quoted in Wheatley and Cunningham, *London Past and Present*, I, 200–201. This letter is dated March 23, 1637: quoted by Gildersleeve, *op. cit.*, p. 214.

all, equipped with the Master of the Revels' licence, could travel and set up their 'bills' at will without fear of penalties under the *Act for Punishment of Vagabondes.**[61] Privilege of this kind begets resentment, and resentment invents its own means of redress. In the provinces one form which this redress took was to obey the letter of the law and defy the spirit: to pay actors the fee normal for a performance and require them to leave the town without giving it. This subject is discussed in detail in Chapter IV.

In London such tactics could not work. The City seems to have accepted its defeat and to have been prepared to bide its time. Yet, in one sense at least, James' whirlwind dealings with the theatre, however autocratic in both concept and execution, must have given the City some cause for pleasure. Either he himself or his Council working with him had acted with startling clarity and firmness: whatever he had appropriated in the interest of the Court brought with it substantial advantages to the City. If three playing companies had to be accepted in London, at least their monopoly prevented the city itself being invaded by less reputable companies; if the City had failed to get the public theatres in the city liberties and in the suburbs destroyed, as had been promised in 1597, nevertheless James had restricted the licensed companies to 'their usual houses' and had consequently reduced the risk of Inns and other buildings in the city itself being appropriated for use as playhouses. The city was further assured that the Privy Council and its executives in the Revels Office were fully alerted to the dangers both of public assemblies in time of plague and of religious polemic in play-scripts. And James himself had made a gesture to Puritan sentiment immediately upon his accession in forbidding by Proclamation all Sunday play-acting, a gesture which was confirmed and ratified by Charles I in an Act of Parliament.[62]

Thus, to a large extent, James' actions had brought those ends which the more liberal-minded of London's merchants and divines had for so long been striving to obtain within sight of fulfilment. Only those acting companies which, in their standards and reputation, had proved themselves the most experienced and reliable were now allowed to perform. Reasonable provision for discipline in London's auditoriums and for preventing the spread of infectious diseases had been made. A system existed to banish

---

* On the other hand, in some areas, the law itself could not have been very well known; for some noblemen's companies continued to present plays despite having been officially disestablished, while in the extreme North Western counties performances of Miracle Cycles by local companies were given, despite the penalties, as late as 1612.

seditious, blasphemous, and other controversial subject-matter from the stage. What survived in terms of theatres, plays and players could hardly be said to amount to more than what anyone might legitimately wish to visit in pursuance of 'honest recreation'.

In attempting to explain the curious silence which descends on the Councils of the City of London in respect of the theatre after James I's accession, I incline to think myself that, whether the city was consciously aware of the fact or not, James' actions had already sealed the theatre's fate. A control of the drama so absolute as that exercised by James, his family and his immediate Court advisers could not but serve to divorce the theatre from the popular audience on which it had previously been based and from which it had drawn its vigour. The actors and their playmakers, as royal servants, could scarcely avoid aligning the subject matter of their plays in future to suit the tastes of their patrons and protectors in preference to that of humbler citizens: just as relevant, the most topical of all subject matter, the relationship between Church, State and individual human being—the topic which had kept English drama so vividly in touch with life in the Tudor era—was the very subject matter which the whole machinery of censorship and control had been devised to license and suppress. And suppressed it most surely was. The decadence in Jacobean and Caroline dramatic writing which has so frequently been remarked and debated by literary critics is thus, in my view, due in far greater measure to the censorship (in the widest sense of that word) as exercised by early Stuart governments than to any particular failing in the writers themselves. I believe, further, that this steady weakening of the relationship between the realities of religious, political and social life in England and the reflection of them upon the stage made it very much easier for the architect-painters to capture the interest of audiences at the expense of dramatic poets than might otherwise have been so. Foxe in his *Acts & Monuments*, printed in 1539, had said that

'players, printers and preachers be set up of God as a triple bulwark against the triple crown of the Pope, to bring him down, as, God be praised, they have done meetly well already.'[63]

It is an ironic paradox, indeed, that within almost exactly one hundred years players could be so abhorred by Foxe's successors among the most zealous of Protestant Reformers as to warrant extermination by Act of Parliament. In 1642 the theatres were formally closed and acting forbidden for a period of five years.

'Whereas . . . the distracted estate of England, threatened with a cloud of blood by a civil war, call for all possible means to appease and avert the wrath of God appearing in these judgments: . . . and whereas public sports do not well agree with public calamities, nor public stage-plays with the seasons of humiliation, this being an exercise of sad and pious solemnity, and the other being spectacles of pleasure, too commonly expressing lascivious mirth and levity: it is therefore thought fit and ordained by the Lords and Commons in this Parliament assembled, that while these sad causes and set-times of humiliation do continue, public stage-plays shall cease and be forborne.'[64]

In 1648

'All stage-players . . . whether they be wanderers or no, and not-withstanding any License whatsoever from the King or any person . . .' are forbidden to act, and for better assurance the Lord Mayor and the Justices of the Peace are ordered to 'pull down and demolish . . . all Stage-Galleries, Seats, and Boxes, erected and used for the acting or playing, or seeing acted or plaid, such Stage-Playes'.[65]

Much of the blame, if blame is the right word for these measures, must attach to the closeness of the bonds associating the Jacobean and Caroline theatre with the Royal Family: and it is hardly sur-prising that only one actor is known to have fought in the Civil War on the Parliament side.[66] The remainder of the feeling generated against the theatre in Elizabethan England and smoul-dering steadily under James and Charles was derived from mis-guided interpretations of Christian writings—the Bible, the works of the Fathers of the early Church, and laws of Church Councils—and garbled versions of Plato, Cicero and other classical writers. The classic summation of all these anti-theatrical rumblings is Prynne's *Histrio-Mastix*, published in 1632, which sets out to prove 'that popular Stage-playes (the very Pompes of the Divell which we renounce in Baptisme, if we beleeve the Fathers) are sinfull, heathenish, lewde, ungodly Spectacles, and most pernicious Cor-ruptions; condemned in all ages, as intolerable Mischiefes to Churches, to Republickes, to the manners, mindes and soules of men. And that the Profession of Play-poets, of Stage-playes, are unlawfull, infamous and misbeseeming Christians.'[67]

This language is of course as intemperate as that of Ben Jonson's Zeal-of-the-Land-Busy, quoted extensively in Chapter II. Like Busy's, such utterances were based on 'inspiration' rather than on reason; but on that very account these sentiments were the more passionately *felt*. The wheel has indeed come full circle when governments that sought to muzzle the stage for fear of breaches of the peace because they might lead to civil dissension have come to be replaced by a government that is ready to face Civil War for a cause that lists among its objectives the abolition of dramatic performances.

Postscript

With the Restoration of the Monarchy in 1660 came the restoration of the theatre: but, after the century of State Control which we have just traced, the theatre which was revived and licensed to new life could never hope to resemble its predecessor in anything but externals.

In the first place some eighty years had passed since the last performances of those religious plays from which the Tudor drama had drawn its scope and its conventions and from which the early Stuart drama, despite the censorship, had still in large measure drawn its inspiration. Time enough had passed for all eye witnesses of such performances to have died, for such plays to be dismissed by the advocates of 'progress' as idle, superstitious, or vain fancies of an ignorant and barbarous past, without exciting any contrary opinion. With the disappearance of the religious stage, that spontaneous, personal and universal appreciation of dramatic art as an integral part of national life, to which all had contributed in some measure as a natural expression of their emotions, also disappeared. Theatre in the provinces ceased to exist as a serious, well organized activity: in London it was reduced to the status of a toy for killing time.[68] Its scope had dwindled to satirizing the quirks of men and manners or to refreshing the spirits of a leisured few with song, dance and costly spectacle. This small, literate and sophisticated audience—and it is important to realize that the two theatre managements of Restoration London, and their respective companies, had no other audience from whose support to draw their pay—this audience, devoted to the formalism of classical theorists, absorbed in its own private jokes and personal vendettas, and unable to forget the years of exile among the savants in French salons, cared little, if at all, for the popular theatre of former times. Managements, actors, and theatre craftsmen therefore had little incentive to preserve, for their own sake, anything of the stage conventions inherited from the past. Only those aspects of them which still suited the new modes were likely to possess much interest: and the probability is that practical expediency dictated their survival or eclipse. Any possibility of a reversion to a popular theatre that might have sprung up spontaneously was doomed from the outset by Sir Henry Herbert's efforts to re-establish himself as licenser of plays, players and playhouses in his capacity of Master of the Revels: for however desirable or undesirable continued censorship may have seemed on ethical grounds, the Office of Censor had proved itself to be too valuable a source of private income to be dispensed with either by courtier or monarch, lessee and lessor respectively. Herbert valued his loss at £4,000 a year. [69]

IV

ACTORS, PLAYMAKERS AND THEATRES UNDER STATE CONTROL

1 Precedence

IN THE previous chapter I have tried to outline the actual progress of stage-censorship in England from its comparatively
harmless beginnings under Henry VIII to its disturbing and dis-
rupting zenith in the Commonwealth era. What started as a
well-intentioned attempt to free English audiences from any responsibility to the Pope in far-away Rome, and to protect persons
and property from the effects of unruly conduct in or about the
stage and auditorium, became at once something so much more
serious and far reaching as to have governed the attitude of English
people to the theatre until the present time. The theatre's roots in
Catholic worship and observances involved it inescapably in the
political controversies of the Reformation and Counter-Reformation: once entangled in this treacherous web, it became a battle
target between two rival factions, neither of whom could isolate it
from other issues of the day. The most ardent of Reformers, reinforced with the verbal ammunition of Calvinist theory on the
subject, sought to obtain control of the theatre in order to suppress
it. More moderate, as well as reactionary opinion, reinforced with
humanist arguments based on the literature of the Roman theatre
(and vaguely of the Greek) sought to obtain control of the plays
and performances in order to transform both into splendid ornaments of Court and State. This much I hope I have established.
What still requires scrutiny is the impact of this ideological tug-o'-
war upon the theatre itself; the consequences of this clash of
'mighty opposites' for the actors, for the playmakers and for the
managers who tried to provide buildings in which performances
could be given despite it. This is worth study for the light it

throws both upon dramatic performances and composition in an epoch of our history that has since become world-famous for its drama. It also has a marked bearing on the building of public theatres in London and on the design adopted for their construction.

I have chosen to give precedence to the predicament of the actor since, in so far as the theatre of the sixteenth century was sufficiently homogeneous to have organized a self-conscious defence against its opponents, the actors provided the mainstay of that defence: had the acting companies in the crucial decade of the seventies decided to betray their calling and thus escape the difficulties and dangers which persevering in it by then involved, English literature would probably have lacked Shakespeare's plays and the distinguished dramatic compositions of his younger contemporaries. And if the stand of the acting companies in the seventies is greatly to their credit, the fact that they emerged triumphant from the assaults made upon their profession and their livelihood in the nineties is a minor miracle.

By the start of the seventeenth century virtually all amateur play production (excepting that among courtiers and students) had ceased. In the provinces, even companies of local quasi-professional actors were deprived of the right to act, and the letter of the law was enforced with sufficient vigour for proceedings to be taken against offenders.[1] At the same time the professional actors of the metropolis, thanks to the growth of royal patronage, entered upon a period of comparative security. It cannot be overemphasized to what extent the Elizabethan and early Stuart theatre was professional in its composition and its outlook. It is as well therefore to be clear about the connotation to be given to these words 'amateur' and 'professional' in subsequent discussion of the actor's status. In respect of the word professional, I cannot myself improve upon what Sir Edmund Chambers describes as,

'. . . a regular profession, in which money might with reasonable safety be invested, to which a man might look for the career of a lifetime, and in which he might venture to bring up his children.'[2]

If we need a similarly apt assessment of amateur status, we could do worse than accept that supplied by William Fleetwood, Recorder of the City of London, in 1584.

'It hath not been used nor thought meet heretofore that players have or should make their living on the art of playing; but men for their livings, using other honest and lawful arts, or retained in honest services, have by companies learned some interludes for some increase to their profit by other men's pleasures in vacant time of recreation'.*

Fleetwood wrote this as part of a very detailed reply to a request from the Queen's players for performing facilities in London which would accord with their status as professional actors.[3]

The fact that the Corporation of London dared to adopt so contemptuous an attitude towards one of the leading companies of the day and at so late a date as 1584 is interesting in itself; but the fact that the Recorder has to call on past precedent—'it hath not been . . . thought meet heretofore'—illustrates the nature of the challenge that he and his fellow Aldermen were being called upon to face. The challenge stems directly from acting companies who already worked in theatres designed and constructed at least in part to meet their needs, and who commissioned and owned the plays which they performed in them. The companies existed before the theatres, and both existed before most of the plays known collectively to us as Elizabethan drama. This order of precedence, which has been blurred for us by time and scholarship, is one that I hope I may do something to restore in the course of this chapter. It is on this premise at least that my whole approach to the problems of Elizabethan and Jacobean stagecraft is based, and against which the reconstructions of theatre practice and its development set out in subsequent chapters must be judged.

2 Actors at large

The beginnings of acting as a profession in England are not directly traceable to a single source, but rather to five independent and spontaneous sources of great antiquity which interacted upon one another as they developed and finally coalesced in the early seventeenth century under the external pressures of censorship, 'police' action and patronage.

The five sources are (i) the monastic and cathedral choirs (with the schools that provided the choristers) who performed the liturgical offices of early Christian worship, (ii) the peasant buffoons who played mimetic games on the chief holidays of the agricultural year, (iii) the minstrel troupes of acrobatic and musical jongleurs led by their poet-singer, the trouvère, (iv) the artisans of the larger towns who did their duty by God, sovereign and fellow townsmen in sacred drama and civic Pageant when occasion demanded, and (v) the wealthy, privileged and sophisticated young

* Spelling and punctuation modernized.

people who in Tournament and masked ball acted out the elaborate and highly decorated rites of courtship and marriage before their parents and relations.

By virtue of its spontaneity all this acting was amateur in the first instance, and either devotional or recreational in purpose. The Romans built theatres in England, and it must be assumed that professional mimes performed in them. No evidence exists however of how many of these actors stayed on as immigrants, or of whether they established anything that could be described as a tradition of acting. For the present therefore their influence must be discounted.

I have given some account in Volume I of the early contributions of all these groups to the formation of something resembling a regular drama in England in the fifteenth century. It suffices to say here that each of them continued, in the sixteenth century, to make some independent and individual contribution to the art of the stage play—though by then it must be assumed that each group was sufficiently self-conscious, both in its purpose and of its prowess, to be casting eyes upon its rivals, borrowing techniques of presentation here, and improving upon its artistry there. The choir schools in and about London, for instance, came frequently to be called upon by both Henry VII and Henry VIII to give performances at Court, sometimes of Latin plays in imitation of those fashionable in Italy, sometimes of plays specially written for them by their masters.[4] In this they became the rivals, in an evening's or a season's 'Revels', of both the professional minstrel troupe of the Royal Household (by then known as the players of Interludes) and the courtly amateurs in their spectacular Disguisings and Masks. May games and other holiday sports keep the courtly audience in touch with the mimetic *ludi* of humbler folk, with Robin Hood, St. George and the May King.[5] Tournaments change their style but lose none of their popularity.* Coronations and the visits of distinguished strangers are greeted with the accustomed pageantry, and to this is added a special annual show to mark the election of London's Lord Mayor.† Miracle Cycles, Morality Plays and Saint Plays ever more spectacular in scale and scope, give provincial towns a drama that taxes their financial and organizational strength to the utmost, but do not exclude either humbler dramatic games or occasional visits from small groups of professional players. Professional players are sometimes employed to fortify the casting of the Miracle Cycles: and wherever there is a Cathedral school or a

* See Ch. VI, pp. 229–236 below.
† See Ch. VI, pp. 209–210 below.

monastery, learned men are to hand to devise plays and entertainments appropriate to every occasion, helped by clerks able both to copy out actors' parts and to acquit themselves as performers if required. Dramatic activity during the early sixteenth century, viewed in this general context, was a nationwide pastime of unrivalled popularity: and, provided it was not accompanied by drunken brawls or vicious thieving, it everywhere received the approval and encouragement of both civic and ecclesiastical authority. As we have observed, the coming of plays of religious polemic changed all this: and so, I believe, did the dissolution of the religious houses. It is to be noted that in Spain, where the development of the drama was not affected by any such conflict with religion, the building of theatres for professional performances spread from the capital to the provinces:[6] in England, despite the notoriety of the London theatres, no such development took place in the provinces. How, then, were actors affected? The short answer is that the amateurs among them were crippled, the professionals enormously strengthened.

It is clear from the evidence presented in Chapter III that, by the fifteen-forties, acting, whether professional or amateur, had begun to be a dangerous occupation. As early as 1527, Cardinal Wolsey had clapped Sir John Roo—the author of a play about 'Lord Governannce' and 'Lady Publicke Wele'—into the Fleet prison, and had rebuked the young gentlemen of Gray's Inn who had performed it: * Bishop Gardiner had reacted almost as sharply to the acting of *Pammachius* at Cambridge in 1537, describing it as 'soo pestiferous as were intolerable'.† In country towns many Mayors and their councils had taken it upon themselves during the fifteen-thirties to order the discontinuance of civic dramas, an example followed by others who included ecclesiastics among their supporters, when the official suppression of the Feast of Corpus Christi made the local plays associated with the Festival appear redundant. ‡

As from 1543, participation in any play, whether long established by tradition or newly written, which presumed to 'medle with interpretacions of Scripture, contrarye to the doctryne sett foorth or to be sett foorth by the Kinges Mayestie' became by Act of Parliament a punishable offence.§ I have already supplied examples of individual actors whose lack of circumspection (or deliberate re-

* See *EES*, i., p. 237.
† See Ch. III, n. 9, p. 351 below.
‡ See p. 69 above.
§ See pp. 15–16 and 63 above.

bellion) brought the grim penalties of this law upon themselves. It is worth adding here that in London two companies of actors were suppressed on orders from the Privy Council in April 1543. One was an amateur company—'certain joyners to the number of xx'—and the other a professional company of four players—'belonging to my Lord Warden': the joiners had offended by acting on a Sunday, 'without respect either of the day or the order which was known openly the Kings Highness intended to take for the repressing of plays': the professional actors were in trouble 'for playing contrary to an order taken by the Mayor'. The professionals were committed to the Counter, and the joiners to the Tower. [7]

Under Edward VI's Protestant government and under Mary's Catholic rule, criminal proceedings against actors continued; but they appear still to have been directed against participants in plays of religious polemic. One edict survives however from London's Court of Aldermen, dated 23rd December 1550 and directed against 'certein comen plaiers of interludes' which indicates that actors already had cause to be more careful in their choice of play than simply establishing its religious orthodoxy.

'At this Courte, certein comen plaiers of interludes within this Citie were bounden by Recognisaunce as herafter insuythe:

Item, Johannes Nethe, Robertus Southyn, Robertus Drake, Robertus Peacocke, Johannes Nethersall, Robertus Sutton, Ricardus Jugler, Johannes Ronner, Willelmus Readyng, Edmundus Stokedale, Johannes Rawlyns, Johannes Crane, Ricardus Gyrke, Johannes Radstone, Oliuerus Page, Ricardus Pokeley, Ricardus Parseley, & Willelmus Clement, recognoverunt se & eorum quemlibet, per se debere domino Regi xx li, bonis etc soluendis etc: The condicion, etc, that yf the above bounden John Nethe, Robert Southyn etc & eny and euery of them, do not at herafter play eny interlude or comen play within eny of our Soueraygn Lorde the kynges domynyons, without the especiall licence of our seid Soueraygn Lorde, or of his most honourable Councell for the tyme beyng, had & obteyned for the same, And also yf they the seid Recognytours, & euery of them, do att all & euery tyme & tymes herafter, when they or any of them shalbe, by the seid Counsell or eny of them, sent for, personally appere before the seid Counsell or some of them, that then, etc, or els etc.' [8]

The affair of Sir Francis Leek and his players in 1556, discussed in Chapter III, indicates just as forcefully that not only the actors but their patrons were liable to be disciplined under the law for offences against the censorship imposed by the central government.* The letter from the Privy Council to the Lord President of the North demanding action against Sir Francis Leek and his players has additional interest for us in that it points directly at the prime instrument that governments of the second half of the century were to use to bring the nomadic acting companies under their control.

'... at any tyme hereafter', reads the letter, '... yo(u)r L(*ordship*) shall do well to gyve the Justices of Peace in charge to see them (*actors*) apprehendyd owt of hande, and punished as vagabounds, by vertue of the statute made agaynst loytering and idle p(er)sonnes.'[9]

The statute in question is that of 22. Hen. VIII c. 12 which had been revised on several occasions, the last being in 1553.[10] The act in that form, and as continued by Elizabeth in 1563, not being designed as an instrument against actors—was so vague in its application to the stage that both actors and their patrons could well imagine themselves exempt and make it difficult for any prosecutor to prove that they were not.† Any doubts however which actors may have entertained about their liberty to pursue their calling without let or hindrance must have been finally dispelled by the wholesale revision of the Act in 1572. The position in Elizabethan England prior to this time is summed up admirably by Miss Gildersleeve as follows:

'... though no licence was explicitly required, something like a licensing system had grown naturally out of existing social conditions. Players who wandered abroad needed to have their legal status certified to by connection with some town or some person of rank. Otherwise they were liable to be treated as vagabonds, like other masterless men.'[11]

This degree of tolerance was subsequently reduced in four fairly distinct phases. In 1572 the privilege of keeping a private company of players was withdrawn from Baronets and gentlemen and left only to 'any Baron of this Realme or ... any other honourable Personage of greater Degree'. ‡ The object of this change was to ensure that actors, as a professional class, should be sufficiently well organized to be immediately recognizable to officers of the law for

---

* See pp. 72–73 above.

† In *Love's Labour's Lost*, Costard's justification before the King of his conduct with Jaquenetta proceeds on just such lines. (I: lines 272–290).

‡ The relevant passages of this Statute are printed in Appendix E together with the revisions made in 1597/98 and again in 1604. See pp. 335–336 below.

what they were, instead of providing beggars, tramps and criminals with an alibi under which to masquerade and thus escape from justice: and to that end, Elizabeth I and her Council sought to place professional actors firmly under the control of responsible gentlemen who could themselves be brought to account for any indiscretions committed by their servants. If actors, however, were neither outlawed nor reduced in number, the result of this change was to disenfranchise all of the smaller companies of professional actors as effectively as the clerical actors had been deprived of security in their vocation when the religious houses were dissolved. Gentlemen's companies were left with the alternatives of choosing some other occupation or of obtaining a licence to perform from 'two Justices of the Peace at the least, whereof one to be of the Quorum, where and in what shire they shall happen to wander.' In practice, this could only mean that these actors were obliged to abandon acting, or, if they were to continue, then they must do so either as resident amateurs or as professionals with rights of travel so sharply curtailed as to prohibit 'happening to wander'.

The second blow fell in 1597/98 when even this slender, remaining privilege was withdrawn from Gentlemen's Companies. From then until the end of Elizabeth's reign only those companies licensed in the name of the sovereign, and of a few great nobles of sufficient consequence at Court to warrant the privilege, were legally free to perform plays in England. Nevertheless, enough ambiguity still existed in the interpretation of the Statute for James I to make a further revision of it one of the first priorities of his reign. Because of 'divers Doubtes and Questions . . . moved and growen by diversitie of opinions taken in and upon the letter of the saide Acte' (1572), James' first Parliament enacts in 1604 that 'no Authoritie (is) to be given or made by any Baron of this Realme or any other honourable Personage of greater Degree' which can free actors from the 'Offence and Punishment of the same Statute'.[12] James' intention is quite clear: actors act by his authority or not at all. In other words, all extensions of the royal prerogative to license players as household servants which had grown up during the fifteenth and sixteenth centuries are to be swept away. The spirit of the new Act is made obvious by James' subsequent actions in issuing Letters Patent to acting companies in his own name, in the Queen's name, in the names of his children, and to no one else. The letter of the Act, however, was still ambiguous enough for the more powerful nobles, especially those in East Anglia and the North, to defy it for some time to come on an occasional basis and in provincial districts remote enough from London to escape detection.* Never again, however, was any nobleman's company of actors able to venture a performance at Court: and if the sovereign should go on Progress into the provinces, it was assumed that his own company, as members of his household, would accompany him, taking their orders from the Lord Chamberlain.

The fourth and final phase of this long-drawn-out process of inhibition is not marked by any particular legislation but by the determination of local authorities in the provinces to challenge the right of actors travelling under royal Letters Patent to perform in places that came within their own jurisdiction. A discovery was made in mayors' parlours up and down the country that means existed to defy the spirit of the law without breaking the letter: to pay those actors licensed in their profession a gratuity to refrain from performing in the town. The Treasurer's Account Book for the city of Bristol contains this entry under the 4th Quarter of the year 1634/35:

'Item paide to one Perry a plaier by order of Mr Mayor for (tha)t hee should not sho(w) his skill heere in this citty—£2.'

When Parliament finally suppressed acting in London by closing the theatres in 1642, this practice had become so widespread that no hope was left of an alternative livelihood in tours of provincial towns.

3 The Right to Act

At Henry VIII's accession an Englishman's right to act in a play if he wanted to had come to be as widely recognized in Church and State as it had come to be assumed by nobleman and commoner throughout the land. Denunciations of acting—more particularly of persons who turned mimetic talent to personal gain—from a succession of mediaeval preachers and thinkers alarmed at the prospect of a world racing so rapidly to ruin had proved too sporadic to result in any inhibitive legislation against it. Amateur acting associated with personal recreation and civic welfare had established itself in town hall, on village green, in market square and even in church or chapel as a normal accompaniment of public festivals and holidays. The Royal prerogative of maintaining a

* See 'Companies of Players Entertained by the Earl of Cumberland and Lord Clifford, 1607–39', MSC, v, pp. 17–28.

company of professional entertainers had been extended to courtiers, nobles and gentry over the centuries and on an equally wide scale. Moreover, it had come to be tacitly admitted that these companies could perfect their skills as well as meet some of the expense of their maintenance, by performing in public places alongside of the amateurs when not required at home by their masters.* Thus it had come about that the royal licence to keep a company of players had come also to serve as a badge of control: for all professional actors were answerable either immediately, or indirectly through their master, to the Crown.

Prior to 1572 there is no evidence that any other attitude was officially adopted towards acting or actors; those actors and those patrons of actors who found themselves in trouble with the government did so either on account of their association with an offensive text or because of their connection with some breach of the peace in the auditorium.† In 1572, however, Baronets and gentlemen were stripped of their right to maintain companies, and the instrument employed to effect the change, as we have seen, was 'An Acte for the punishement of Vacabondes'. By no reasoning can one regard this action as anything but a change in the official attitude to acting. Acting itself, as opposed to the acting of certain types of play, had clearly come to be regarded, at least by the central government, as something other than an Englishman's right. Regardless of past precedent, it was henceforward to be viewed as an activity conditional upon and regulated by Parliamentary Statute. Nothing is said in the Statute of 1572 about amateur acting: only the professional itinerant companies are mentioned.‡

What occasioned this change of attitude? And what suggested that the change be expressed in the form of Poor Law legislation? Although I have no evidence approximating to proof, I cannot but wonder whether it was not as much the dissolution of the monasteries and religious fraternities as the intrinsically nomadic existence of the professional ministrels-cum-interluders which gave occasion for actors to become associated in the public mind with indigents and criminals; and, in consequence, for the government to become alarmed enough to take action to control their movements. At least there is a striking parallel with the condition of music and musicians in England at that time which renders this

* Anthony Munday wrote scathingly about this practice in 1580. See p. 116 below.
† See pp. 60–75 above.
‡ See p. 80 above, and Appendix E.

suggestion highly plausible. Thomas Whythorne, a musician by profession, writes reproachfully on the subject in his autobiography (c. 1570).*

'In time past music was chiefly maintained by Cathedral Churches, Abbeys, Colleges, Parish Churches, Chantries, Guilds, Fraternities etc., but when the Abbeys, and Colleges without the Universities, with Guilds and Fraternities etc., were suppressed, then went music to decay. To speak of music in [private] houses, ye shall understand, that divers noblemen and women, in time past, imitating the prince, would have Organists, and singingmen to serve God after the manner of that time with music in their private chapels. But that imitation is also left. Then for such as served for private recreation in houses, which were for the nobility and worshipful, these were no less esteemed than the others, till time that the rascal and off-scum of that profession, who be, or ought to be called minstrels (although now a days many do name them([?] selves) musicians) these I say did and do make it common by offering of it to every jack, going about every place and county for the same purpose. . . .'

Whythorne then recounts a lengthy anecdote of an encounter between a minstrel and a beggar, concluding,

'. . . by this you may see in what state the minstrels be in when as beggars and rogues do account them to be their companions and fellows.'[13]

That the larger religious houses possessed their own actors as well as their own musicians has never been in doubt; and it is equally certain that in many towns the great cycles of religious plays were produced and acted by clerical guilds; nor is there any good reason to suppose that these practices had ceased before the start of the sixteenth century. The Pre-Reformation Banns of the Chester plays state specifically that as well as the Cycle at Whitsun,

'Appon the day of corpus (ch)r(ist)i
The blessed Sacrament caried shalbe
And A play sett forth by the clergye
In hono[r] of the fest.'†

In Lincoln, the play of the Assumption in the St. Anne Cycle was the responsibility of the Cathedral Chapter.[14] Cardinal Wolsey was sufficiently concerned about the time and energy devoted to

* The spelling and punctuation in the following quotations have been modernized.
† See *EES*, i, pp. 346–7.

acting by the monks of St. Austin for him to issue regulations forbidding them to tour the countryside for gain as *lusores aut mimici*.[15]

What happened then to these histrionic clerics when they were dispossessed of their houses, turned out upon the roads without the identity of a recognized trade, and obliged to earn a living on their own initiative? Social historians have long been agreed that these multitudes of men and women, deprived of one means of livelihood without being trained for another, created a major social problem in Tudor England. Is it not to be presumed then that many of those possessed of proven acting talent should have decided to change the religious life for that of the public stage? An offer of employment could at least be anticipated from the upstart Tudor 'gentlemen' who were anxious to dignify their personal household by adding to it a private company of players, or from the mayor and aldermen in those towns where, as clerical actors, they had given pleasure in earlier years and already possessed an enthusiastic local audience. This hypothesis would also serve to explain the sudden increase of polemical religious plays which is so noticeable a feature of English literary history in the fifteen-forties and -fifties, since these some-time clerical actors, in forming themselves into companies, could reckon upon the continuing services of those authors and copyists who had supplied them with scripts and actors' copies in their respective monastic institutions.[16] If then in addition to the problems of textual censorship occasioned by the religious and political difficulties of the times, Tudor governments under Edward VI, Mary and Elizabeth had to contend with those resulting from a sudden and huge multiplication of the number of acting companies touring the country for a living, it is at least possible to understand why legislation directed against riots and vagabondage should have been stretched to take in theatrical performances and acting. I am myself disposed to think that this legislation was thus occasioned and was designed to protect *bona-fide* actors and performers from abuse by impostors: but the procedures adopted had the sorry consequence of providing Puritan opinion hostile to the theatre with a formidable weapon against it. For what could better suit the drama's enemies than the association, however indirect, of actors with beggars and criminals, and the coupling of play-acting with violence to persons and property? Philip Stubbs illustrates the point succinctly: writing of actors in 1583 he asks,

'live they not upon begging of every one that comes? Are they not taken by the lawes of the Realm for roagues and vacaboundes? I speak of such as travaile [*travel*] the Cuntries [*counties*] with playes & enterludes, making an occupation of it. . . .'[17]

To this smear another could easily be added—association with Roman Catholicism. The link that I have suggested between the dissolution of the religious houses and the inclusion of actors in the legislation against vagabonds is taken for granted by the Puritan preacher William Crashaw. Preaching at Paul's Cross in 1608, he thundered rhetorically,

'The ungodly Playes and Enterludes so rife in this nation: what are they but a bastard of Babylon, a daughter of error and confusion, a hellish device (the divel's owne recreation to mock at holy things) by him delivered to the Heathen, from them to the Papists, and from them to us?'[18]

If Crashaw's assumption can be regarded as bearing a close resemblance to remembered fact in Elizabethan and Jacobean England, then it is easy enough to understand why Puritan hostility to acting as a profession was so vituperative and implacable.

While these ideas must remain largely speculative, we have proof from other sources of a gradual change of attitude to acting. The exile of the most ardent English reformers in the early fifteen-forties and again in Mary's reign brought them into direct contact with the views and practice of continental reformers, notably Calvin's: and on their return to England they voiced these experiences in sermons, in pamphlets and in verbal advice to councillors of Church and State. The importance of these views, both at the time and to this enquiry, lies in a subtle shift of approach; they placed the moral and ethical grounds for permitting acting within the nation on an equal footing with the expedient practical considerations of law and order which were currently exercising government officials.

This attitude is conveniently epitomized in a chapter headed 'on the propriety of plays' (*De honestis ludis*) in the *De Regno Christi*, written for Edward VI by the Regius Professor of Divinity at Cambridge, Martin Bucer, and presented as a New Year gift in 1551. Bucer's views are liberal in that he does not seek to suppress acting; but the grounds on which he justifies it are primarily those of advancing instruction in the articles of the Christian faith; precisely those, in short, which had governed the religious stage since the fourteenth century and which would be invalidated immediately plays of religious polemic became too dangerous for governments to tolerate. It is ironic, therefore, that Bucer should have himself suggested in this same chapter the very means which were so soon to be used to put an end to religious plays.

'In order that Christ's people may profit from religious comedies and tragedies men will have to be appointed to the task of preventing the performance of any comedy or tragedy which they have not seen beforehand and decided should be acted; they must be men both outstanding in their knowledge of this kind of literature and also of established and constant zeal for Christ's Kingdom.'*

Just as serious for the future was the attack launched upon acting itself, for which Calvin's sermon on the following verse in the Bible served as prototype.

'The woman shall not wear that which pertaineth unto a man, neither shall a man put on a woman's garment: for all that do so are abomination unto the Lord thy God.' (*Deuteronomy*, XXII, 5.)

Stephen Gosson paraphrased this text in his *Playes Confuted in five Actions* (1582) in these words. 'The Law of God very straightly forbids men to put on womens garments.'[19] One has only to look at the surviving cast-lists of sixteenth-century plays or to consider to what extent play-acting was used as an instrument of education in Tudor boys' schools to realize what damage Calvin's sermon of 1556 could do to the actor's profession among those disposed to take it literally. *Twelfth Night, As You Like It, The Merchant of Venice* and a host of other plays offend directly; for no matter whether the female parts are played by boys or women, the scriptural injunction cannot but be broken.

The steady growth of opposition to acting on ethical grounds, as opposed to those of political expediency, was countered somewhat unevenly by the formulation and advancement of critical theories based on grounds of antiquity, academic instruction and moral worth. Where Calvin's appeal was to the Hebraic past, and Luther's to the early Christian Fathers, the humanist scholars made their appeal to the precedents of Greece and Rome. Aristotle, Seneca and more particularly the *Ars Poetica* of Horace, provided them with the ammunition of apology for acting.

It is on these grounds that Richard Edwardes, Master of the Children of the Chapel, commends his *Damon and Pithias* to his audience and readers in 1571.

* See Appendix C, pp. 329–331 below.

So correspondent to their kinde their speeches ought to bee.
Which speeches well pronounste, with action lively framed,
If this offende the lookers on, let *Horace* then be blamed,
Which hath our Author taught at Schole, from whom he doth not swarve,
In all suche kinde of exercise *decorum* to observe,
Thus much for his defence (he sayth) as Poetes earst have donne.[20]

However, as I have argued in Chapter II, the appeal to Rome was a double-edged weapon in the hands of English humanists when the sponsorship of Latin could just as easily be interpreted as the badge of Papistry as of scholarship. *

The urging of classical authority has a twofold importance, for it affected the development of the ethical debate about acting in England in point both of quality and quantity. The suspicion attaching to Latin accelerated the organizing of opinion assembled to denounce acting and retarded the formulation of the case for the defence. Of still more consequence in the long run, the case against acting went virtually unopposed in the provinces where the dissolution of the monasteries had stripped the countryside of centres of learning equivalent to the Inns of Court and the two Universities where Latin could still be studied on grounds of practical necessity and where neo-classical enthusiasms could grow in comparative safety.

When therefore this verbal battle was joined in earnest in the fifteen-seventies, the attack on the ethics of acting got off to a flying start. Any good Protestant was bound at least to listen to the exhortations of his ministers in sermon and pamphlet to question his former assumptions about acting. No such obligation bound him to listen to university dons or Court poets. Moreover, an appeal to eschew acting based on the Bible and the writings of the Fathers automatically carried more weight among Christian merchants and artisans with no Greek and very small Latin than any exhortation to support acting grounded on classical authority. Any tendency for such humanist exhortations to reach the provinces in diluted form was counteracted by their coinciding with the central government's suppression of the religious stage: for to this extent Puritan sentiment was reinforced by government action. In the provinces then, greater need existed than in London, Oxford or Cambridge for a rational and carefully organized reply: yet it was precisely there that neo-classical apologists could least hope for local support. I am myself of the opinion therefore that the Puritan onslaught on acting (if I may here equate the word

* See pp. 25–30 above.

Puritan with attack on moral grounds) achieved an immediate and decisive victory in the provinces. After 1580, the time at which in London and in the two Universities, the humanist counter-attack began to make some headway, acting is still to be witnessed in many provincial towns; but seldom can this acting be described as the spontaneous exercise of a natural right. From this time forward local citizens appear to have been either too bewildered or too frightened to test their right any further. The right to act, when exercised in provincial towns, has passed from the hands of local amateurs into those of strangers, men who were at once outsiders and visitors, permitted to be present on the mayor's sufferance.

The letter from Edward Alleyn quoted in Volume I (p. 270) shows that in 1593 one of the best London companies was not only on tour but was on the point of visiting those very cities where the old amateur acting tradition had flourished with outstanding success—Shrewsbury, Chester and York: and there is record of frequent visits to other towns, and by other companies, both before and after this date. Nevertheless this is a fundamentally different situation. In the first place, citizens who had lost their own plays and the right to act them under threat of fine, imprisonment and execution could never again regard dramatic performances as either an enjoyable duty before God or an innocent recreation among men. Secondly, the professional companies themselves, with their economy based on London property, could never regard provincial performances as anything more than an uncomfortable expedient for raising money when temporarily obliged to vacate the capital. Given these conditions and the spread of Puritan preaching and literature against the stage, it should come as no surprise that in the early seventeenth century the Mayors of many towns could pay a professional company a sum of money not to perform and rest safe in the knowledge that a direct appeal by the actors to the citizens would not arouse enough enthusiasm to warrant their challenging his authority.

In London and the Universities the right to act found varied and able support, not least from men of considerable education who were themselves dramatists. Nevertheless, the element of special pleading which this support represented served to make the debate more satirical and bitter. Lodge, Nashe, Jonson and Heywood, in pleading for their own profession, could hardly fail to colour ethical arguments with their own commercial interest and with satire at the expense of their personal enemies: and to this extent such support was as much of an embarrassment to the detached intellectual apologists—Ascham, Sydney, Puttenham, Harrington and others—as it was of genuine use.*

I have isolated these ethical arguments and the order of their growth deliberately in this narrative, because I believe that just as it was in the nature of the times for governments to seek to place the theatre under a measure of control in the interests of law and public order, so this moral debate would have arisen at this time in Tudor England regardless of the particular quality of the drama or the physical conditions of the theatre. In short, I am arguing that Reformation and Renaissance concepts of government, including concern for the policing of society and for the ordering of its moral welfare, enmeshed the English theatre like some bird in a net, and that only when in the net did the true nature of the bird become apparent to its captors. Once entangled in the web of political and ethical controversy, theatrical practice, from its own strength and resources, began to exercise a dominant influence upon the actual direction of both debates: and central to this process was the widespread popularity of acting, together with the commercial returns known to be related to it—both of them legacies from the mediaeval past. As we have seen, the police action against the theatre under Henry VIII, Edward VI and Queen Mary—however well intentioned and directed—was singularly ineffective because neither the nature nor scope of the place which the theatre held in the life of the community had been adequately assessed. For the same reason, the initial phases of the ethical debate on the propriety of plays and acting were inconclusive. Only when the stage itself had fully declared its nature, potentialities and intentions could its future place in society be debated as a matter of national rather than local importance and with its survival or suppression as the single clear-cut issue.

In the event, as we know, Elizabeth, James I and Charles I gave their patronage to the theatre's apologists, while opponents of the stage found their champions in the representatives of extreme reformist and democratic opinion in Church and Parliament. At the sole point in the period when both sides argued in concert—in exterminating the religious stage during the fifteen-seventies—the amateur's right to act (except in the schools and Universities) was irrevocably prejudiced. From then on discussion of the right to act, in practice if not in theory, concerns professional acting. Gosson

* The cases of Stephen Gosson and Anthony Munday are notable examples, 'playwrights' as Chambers observes, 'who had embraced conversion, and had the advantage of speaking from inner knowledge of the profession they were attacking'.[21]

acknowledges as much in advising London's Lord Mayor in 1579 that 'if their letters of commendation [*i.e.* the actors'] were once stayed, it were easie for you to overthrow them.'[22]

The actor's case (political and ethical considerations apart) rested on grounds which would obtain a sympathetic hearing in our own 'free-enterprise' society: 'let our right to act be conditioned by the willingness of audiences to support our plays'. This attitude was one which, at that time too, was probably endorsed by the majority of the population who were not *as individuals* actively engaged in or exercised by either the political or ethical controversies about stage plays: but the physical conditions of professional performances intervened at this point and presented many such neutrals with questions to answer which were to have a marked influence upon the argument.

The first group whose viewpoint we may consider in this light are the Mayors, Aldermen, Magistrates and Judges throughout the land who were responsible both for interpreting and enforcing the law and for safeguarding the local interests of the citizens who had either elected them to office, or whose lives and property had been entrusted to their care by the central government. To them a professional theatre, judged by the standards of conduct which it set itself, presented many problems.

The professional actor was for ever exercised by three questions of paramount importance to his livelihood: the frequency of performances, the availability and security of the place of performance, and the size and regularity of attendances at those performances. And on each of these counts his needs were liable to conflict with the private interests of his neighbours. When conflict became acute enough to lead to a dispute, City Fathers or county magistrates were in duty bound to resolve them.

My purpose in what follows is not to supply the reader with an exhaustive list of all such disputes relating to the right to act, but simply to indicate how disputes, of minor consequence if taken in isolation, came to attach themselves to the larger political and ethical arguments concerning the future of the stage in English life.

Central to all these disputes, at least from 1570 onward, was the theatre's increasing reliance upon capital investment. The money needed by a company of professional players in Tudor times to finance the production of their plays grew in volume in proportion both to the number of actors employed and to the number of plays commissioned: and costs on both counts were subject to any fluctuation in the number of performances given. John Stockwood in an attack on the theatre in 1577 estimated that there were eight 'ordinarie places in the Citie' known to him where plays were given twice or three times a week bringing in an annual profit to the actors of £2,000 a year.[23]

Since an actor's right to perform was itself dependent upon his employment as a servant in the household of a gentleman 'or person of greater degree', his elementary wants—a suit of clothes, meals, bed, and a small annual salary which cannot have amounted to more than a retaining fee—were in theory guaranteed. From the patron's viewpoint however the ability which such servants possessed to contribute to their own maintenance, if allowed to perform for monetary gain in other people's houses, could scarcely be overlooked: nor can there be much doubt that these actor-servants could enjoy a far higher standard of living when the elementary needs provided by the patron were supplemented by the moneys received from performances in other towns and counties. This pattern of life had been established by the mediaeval minstrels and was bequeathed by them to the 'players of interludes' in the fifteenth century as an unquestioned right. John English and the actors who worked with him in Henry VII's personal company of players not only received money for their performances when travelling in the provinces but from their master's Privy Purse in reward for performances at Court.* Money therefore had come to count, by then if not earlier, for more than everything else offered by the patron, with the notable exception of that patronage itself. Nearly a hundred years later Anthony Munday had this to say about the practice.

'. . . but since the reteining of these Caterpillers [Actors], the credite of noble men hath decaied, they are thought to be covetous by permitting their servants, which cannot live of them selves, and whome for neerenes they wil not maintaine, to live at the devotion or almes of other men, passing from countrie to countrie (i.e. *county to county*), from one Gentlemans house to another, offering their service, which is a kind of beggerie. Who in deede, to speake more trulie, are become beggars for their servants.'[24]

In Henry VII's lifetime, English and his men were each in the habit of receiving a yearly 'basic' wage of £3 6s. 8d. (five marks) in two instalments, one at Easter and the other at Michaelmas. Under

* His fellows were Edward Maye, Richard Gibson and John Hammond. It is possible that Gibson took over the leadership of the company from English at some point. English is not mentioned in the surviving records after 1531. Gibson became Sargeant of Tents in 1510, an office which he held until 1530.

Henry VIII the total Exchequer allowance for the 'Players of the king's Interludes' was increased from twenty to forty marks of which English's share was £6 13s. 4d. To this were added additional sums from the Privy Purse as occasion warranted.[25] English, for example, received £6 13s. 4d. on 26th October 1501 'for his pageant', a personal gratuity of 10 shillings on 7th January 1502, and 'for a rewarde' to be shared with his fellows £2 on 7th January 1509.[26] Glimpses of other sources of monetary reward reach us from the chance survival of sundry documents. From a law suit of 1528 we learn that the king's players made a profit of £30 on a provincial tour. Their reward at Durham Priory in 1532 was 15 shillings. In the same year they received 6s. 8d. from Selby Abbey, while for playing on 25th July and again on 8th August five years earlier they had been given 13s. 4d.[27] On the debit side of their balance sheet they had to meet a variety of expenses which may be briefly summarized as production and travel cost. Although largely subsidized by the Great Wardrobe and the Office of Works in respect of costumes, stage and scenic requirements when performing at Court, it is on record that the company had to pay hire costs to the Wardrobe in 1546/7.[28] When on tour in the provinces they had their living and transportation costs to meet.

These rather dreary figures can have little meaning for us; but they suffice to illustrate, long before Elizabeth's accession, that money had already come to assume an important place in a professional actor's attitude to his work. A further small point of some note is that in 1527 two members of this company, George Birche and George Mayler, are cited in a lawsuit about the value of stage costumes as 'coriar' and 'merchant tailor' respectively.[29] This knowledge suggests at least one alternative source of earning power and, more particularly, a source for the borrowing of capital should more money be required for a particular enterprise than a company could raise from its takings at its normal performances. *
If I may jump forward half a century for a moment, it is also as 'citizen & Inholder of London' that we find John Alleyn (Edward's brother) described in 1586 although we know him to have been

---

* I hope I am not pressing slender evidence further than I ought in emphasizing here the connection that existed between some professional actors and the Livery companies of London, as I have already emphasized the link simultaneously connecting some professional actors and the Royal Office of Pavilions and Tents: for to my mind these links helped to keep the professional stage in contact with both Civic Pageantry and with Tournaments, and served thereby to augment the spectacular potentialities of dramatic entertainment with corresponding increases in production costs. See Ch. VI, pp. 240–242 and Ch. VII, pp. 267 et seq.

a member of the Admiral's Company of actors at that time.[30]

This rise in production costs may be attributed in general terms almost wholly to the actors' determination to contest the mounting opposition to their right to act. The first expensive step in that direction was the decision, taken in the fifteen-seventies, to seek public playing places in London which were reserved to that purpose in the first instance (i.e. rather than hiring public halls, inns or private rooms which only served as theatres in the second instance) and which, at the same time were free from interference direct or indirect by the Court of Aldermen. The decision to enlarge the membership of the acting companies, taken at about the same time or shortly afterwards, was another. Both of these essentially Elizabethan innovations cost money involving heavy capital expenditure. Burbage met his obligation in respect of the building of the Theater by borrowing most of the sum required from a merchant, John Brayne.[31] The more spectacular productions which the existence of the Theater and the Curtain allowed brought box office returns that could be devoted to financing structural improvements and enlarging membership of the companies.* We have no records of early receipts to prove this, but we have other information which amounts to proof. The first is the readiness of Innkeepers to allow regular performances on their premises, together with the interest of speculators in theatre building in and round London: the second is the ability of the companies to increase their numbers: the third, the satirical comments from contemporaries about the spectacular nature of theatre decoration and the extravagance of actors' clothes.

'Beholde' wrote Thomas White in 1577, 'the sumptuous Theatre houses, a continuall monument of London's prodigalitie and folly'.[32]

Stephen Gosson is just as scathing about the parvenu actors in his *School of Abuse* of 1579.

'Overlashing in apparel is so common a fault, that the very hyerlings of some of our players, which stand at a reversion of vi.s by the weeke, jet under gentlemens noses in sutes of silke, exercising themselues too prating on the stage, and common scoffing when they come abrode, where they looke askance ouer the shoulder at euery man, of whom the Sunday before they begged an almes'.[33]

Robert Greene, in 1592, says of an actor that his

'share in playing apparrell will not be solde for two hundred pounds'.[34]

* See Ch. VIII, pp. 297–307 below.

Gosson, in his contemptuous reference to hirelings, and Greene, in his comment about an arrogant 'sharer', between them inform us how the acting companies supplied the capital to purchase their equipment and how they enlarged their own ranks. The sharer system was almost certainly a legacy of the early Tudor professional interluders to the Elizabethan companies: a nucleus of some four, six or at most eight actors pooled their resources to provide the initial capital for financing their productions and then shared the takings from performances on a basis proportional to their initial investment. All capital assets subsequently acquired—playbooks, costumes, scenic units and, later on, even theatre buildings —were similarly divisible among the sharers. A small company of this sort, once it could show a net profit on its investment, could consider increasing its numbers by employing additional actors on either a part-time or a full-time basis: these actors, supernumerary to the original sharers, were known as hirelings: they received a wage (said by Gosson to be six shillings a week in 1579) and could hope, with luck and adequate talent, to graduate in time to the status of sharers. [35]

Share-capital provided by the companies themselves and capital borrowed from speculators gave the Elizabethan theatre both the financial strength and the interest in self-preservation needed to acquire regular professional status despite the powerful factions combining to oppose it.

It is all too easy to lump all signs of hostility to the theatre together as evidence of Puritan antipathy: yet, as we have seen, the government could be as sternly opposed to theatrical performances as any Puritan where theatre practices of the day conflicted with its own responsibility for public health and public order. Epidemics of plague and riots associated with public assemblies were too frequent and too dangerous to be treated lightly. Both Whitehall and Guildhall thus found themselves working in this instance in concert with Puritan opinion whether they wished to or not. To modern minds it may seem strange that plague could be thought to originate and spread among theatre audiences while withholding its visitations apparently from assemblies of worshippers in Churches: but, to Elizabethans, plague itself was a direct sign of God's wrath, and plays were said to provoke that wrath.[36] And if sermons were not as well patronized as those who delivered them would have wished, young apprentices were similarly inclined to prefer dramatic entertainment to the tasks their masters appointed for them. These young absentees, however many pennies they contributed to enter the theatres, were a mixed blessing to the owner-sharers, for, in a manner familiar enough to us today, they formed themselves into gangs whose rivalries could easily be played upon by unscrupulous layabouts and quickly whipped up into sizeable riots.

'The beginners', writes Henry Chettle in 1592, 'are neither gentlemen, nor citizens, nor any of both their seruants, but some lewd mates that long for innouation; & when they see aduantage, that either Seruingmen or Apprentises are most in number, they will be of either side, though indeed they are of no side, but men beside all honestie, willing to make boote of cloakes, hats, purses, or what euer they can lay holde on in a hurley burley. These are the common causers of discord in publike places.' [37]

The actual siting of so many of London's theatres as near neighbours to London's most notorious brothels cannot have helped to improve the opinion held of them by honest and sensible citizens genuinely concerned for the standards of public order and decency; and there can be little doubt that pimps and procurers found the theatres as convenient a place to obtain customers as certain public houses and clubs have been made by government action in our own times. The Cockpit Theatre in Lincoln's Inn Fields was even said by Middleton to have been ill-fated from the outset for 'a my Conscience, some Queane pist upon the first Brick'. [38]

At the Blackfriars theatre it was the noise and inconvenience of traffic congestion which caused residents in the neighbourhood to petition the Lord Mayor to forbid acting there. [39] In the provinces similar inconveniences of a strictly local kind account for many of the inhibitive measures taken against actors. In Southampton the Town Hall was banned to actors for performances in 1623 'from henceforth' on the grounds that such use interfered with the conduct of 'the Kinges Courtes'. [40] Chester City Council, for identical reasons, had in 1615 forbidden the use of the Town Hall to actors 'in the night time or after vi of the clocke in the eveninge'. [41] From Norwich we learn of injunctions against performances: in 1611 because their licence appeared to be forged; in 1624 because the company of actors, having come from London, were suspected of carrying plague. [42] Many another case could be instanced from the surviving records, but I trust I have cited enough to support my contention that the change over from a primarily amateur theatre to an exclusively professional one during the reign of Elizabeth I provoked a wide variety of emotional reactions against it which at least in the first instance had nothing to do with the theological principles of avowed Puritans. Puritans in positions of authority however could very easily reckon to muster many of these private animosities to the service of their own cause. By continually fanning the flames of envy, jealousy, indignation or simple irritation created against actors by some small local incident or other, it became possible throughout the nation to open to question their right to act: and once this right had been conveniently exposed by the central government to exist only in Royal Letters Patent, it was not difficult to translate the issue into one of monarchical tyranny versus the voice of the people, or as John Cocke put it,

'howsoever [a common Player] pretends to have a royall Master or Mistresse, his wages and dependance prove him to be the servant of the people. . . . Hee is politick also to perceive the common-wealth doubts of his licence, and therefore in spight of Parliaments or Statutes hee incorporates himselfe by the title of a brotherhood.' [43]

On 22nd October 1647, 'an Ordinance of the Lords and Commons, assembled in Parliament' was sent to 'the Lord Mayor of the City of London, and the Justices of the Peace', authorizing them to arrest any 'common Players or Actors . . . to commit [them] to any common jail or prison, there to remain until the next general Sessions of the Peace . . . there to be punished as Rogues, according to the Law'.[44] It is signed Jo. Brown, Cleric. Parliamentorum, Hen. Elsynge, Cler. Parl. Dom. Com. Within a little more than a year the king was executed, ironically enough on a stage built in the street outside Inigo Jones' Banqueting Hall in Whitehall. (See Plate XXXII.) With him vanished, *sine die*, the Englishman's right to act.

4 *Playmakers and Dramatick Poets*

Between acquiring full professional status through the Letters Patent received from James I and losing the right to exercise their profession at the hands of the Long Parliament, the story of actors and acting becomes increasingly of interest for the light which it throws on the men who wrote the plays to be acted and the men who governed the theatre buildings in which they were acted. This short forty-year period marks an astonishing change in the status of the dramatist and a growing tendency towards monopoly in theatrical management which after 1660 became total. The key figures are, respectively, Ben Jonson and Philip Henslowe. Although the very homogeneity which characterizes the relationship between actors, dramatists and managers in the theatre of the time was one of its principal strengths then and must not be lost sight of now, clarity demands some separation both of function and treatment in this narrative; and for the present I wish to transfer attention from the fortunes of the actor to those of the dramatists.

In using the word dramatist it is important to recognize that this word only finds its way into our vocabulary towards the end of the seventeenth century. I stand open to correction from philologists, but as far as I am aware, dramatists throughout the sixteenth century are described as

1. makers of enterludes, or interludes
2. play-makers
3. makers of stage plays

and, starting late in Elizabeth's reign,

4. stage-poets
5. authors.

Ben Jonson is the first writer of plays to use the term 'dramatick, or (as they terme it) stage-poetrie'. The phrase occurs in his dedication of *Volpone* (1608) to 'THE TWO FAMOUS UNIVERSITIES'.[45] Puttenham had used the phrase in *English Poesie* of 1578, but in the context of the plays of ancient Greece and Rome. It is Jonson too who in 1616 first uses the word 'drama':

> 'I cannot for the stage a *Drama* lay
> *Tragick*, or *Comick*; but thou writ'st the play.' (*Epigrams*, cxii)

So universal has Shakespeare's fame become since then that one may legitimately wonder what any school of English literature would amount to today if stripped of the study of his work: yet it behoves us to remember that rather less than half of his plays were read in his lifetime by anyone other than the actors who performed them, and of those that did find their way into print, the majority were pirated and published without either his own or the actors' consent.* The fact has to be faced that the society in which Shakespeare lived did not admit plays as literature. This was a dignity reserved to Philosophy, Theology, History and Poetry. Shakespeare, along with countless other writers for the theatre, was thought of as a playmaker. His literary standing as a dramatist only begins to become of consequence with the publication of the First Folio seven years after his death; and it is to be doubted

* See A. W. Pollard, *Shakespeare's Fight with The Pirates*, 1917.

whether his fellow actors, Heminges and Condell, would have taken this momentous step without the precedent set by Ben Jonson who had ventured upon the innovation of personally supervising the publication of all his own writings, including plays and masks, under the title of *Works*, in 1616. In the theatre this was indeed a remarkable year, for in the course of it the death of both Shakespeare and Henslowe marks the end of one order, while the royal pension and laureateship bestowed on Ben Jonson proclaims the start of another.

Jonson's triumph was not won without careful preparation and much subsequent acrimony, both typical of the man. In the epistle dedicatory to *Volpone* we may catch a glimpse of his thinking.

'I cannot but be serious' he protests, 'in a cause of this nature, wherein my fame, and the reputations of divers honest, and learned are the question; when a Name, so ful of authority, antiquity, and all great marke, is (through their [i.e. stage-poets'] insolence) become the lowest scorne of the age: and those men subject to the petulancy of every vernaculous Orator, that were wont to bee the care of Kings, and happiest Monarchs. This it is, that hath not only rap't me to present indignation, but made me studious, heretofore; and, by all my actions, to stand off, from them.'

Of *Volpone* itself, he adds that it has been his object 'to reduce, not onely the ancient formes, but manners of the *scene*, the easinesse, the propriety, the innocence, and last the doctrine, which is the principall end of *poesie*, to informe men, in the best reason of living.'[46]

Jonson has a twofold purpose here: on the one hand to claim recognition as a poet writing for the stage who disassociates himself from other playmakers of the time, and on the other hand to establish that claim by a direct appeal to the 'dramatick' poetry of antiquity. Since the appeal is directed to readers in Oxford and Cambridge, he might well hope that his claim would gain support among intellectuals elsewhere. Nor is it only *Volpone* that he dedicates with care in this way: *Every Man Out of His Humour* is dedicated to the Inns of Court, *Cynthia's Revels* to the Court itself, 'the fountain of manners'.[47] His individual patrons are no less distinguished and influential. Camden is chosen for *Every Man in His Humour*, the Lord Chamberlain for *Catiline*, and Prince Henry for *The Mask of Queens*.[48] Jonson's action in this respect, if not unprecedented, was both deliberate and frequent enough to establish for others what Nichol Smith called 'the habit of offering to a patron the published version of a successful play'.[49] The contrast with Shakespeare, who did not dedicate a single play to a patron, is so striking as to oblige us to seek some reason to explain this difference in conduct. I am myself convinced that Jonson's object was the defence of his status as a playmaker partly against the spate of pamphlets and sermons (precipitated by Gosson's *School of Abuse*) designed to bring all plays and their authors into contempt, and partly against the habit of collaborative playwriting.

Apart from the fact that Shakespeare does not appear to have been possessed of the crusading spirit that forms so important a part of Jonson's character, his financial situation as an actor/sharer in the Globe/Blackfriars syndicate was far more comfortable than Jonson's, and his ambitions probably more modest.* Jonson confessed in 1619 that he had not earned as much as £200 from all his plays, a sum smaller than Shakespeare's annual income, estimated at £300.[50] Since Jonson lacked any steady income from other theatrical sources, once he had abandoned acting, his indebtedness to patronage is obvious. Henslowe loaned him the capital to buy an actor's 'share' in the Admiral's Company and the Earl of Pembroke gave him a regular New Year's gift of £20 'to buy books'.[51] In 1616 James I granted him by Patent, 'a certaine an(n)uytie or penc(i)on of one hundred markes of lawfull money of England by the yeare' and promised him the reversion of the Master of the Revels in which, however, he was to be disappointed.[52] In 1628 he was appointed Chronologer to the City of London at a fee of 'one hundred nobles p(er) Anu(m)'; a post left empty by the death of another dramatist, Thomas Middleton.[53] And as Jonson succeeded Middleton, so, in 1637, he was himself succeeded as Poet Laureate by another dramatist, William Davenant. The laureateship thus came to be bestowed on a playmaker not only for the first time, but twice in succession: and thus, although Jonson was himself in financial straits for much of his life and died in stringent poverty,[54] his fight to improve the status of playmakers in society resulted in a victory of revolutionary proportions. From this time forward the dramatist could legitimately regard himself as a man of letters to whom the highest national rewards were open as of right.

In the earliest days of English drama the playmaker had so little literary standing that as often as not his name did not appear on the

* Having removed the stigma of his father's bankruptcy, acquired a coat of arms and bought New Place for his family he might well consider himself fortunate. He is reputed (at second-hand *via* Sir William Davenant) to have received a gift of £1,000 from a patron for a purchase he was especially interested in making. Heminges and Condell dedicated the First Folio to the Lord Chamberlain.

'original' or 'register', as his manuscript was then called. Yet once this manuscript existed, it was thought valuable enough by the actors whose property it became to be stored with care for use again and again—for their own use, that is, not use by others.* We have seen with what scant respect the unfortunate author of the *Mystère des Trois Doms* was treated in 1509 by those fellow townsmen who commissioned his epic of three days duration.† Others fared better, notably the schoolmasters and choirmasters of early Tudor times who made interludes for their pupils. At least most of them escaped anonymity and wrote what they pleased.

The first maker of any dramatic entertainment in England that included a written text, and who is known to us by name, is John Lydgate.‡ It is significant that the seven texts for indoor revels surviving from his pen are the work of someone who was both the most notable poet of his time and a cleric; for one or other or both these features repeat themselves over the next hundred years, and in large measure account for the nature of the subject matter treated.

Barclay, Skelton, Medwall, Bale and Udall all held office in the Church, two of them as Bishops. Sir David Lyndsay was Lyon King of Arms and a notable poet as well as a maker of interludes. There is evidence that an ability to make plays was a normal qualification for employment as a chaplain in a large household.[55] With the coming of the censorship however, and as a result of the dissolution of the religious houses, change became inevitable. Outside Oxford and Cambridge, only London could rely on a constant supply of playmakers. Elsewhere, the organists, choirmasters, lawyers and schoolmasters who might be called upon to 'make' interludes when occasion demanded, while certainly learned men by the standards of the times, were not necessarily either divines or poets: and by the close of the sixteenth century no one with a talent for playmaking had much chance of exercising it except in association with the professional acting companies in the capital.§

A factor which could have been very important in advancing the literary standing of the early Tudor playmakers was the invention of printing with the possibilities which that offered for the wider

* See *EES*, i, pp. 302–305.
† See *EES*, i, pp.191 *et seq.*
‡ See *EES*, i, pp. 191–207.
§ See Ch. III, pp. 90–93. In 1578 the scholars of the free school in Chester performed a 'comedy', and I have myself received, on loan, the MS of a hitherto unknown Elizabethan play, *Oedipus, with a Song*, written by a schoolmaster and performed between 1581 and 1605 in the North-East of England.

circulation of plays, both English and foreign. However, apart from the natural reluctance of the acting companies to relinquish their copyright in their own plays, any tendency on the part of authors to press for the printing of their plays in England was seriously handicapped by the laws and edicts associated with government censorship of publishing after 1538. Like the censorship of plays for performance, the early censorship of books was not launched on doctrinal grounds. Discussing its operation R. B. McKerrow sums up the matter by remarking that

'there was nothing of religious bigotry, or even of the desire to save souls; the intention was throughout political, to avoid the danger of civil dissension.'[56]

With the Incorporation of the Stationers' Company in 1557 and the confirming of its charter in 1559, the censorship of books became far more effective than it had been during the preceding twenty years.[57] Thus the licensing of texts served to strengthen the acting companies' proprietary interest in their own plays and to impede the playmaker from establishing himself in public esteem as a man of letters. Any success that he might claim on that account had to be earned by other literary pursuits. The MSS of plays were in some instances not even recognized by the government as books: for certain texts, among which are grouped plays and pamphlets, had to be submitted to three members of the Court of Ecclesiastical Commission for licensing instead of to the normal body consisting of the Archbishops of Canterbury and York, the Chancellors of Oxford and Cambridge Universities, the Bishop of London and the Ordinary or Archdeacon of the place of publication.[58] Either way, however, this evidence provides conclusive proof that the Church retained its control over the texts of plays, religious and other, until the end. * Furthermore, it must be added that printing of any sort was forbidden to provincial cities with the exception of Oxford and Cambridge. This knowledge substantially reinforces Warton's contention, cited above, that provincial ignorance in the mid sixteenth century became universal:† it also serves to explain why the citizens of Coventry when their own Miracle Cycle was suppressed had to go to Oxford to engage a Mr. Smith to write *The Destruction of Jerusalem* which replaced it in 1584. ‡

Broadly speaking then, I think we may say with some confidence that the playmaker owed such status as he enjoyed in English society

* *EES*, i, p. 119, and pp. 55–56 above.
† Ch. II, p. 26.
‡ See *EES*, i, p. 301.

until Elizabeth's accession to his ability to supply actors with material which *they* deemed likely to meet with the approval of *their* audiences. Plays prepared for Court audiences or for scholars, like Medwall's *Fulgens and Lucrece* or Redford's *Wit and Science* are noticeably more literary than the more polemical interludes of the period: but the essentially emblematic quality of the mediaeval Miracle Cycle and Morality Play continued to distinguish Tudor plays. The reliance of these plays (childlike in its faith) upon narrative, debate, and the imaginative perceptiveness of the beholders gave a freedom to the actors in performance which ensured that the success or failure of the play was rated in terms of their achievement rather than in that of the author. This is reasonable enough when so many plays were not original, but redactions of earlier plays upon the same subject. The exception was closet drama, of which scholarly translations of Latin plays provided the most usual examples in the period.

However, as I have already indicated,* the government, in suppressing the religious stage, inadvertently went a long way to change the status of the playmaker in relation to the acting companies. During the rest of Elizabeth's reign his status remained that of a servant to the actors providing them with their scripts; but gradually his services became so much more valuable as to warrant a change of status. There are at least three reasons for this change. In the first place, new plays had to be written which would survive the scrutiny of the licensing authorities: secondly, with regular weekday performances now permitted in London, more plays were suddenly wanted than had ever been needed before: thirdly, some two generations of writers had grown to maturity whose education had not been received at clerical hands and who were not themselves in holy orders. By 1590, with the Armada defeated and Mary of Scotland in her tomb, ideas of Italian inspiration were once again making rapid and fruitful growth on English soil. Men therefore with a University background and a reputation as poets or novelists among the wealthier patrons of the theatre became as welcome to the actors in the capacity of playmaker as men of humbler academic attainment among their own ranks. In consequence, we may see developing both a change in the balance of theatrical power between authors and actors and a feud between authors of different background and aspiration.

The playmakers knew well enough how comfortable an income the actor sharers were making from their theatrical investment,

* See Ch. II, pp. 40–43 above.

compared with their own earnings; and at the same time they were beginning to sense the degree of bargaining power latent in the actors' indebtedness to them. Greene thus satirizes actors as 'Puppits . . . that speake from our mouths'. His indignation is only further provoked by the knowledge that some of these upstart crows of actors can beautify themselves with the feathers properly belonging to recognized men of letters. [59] The case is stated neatly, probably overstated, in the Cambridge satire *The Return from Parnassus* of 1601/02.

> 'Vile world, that lifts them [actors] up to hye degree,
> And treads us [scholar-poets] downe in groveling misery.'[60]

The only concession which the actors appear to have made to unattached playmakers in Shakespeare's working lifetime is to have increased the lump sum paid them in exchange for their plays, by doubling it from some £10 to some £20 for each play. Once the play had been handed over, however, the copyright as in earlier times became the actors', and the dramatist was not allowed either to supply copies to other companies or to a printer. [61] Squabbles on this count were frequent, and it will suffice to note that the king's men sought the Lord Chamberlain's help on several occasions in preventing other companies from acting any of their plays 'purchased by them at Deare rates'. [62] Further evidence of the value of plays to the actors is provided in the disaster which overtook the Admiral's Company in 1621 (by then they were licensed as the Palsgrave's men) when they lost their entire stock of plays in the fire which destroyed the Fortune Theatre. Since the Fortune was immediately rebuilt, it was in all probability the loss of their repertoire (combined with two bad plague years) which crippled the company in its struggle to compete with the King's Men for the favour of the town.[63] Dramatists of the late Elizabethan and Jacobean period knew well enough what they were allowed to write about and what they were not: and in most instances the scrutiny of every play by the Master of the Revels before it was acted, and by the Warden of the Stationers' Company before it was printed, served to keep the dramatists clear of the law. Attention will be drawn later to some notable exceptions. *

A dramatist's individual worth to a company was rated in part by his promptness in delivering his scripts and partly by the success which they met in performance. As a result, companies of actors sought to shackle a promising dramatist to their exclusive service

* See pp. 130–132 below.

and were none too scrupulous in their methods. The story of Henslowe's dealings with authors, especially the system he employed of putting them so deeply into his debt as to be obliged to write for his company and no other, is too well known to require restating; but before we wax too indignant about either, we would do well to reflect on the morality of many of our own hire-purchase or 'no down-payment' dealings.[64]

A much more serious charge that can be levelled against the actors and 'bankers' of the time in their relations with authors—at least from any aesthetic or literary standpoint—is the habit of obliging syndicates of needy authors to rush a story into play form with speed of completion as the principal objective. In the instance about which most is known the text of the play itself is unfortunately no longer in existence. In September 1624 Sir Henry Herbert's register of licences records the entry of a play called 'A new Tragedy, called *A late Murther of the Sonn upon the Mother*', with sub-title 'Keep the Widow Waking'. Thanks to the researches of Professor C. J. Sisson into the law suit which followed the performance of this play we know both who wrote it and how the labour was divided.* The authors were Dekker, Ford, Rowley and Webster. They dramatized two recent and notorious crimes, one being Nathaniel Tindall's murder of his mother in April, and the other concerning a certain Tobias Audley's scandalous relations with a Mrs. Anne Elsden, a wealthy widow. Mrs. Elsden's son-in-law brought an action against the authors, and it is as a defendant in the case that Dekker gave the following testimony:

'. . . true it is, Hee wrote two sheetes of paper conteyning the first Act of a Play called The Late Murder in White Chappell, or Keepe the Widow waking, and a speech in the Last Scene of the Last Act of the Boy who had killed his mother. . . .'[65]

The presumption is that Ford, Rowley and Webster similarly contributed an Act each together with a part of the final Act. Dekker testifies further that they

'. . . did make and contrive the same [play] uppon the instruc-c(i)ons given them by one Raph Savage. . . .'[66]

The play was certainly acted at the Red Bull where Savage was apparently serving as manager at the time. The dates of the two

* See *Lost Plays of Shakespeare's Age*, 1936, pp. 80–124; also G. E. Bentley, *J. & C. S.*, i, pp. 208–9 and iii, pp. 252–6.

crimes, April and July/August, compared with that of the licensing of the play, September, provide the obvious reason for Savage's interest in this collaborative effort. It is probable that a second company was preparing a play on this topical subject at the same time. The practice certainly had ample precedent, Ford, Rowley and Dekker having collaborated only three years earlier on the equally topical *The Witch of Edmonton*,[67] and a casual glance at Henslowe's Diary indicates that a large majority of the plays which he commissioned were written (or 'made') by two, three or four collaborators.[68] Nor is it unfamiliar to those who write scripts for the cinema and television today.

That Jonson with his strong vested interest in improving the literary standing of the playmaker should abhor the practice is understandable: but it may be remarked that the new literary status which he won for his successors did not result in a more remarkable repertoire of plays than that produced by his predecessors. The leading dramatists of the Caroline period lived more comfortably than they could have hoped to do in earlier times, largely by virtue of the greater stability of the acting companies and the higher premium which the companies were obliged (in their quest for new plays) to place upon their services. They were moreover better off than the majority of the actors who by then were complaining about the monopolistic tendencies among the sharers.[69] Herbert's licences furnish us with a remarkably clear picture of the market for plays at that time. Beaumont, Fletcher and Massinger wrote for the King's Company, Lady Elizabeth's and Queen Henrietta's, averaging slightly more than two a year between 1620 and 1640. Davenant averaged a play a year for the King's Men between 1630 and 1640, while Queen Henrietta's Company provided both Heywood and Shirley with their best market.[70] The relations of all these dramatists with the licensing authorities were no less comfortable and relaxed than with the actors. There is no evidence that any of them tried to defy the censorship after Middleton's notorious *Game at Chess* (1624) had forced him to seek temporary cover in the country and occasioned the actors (King's Men) to be restrained from acting while the affair was under investigation.[71] Rather did they abandon all efforts to write about religion or politics from a national standpoint. Even the long-standing habit of cloaking topical subject matter in parable or allegory seems to have declined in its general use. The King's Men were in trouble in 1632 for interpolating matter of their own into Jonson's *Magnetick Lady*.[72] Davenant's *The Wits* (1634) offended Herbert in point of certain oaths used, but on representations being made to Charles I many of Herbert's deletions were restored.*

'This morning,' Herbert records 'being the 9th of January, 1633, the kinge was pleasd to call mee into his withdrawinge chamber to the windowe, wher he went over all that I had croste in Davenants play-booke, and allowing of *faith* and *slight* to bee asseverations only, and no oathes, markt them to stande, and some other few things, but in the greater part allowed of my reformations. This was done upon a complaint of Mr. Endymion Porters in December. The kinge is pleasd to take *faith, death, slight,* for asseverations, and no oaths, to which I doe humbly submit as my masters judgment; but, under favour, conceive them to be oaths, and enter them here, to declare my opinion and submission.

The 10 of January, 1633, I returned unto Mr. Davenant his playe-booke of *The Witts*, corrected by the kinge.

The kinge would not take the booke at Mr. Porters hands; but commanded him to bring it unto mee, which he did, and likewise commanded Davenant to come to me for it, as I believe: otherwise he would not have byn so civill.'[74]

Charles was not so temperately minded in respect of Massinger's *The King and The Subject* written in 1638. Herbert gives a clear account of what occurred. Some friend of his, sensing that trouble might follow if it were performed as it stood, warned both Herbert and the King. Herbert insisted that the title be altered and 'the reformations [i.e. his own] most strictly observed'. The King sent his views back to Herbert who wrote,

'Received of Mr. Lowens for my paines about Messinger's play called *The King and the Subject*, 2 June, 1638, £1.0.0.

The name of *The King and the Subject* is altered, and I allowed the play to bee acted, the reformations most strictly observed, and not otherwise, the 5th of June, 1638.

At Greenwich the 4 of June, Mr. W. Murray, gave mee power from the king to allowe of the play, and tould me that hee would warrant it.

> 'Monys? Wee'le rayse supplies what ways we please,
> And force you to subscribe to blanks, in which
> We'le mulct you as wee shall thinke fitt. The Caesars
> In Rome were wise, acknowledginge no lawes
> But what their swords did ratifye, the wives
> And daughters of the senators bowinge to
> Their wills, as deities,' &c.

* A similar objection in point of profane language had occasioned Fletcher's *The Woman's Prize* or *The Tamer Tamed* to be suppressed and reformed.[73]

This is a peece taken out of Phillip Messingers play, called *The King and the Subject*, and entered here for ever to bee remembered by my son and those that cast their eyes on it, in honour of Kinge Charles, my master, who readinge over the play at Newmarket, set his marke upon the place with his owne hande, and in thes words:

"This is too insolent, and to bee changed."

Note, that the poett makes it the speech of a king, Don Pedro, king of Spayne, and spoken to his subjects.'[75]

If Massinger's sentiments were bold and rash, they are probably as nothing to what might have been written at this time in Lincoln, Coventry, Hereford or York had there been any play-makers left to write plays or local actors to act them: but there were neither and remembrance of both had virtually passed out of living memory.

5 Bankers and Managers

It will have been noticed that a key figure in regulating the balance of power between the actors and the playmakers was the 'business manager', banker or capitalist-owner of theatrical pro-perty. From the days of the trouvère, the head of a professional troupe of entertainers (first minstrels, then interluders) had given the troupe its name, secured the right to perform and received the financial reward for performances. It is this form of professional dis-cipline that we encounter among the players who visit Hamlet at Elsinore: and as a system of management it sufficed until the capital outlay required to finance the building of a permanent play-house obliged the actors to seek the interest of speculators. The three most notable capitalists of Elizabethan times who adopted an interest in theatre business were John Brayne, the wealthy grocer who loaned Burbage the money to build his Theater in 1576, Francis Langley, the builder of the Swan, and Philip Henslowe, the builder of the Rose, the Fortune and, in 1614, the Hope. Henry Lanman owned the profits of the Curtain in 1585 and probably financed its erection eight years earlier. The Red Bull was built *c*. 1605 by Aaron Holland, a yeoman described as 'utterly un-learned and illiterate, not being able to read'.[76]

This is not the place to discuss questions of the design, con-struction or stage practice of the theatres; but as the siting of most of them was directly connected with the laws governing the con-duct of actors and the licensing of plays, some brief mention at least must be made here of the means adopted by these financiers for securing their large speculative investments against the recurring risks of conflict with the licensing authority and county magistrates. Nor can we overlook the lasting effects of these early capital speculations upon the fortunes of actors, dramatists and painters in the English theatre.

There can be little doubt that the acting companies of the early part of Elizabeth's reign encountered pressures of a new and extreme sort to cause them to place their future in the hands of money-lenders. The reason usually given to explain the spate of theatre building which marks the last two decades of Elizabeth's reign is the growing determination of the actors to escape from the control which the Court of Aldermen exercised over their activities in the London Inns. To this end, it is said, they built the new theatres on land outside the jurisdiction of the City Fathers yet as close to the City as they conveniently could. I have no evidence to suggest this view is mistaken; but, as I have argued elsewhere, the change over from occasional performances on public holidays to regular performances on weekdays, signalized by Elizabeth's Patent to Leicester's Company in 1574, was enough in itself to prompt the acting companies to free themselves from their dependence upon the goodwill of Innkeepers and others who leased halls to them by finding premises which could be devoted to exclusively theatrical purposes.* This is an attitude of mind which many an amateur dramatic society of our own time can readily vouch for. Yet, this objective, however desirable in principle, was by no means easy of attainment in a rapidly expanding city where building sites were both rare and expensive. The dissolved religious houses within the city, the traditional playgrounds in the Fields to the North and across the river on the South Bank were the most likely places for a site to be available at a modest price.

This problem of real estate provoked in the solution adopted much of the subsequent hostility displayed towards the theatre on moral grounds. Those theatres which were established in disused religious houses in the city, Blackfriars and Whitefriars, strengthened the Puritan argument that theatres represented a perpetuation of Popery, but were significantly free of those more serious disorders associated with the playhouses in the fields. Not only was the policing of remoter suburban areas more difficult, but the proximity of gambling houses, places for martial exercises and, above all, of the brothels, tarred the new enterprises from the outset with all the most vicious features of the old. In calling theatres

* For the City Edict of 1582–84, formerly dated 1574–76, see p. 85 above.

'Satan's palaces' the Puritans had ample evidence to substantiate their point; evidence of a sort, moreover, that would alarm men responsible for public order, health and decency whatever their position in religion and politics. *

Because we are wise after the event, it is hardly fair to blame the building speculators and acting companies of the time for their lack of foresight in this respect. Most of them in any case got their fingers badly burned in consequence. I have already remarked on the partial destruction of the Cockpit by rowdy apprentices,† and the fire which destroyed the Fortune,‡ calamities in any event for the actors, but far more serious for the owners in days when no insurance cover could be expected. Plague and restraint from the licensing authorities were other hazards to receipts from theatrical investment. Francis Langley's adventure with the Swan foundered on this account. Opened *c.* 1594 and leased to Pembroke's Men, this theatre lost its licence as a result of the performance of *The Isle of Dogs* in 1597: it remained closed on account of plague for several months and was never again officially allowed to function as a regular theatre.[77] John Brayne, who enabled James Burbage to build the Theater, had similar reason to regret his investment. It suffices to say that our knowledge of the relations between the two is based wholly on a series of cross-suits in Chancery all of which have been admirably set out by Sir Edmund Chambers.§ Brayne attested that he was talked into the original agreement very much against his will by Burbage who turned out to be a double-dealer and quite unreliable in his estimates: but since Brayne had had a capital interest in plays at the Red Lion inn before he joined Burbage in this enterprise, he cannot be wholly exculpated from money-grubbing motives himself.

Of all the capitalist outsiders, only Philip Henslowe was consistently successful in his theatrical speculations. From an interest in the building of the Rose starting *c.* 1587, he progressed to ownership of the Fortune (built 1602) and the Hope (built 1614) and to a leading interest in both the Swan and the Whitefriars. This must be attributed to superior capital assets enabling him to weather financial storms which broke other men; to his close association with Edward Alleyn, the most reputable actor of the time in respect of both profession and personal integrity; and to his careful courtship of influential patrons in the City and at West-

* See pp. 85–87 and 118–119.
† See p. 120.
‡ The first Globe was gutted by fire in 1613.
§ *ES*, ii, pp. 387 *et seq.*

minster. His so-called diary shows how he succeeded, by recourse to a long series of loans between 1597 and 1603, in keeping continuity within his companies, paying actors' debts, bailing out dramatists from prison, and meeting his obligations to the Revels Office in respect of licence fees. In 1592 he married his daughter to Alleyn. In Elizabeth's Household he had enjoyed the rank, first of groom of the chamber, then that of a Sewer; and in 1604 he obtained for himself and Alleyn the Mastership of the Royal Bears from James I.[78] To me, it appears no coincidence that the two acting companies in which Henslowe had a controlling financial interest, Worcester's and the Admiral's, were among the three which survived from Elizabeth's reign and were granted Patents in the service of the Royal Family by James I. Both thus safely escaped the inhibitions of the Statute of 1604, thereby securing themselves in their profession and Henslowe and his son-in-law in their investments.

The third company succeeding to this good fortune was that which James I took over from the Lord Chamberlain's service and put into his own, and in which the Burbage family had a controlling interest. Despite their calamitous relations at the Theater with their financier Brayne, and later with their ground landlord Giles Allen, James Burbage and his sons Richard and Cuthbert transferred their old interest in 1598 'with more summes of money taken up at interest, which lay heavy on us many yeeres' to the building of the Globe and the refurbishing of Ferrers' theatre in the Blackfriars.[79] Where the Globe was concerned, they provided 50 per cent. of the share-capital themselves, the rest being supplied by Shakespeare, Heminges, Philips, Pope and Kempe. The Blackfriars had been bought two years earlier at a cost of £600: the capital was apportioned between Richard and Cuthbert Burbage (James having died) and the actors on the basis of seven equal shares. An interesting if minor point is that Shakespeare, since the shares covered all theatrical property as well as the buildings, was one of the very few dramatists, in these early days, who held a reversionary interest in his own plays.

The financial strength which these arrangements gave the company to meet a crisis, like the burning of the Globe in 1613 or a restraint on playing of as much as a year's duration on account of plague, can scarcely be exaggerated. Even so, disaster would have overtaken the company on several occasions had it not been for the private bounty of their two Royal Patrons, James I and Charles I, and the special protection on which they could rely in safeguarding their copyright in plays against other companies and unscrupulous publishers.

The moral to this brief survey of managerial conditions in London is obvious enough. In seeking to escape from the irksome and inhibiting effects of censorship and control inside the city limits, the adult companies transferred their activities to localities which invited criticism on moral grounds. To the fire of ethical opposition to professional acting they thereby caused the fuel of much magisterial and commercial enmity to be added; and, in doing so, they alienated a growing body of bourgeois opinion that might otherwise have remained neutral. It is this combination of forces that petitions the Court of Aldermen, the Bishop of London and Archbishop of Canterbury and finally the Privy Council to suppress all theatres during the fifteen-eighties and fifteen-nineties.* Faced with this situation, the speculators could hope for little redress against defaulting actors or other emergencies unless they were provided with direct lifelines to the Privy Council or the Royal Household. James I, at his accession, by taking only the best organized companies into the service of his own family and by licensing only those theatres in which their capital was invested, merely put a seal of regularity on this position.† The authority of the Crown sufficed to preserve it until Parliament grew powerful enough to reverse it.

Before leaving the subject of management, a word must be said about the effects of managerial conditions upon the physical conditions of the theatre buildings, their shape and appearance. We have no evidence to show that the Elizabethan building speculators who went into partnership with the acting companies had any more serious interest in the artistic, educational or moral value of drama to the community than have the managers of commercial radio and television companies of the present day. The primary object of lending money then to be invested in the building of playhouses was the promise of high box-office returns which the growing popular appetite for stage-plays might be expected to bring in. This factor above all others created a pressure towards the building of large-capacity auditoriums, and must be held responsible for the decision to reject small, intimate, roofed-in halls in favour of the grander, three-story, open-air playhouses. In the seventeenth century, the King's Men could reckon to take more money from a performance at their 'private house' in the Blackfriars than from one at the Globe: but by then they had earned a reputation which enabled them to price admission in terms of shillings instead of in pence. In the fifteen-seventies the capacity of the house as a whole,

* See Ch. III, pp. 85–86 and 93.
† See Ch. III, p. 90 above.

136

rather than the maximum price that could be put on an individual seat, was what counted.

Scarcely less important was the need to secure the investment in the buildings against the risk of a total prohibition of all stage plays. A building devoted exclusively to this purpose could become a total loss, virtually overnight, if the government should decide to join forces with the City in suppressing secular plays (as it had already joined forces with the Church to suppress the religious stage) unless steps were taken to ensure that the building could contain other forms of popular entertainment as readily as stage-plays.

In short, I think we must envisage the probability that the early theatres were never designed as theatres in our sense of that word, but instead as multi-purpose amusement houses. Only after it had become clear that stage-plays were more profitable than any other form of entertainment in their drawing-power, and that the Privy Council was not going to allow them to be banned, was it possible to contemplate designing a building devoted exclusively to actors' and dramatists' specifications. It seems to me therefore that the Globe (1598/9) and the Fortune (1601/2) were likely to have differed on this account from the design of their predecessors, just as the later Blackfriars, Salisbury Court and other theatres built in Stuart times differed from the Globe and Fortune because of changes in the political, social and financial climate of the times.

6 Royal Slaves

The last words, like the first in this chapter, must rest with the actors; for it was in their persons rather than anyone else's that such traditions of play performance as were transmitted from Caroline to Restoration times reached the new audiences. The readmission of theatrical performances under Charles II's rule represents a fusion of two pre-Civil War traditions of dramatic entertainment rather than a fresh start imported from French, Italian, German or other foreign sources eclipsing everything known to pre-Commonwealth London.

Davenant and Killigrew* who by November 1660 had succeeded in extorting a monopoly in theatrical management from Charles II, were both courtiers in Caroline times and had both written plays for the Royal companies.[80] Both had worked with Inigo Jones and

---

* Thomas, fourth son of Sir Robert, and brother of Sir William: Davenant was knighted by Charles I in 1643 after the battle of Gloucester.

knew everything there was to be known about the Court Masks. Jones' pupil, John Webb, joined Davenant and was made responsible for the staging of his first music drama on return from exile, *The Siege of Rhodes*.[81] Both Davenant and Killigrew had to fight Sir Henry Herbert who, as Master of the Revels, had survived the war and sought to impose upon them the rights of control formerly vested in his office.[82] Davenant had been given a Patent by Charles I in 1639 to build a theatre of his own in Fleet Street, primarily for use as an opera house, but he did not proceed to build it: instead he took over the management of Inigo Jones' Cockpit-in-Court in 1640.[83] This theatre survived destruction during the Civil War and Commonwealth, as did the other Cockpit (situated in Drury Lane and known in Caroline times as The Phoenix), the Red Bull and Salisbury Court: and at all four theatres actors who had served the new king's father on stage and battlefield were already performing illicitly when Davenant and Killigrew secured their managerial monopoly.[84] These actors were faced with a choice of relinquishing their hard-won freedom to resume their calling or accepting one of these two men as their new master. Most of them joined Killigrew and once again resumed the title of the King's Company. Davenant elected to muster the younger men behind him and they were granted the title of the Duke's Company. Although the first play after the Restoration to be performed before the King was given by Killigrew's company at the Cockpit and introduced by a splendid Prologue written by Davenant, both managers opted to abandon the surviving theatres and to build new ones. The reason for this was to bring English theatre practice into line with that of Italian opera and French Ballet, or in other words to incorporate into licensed public theatres the scenic stage of the Caroline Court Masks. Never again could England afford the opulent extravagance of Masks, but there was every reason, granted the chance of a new beginning, to make provision for the staging of operas and ballets derived from the Mask in repertoire with stage plays.[85] The Duke's Theatre in Dorset Gardens, for the building of which Davenant was responsible, and the Theatre Royal in Bridges Street, which Killigrew erected, thus became the prototypes respectively for the two theatres Royal in Covent Garden and Drury Lane which were to dominate English theatrical history for the next two hundred years.[86] The style of acting however that was to grace the new theatres could hardly differ much from that which had been familiar in the old days when the companies were headed by Rhodes, Mohun, Hart and others who had received their training in pre-war days and had exercised their art with surprising frequency despite war and parliamentary restraint.[87] The companies had lost most of their playing gear over the war years, but this could be remedied by loans and subscriptions. A much more serious loss was the break in continuity which lack of boy apprentices occasioned: this was a war-scar that could not be concealed. Some of the younger actors were pressed into female roles between 1656 and 1663, notably Kynaston whom Pepys thought 'made the loveliest lady that ever I saw in my life' as the Duke's sister in Fletcher's *The Loyal Subject*; but the straits that the companies were in is amusingly illustrated in these lines:

> 'Our women are defective, and so siz'd
> You'd think they were some of the guard disguis'd;
> For to speak truth, men act, that are between
> Forty and fifty, wenches of fifteen;
> With bone so large, and nerve so incompliant,
> When you call DESDEMONA, enter GIANT.'[88]

This was a difficulty that Davenant and Killigrew determined to put right by calling on their experience of the Court Mask and the French stage,

> 'Shall we count that a crime, France counts an honour?
> In other kingdoms husbands safely trust 'em;
> The difference lies only in the custom.'[89]

The matter was finally disposed of in Davenant's articles of agreement with his own company when it was specified that seven of the fifteen shares were to be set aside to provide a fund for the payment of the actresses.[90] Killigrew similarly took advantage of the royal licence in his Patent to employ women.[91] If this measure was likely to scandalise opinion in some quarters, it at least did away with earlier Puritan objections to men and boys assuming female dress on the stage.* The public quickly accepted the change and there is no reason to think that the men who enjoyed their former privileges both as members of the Royal Households and as sharers would allow the women (who as 'hirelings' enjoyed neither status) to rehearse under different conditions or in a different style from the boys they had replaced: and some of these men, be it remembered, had played women's parts themselves with notable success.

* See p. 111 above. The Patent of 1662/3 reads 'That whereas the women's parts in plays have hitherto been acted by men in the habits of women, at which some have taken offence, we permit and give leave for the time to come, that all women's parts be acted by women.'

The introduction of 'sceanes'—or as we would say, scenery—to the public theatres very evidently occasioned changes with the past since both Killigrew and Davenant found it necessary to build new houses to accommodate them. Yet the evidence, both pictorial and in stage directions, relating to Davenant's *The Siege of Rhodes* makes it amply clear that in many respects the new 'sceanes' were as emblematic as the former scenic units.[92] In intention they substituted 'landscapes' for *'aedes'* or 'houses' of the old public theatres, and were of course far more spectacular: but painted in perspective or no, and with or without 'changes', they remained essentially pictorial illustrations of the action presented by the actors and discussed in the dialogue.

In his *History of Sir Francis Drake* (1658), Davenant prescribes by way of stage-direction for the scenery of the 'first entry',

'a Harbour . . . where two Ships are Moor'd, and Sea-Carpenters are erecting a Pinnace, whilst others are felling Trees to build a Fort . . . on the top of a high Tree, a Marriner making his Ken. This Prospect is made through a Wood, differing from those of European Climats, by representing of Coco-Trees, Pines, and Palmitos. And on the Boughs of other Trees are seen Munkies Apes and Parrots.'[93]*

The Sailor in the tree who is thus painted in the landscape is shortly to be addressed directly in the dialogue, and when his cue comes he is spoken for by an actor in the wings. The painted 'sea-carpenters' are likewise constrained to remain immobile throughout the scene; and no matter what action may proceed on the fore-stage among the protagonists, one thing is certain—the 'pinnace' will be no nearer completion at the end of the scene than it was at the start.

As yet, therefore, there was no reason for the actors to compromise their former style in the direction of what I can best call 'behaviourism' in the interest of strict verisimilitude. Nevertheless, under the twin pressures of the newly designed buildings (too expensive to alter) and of French dramatic theory concerning unity of place, both actors and dramatists were now irrevocably launched on that slippery path (as Ben Jonson had prophesied would happen) whether they knew it or not.[94] Scarcely less important, the survival of censorship and Royal prerogative in respect of plays and acting ensured that all former connections with the religious origins and philosophy of English drama were effectively cut. The stage of social recreation, for so many generations the rival of the

* See Ch. VII, pp. 267 *et seq.* below.

theatre of worship, had won a resounding victory, the fruits of which are still with us today.

7 Country Cousins

'This truth we can to our advantage say,
They that would have no KING, would have no Play:
The Laurel and the Crown together went,
Had the same Foes, and the same Banishment.'[95]

The lines are Davenant's and taken from the Prologue written by the Poet Laureate to celebrate the first performance of a play presented to the king after the Restoration of the monarchy. If the 'banishment' of the stage in London was 'more honoured in the breach than the observance', in the provinces it was total.* Moreover, it was not destined to be readily repealed.

The primary reasons for the collapse of the provincial theatre have already been given. It may be helpful if I briefly recapitulate them here:

A. *Amateur drama*

1. The blows to provincial playmaking occasioned by Henry VIII's dissolution of the religious houses, his suppression of the Feast of Corpus Christi and ban on the establishment of printing presses outside London, Oxford and Cambridge.

2. The suppression of the religious stage, achieved during the remainder of the Tudor epoch through the censorship or confiscation of the manuscript playbooks and by the imposition of penalties ranging from fines to execution on anyone convicted of acting them or permitting them to be acted.

B. *Professional*

1. Elizabeth's withdrawal from country gentlemen of the privilege of maintaining a private company of professional players.

2. James I's withdrawal of this privilege from the nobility.

3. The discovery by City Fathers that even Royal Patents giving actors the right to perform in the provinces could be ignored with impunity, provided the actors were rewarded with a gratuity equivalent to their playing fee for leaving the town without performing.

* The only exception was those cities, notably Oxford, where Charles I was in residence between 1642 and 1648.

4. The fear lest licensed professional actors (whose interest in provincial circuits only waxed keen when plague was raging in London) should prove to be carriers of infection.

In the years between 1604 and the Civil War only two provincial cities were deemed worthy of the privilege of a resident company of actors, Bristol and York. The former players were licensed in 1618 as 'Her Ma(jes)ties servants of her Royall Chamber of Bristoll' to perform locally and wherever else they pleased provided that they showed their licence, behaved in an orderly manner and did not stay more than fifteen days in one place or play on Sunday or at times of divine service.[96] Unfortunately, beyond a letter of complaint from the Mayor of Exeter to the Privy Council virtually nothing is heard of them.[97] The York proposals never materialised. William Perry obtained a licence to form a company 'by the name of His Majesty's servants for the city of York' in September 1629; but on receiving a licence two months later to manage the company at the Red Bull he apparently chose not to proceed further in the collecting of a company for the North.[98]

Important researches are proceeding at the moment under the auspices of the Malone Society about performances in provincial cities and noblemen's private houses. For the present however J. T. Murray's *English Dramatic Companies* and G. E. Bentley's *Jacobean and Caroline Stage* remain the standard works on the subject. Bentley's work has shown that many of the provincial performances which Murray took to have been given by the London Companies on tour were actually given by subsidiary companies carrying duplicate licences who in fact spent their whole time in the provinces.

An unfortunate feature of these duplicate licences was the opportunity which they afforded to mayors and magistrates for challenging all licences. Events in the City of Norwich during the year 1623 may serve here as a convenient example. An entry in the Mayor's Court Book under 31st May reads:

'This day Gilbert Reason brought into this Court a duplicate or exemplificacon of A Patent made to him & others Teste xxx⁰ Marii Anno octavo Regis Jacobi And the exemplificacon beareth Test xxxi⁰ die Maii Anno vndecimo Jacobi Regis. Whereby they are lycensed to play as servants to the Prince by the name of Charles Duke of Yorke wᶜʰ exemplificacon ys crossed by a warrant from the Lo: Chamberlyn dated the xiiᵗʰ of July 1616 wᶜʰ warrant ys entred verbatim in the end of Sʳ Thomas Hyrnes yeare of

Maioraltie in the Court Booke. Hee & his Company are denyed to play by reason of the want of worke for the poore & in respect of the contagion feared And for many other Causes, but was offered a gratuitie wch he refused.'[99]

The genuineness of the reason behind this refusal is opened to question by the next entry, dated 14th June 1623:

'This day Nicholas Hanson brought into this Court a Bill signed vnder his Maties hand authorisinge him & others to play &c Test 28 Maii 1622 wherevpon the Letters of the Lords of his Maties most hono^ble privie counsell was read vnto him, wherevnto he gave answer that he will play vnles he see the Kings hand to the contrary.'[100]

The letters in question from the Privy Council have fortunately been preserved in the *Liber Ruber Civitatis*. Dated '21 Jas 1. 1623. May 27', it reads:

'To our very loving friends the Mayor and Justices of the City of Norwich.
After our very hearty Commendations; whereas we have received information from Mr. Gleane one of your aldermen that you have been of late years, and are at this present, much pestered and disquieted in the orderly government of your City by the reason of several companies of players, tumblers, dancers upon the ropes and the like, the suffering whereof is alleged to be more inconvenient and prejudicial to that City more than other places; by reason it consists altogether of much and several manufactures, wherein multitudes of people and families are set on work, who being apt to be drawn away from their business and labour by their occasion the sayd manufactures are in the mean time in such sort neglected as causeth daily very great and apparent losses and damage to that city in particular and by consequence no small hurt and prejudice to the commonwealth in general. We taking the same in our consideration and finding cause much to condemn the lawless liberty taken up and practised in all parts of the kingdom by that sort of vagrant and licentious rabble by whose means and devices the purses of poor servants and apprentices and of the meaner sort of people are drained and emptied and which pinches so much the more in these times of scarcity and dearth and we tendering the good and welfare of your city in particular have thought good hereby to authorize and require you not to suffer any Companies of players, tumblers or the like sort of persons to act any plays or to shew or exercise any other feats and devices within that city or the

143

liberty of the same until you shall receive further order from this Board. So we bid you very heartily farewell.

From Whitehall 27 May 1623

Your very loving friends

Midlesex, Mandeville, Arundell and Surey, G. Cant, F. Edmonds, Jull Cesar.'[101]

The absenteeism which had occasioned complaint in London in Elizabeth's reign is here a primary cause of concern to the good-men of Norwich.* That the actors appreciated the crucial nature of this trial of strength is clearly documented by the Norwich records in the following year, 1624.

On 24th April Francis Wambus asked leave on behalf of the Lady Elizabeth's Company to play in the town and presented a Patent 'dated the xx[th] day of March 1621' in support of his request. He too was shown 'the Letters directed from the Lords of his Ma(jes)ties most Honorable privie Counsell' quoted above: but where Nicholas Hanson in 1623 had apparently been content to issue a threat, Wambus was determined to put the matter to the test. The Mayor's clerk records in outraged tones:

'the said Wambus pemtorily (sic) affirmed that he would play in this City & would lay in prison here this Tweluemoneth but he would try whether the kings comand or the Counsells be the greater. And this entry beinge redd vnto him he sayd he denyed nothinge of what was here sett downe And therevpon the said wambus was accordinge to the Counsells order comanded to for-beare to play w(i)thin the liberties of this City And he neu(er)-theles answered that he would make tryall what he might doe by the kings authority for he said he would play.'

Two days later a note was found fastened to the gate of an inn called 'the white horse nere Tomeland in Norw(i)ch', which was taken to the Mayor. It said:

'Here w(i)thin this place at one of the clocke shalbe acted an excelent new Comedy called the Spanishe Contract By the Princesse servants / vivat Rex /.'

The Mayor gave immediate order that the actors appear before him. Only Wambus could be found and, on being asked whether he had written the offending note, he not only admitted it but 'accused Mr. Maior to his face that he contemned the kyngs

* See pp. 84–85 above.

144

authority'. Wambus was promptly committed 'untill he should finde suerties for his appeerence at the next Sessions'. On 24th May he appeared before the Mayor and Justices of the Peace thanks to pleas on his behalf by a certain Mr. Rosse.[102] Two days later he was released from prison. On 28th September Wambus, accompanied by his fellow actor Mr. Townshend, returned to Norwich and tried to sue the Maior for wrongful imprisonment![103] He lost his case and, as far as is known, did not visit the town again. Nevertheless it was a spirited stand and one which must have given heart to other actors encountering difficulty there and elsewhere: for, ten years later, we find the Aldermen of Norwich despairing of firm action against Players from the Privy Council and taking steps to discover 'whether yt be fitt to complayne by peticion to the kinge'.[104] It was decided that this was a proper course of action, but that it would be as well to inform the Privy Council at the same time lest the King should refer the matter to them. Both were accordingly informed 'that the maintenance of the Inhabitants here [i.e. of Norwich] doth consist of worke & makinge of manufactures', activities which were interrupted by the competition of plays.

A number of important issues emerge with the greatest clarity from the Norwich records. First, the closeness with which stage and Court were associated in provincial minds cannot be doubted. Secondly, popular support for the stage was evidently still substantial: otherwise city merchants would not have been so active in their efforts to suppress it. Thirdly, it was the Mayor's jurisdiction over the place of performance, surviving from mediaeval times, which sealed the fate of the theatre in the provinces. It will be remembered that in London James I, in issuing Patents to the Royal Companies, had taken into his own hands the right to license the theatres in which they were permitted to perform by naming both in the Patents.* In effect this meant that no one could challenge their right to use these buildings other than the owners who in any case expected to profit financially from such use. Theoretically the same authority existed in the Patents to use convenient buildings in provincial cities.* In practice, however, what the Patent ordered in respect of a Townhall and what a city council found it convenient to allow frequently conflicted. It was this divided authority over the building in which performances were to be given which proved the undoing of the actors, and through which the central government's intention was contradicted by the local authority's action.

* See p. 90 above.

If it were complained in Norwich that the actors, by giving performances in daylight hours, were drawing citizens away from their work, it was objected in Chester that performances by night provoked riots. The following document from Southampton, dated 6th February, 1623, provides further grounds for disapproval.

'Stage Players. Forasmuch as the grauntinge of leave to stage players or players of interludes and the like, to act and represent theire interludes playes and shewes in the towne-hall is very hurtfull troublesome and inconvenyent for that the table, benches and fourmes theire sett and placed for holdinge the Kinges Courtes are by those meanes broken and spoyled, or at least wise soe disordered that the Mayor and bayliffes and other officers of the saide courts comminge thither for the administracion of justice, especially in the Pipowder Courts of the said Towne, which are there to bee holden twice a day yf occasion soe require, cannot sit there in such decent and convenient order as becometh, and dyvers other inconvenyences do thereupon ensue, It is therefore ordered by generall consent that from henceforth no leaue shall bee graunted to any Stage players or interlude players or to any other person or persons resortinge to this towne to act shewe or represent any manner of interludes or playes or any other sports or pastymes whatsoeuer in the said hall.'[105]

In Worcester it is 'the upper end of the Town-hall' that is banned to players together with all council chambers.[106] In 1627 the council complain that they 'finde the glass windows in the Council chamber to be much broken' and blame it on the actors and drunks in the audience.[107] Recurring costs for such 'reparacions' provided yet another irritant to back up the case against play-acting: for this was an expense additional to the gratuity with which by tradition the Mayor had to reward the players.* And financial penalties attaching to the fulfilment of any compulsory obligation is something which rankles with many people today as much as it did with the Aldermen of Leicester in 1607.[108] These at any rate are some of the reasons which underlie the bitterness of phrases accompanying such entries in city records of payment to actors as 'to send them out of this citty' (Bristol, 1631), 'to ridd them out of the Town' (Bristol, 1634), 'to dep(ar)t the Cittie and not to play' (Canterbury, 1625), or 'for putting off a Companie of plaires' (Exeter, 1635) or 'dismissed without playing' (Southampton, 1635), 'to prevent their playing in the city' (Worcester, 1634).[109]

Not all cities adopted this attitude; Dover, Leicester and

* See note 108 and pp. 178–185 below.

Gloucester being notably co-operative. It is particularly pleasing to be able to record that the municipal authority which in our own time has been the first in England to build and subsidize a civic theatre also represents a city which as late as 1640 was still ready to accord a welcome to the players. Both honours go to Coventry, famous in any event for its long and distinguished support of the early religious stage and pageantry.

Why, it must be asked, did Elizabethan and Jacobean actors not build theatres in provincial cities as they did in London and obviate their dependence on the goodwill of local authorities for a place in which to perform? I see three reasons for their apparent inability to do so. It is to be doubted, first, whether they could have raised the capital for such an expensive undertaking.* The money would have had to be raised locally and, following so closely upon the suppression of the local plays and local amateur companies, it is hardly likely that the money would have been forthcoming for the benefit of total strangers. Secondly, the local amateurs having lost their plays and playmakers lacked the organizational strength to risk adventuring upon an enterprise of this sort in the face of the known clerical and municipal doubts about play-acting. Finally, it must sadly be admitted that in the light of the Elizabethan actors' general record among Londoners for conceit, greed and fecklessness in business, it is unlikely they ever gave a thought to the provinces except when plague made it expedient for them to do so.[110] When therefore the tables were reversed, their country cousins cannot be wholly held to blame for ceasing to interest themselves in the actors.

The war over and the monarch restored to his own, attempts were made in 1660 to revive provincial performances, but were resisted. On 8th October, the Mayor and Recorder of Maidstone wrote to Sir Henry Herbert pointing out that, Master of the Revels or no, he had made a mistake in licensing 'Jacob Brewer, &c.' to give performances outside 'the verge of his Majestie's Courte'. Herbert, furious, replied a day later in terms which are worth quoting.

'. . . And you may be asured by me that you are the first Mayor or other officer that ever did dispute the authority, or the extent of it, for to confine it to the verge of the court, is such a sense as was never imposed upon it before, and contrary to the constant practice for several grantes have been made by me, since the happy restoration of our gracious sovereign, to persons in the like quality,

* The actor Wambus, being a stranger in Norwich, found it hard to bail himself out of prison.

and seriously therefore, admitted into all counties and liberties of England without any dispute or molestation.'[111]

He goes on to threaten the Mayor with a summons if he should continue to 'delighte in oposition and obstinacy to lawfull authority'. If this letter was calculated to forward the cause of resumed provincial performances it could hardly have served its purpose worse. What other companies the 'several grantes' were made to we do not know. Herbert, in his anxiety to re-establish his own authority and the personal income derived from it, was possibly exaggerating there as he is known to have done in other matters. *
The only other person for whom a Patent survives is George Jolly, an actor who had served Charles as Prince of Wales in Paris until 1646 and then enjoyed a successful career in Germany.[112] He returned to England in 1660, and on 24th December was given authority by the king to build a playhouse in London and to raise a company to fill it.[113] On 1st January 1663, he received a licence from Herbert to raise a company of actors to tour the provinces. I need not here retrace the steps by which Jolly was cheated of his London hopes by Davenant and Killigrew. Jolly's licence to 'act Comedies &c throughout England with exception onely to *the* Cities of London and Westm(inster) and the suburbs of each respective citty' was reinforced by a set of instructions from the king to the municipal authorities to permit him to play in town halls and elsewhere as in former times.[114] We know nothing about the use he made of these warrants beyond the fact that he was absent from London for about a year, by which time Davenant and Killigrew had tricked him out of his London dues and forced him to devote his time to recovering his losses.[115] However the die was already cast. The new London theatres were designed and built to accommodate 'scenes'.[116] The plays that were to be written and talked about were devised by men who were required to take this into account and to remember that they were writing to please small audiences of courtiers. Since no small talk could be more parochial than that of 'the town' and since no theatres existed in the provinces which could accommodate scenic machinery, London and the provinces as far as the theatre was concerned became two separate worlds. The legacy of hostility to the theatre left in the provinces sufficed to ensure that this situation would not change for many years to come: and, in fact, more than a century had to pass before strolling players could exercise their calling with any regularity and within the law.

* See Ch. III, n. 69, p. 354 below.

8 *Conclusion*

From my own reading of the evidence relating to actors, plays, playmakers, theatres, managers and censorship, I deduce a fairly simple pattern of change in English theatre practice in the period 1530–1660.

A theatre which for generations had been allowed to develop in freedom came to be regarded at the Reformation, because of its religious character, first as a political nuisance and then as a serious threat to social stability. For some forty years after Henry VIII's break with Rome more or less intensive efforts were made to bring the stage under the control of the central government in Westminster. Simultaneously with these endeavours to control the stage on grounds of political expediency, a debate began about the ethics of stage-performances which engaged the attention of all thinking people at the time. Harried by the effects of government action and directly threatened in their calling by some of the arguments used in the ethical debate, the actors and playmakers found themselves forced to fight for very survival. The amateurs lacked the organizational strength to fight for long and had virtually abandoned the struggle by the close of the Tudor epoch. The professionals however found champions among both the capitalist-speculators of the merchant class and the educated nobility in touch with continental theory and practice in respect of the theatre. Helped by these allies, the theatre declared itself, under duress, to be a commercial metropolitan organization designed for leisure recreation instead of an occasional national pastime organized as a component part of all festive celebrations. Despite this transformation, however, the new theatre which Elizabeth I bequeathed to James I preserved one vital feature of its former self, its wide popular appeal: and this it was destined to lose under the Stuarts. Patronized both in London and the provinces by the nobility and the agricultural and industrial labourers, the professional theatre, under twin political and economic pressure, lost the support of those classes in English society lying between these extremes. By the time that Civil War descended on the country the theatre had come to be regarded either as a wasteful extravagance exclusive to royalty, or as an equally wasteful distraction, leading simple minds away from both the benefits of common toil and the profits of true religion. And despite all the arguments of learned apologists to the contrary, after the Restoration of the monarchy, this verdict on the theatre was the one which stuck.

BOOK TWO

Emblems and Images

V

PLAYHOUSES

'History has its laws of sequence, of cause and effect, as well as other sciences.' T. F. Ordish, *Early London Theatres*, 1894, p. 144.

---

1 *Introduction*

HISTORIANS have usually assumed that James Burbage's building of The Theater in 1576 marks the start of a metropolitan centred national drama of secular content and professional character. The idea takes its substance from the claim made by Cuthbert Burbage in 1635, that, 'the father of us, Cut(*h*)bert and Richard Burbage (i.e. James Burbage), was the first builder of playehowses, and was himselfe in his younger yeeres a player.'[1]

There is no reason to query the accuracy of this claim *per se*, but there is every reason to question the accuracy of the emphasis which historians have since placed upon it. For it is from this claim above all that such firmly rooted notions have grown up as that Burbage and his fellow actors were the first professional company in England, that The Theater was a novelty with only the mountebank conditions of the inn-yards for precedent in its architecture and its stagecraft, that subsequent public theatres built in Elizabethan and Jacobean London were largely derived from it, and that the professional theatre which fostered Shakespeare and his fellow dramatists was one of exclusively metropolitan inspiration and composition. All these notions, and more like them, have compounded to sever the theatres and stages of Elizabethan and Jacobean London from their Tudor antecedents in England as a whole (let alone from those of earlier times) and thereby to present the historian of the stage with two apparently insoluble problems. Where did so startlingly original an idea as the Globe style of Playhouse spring from, and why did it appear at this particular moment in time?

Various Elizabethan and Jacobean maps of London have told

scholars that these theatres were circular or octagonal in external appearance, an image contradicted by the rectangular shape of the inn-yards from which the theatres are assumed to have been adapted, yet confirmed by the one and only contemporary picture of their internal appearance, De Witt's famous drawing of the Swan. This picture is not altogether reliable. No one knows whether it was made on the spot at a rehearsal or at a performance, or sketched from memory afterwards. It is corroborated in some details and contradicted in others by two builders' contracts (one late Elizabethan and one early Jacobean) and by two Caroline frontispieces to printed copies of plays—*Roxana* and *Messalina.* * A difficult subject is still further complicated when any attempt is made to elucidate this pictorial evidence by recourse to the stage directions of those plays which have survived to us. G. F. Reynolds has postulated in definitive manner all the dangers surrounding literal interpretation of Elizabethan and Jacobean stage directions, and it suffices here to repeat that what may appear in an edited version of any play as evidence of stagecraft can represent the hand of the author either in his original MS 'prompt-copy' or as revised for readers, or it may represent the hand of the prompter in a theatre, or that of a printer lacking first-hand knowledge of stage practice, or of a subsequent editor working from the stage practice of his own day and age. Even when all this has been taken into account, allowance has still to be made for possible differences of physical shape and equipment as between one theatre and another. And all the while there is the spectre at the back of the historian's mind of the Court Theatre (as opposed to the public and private playhouses) which, by 1605, had been equipped with a proscenium arch derived from Italian research and experiment and, by 1611, with settings that could be changed in the course of the dramatic action to accord with changes of place.[3]

An obvious temptation that must result from supposing that Burbage initiated a metropolitan professional theatre in 1576 is to assume that the thirty years which intervene between this initiative and the advent of Inigo Jones' proscenium arched stage with its perspective settings at Court must span some logical progression from the sparsest simplicity of an inventor's first essay towards the mechanical complexities of changeable scenery destined to endure into modern times. It is this idea of the necessity of progression from the one into the other, based ultimately on the concept of progress, which underlies all those reconstructions of Elizabethan

* There is also the frontispiece to Kirkman's *The Wits* of 1672; but this depicts a roofed-in theatre employing artificial light.[2] See Plate VIII No. 11.

and Jacobean stagecraft that endow the actors, dramatists and stage managers of the time with an ideal of self-consistency in production techniques comparable to that current in more recent times.

This concept of progress and direct progression from the Elizabethan theatre into the Restoration theatre via the Court Masks is one which I feel obliged to challenge in the sharpest way I can. No one questions that the Monarchy which was restored in 1660 was very different in kind from that which preceded the period of the Commonwealth: in other words, that with the execution of Charles I, one kind of government ended and another began; and that where many of the outward emblems of the old monarchy were later restored, this new monarchy was grounded on fundamentally different principles from the old. Is it so very strange then to suggest that a change, just as radical in its implications, overtook the theatre, the mirror of this society, at this same time? In putting this question, my object is to challenge the view that a satisfactory idea of Elizabethan stagecraft may be gleaned from studying it in a context restricted to that of progression from Burbage's Theater to Jonson's *Mask of Blackness*, or in that of plays written for the Globe Theatre, or even in terms of the public theatres alone within the period 1576 to their enforced closure in 1642. Instead, I wish to argue that what we are really confronted with is a conflict between an emblematic theatre—literally, a theatre which aimed at achieving dramatic illusion by figurative representation—and a theatre of realistic illusion—literally, a theatre seeking to simulate actuality in terms of images. The former kind of theatre, as I have argued in Volume I, grew up spontaneously during the Middle Ages and, as I shall argue now, reached its climax in the style of public building depicted by De Witt in his sketch of the Swan. It was an actor's and a poet's theatre which received its death warrant, when all is said and done, from the Lord Chamberlain and his agents in the Revels Office.* The new theatre which achieved supremacy in its place was a sophisticated, theorist's theatre, brought to birth by architect-painters; and although it resembled the old in many externals, just as the restored monarchy had much in common with its predecessor, it was nevertheless no longer an emblematic theatre concerned with man's relations to God and society, but a theatre striving to imitate actuality within the more limited terms of reference permitted by images of fashionable conversation and backgrounds of painted perspectives.

In making this claim, I might as well state frankly that in the

* See Ch. III above.

course of my own researches I have not had the luck to discover any new drawings or documents directly depicting or describing the Elizabethan and Jacobean public playhouses with which to startle myself or the world. Such information as the following chapters provide which may have the air of novelty about it results directly from examining the data presented by others in a wider context than they themselves chose to do.

Broadly speaking, any scholar or producer in the last thirty years sufficiently interested in these matters to pursue them for himself has had a choice of two alternative starting points. He could either adopt the orthodox viewpoint established by Lawrence and Chambers* that while staging methods at court on the one hand and those used in the theatres on the other differed radically from one another, each type was at least consistent to itself as from one play to the next. Or he could approach the problem of stage conventions from the standpoint argued by G. F. Reynolds in his study of conditions at the Red Bull Playhouse,† in the introduction to which he wrote:

'I have seen no real objection (i.e. critical rejoinder) to Sir Edmund Chambers' idea that simultaneous settings were used at the private theatres and at court, but never in the seventeenth century at the public theatres. How such a distinction could possibly exist when numerous plays were given interchangeably at these producing centers has not been made clear. Certainly such a divergence seems highly improbable.'[4]

Of the important contributors to the subject since then, J. C. Adams and G. R. Kernodle have tended to follow Lawrence and Chambers in seeking to establish some form of consistency in the production methods of the public theatres, while C. W. Hodges and A. M. Nagler have tended to follow Reynolds.‡ I have myself found it easy to accept Reynolds, Hodges' and Nagler's outlook as a starting point. Less easy to place or accommodate are the three notable books published by Dr. Leslie Hotson. *The Commonwealth and Restoration Stage*, 1928, remains a goldmine of factual information, not only for the period of the label, but in respect of the

---

* W. J. Lawrence, *The Physical Conditions of the Elizabethan Public Playhouse*, 1927: E. K. Chambers, *The Elizabethan Stage*, 1923, Vol. iii, pp. 1–154.

† *The Staging of Elizabethan Plays at the Red Bull Theater, 1605–1625*, 1940.

‡ J. C. Adams, *The Globe Playhouse*, 1942; G. R. Kernodle, *From Art to Theatre*, 1944; C. W. Hodges, *The Globe Restored*, 1953; A. M. Nagler, *Shakespeare's Stage*, 1958.

stagecraft of earlier times as well. As for *The First Night of Twelfth Night*, 1954, and *Shakespeare's Wooden 'O'*, 1960, while I have found both eminently readable and highly stimulating, I cannot myself take seriously the viewpoints postulated in either of them on account of the short-shrift meted out to all evidence that happens to conflict with or to contradict his own arguments. I have not therefore felt obliged to regard any particular point in either book as something requiring specific support or contradiction in this study, preferring to let the reader ponder and assess both for himself bearing this warning about the use of evidence in mind.

If I can claim any originality of approach for myself, it is in having questioned the validity of the widely held belief that the prototype of the Elizabethan public theatres is to be found in courtyards of town and country inns: if this were really true, then is it not curious that the Fortune Theatre, built as late as 1601/02, should have been the first out of six or seven playhouses to adopt a rectangular ground plan for its auditorium? Finding no satisfactory answer to this conundrum, I have followed up a suggestion, made in 1894 by T. F. Ordish, that perhaps precedents other than the inn-yards existed in 1576 for Burbage's Theater and for the Curtain, the Rose, the Swan, the Globe and possibly the theatre at Newington Butts.

This chapter therefore is devoted to an examination of architectural precedent. I have chosen first to look at the Elizabethan public playhouse as a building designed to accommodate spectators assembled to view an entertainment in return for the money paid to enter that building, and to scrutinize it in the context of the property market of that time. The next section of the chapter is devoted to the sort of copy-book precedents which carpenter-builders like Burbage, Street and Katherens (as opposed to architect-designers like Palladio, Scamozzi or Inigo Jones) had ready access. Still looking at the auditorium rather than the stage, I have then conducted a long survey of all those localities, including inns, in which plays are definitely known to have been presented both in London and the provinces between approximately 1530 and 1630. From this it becomes abundantly clear, however surprising it may seem, that the professional acting companies had a marked preference throughout the whole hundred-year period for indoor performance, and that the evidence for performances having been regularly conducted in inn-yards either before or after 1576 is of the slenderest. The final section of the chapter is accordingly devoted to a reappraisal of De Witt's drawing of the Swan in terms of what we know of the Tudor Hall instead of in those of the usual attempted equation of the drawing with either an inn-yard or the Serlian Court Theatre or some compromise between both. From the inn-yard stems the black and white beam-and-plaster appearance of the reconstructions, and from the Serlian theatre springs the concept of the 'inner-stage' both of which are so conspicuously missing from De Witt's sketch. With the banquet-hall as the *fons et origo*, both of these discrepancies vanish.

2 *Building Sites and Architectural Precedents*

The most important single fact about the public theatres of Elizabethan and Jacobean London of which we can be certain is their professional character. By 'professional' I mean their use by companies of actors who reckoned to earn a living from presenting plays regularly to a public that paid cash to gain admission to see them. This single and simple fact not only differentiates Elizabethan drama from most of its mediaeval antecedents, but governs both the nature of the auditorium and the stage to which that auditorium was linked—the 'howse and stadge for a Plaiehouse' of the Fortune contract. Here then is something new, something in which James Burbage could justifiably claim to be a pioneer and innovator; provision of an auditorium and of a stage within that auditorium, regularly available for professional actors.

The question to be asked of this fact is: What pressures were working on Burbage to persuade him to take this very sensible step at this particular time? Why in 1576? The answer, as I think, is self-evident: the suppression of the religious stage and the gift of its large popular audience to the professional actors coupled with the permission given by Letters Patent two years earlier to the Earl of Leicester's company, of which Burbage was a leading member, to give regular performances on weekdays throughout the year in London. A professional company of players possessed of this unique privilege had a unique reason for wanting a home of their own in which to exercise it. Granted this initial compulsion to seek a home, and a large one at that, the company would next be exercised by the equally relevant pressure of choosing the most favourable site for this home. At first glance it might seem that a site as near as possible to the centre of the city would be preferred to any other, the more especially since professional acting companies were already accustomed to performing in London halls and taverns, and since audiences were already in the habit of attending them. It must be remembered, however, that the individual citizens composing these audiences were just as accustomed to journeying the short distances into 'the fields' beyond the walls marking the city boundaries for a wide range of other diversions and recreations, and that some of the inns used for plays were situated in these recreational areas.* To the West and North-West they had walked through Ludgate and Newgate to Clerkenwell and Skinners Well to see the Miracle plays performed by their own guild of Parish Clerks. Not far distant lay the great fairground of St. Bartholomew adjacent to which was Smithfield, the traditional site of countless Tournaments. A similar short journey through Moorgate or Bishopsgate to the North led them out into Moorfields, the parade ground of the city musters and one of London's two archery practice-butts. Bordering on Moorfields to the East lay Finsbury Fields and Shoreditch, another traditional area for the exercise of arms and other athletic sports. South of the river lay Southwark which, in its turn, was flanked by 'fields', time out of mind employed for recreational pastimes. To the South-East lay St. George's Fields and the archery butts at Newington: to the West the liberty of the Clink and Paris Garden where the Royal bulls, bears and mastiffs were kept caged, and were baited in public when not required across the river at Westminster and Whitehall. Any of these sites was as likely to serve its purpose as a more centrally positioned theatre, if only because all of them were already the habitual haunts of pleasure seekers.

Two other factors had to be taken into account at the time that the choice of site was being debated: first, the availability of land on which to build and, secondly, the measure of opposition likely to be encountered from the City Council to any proposal for appropriating land in the city for this purpose. On the second count, companies of players had ample evidence behind them of the sort of treatment they might anticipate were they, like Daniel, to take up residence in the lion's den: and as far as availability of building site was concerned, the most likely spots, the halls of dissolved monastic foundations, were either relegated to private domestic use or had already been appropriated to this purpose. The buildings attached to St. Paul's Cathedral were occupied by the scholars and choristers, one of them, circular in shape, as a theatre.[5] The Blackfriars, occupied from 1540 by the Revels Office until its removal to Clerkenwell in 1560, was in the process of being taken over by Farrant and his company of boys.[6] The Whitefriars had been given to Thomas, Lord de la Warr, by Henry VIII in 1544, and from his family it passed into the hands of the Sackvilles who, in their turn,

* See pp. 177, 186 et seq., and Fig. 6, pp. 50–51.

appear to have leased rooms for play-acting to the Children of the Chapel.[7] The fact that James Burbage's sons, Richard and Cuthbert, negotiated successfully for the lease of the Blackfriars in 1596 when the City Council's campaign against the actors was even tougher than it had been in 1576, suggests to me that in deciding where to site their first theatre simple availability of site took precedence over speculation about tenure: and if I am right in thinking that a determining factor was the need to exploit the financial potential of a large, newly acquired popular audience, then building land in the suburbs clearly offered better prospects than any conversion project in city tenements. At any rate it was for Finsbury Fields and the dissolved Priory of Hollywell in adjacent Shoreditch that Burbage settled in the event, where he was free to build as he chose and to accommodate as many thousands of spectators as he could contain hundreds in the halls or inns of the city.[8]

Having discussed the company's motives in electing to build a large theatre of their own, and having considered the possible reasons for the choice of site actually made, we must now turn our attention to the design of their new home. Granting the novelty of the idea of a large, permanent performing place around the years 1574–76, must we also assume that the physical design of this performing place was as novel as the notion? I think we must, *unless* we can prove beyond reasonable doubt that sufficient traditional precedent existed to make a wholly original prototype as unnecessary as it would seem unlikely when Burbage's previous architectural background and experience are taken into account. As far as we know he was by upbringing a joiner, that is, a carpenter; the sort of man who might reasonably be expected to know how to use a copy-book for building in timber and much more likely to make use of traditional skills handed down from father to son than to be inspired with ideas of theatre building that elsewhere in Europe were the prerogative of the most highly trained and inspired Italian architect-painters of the day. Indeed, were James Burbage (or, for that matter, Peter Street and Gilbert Katherens after him, in terms of the Globe, Fortune and Hope) to have been a man of the latter ilk, then Inigo Jones could scarcely have been hailed as the pioneer of British architecture—Vitruvius Britannicus—as in fact he was.[9] Supposing, then, that Burbage was not working from Serlian or Palladian blue-prints of Italian origin (and work on the Teatro Olimpico in Vicenza did not start till 1580), the next step would seem to be to enquire what sort of plans, what precedents Burbage and his friends could have obtained from contemporary copy-books or extant edifices in England on which to model their own enterprise. And here the choice strikes me as having been much wider than has generally been supposed.

'There was an obvious precedent for the amphitheatrical form', wrote Sir Edmund Chambers in 1923, 'in the bear and bull rings which preceded the public theatres.' So far so good; but he follows up that sensible observation with a more dubious dictum. 'I do not know that we need go back with Ordish (*Early London Theatres*) to a tradition of round mediaeval play-places, Cornish or English, or to the remains of Roman occupation. A ring is the natural form in which the maximum number of spectators can press about an object of interest.'[10] This last sentence is unexceptionable in itself provided one is consistent and regards Elizabethan plays as designed for acting in the ring or arena postulated in the manner of *The Castle of Perseverance*: but then neither Chambers nor those who followed him were consistent in this respect, choosing rather to regard the stage as 'forming a chord to an arc of the circular structure of the play-house' and allowing room for spectators 'on three sides'.[11] Three sides is surely a curious phrase to use of a ring? Lest it be thought that I am being unnecessarily pedantic in querying this point, let me illustrate it diagrammatically.

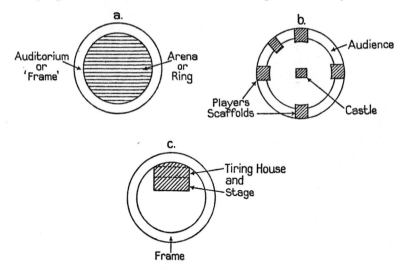

Fig. 7. Three circular 'game-places' or 'play-houses'.

a) Bull or bear baiting arena.
b) Ground plan of stage and seating for *The Castle of Perseverance*.
c) The Swan Theatre in ground plan.

Given these three diagrams it is at once apparent that plays written for performance 'in the round' like *The Castle of Perseverance* or the

Cornish Miracles can be presented to an audience virtually without modification in the Bull-ring type of arena (*Fig. a*) but only with substantial rearrangement of the scenic units and replotting of the actors' moves on the stage of the De Witt sketch (*Fig. c*). Chambers, as it seems to me, was inconsistent in asking us to accept *Fig. a* as the precedent for *Fig. c* in respect of both auditorium *and* stage: for the diagrams show quite clearly that the vision of the audience in *Fig. a* is unrestricted and free to focus where it likes, whereas the vision of the audience in *Fig. c* is both restricted and focused constantly upon a comparatively small part of the arena. Where stage production is concerned this is a cardinal point of difference. I must say therefore, with all the respect due to an historian who was as exceptionally well informed in the development of the mediaeval stage as in that of the Elizabethan era, that I think it unfortunate that Chambers should have dismissed Ordish's suggestions so peremptorily:* for the very authoritativeness of so much of Chambers' work has put the sharpest of brakes on speculation about the likelihood of continuity in stage architecture, convention and practice between the mediaeval and Elizabethan theatres. That is unfortunate in itself; but if, as I believe, he made a major mistake in interpreting the De Witt sketch of the Swan to represent the back of the stage as 'forming a chord to an arc of the circular structure of the playhouse', then it is more than high time to set speculation flowing again. For whatever else may be in dispute about the interpretation of the Swan drawing, only wilful distortion of the horizontal lines describing the limits of the stage and tiring-house façade can make them join up with the lines describing the galleries of the auditorium. Yet this distortion has been connived at or indulged in by all reconstructors of Elizabethan Playhouses with the exception of Hodges (*The Globe Restored*). As a result, the stage gallery or gallery above the tiring-house has been incorporated within the second gallery of the auditorium. De Witt however was at pains to show it as wholly independent of the auditorium or 'frame' of the playhouse, both by his alignment of the horizontals in his sketch and by the shading in the angles between the circumference of the arena and the stage-and-tiring-house unit where the two meet. (See Plate VIII, No. 11.)

The significance of this important matter is fully discussed later in this Chapter (pp. 204–205). Thus it can suffice at present to note that a case exists for considering the 'frame' or auditorium on the one hand and the stage and tiring-house on the other as separate

* *Early London Theatres*, 1894, pp. 11 *et seq.*

units, possibly with independent histories, and possibly brought together by chance rather than by deliberate design. On this presupposition, I can still accept Chambers' suggestion that the bull- and bear-baiting arenas offered Burbage a prototype for the frame of his Theater, but I cannot dismiss as he does the earlier precedents for these arenas: for in them, as I believe, lies an explanation of how the stage and tiring-house of De Witt's sketch

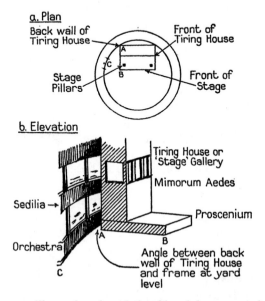

Fig. 8. Diagrams illustrating the relationship of the stage and tiring-house to the 'frame' of the auditorium in the Swan Playhouse.

found their way into these arenas and thus obliged the acting companies who used them to depart from the staging methods revealed to us in the ground plans and stage directions of *The Castle of Perseverance* and the Cornish plays, as well as from those of the perambulatory pageant-waggons.

3 Ludus, plega, *game and play*

(a) *Roman Amphitheatres, Round Tables and Wooden Os*

In Volume One I have already instanced a remarkable building constructed in 1571 in London for a Trial by Combat. The reader must excuse me if I now repeat that quotation because of its paramount importance to my present argument.

'In Tuthill Fields . . . was prepared one plot of ground one and twenty yards square, double-railed for the combat, without the West square a stage being set up for the judges, representing the court of Common Pleas. All the compass without the lists was set with scaffolds one above another, for people to stand and behold. There were behind the square where the judges sat two tents.'[12]

The tents were provided to accommodate the defender and the challenger with necessary dressing-rooms. It is the more interesting therefore that the champion for the defender (T. Paramore) was 'Hen. Nailor, master of defense, and servant to the right honourable the Earle of Leicester',—a member in fact of the same noble household as James Burbage and his fellow actors, and a person who might well be reckoned to share with the actors the duty of entertaining their noble master. For who was better qualified to lead those 'feats of activity' so frequently coupled with Elizabethan stage plays than this 'proper, slender man', Henry Nailer, the master of defence?* The tents are also worthy of remark, since, as dressing-rooms for the protagonists in the action, they have their antecedents in the tent of the stage directions of *The Castle of Perseverance* and of Lydgate's Troy Theatre.[13] The auditorium provides a magnificent prototype for the Fortune Theatre if not for the circular Swan: if, however, we want precedent for that, we possess pictorial evidence to prove that two circular auditoriums existed across the river from Tuthill Fields at least two decades earlier which were probably still standing when this Combat arena was built. They are shown on Aga's map (*c.* 1560), and reappear on Höfnagel's map (*c.*1570); positioned slightly to the West of London Bridge, they are labelled 'The Beare bayting' and 'The Bolle [bull] bayting'.† One of them, the bull-ring, appears still earlier on a Southwark map of 1542.[14] Beyond that date examples must be taken from the Tournament,‡ in which context, via Chaucer's *Knights Tale*, we can get back to the late fourteenth century. The best example post-1571 known to me is that instanced by Sir John Ferne in his *Blazon of Gentry*, published 1586. He describes lists for Trial by Combat as

'a place circuler and rounde, compassed in with lowe rayles or pales of wood, painted with red'.[15]

---

* See p. 195 and Ch. VI, p. 240 below.

† Both are reproduced by Ordish, *Early London Theatres*, facing p. 1 and p. 126.

‡ See *EES*, i, Plates VIII and IX and Figs. 2, 3 and 4.

What then are we to make of the puzzling evidence of the 'rounds' in Cornwall, and the circular ground plans for the Cornish Miracle Cycle (MS. of the late sixteenth century) and *The Castle of Perseverance* (MS. of the early fifteenth century)?* Does any connection exist between these 'round' theatres for plays and the Tournament arenas? And are both related to the theatres built to accommodate stage-plays and feats of activity in Elizabethan and Jacobean London? The intimate connection between the sophisticated indoor Tournaments (Jousting at Barriers) and the Court Disguisings and Masks, and the no less intimate association of fencing, wrestling and bear-baiting contests with popular stage-plays has for long suggested to me that it does.

Presupposing the existence of a link—and the reader is at liberty to skip the next few pages if he is disinclined to bear with me in such speculation—then the most likely point of common contact lies to hand, as Ordish suggested, in the circular and elliptical theatres and amphitheatres of Roman times.[16]

What were these Roman amphitheatres designed to accommodate? One of their functions was to contain the *ludus gladiatorum*: another to accommodate the *venatio* or baiting and killing of wild animals for public amusement. The former spectacle finds its Elizabethan parallel in the trial by combat: the latter in the bear- and bull-baiting arenas of Höfnagel's and Agas' maps, both sports having almost as long a history in England as Tournaments. Moreover, should it be argued that both these parallels, by ante-dating Burbage's building of his Theater, are to be regarded as mere relics of outmoded precedents, Sir John Ferne's description of the lists required for Trial by Combat published in 1586 finds its more graphic equivalent in the bear-baiting arena of Norden's map of 1593. Either way a firm answer can be given to my earlier question: what sort of copy-book precedent existed for a carpenter-builder like Burbage to model the auditorium of his Theater upon in 1576? My purpose in endeavouring to establish this point with the maximum of emphasis is to free the student of the Elizabethan drama from any further *obligation* to regard the public theatres as necessarily either derived from local inn-yards or copied from the neo-classical experiments of Italian architect-painters. If the design actually adopted for the auditorium of the Theater, the Curtain, the Rose, the Swan and the Globe is considered strictly in terms of the capabilities and social reputation of the builders and the circular

---

* See Richard Southern, *The Medieval Theatre in the Round*, 1957; and Edwin Norris, *The Ancient Cornish Drama*, 2 vols., 1859.

as opposed to rectangular appearance of the buildings, then it is much harder to substantiate any close connection between these theatres and either the inn-yards or Italian court theatres than it is with amphitheatres built for games of animal baiting or the Tournament arena. This point I shall now follow up in detail.

(b) *Play-places and Game-houses*

One major advantage of at least reflecting along these lines, whether you chose to accept or dismiss the foregoing suggestions, is that it immediately opens up a seam of information which has a marked bearing on the conditions of performance within the amphitheatres. Why were they *not* called 'amphitheatres' or 'arenas'? And why *were* they called 'playhouses'?

Our English word *play* is derived from the Anglo-Saxon *plega*, and both are identical in meaning with the Latin *ludus*.[17] *Ludus*, with its plural *ludi*, was a word of wide application in Roman times. It could mean 'activity' of any sort and activities of many particular sorts—games, sport, jokes, dramatic entertainment, athletics, military exercises—normally carrying with it the general sense of 'recreation'. Sometimes however it was necessary to specify the particular nature of the recreation or activity as in *hastiludium*, spear-play, or as in Vergil's Georgics, *veteres ineunt proscaenia ludi*, 'the old plays appear on the stage'.[18] The same freedom of use may be observed in respect of the Anglo-Saxon *plega*. *Hastiludium* has its equivalent in *aesc-plega*, 'spear-play'; *lusoris*, meaning 'player' or 'entertainer', in *pleg-mann* meaning 'player' or 'athlete'.[19]

The relevance of this philological discussion becomes obvious with the citing of two other *plega* hybrids: *pleg-stów* and *pleg-hús*. *Pleg-stów* is defined in the dictionary as 'A place for play, a gymnasium, wrestling place, amphitheatre', and has its ancient Cornish equivalent in Plain-an-Gwarry, the word used to describe the amphitheatres at St. Just and Perran.[20]

Pleg-hús, game-house or play-house, brings us directly into touch with Tudor England and thus with Elizabethan London and the Burbage family. In 1538/39 a 'Game House' was built in Great Yarmouth by the Corporation and leased on 15th March to one Robert Copping on the stipulation that he should 'permitt and suffre all such players & ther audiens to have the pleasure & ese of the said hous & gameplace, att all suche tyme and tymes as eny interludes or playes ther shal be ministered or played at eny tyme withought eny profight thereof by hym or his assigns to be taken.'

This 'Game House', interestingly enough, was erected on a portion of the garden of the Priory adjoining the town wall near Porden Gate.[21] Here then, astonishing as it may seem, we have a municipally subsidized theatre legally established in a provincial city nearly forty years before Burbage, with the aid of private-enterprise capital, erected his metropolitan house: the Yarmouth gamehouse, like the Shoreditch playhouse, was built within the precincts of a dissolved Priory. Players visiting the town, however,

FIG. 9. Sketch of the amphitheatre (*Plân au guare* or level place for games) at St. Just, Cornwall, as it appears today.

probably gave their first performance in the Guildhall before the Mayor as was normal elsewhere; for there is an entry in the assembly book under March 11th, 1595, which reads,

'Game players having been heretofore licensed to play in the Guildhall, ordered that the Bailiffs shall not suffer the players to play there for the future.'*

The last links in this curious chain of circumstantial evidence are supplied by John Stow in the MS. of his *Survey of London*, and in the first edition of his *Annales*. In the former he describes the Theater and the Curtain as,

'. . . two houses for the shewe of Activities, comedies, tragedies, and histories for recreation'.[22]

In the latter he writes of

---

* See note 21 above and pp. 178, 183–185 and 359 below.

'. . . the play-house or Theater, called the Globe . . .'[23]

Thus, what Burbage and his fellow-actors were called upon by their financier to build in Shoreditch and on the Bankside, and what they did build, were playhouses in the literal and traditional sense of that word—houses for plays; i.e. for recreation, for 'feats of activity', for entertainment including stage-plays. In building his Theater in Finsbury Fields therefore Burbage was in one sense at least no innovator: for he was simply copying what had been done several times already in respect of recreational activities in Tuthill Fields and in Southwark. On the other hand, in another sense he may well have been the pioneer that his son Cuthbert claimed in devoting his playhouse predominantly to stage-plays as opposed to other kinds of play. The point is supported by the modifications Stow chose to make to the phrase about the early playhouses in the printed editions of his *Survey*: also by a curious phrase in a polemical sermon preached by the noted Puritan, John Stockwood, in 1578.[24]

'I know not how I might . . . more discommende the gorgeous Playing place erected in the fieldes, than to terme it, as they please to have it called, a Theatre.'

The irony implicit in this passage, if lost on many today, would not have been wasted on 'the godly-learned' to whom it was 'especially' addressed: if Elizabethans erect artifically constructed playing places or playhouses, and think to cloak their folly under a classical name, then they should remember, as citizens of a Christian Commonwealth, what the Fathers had said about Roman theatres and the *spectacula* presented in them.

It only remains to add that nearly forty years after the preaching of this sermon and the building of this Theater, a contract was signed for the construction on the South Bank of

'. . . one other Game place or Plaiehouse fitt & convenient in all thinges, bothe for players to playe In, And for the game of Beares and Bulls to be bayted in the same, And also A fitt and convenient Tyre house and a stage to be carryed or taken awaie . . .'

I quote this extract from the Hope Contract in my own transcription of Dulwich College Muniment 49, as it actually reads, and not in the transcript Sir Walter Greg printed in 1907 in *Henslowe Papers* (pp. 19–22) which has been followed as gospel ever since. Greg mistook 'G' for 'S' and thus read 'Same' instead of 'Game' in lines 14/15 and 20/21 of the Contract.[25] This Contract was drawn up between the builder, Gilbert Katherens, and Philip

Henslowe and Jacob Mead in 1613—only two months after the destruction of the first Globe and almost simultaneously with a start
being made on the second. What is perhaps even more remarkable
is that so experienced an impresario as Henslowe should have
entered into a contract which uses the words 'game-house' and
'play-house' as alternatives in order to specify his intention of
alternating the 'game' with the 'play' (or the *venatio* with the
'*proscaenium*' *ludus* or stage-play) in his new amphitheatre nearly ten
years after Inigo Jones had introduced the proscenium arch and
perspective settings of the Italian academic theatre to Whitehall.[26]
I am forced, therefore, to conclude that the circular (and poly-
gonal) auditoriums of the period 1576–1614, and the arenas which
they bounded, were architecturally backward-looking in both
spirit and design. This is not to dispraise them. In one respect at
least they set a pattern which the rest of Europe was later to copy
in preference to neo-classical prototypes. In so far as the word
'Theater', as a translation of the Latin *theatrum*, reflects renaissance
interest in classical precedent, it is with the Coliseum rather than
with Hellenistic theatres that comparison should be made. Unlike
the *Teatro Olimpico* or the *Teatro Farnese* or other early Italian
theatres where the auditorium swept upwards from the orchestra
floor in a single rising tier, the frame of the early English playhouses was divided vertically into galleries built directly over one
another. When this style of auditorium first makes its appearance
in Italy, significantly it is still in terms of a Tournament—at
Bologna in 1628 (see Plate IX, No. 12).[27]

I suggest therefore that in approaching problems of Elizabethan
theatre-building and stagecraft we do not tie ourselves in advance
either to Italian academic precept or to the shape and appearance
of Tudor coaching-inns or to modern notions of the requirements
of a professional acting company. In place of these, I suggest that
we consider the far-from-novel, circular *pleg-hús* or game-house,
adapted and sophisticated over the centuries from the circular *pleg
stów* or fortress-come-recreation ground, and stretched both in its
meaning to include performances of stage-plays, and in its physical
appearance to admit the addition of a raised stage and tiring-house:
for however sketchy the middle portion of this genealogy still is,
the Roman and the early Tudor extremities are firm enough.

This stretching of an old name to include within its meaning and
function a place for interludes, alias '*proscaenium*' *ludi*, alias stage
plays, occurred at a point in time when professional actors needed
homes of their own within which to take advantage of their newly
acquired right to perform regularly in London on weekdays. I

believe these to have been the circumstances which confronted the Earl of Leicester's servants when first possessed of their Patent in 1574 and which accordingly played a part in persuading Burbage and his financier John Brayne both to erect their playhouse called The Theater in the recreation grounds of Finsbury Fields and to copy the traditional game-house when designing the frame. Once this initiative had been adopted, its plain common sense (not to mention its commercial success) quickly persuaded other actors and building speculators to imitate this example both nearby and elsewhere.[28]

If this argument can be conceded, then I think it will be agreed that the principal professional tasks necessarily facing the London acting companies over the next thirty to forty years were those of learning how best to adapt their former stage technique to their new environment and of modifying the frame, or auditorium, to make it serve their own acting skills to maximum advantage. The firm evidence that we possess of the modelling of the first Globe (1598) upon the Theater (1576), and of the second Globe (1613/14) upon the first, of the copying of the first Globe stage in the Fortune (1601/02), of the basing of the design of the Hope (1614) on that of the Swan (1596) and, finally, of the rebuilding of the Fortune (1621) along the lines of its predecessor, all clearly suggests continuity of thought and action within closely restricted architectural terms of reference. Yet the evidence of a readiness to alter features of the prototype to improve the model in hand is just as firm. Perhaps the most detailed and significant instance is the phrase in the Hope contract specifying that,

'. . . the Heavens all over the saide stage, [are] to be borne or carryed without any postes or supporters to be fixed or sett uppon the saide stage'.[29]

Knowledge that the second Globe was to be 'fairer' than its predecessor and the wording of much of the Fortune contract confirm the impression that the lessons of practical experience were put to use within each new 'frame' as it was erected.

We may conclude therefore that the auditoriums of the public playhouses were

(a) built to a traditional copy-book pattern
(b) built to a pattern evolved to suit many forms of recreation rather than stage-plays alone
(c) adapted progressively with time to meet the needs of stage-plays as they came to take precedence over other forms of entertainment in popular appeal.

We have no right however to assume that the stage and its furnishings either dictated the design of the auditorium at the outset or formed an integral part of the frame. Professional actors had been giving performances in enclosed spaces for more than a hundred years before committing themselves financially to the construction of theatres of their own. The price to them of securing the necessary capital to indulge in this luxury was to accept an alliance with masters of defence and ring masters whose technical skills and interests had to be catered for and assured as those of partners within a single enterprise. Stage-plays, it must be remembered, were at this time under severe attack from Church, City and State. From the standpoint of any one with capital to invest therefore they represented a very dangerous risk; and especially so after 1570 in view of the determined government action following the excommunication of Elizabeth as demonstrated in Chapters III and IV. Popular enthusiasm for stage-plays was keen enough to make substantial investment of capital in them a very enticing proposition, but the speculator who was willing to take the initial risk of putting his money into a building devoted to the acting of these plays had the strongest possible incentive to ensure that, should stage-plays be finally banned, his auditorium was so situated and so designed that it could continue to bring in a dividend from other forms of play, game or recreation. In the years 1574 to 1576—the years, that is, immediately prior to the building of the Theater and the Curtain—these scales could not have been more delicately balanced. The government, with the full endorsement of the Church, had finally declared its hand in respect of the religious stage. Yet in dealing out threats and punishments with the right hand, it had slipped a clear hint in the left hand (by granting a Patent giving Leicester's actors permission to act regularly on weekdays in London) that the City's threats to suppress all plays need not be taken too seriously.[30] Burbage and Brayne, and Henry Lanman (the owner of the Curtain)* must be credited with a knowledge of these issues and of the bearing they were likely to have on their own proposed investments.

Before, therefore, we attempt to pronounce upon the nature of the stage, its relationship to the frame and its use in performance, we must examine those traditions of performance which the professional acting companies had acquired during the fifteenth and sixteenth centuries and for which they staked out a claim when talking business with their financial backers and the other professional entertainers who, as partners, were to serve as security

* Sometimes spelt as Laneman.

against the future. Stated in the most brutal terms, the financiers were interested in the box-office returns of game-houses, that is to say in a multi-purpose arena bounded by a large-capacity auditorium: they recognized the scale of the dividend that mounting popular enthusiasm for stage-plays might bring them, but had to protect themselves against the risk that stage-plays might be suppressed. The actors, armed with a Patent and the implications of that document, had to persuade the financiers to give them as much by way of stage and dressing-room facilities within the multipurpose arena and its frame as was consistent with both their own needs and this risk. What we must endeavour to determine now is, first, the nature of the stage facilities asked for by the actors, and secondly how much of what they asked for they were in fact granted.

4 *Church, Street, Yard and Chamber*

i. *Regular performances and special occasions*

One consequence of simplifying the development of English mediaeval drama to the point where religious plays written for performances in church are said to have been first, 'secularized' by contact with the market place, and then superseded by Elizabethan histories, comedies and tragedies, is to endow the respective places of performance with a far sharper distinction than ever existed in fact. Liturgical plays, by this reasoning, become church plays; miracles and moralities become plays for street and market place performance; Elizabethan plays become genuine theatre plays. Students brought up through school textbooks in this faith are startled, or so I have found, to learn that performances of indisputably secular plays were given in churches in Elizabethan, and even quite late in Jacobean, times. Scholars, equally, who are very well informed in the stage directions of Shakespeare's plays and in other evidence pertaining to the public playhouses of his day, often exhibit a marked reluctance to acknowledge that those same Elizabethan and Jacobean audiences who continued to support dramatic and quasi-dramatic entertainments performed in circumstances normally associated with the outmoded Miracles and Moralities—streets, village greens, market squares, townhalls or inns—could have accepted the stage conventions associated with them in the regular playhouses. And yet this confusing and at times contradictory attitude of audiences is itself a factor of major consequence to any understanding of the theatre and its conventions of those times.

Elizabeth I, for example, while ready to support the censorship and eventual suppression of the religious stage in the name of true religion took no offence at being required to sit in state on a stage in King's College Chapel to watch, of all things, a performance of Plautus' *Aulularia* (1564).* The Earl of Leicester, so intimately associated with James Burbage and the building of The Theater, saw nothing inappropriate in entertaining his sovereign with a folk play in his park at Kenilworth (1575) sandwiched between pastoral playlets devised by such sophisticated authors as Hunnis, Gascoigne and Mulcaster. Jonson, Dekker and Middleton were flattered rather than displeased to be asked to write verses for London's reception of James I in the city's streets and took as much trouble in recording the visual appearance of their handiwork as Daniel, Campion and other librettists of the Court Masks did in editing their respective texts.† Sydney, Essex, Fulke Greville and other intellectual courtiers, who of all people knew most about renaissance theories of propriety in dramatic entertainment, took the initiative in perpetuating the quasi-dramatic tilt and combat at barriers. The Elizabethan acting companies, as we have seen, justified their week-day performances in the public theatres by claiming that only by such 'rehearsal' could they perfect themselves for command performances before the Queen in Palace halls. Even the professional actors of the Jacobean and Caroline royal companies, accustomed as they were to the staging facilities of both public playhouses and the Court banqueting halls, were seemingly incapable of remedying the makeshift conditions of townhalls, inns and other fit-up stages when away from London on a tour of the provinces.

The plain fact is that despite the change in the actors' status and economy from a predominantly amateur to a strictly professional way of life, Elizabethan and Jacobean society had as much use for occasional entertainments as had its ancestors. The Lord Mayor's Show in London, the Midsummer Watches in Chester and other provincial cities, Royal Progresses with prolonged halts at favoured towns, in the Universities, and in baronial manor houses, and the continuing festivities associated with the Christmas season in villages and private homes up and down the land, all provoked a demand for dramatic entertainment and decoration which had to be met, with or without the sort of stage equipment that could be installed in a professional playhouse. In meeting the demand for these entertainments the devisers of the scripts, the actors and decorators were inevitably thrown back on those traditional and

* See *EES*, i, p. 248 *et seq.*   † See *EES*, i, pp. 82–88 and 107–108.

emblematic methods of presentation associated with these conditions of performance time out of mind. This knowledge corro-
borates that of the readiness of audiences to accept great diversity
of both environment and convention in performances and is itself
a factor of major importance when considering the nature of the
regular London playhouses; for no acting company could have
afforded to gear its repertory of plays so closely to the physical
features of its own London public playhouse as to be unable to
mount these plays at Court or in the provinces: in other words, the
conditions governing the staging of plays and other entertainments
outside the public theatres were still of consequence enough both in
variety and frequency to have exercised a pressure of their own
upon those in the theatres. I propose therefore to examine next the
sort of stages and auditoriums, other than those of the public
theatres, which were used by the acting companies: and in doing
this it is probably wise to try to distinguish between performances
given before 1576 and those given after that date.

ii. *Open-air performances*

Any reader of John Nichol's well-known *Progresses of Queen
Elizabeth* (3 vols., 1788) and the less well-known *Progresses of
James I* (4 vols., 1828) will be familiar with the sort of bizarre
entertainments which were prepared for these two monarchs by
obsequious courtiers, nervous officials and loving subjects in streets
and parks and on ponds and rivers. Just as familiar to many are the
curiously theatrical demonstrations of civic pride provoked by the
election of a Mayor or the visit of a distinguished stranger.
Possibly just because these entertainments were occasional and not
regular, it has not been usual for historians to study them collectively or to couple them with the sporadic revivals of religious
plays. Yet taken as a composite group they make up a formidable
list, as the following abbreviated table shows at a glance.

TABLE A

Typical open-air entertainments 1530–1660 [31]

Date	Occasion	Type	Place	Author, Performer, &c.
1533	Coronation of Anne Boleyn	Royal Entry	London	Street and water shows: verses by Nicholas Udall
1539/40	Summertime	Morality Play	Edinburgh	Sir David Lyndsay's *Thre Estatis* in 'playfield'

Year	Occasion	Type	Place	Notes
1545	Lord Mayor's Show	Civic Riding	London	Becomes an annual event from this year on
1547	Edward VI's Coronation	Royal Entry Jousting	London Shoreditch	See *EES*, i, p. 98.
1557	Feast of Corpus Christi	Miracle Plays	London, at Greyfriars	See p. 70 above.
1561	Lord Mayor's Show	Civic Riding	London	Children of Westminster used as actors
1563	Sunday after Midsummer	Play	Chester	*The History of Eneas and Queen Dido* in the open air
1574	Queen's Progress	Pageants	Bristol	Street and water shows
1574	Whitsun	Miracle Cycle	Chester	Performed despite official injunction to the contrary. Last performance
1575	Queen's Progress	Entertainments	Kenilworth	Coventry Hox-Tuesday play and other diversions
1578	Queen's Progress	Entertainments	Norwich	Land and water shows by Thomas Churchyard
1581	Accession Anniversary	Tilt	London	Sydney, Fulke Greville and others
1584	Midsummer	Neo-Miracle Cycle	Coventry	The Destruction of Jerusalem by Mr. Smith
1585	Lord Mayor's Show	Civic Riding	London	Verses by Peele
1590	Accession Anniversary	Tilt	London	Verses by Peele
1591	Provincial Tour	Play in Churchyard	Gloucester	Queen's Company
1591	Queen's Progress	Entertainments	Elvetham	Water Show
1603	Reception of James I	Royal Entry	London	Text by Jonson, Dekker and Middleton: designs by Stephen Harrison: Alleyn, one of the actors
1610	St. George's Day	Pageants	Chester	Prince Henry a spectator. Land and Water Shows
1610	Creation of Prince of Wales	Water Show	London	Text by A. Munday. R. Burbage and J. Rice among the actors

1612–1639	Lord Mayor's Show: an annual event. London. Texts by Dekker, Middleton, Webster and Heywood
1660–1662	Reception into London of Charles II and Catherine of Braganza mark a resumption of full-scale land and water Pageantry of the traditional kind.

This list is by no means exhaustive; but it suffices to illustrate four important points. First, the period of maximum variety and activity in these occasional entertainments corresponded with that of the building of the London theatres. Secondly, the leading playmakers, actors and artificers of the day were deeply involved in

175

their preparation. Thirdly, the audiences for whom these open-air entertainments were prepared were not restricted to persons of any one section of society; rather did they serve to unite not only citizens of the metropolis but, often, subjects and sovereign, throughout the nation. Fourth and last, most if not all of them were financed by a private patron or from public funds and not by direct charge to the individual spectators.

In thinking therefore about the design of Elizabethan playhouses we can safely dismiss most of these entertainments as having had no serious influence on the design of the 'frame': for not only was the concept of an auditorium itself generally lacking, but the performers were not immediately dependent on the crowd for their reward: this came instead from the sponsors. Nevertheless these entertainments must have served to convince the entertainers that the securing of an enclosed auditorium with controlled and graded admission was an essential first-step towards earning a living wage by acting alone.

If however we can leave such entertainments out of account when considering the 'frame' of Elizabethan and Jacobean playhouses, we should certainly beware of doing so when considering the techniques of presentation employed in those theatres: for even if these shows often appear esoteric and undramatic to us, they clearly satisfied their own audiences and occurred frequently enough for everyone who patronized the playhouses to be familiar with some of the alternatives provided on festive occasions. If therefore it is reasonable to suppose that the spectacular quality of Masks and other sophisticated Revels influenced the writing of plays for performance at Court, so, by the same token of a common audience, it is not unreasonable to anticipate corresponding affinities at popular level between the occasional entertainments of street and park and the plays presented in the public theatres.

iii. *Indoor performances*

If we eliminate folk plays, civic ridings, and both parkland and water shows when considering the places selected by acting companies for dramatic performances between 1530 and 1640, quite the most startling fact to emerge from the evidence of surviving records is that far more plays were given indoors than in the open air. On either side of the year 1576, open-air performances (other than those given in the London playhouses) were rarities compared with those given in townhalls, private rooms, churches and chapels. Again, a table illustrates the point at once.

TABLE B

Performances in London 1550–1576 the locality of which is recorded, excluding School and Court plays.

Date	Place	Type	Authority
1511	Sheriff's private house	Interlude	Skinners Company
1515–40	Drapers' Hall	Virtually annual performances by leading companies	Drapers Company
1528	Parish of All Hallows in the Wall	Plays from Easter to Michaelmas to raise funds for the Church	Repertory
1529	Parish of St. Catherine, Christchurch	Plays from April to Michaelmas to raise funds for the Church	Repertory
1541	Carpenters' Hall	Polemical Interlude	Foxe, *Acts & Monuments.*
1542	Lord Mayor's injunction against plays in the Common Halls of the City Companies		Journal
1543	Northumberland Place House	Plays prohibited	Repertory
1545	Court of Aldermen's injunction against plays performed elsewhere than in the private houses of civic dignitaries		Repertory
1545–74	Series of injunctions against performances in Vintners' and Victuallers' houses		City Journals, etc.
1557	Greyfriars	Corpus Christi Passion Play	Machyn's Diary
1557	St. Olave's Church in Silver Street	Saint Play	Machyn's Diary
1557	Boar's Head, Aldgate	Sackful of News	Machyn's Diary
1557–68	Trinity Hall, Aldersgate	Hired out for plays annually	Accounts
1562	Barber-Surgeons' Hall	A Play	Machyn's Diary
1574	Innkeepers and others forbidden to permit performances 'within the hous, yarde or anie other place'		Repertory

TABLE C (1)

Provincial Performances, 1530–1640, of which the locality is recorded.[32]

Church	Townhall	Private	Inn	Open air
	Abingdon		Abingdon	
Barnstaple	Barnstaple			
Bewdley				
	Bristol	Bristol		
	Cambridge	Cambridge		
	Canterbury		Canterbury	
	Chester			Chester
	Coventry			Coventry
Doncaster				
	Exeter			
			Folkestone	
	Gloucester			Gloucester
	Ipswich	Ipswich		
Leicester	Leicester		Leicester	
				Louth
	Ludlow	Ludlow		
Lyme Regis				
	Marlborough			
			Maidstone	

177

TABLE C (1)—*continued*

Norwich	Norwich		Norwich	
	Nottingham		Nottingham	
	Oxford	Oxford		
Plymouth	Plymouth	Plymouth		Plymouth
	Reading			
	Shrewsbury			Shrewsbury
	Stratford			
Syston (Leics.)				
	Winchester			
	Worcester			
	York			York

TABLE C (2)

Performances at Inns.[33]

(Provincial)

Date		Town	Company	Inn
	1559	ABINGDON	*Serten Players*	*Newynn*
April	1569/70	DOVER	? Mountjoys	*Sprytweles*
August	1571	NOTTINGHAM	Queen's	*Maister Harpham's*
	1583	NORWICH	Worcester's	Illegally 'in their hoste his hows'
	1600	NORWICH	Hertford's: supplicants	White Horse, Tomeland: refused
	1587	MAIDSTONE	*Players*	*Starre*
	1589/90	LEICESTER	Rope-dancers	*Crosse-Keyes*
December	1603	NOTTINGHAM	*Players*	Illegally, by night at Richard Jackson's
	1609	CANTERBURY	Queen Anne's	*Checkar*
	1610	STOURBRIDGE	Players	Crown: with carts and wagons
	1624/25	NORWICH	Lady Elizabeth's	White Horse, Tomeland: play advertised but not performed

Two warnings must accompany these lists.

1. Where payments to players are concerned (the principal source of information) it is not usual for the clerk to record the place of performance.

2. In provincial towns the licence to perform covers several days, and the performance for which payment is recorded is only that one given in front of the Mayor and Aldermen and for which the Council was financially responsible.

In other words, when assessing the evidence of these tables, the occasions when the place of performance is recorded must be regarded as exceptional rather than routine, and it is quite possible that performances other than those for which payment is recorded could have been presented elsewhere in the same town. There are however two good reasons for regarding the place noted by the clerk when he does note it as being the normal place in that town. The first is that notification of place is much more regular between

178

1530 and 1580 than it becomes afterwards, a fact suggesting that the scribe assumes the place to be known and no longer worth the trouble of recording. The second is that no theatrical company enjoys setting up and striking its stage equipment more frequently than is absolutely necessary. The assumption must be therefore that the company, once in a town and set up to perform, will stay put in that one place unless there are special reasons for moving elsewhere, reasons of a sort which would be significant enough in themselves to occasion notice in the records. The records from Ipswich, which are fuller than most, may serve as example. Among the entries, which run consecutively from 1556–1625, the first to specify a place of performance is for 2nd January 1563–64

'P(ai)d the daye after newe yeres daye to my lorde Rob(er)ts players [i.e. Leicester's] that played at the hall—vjs. viijd.'

The next day they played

'. . . at Mr. Bailiffs com(m)andm(en)t at Mr. Smarts House.'

No place other than the Moothall or Guildhall is mentioned after that with the single exception of a bear-baiting in 1566–67 'uppon the corne hill,' and mention of the hall ceases after 1572.[34]

In general, therefore, I think we can accept the information in these tables as supplying a fairly accurate indication of where performances normally took place both in London and in major provincial towns, and that it is accordingly worth our while to investigate in detail the evidence which we possess about these several localities.

iv. *Performances in the open air and in churches*

Of the open-air performances listed in Tables B & C those given at Chester, Coventry, London, Louth, St. Ives, Shrewsbury and York after 1530 were almost certainly routine representations of local religious plays. The Plymouth performance of 1575–76 was given by 'the players at the broyge [bridge]' and was rewarded with 6s. 8d., the fee normally given to a minor professional company at that time.[35] The performance at Gloucester in 1590 was given by 'the Queenes players which played in the colledge churche yarde' and was rewarded with 30s.[36] Making all due allowance therefore for the destruction of records relating to religious plays during and after the Reformation, it is clear by any reckoning that after 1576 performances of plays in churchyards, streets and market places contracted sharply.

The heyday of the open-air theatre in Britain was unquestionably the late fifteenth and early sixteenth century; for hardly a town of any size then that did not have its own cycle or group of Corpus Christi plays, Whitsun Plays or plays appropriate to Calendar Feasts and local saints. So far as the sadly inadequate surviving texts and the other factual evidence allow us to judge, performance assisted by movable scenic waggons or pageant-carts was more usual than performance restricted to a single stage north of a line roughly from the Bristol Channel to the Wash, while the reverse is

FIG. 10. A German street theatre with raised stage and 'timber-houses' hung with painted cloths.

true south of that line. The reasons for this difference of practice are hard to ascertain with any degree of precision. My own impression is that an explanation may be found in differences in the allocation of responsibility for organizing and presenting the plays. Broadly speaking, perambulatory staging appears to be the rule in places where trade guilds were responsible for financing and organizing production. Where responsibility for these activities was vested in a predominantly religious guild—Corpus Christi, Parish Clerks, Collegiate Fraternities—a single stage was customary. This geographical correspondence admits the further hypothesis that this difference in the conditions of production may stem from a difference of approach to the problems of religious play production in the two ecclesiastical provinces of Canterbury and York. Certainly the unusual degree of freedom allowed by the papacy to archbishops in arranging the particular manner of celebrating the Feast of Corpus Christi within the area of their own jurisdiction encourages this hypothesis:* but that is a matter for the reader to drop or pursue as he pleases.

Despite the glaring gaps in the records, I think we may take it for granted that performance of all these cyclic plays was a fairly regular annual event up to 1530: but that interruptions occasioned by the advance of the censorship became increasingly frequent thereafter, dependent on distance from London coupled with local reformist enthusiasm; and that after the example made of Sir John Savage in Chester in 1574/5 open-air performances of religious plays dwindled from being routine occurrences into highly controversial exceptions. Attempts to substitute Protestant open-air plays on the scale of the Catholic cycles—*Tobias* at Lincoln, *The Destruction of Jerusalem* at Coventry, *God's Promises* at Kilkenny—were not successful. Polemical interludes of both Catholic and Protestant persuasion, which could be performed either out of doors or indoors, had small chance of surviving the censorship for long after 1570.

Thus, as far as stage convention is concerned, we may say that such religious plays as were presented between 1530 and 1570 continued to be given in traditional circumstances, that is:

     (1) in churches
     (2) in church yards
     (3) in halls and private chambers
     (4) in 'play' or 'game' places
and (5) in streets, market squares and fairgrounds.

Of these, many were presented indoors and a large majority on single, fixed stages: furthermore there is no evidence that waggon-stages were used during this period anywhere within a radius of a hundred miles of London.† The clear inference therefore is that in considering precedents for the design of the stages in the London theatres in 1576 and after, we need not pay serious attention to the pageant-carts still in use in the trading cities of Northern and North Midland counties.

In London there are references to churches, in connection with plays, dated 1527, 1529 and 1557. The three early references occur

* See *EES*, i, p. 122.
† I must remind the reader that I am here excluding civic Pageantry from the present discussion.

in licences to two groups of parishioners—those of All Hallows in the Wall and St. Katherine's Christ Church—requesting permission to perform stage plays during the summer months to raise funds for their churches: * but in neither case is the place of performance specified. It is significant however that in none of the many injunctions against plays issued by the City Council after the Reformation do churches figure among the places in which performances are banned. The inference must be that they had already ceased. The only exception is the play of St. Olave of 1557, and that was performed during the Marian reaction.†

In the provinces, however, performances continued to be given in churches long after 1576 (as they had between 1530 and 1576) but these too, if the records are to be trusted, became as infrequent and exceptional as performances in the open-air. Those at Norwich in 1589 and 1617 were clearly unusual. In 1589 Lord Beauchamp's players, having been forbidden to play in the town (but given a gratuity for refraining from doing so) 'did playe in XXe [*Corpus Christi*] churche' in flat defiance of the Mayor's Court: the leader, John Mufford, was imprisoned for this impertinence.[37] In 1617 the Queen's Company and the Prince's Company were both in Norwich in March, but were at first refused permission to perform: subsequently the order was rescinded, 'and theise two Companys [were given] leave to play ffower dayes this next weke but not at Powles [the White Horse Inn] but in the Chappell nere the Newhall'.[38] At Syston in Leicestershire, Lord Morden's players are expressly paid xii^d in 1602 'because they should not play in the Church'.[39] A performance of 2nd August 1574 in Doncaster (although strictly outside the period in question) deserves mention here since the company which was paid xx^d on that occasion by the City Chamberlain 'for playing in the churche' was the Earl of Leicester's—the company which had received the distinction of a Royal Patent three months earlier, of which James Burbage was a member and which was to occupy the Theater two years later.‡ Scanty therefore though the surviving evidence may be, it suffices at least to prove that churches continued on occasion to meet the stage requirements of the professional acting companies of Elizabethan England, when need arose, as adequately as they had

---

* See Fig. 6, pp. 50–51 above, and *MSC II*, pp. 287–288.

A play given in the church at Hascombe, Surrey, in 1578/79 on a Sunday evening was a village King-play: *Med. Stage*, ii, 368.

† See p. 63, n. 12 and p. 70, n. 24 above: also *EDC*, ii, 408.

‡ See *EDC*, ii, 256; *ES*, i, 336 n. 2, and *Med. Stage*, ii, 191.

regularly served the amateur actors of religious plays in earlier times.

v. *Plays in Halls, Chambers and Private Rooms*

By far the most popular place for performances outside London was the Townhall, and a surprising amount of detailed evidence survives concerning the conditions in which performances were given in this favourite building. The Chamberlain's Accounts at Gloucester may serve as a convenient starting point.

1559/60 Also in money payed for an hundred of borde-
nayles to make a scaffolde in the Bothall for the
Quenes Majesties players   vii^d
Also payd to John Battye, carpinter, and his
fellowe for the makinge of the said scaffolde   iiii^d
Also paid at the commaundement of Mr. Mayer
and other the Aldermen of the Citie to the
Quenes Majesties players playeng openly in the
Bothall in the tyme of this accompte   x^s
Also paide in money for a banket the same
day by the said Maire and Al(d)ermen at
the Taverne upon the saide plaiers   v^s vii^d[40]

Two years later payments are again recorded for making scaffolds in the Bothall, the companies being Warwick's and Dudley's (later Leicester's); 3^d is paid to Mr Ingram for providing 'a pounde of candelles'. The payment in the next year (1562–63) for 'makynge of the Skaffold at the Bothall & for nayles there' was 4^d. In 1564/65 it was reduced to 2^d, but there is the additional entry 'Also in money paid for tackinge of the same Scaffold awaye agayne ii^d'.[41] The word 'scaffold' is by itself ambiguous as it could be used to denote a raised dais for spectators just as readily as to describe a stage.* The Gloucester accounts for 1567/68, however, settle that point for us.

'Alsoe paid to Battie for C. and iii quarters of
elme bourdes for a skaffold for playors to playe
one   viii^s
Alsoe paid to hime for a piece of tymber to sett
under the bourdes   ii^s'[42]

---

* See *EES*, i, pp. 31–38.

The last reference to scaffolds in Gloucester occurs under the year 1574–75: the amount is xviii⁸ viii⁴ and includes the cost of wine. After this date the sums disbursed upon the London companies become much larger and should, I think, be regarded as gross payments covering expenses as well as reward and not as net profit.

From Maidstone in 1568 we learn of identical payments for nails and 'for layeing the Tymbʳ off ye stage together.'⁴³ If the similar items entered in the Receiver's Accounts at Exeter in 1604 can be taken to apply to the City Hall (as I think they fairly can)* then we know exactly what this Hall looked like; for it stands to-day unaltered since its reconstruction in 1594. (See Plate VI) The Norwich Chamberlain's Accounts between 1540–1560 are so important in this context that I have reproduced them verbatim in Appendix D. From them we learn that a stage could be made in the Common Hall from twelve long poplar planks: that these were laid on barrels and/or forms: that the stage was made 'at the [far] ende of the halle': that charcoal fires, fumigation and candlelight were provided for the comfort and convenience of the audience; that the Common Hall was not made available to players if their need of it conflicted with city business: and that the players 'gathered' nearly twice as much money from 'amonge the pepyll ther' as they received in gift from the City Chest.⁴⁴

That the far or upper end of the hall was the normal place for the stage is substantiated to some extent by a Jacobean notice from Worcester, penned in a sadly altered tone:

'Item—yt is ordered that noe playes bee had or made in the upper end of the Town-hall of this city, nor council chamber used by any players whatsoever, and that noe playes be had or made in yeald by night time, and yf anie players be admytted to play in the yeald-hall, to be admytted to play in the lower end onlie, upon paine of 40s. to be pᵈ by Mr. Mayor to the use of the citie if any shal be admitted or suffered to the contrary.'⁴⁵

Hints as to the reason behind this action are forthcoming from Bristol as early as 1577.

'It(e)m p(ai)d to my L(ord) of Leycesters players at the end of their play in the Yeld hall before Mr. Mayor and the Aldermen and for lynks [lamps] to give light in the euenyng & the play was called Myngs—the sum of xxii⁸'†

* See *EDC*, ii, *sub* Exeter, 1556–1557 and 1604, pp. 270 and 272.

† This performance was given within a few months of the opening of the Theater.

Two weeks later,

'For men, one party 3 days one 2 days, for mending the bord in the Yeld hall and the doers [doors] there, after my L(ord) of Leycesters players who had leave to play there, at viii^d a day, the others at v^d—amt iii^s vi^d'

Two years later, after a visit from Lord Strange's players

'It(e)m p(ai)d for mending of ii forormes [forms] w(hi)ch were taken ou(t) of St. George's Chapple and set in the Yeld hall at the play, and by the disordre of the people were broken—ii^s v^d'[46]

This sorry story is repeated at Leicester in 1605 and 1609 with broken windows as the chief cause of complaint.[47] In Canterbury in 1595 the town Council restricted players to giving two consecutive days of performance in any one month and then not beyond nine o'clock at night, a line of action which leads directly via the banning of plays in the Townhall at Chester after 6 p.m. to the total prohibition of plays in the Townhall at Southampton in 1623.[48] Worcester appears to have followed suit in 1627, having decreed a year earlier that 'no plaies shall be acted by nyght in the Trinity-Hall . . . upon pain of 40^s'.[49] The ethical and political factors related to these decisions have already been treated in Chapter IV.

Mention of Trinity Hall, Worcester, returns us to London where another Trinity hall, built in the early fifteenth century and occupied in 1446 by the Corpus Christi Guild of the Holy Trinity in the parish of St. Botolph without Aldersgate. C. T. Prouty has ably treated the history of the hall after the Reformation, including its use as a theatre by professional actors and has unearthed a remarkable picture of its interior in both plan and elevation. He is wrong however in saying,

'Aside from one reference to a play in the Carpenters Hall in the reign of Henry VIII there is no other record of plays being presented in a hall or enclosed space until the days of the first Blackfriars, except these accounts of Trinity Hall.'[50]

Plays had been performed in the halls of the lords spiritual and temporal, by travelling as well as local players, for at least a hundred years before the Trinity Hall payments for plays begin in 1557–58. So had they by schoolboys and choristers of all the leading schools in and around London, and at the universities, since the start of the sixteenth century.* Both adult and boy companies too had been performing regularly in the halls of the London Livery

* See pp. 177–8 above and 198 *et seq.* below, and Plate VII, No. 10.

companies from 1485 onwards, if not earlier. The Drapers Company were in the habit of hiring minstrels to entertain them at the feast held annually in their hall to celebrate the election of the Lord Mayor at least as early as 1485; and, by 1515 their clerk is recording payments for plays. From that time forward until the end of Henry VIII's reign it was normal for two plays to be presented on two consecutive nights.[51]

The Skinners Company celebrated Christmas, 1511, with a play in the Sheriff's house.[52] This practice must have become common, for in 1545, when the Court of Aldermen inhibited the Earl of Hertford's players from performing in London, there was the proviso,

'excepte it be in the howses of the lorde mayer, Shreves, aldermen or other substancyall co(mm)i(n)ers.'[53]

Three years earlier the Lord Mayor had ordered all his aldermen to forbid

'any co(mm)en playes or enterludes in any wise to be had or played at ony tyme Herafter w(i)t(h)in the co(mm)en Halles of ony the mysteries companyes or fellowships of this Citee'.[54]

A steady stream of subsequent injunctions attempted to restrain or at least to control performances in 'mansions, houses, yardes, gardens and other places'. *

The point of consequence here is that in London, as in the provinces, records of indoor performances prior to 1576 outnumber those of open-air performances by a startlingly large ratio: for this suggests that the environment of indoor performances was likely to have had a greater influence on the relationship of stage to auditorium in the design of Elizabethan playhouses than precedents drawn from open-air performances. In short, where the 'gamehouse' and combat arena provided the best precedents for the auditorium of the playhouses, the normal physical conditions of performance in the hall provided the model for the design of the stage and its facilities rather than the abnormal and exceptional conditions of open-air performances. The factor which ultimately determines whether or not we can accept this proposition is that of the use made by the acting companies of the inn-yards.

vi. *Inns and Taverns*

That plays were performed in inns both in London and the provinces with sufficient frequency for some of them to be properly

* See pp. 192–196 below.

regarded almost as alternatives to the early amphitheatres is amply substantiated by surviving records. I have myself, however, become increasingly sceptical about the evidence, *contemporary with the plays and performances*, on which Chambers and other inn-yard-style reconstructors of the playhouses saw fit to set performances at inns so firmly in the yard. Discussing the *'planities sive arena'* of the De Witt sketch of the Swan, Sir Edmund wrote,

'This is the space ordinarily known as the 'yard', a name which it may fairly be taken to have inherited from the inn-yards, surrounded by galleries and open overhead, in which, in the days before the building of the Theatre in 1576, more or less permanent play-houses had grown up.'[55]

To equate the two uses of the words 'yard' and 'gallery' and then to proceed to supply the playhouses with all sorts of other features including decoration borrowed from the yards of coaching-inns in the Tudor style is a legitimate course of action *provided* sufficient evidence exists to prove that performances took place more frequently in such yards than anywhere else. But where is this evidence? I have not myself encountered as many as ten references in the whole two hundred year period between the accession of Henry VII in 1485 and the accession of James II in 1685 in which either plays or players are specifically linked with the yard of an inn, and of these only one places performances in the yard alone as opposed to the yard as one of several alternative sites within the inn and its precincts. In chronological order these are:

1. A group of injunctions restraining plays
   (a) 1553. An Act of Common Council
   (b) 1564. Lord Mayor's Precepts
   (c) 1569.   ,,   ,,   ,,
   (d) 1573. An Act of Common Council
   (e) 1574.   ,,   ,,   ,,   ,,   ,,
   (f) 1577. An order of the Court of Aldermen.
2. Notice of the arrival of a group of players with their waggons and carts at Stourbridge, Worcs., 1610.
3. Richard Flecknoe's post-Restoration testimony about two inns in London.

Other references may turn up in the future: but in the meantime we must accept those that we have and work from them.

References associating inns with players and with performances but omitting any mention of the yard are more numerous, both in London and provincial records, than those in which the inn and its yard are linked. Of the former kind, by far the most important are those which couple particular acting companies with named London inns. In Elizabeth's reign the Bull and the Bell are thus associated with the Queen's own players (1583), the Cross Keys with the Lord Chamberlain's Company (1594) and, in 1603, Worcester's with the Boar's Head. These associations however were all occasioned as a result of these particular inns being officially assigned as winter-quarters to these particular companies.[56] This knowledge is interesting in itself, for it should prompt one to ask why three companies, provided by then with regular playhouses, deserted them in winter for London inns unless the inns provided greater warmth and protection from the weather than the theatres. It could be argued I suppose (as Chambers in fact argues)[57] that the change was made to cut out the rough journey into the suburbs through winter snow and mud and that they still played in the yard, open to the sky: but it seems to me just as likely, if not more so, that the companies, being professional, were concerned about the comfort of their patrons during performances and were exchanging a roofed and heated theatre for one open to the sky. Again, it may be that the yards of the inns in question were roofed over: but lacking any evidence to that effect, it seems more probable to me that a hall or gallery within the inn was in fact the theatre.

There are three good reasons to justify such an assumption. The first is one of simple practicality. As I discovered for myself when invited to present a Shakespeare play in the yard of the New Inn at Gloucester two years ago, the yard is virtually the only place in the inn that cannot be closed to traffic without paralyzing all its services. The project in Gloucester had to be abandoned precisely because the proprietor, for all his interest and enthusiasm, could not guarantee to eliminate noise in the surrounding bars and close all doors giving access to the yard during the performance. It may be that Elizabethan playgoers were more tolerant of noise and interruption than we are; but be that as it may, I cannot see any landlord being disposed to paralyze the stable and business traffic of his yard regularly, every day of the working week, throughout the winter months, for the sake of the modest rental derived from its lease to actors.

The second reason for thinking that performances at inns were usually given indoors is the acknowledged fact that the leading companies of James I's reign, when they raised the capital to acquire permanent winter quarters of their own on an exclusive lease, did so in large halls, centrally situated and fully protected from the weather—the Blackfriars, the Whitefriars, Salisbury Court and the Cockpit. I do not believe that this action marks a sudden innovation: rather does it represent a continuance, within buildings of which the companies owned the lease, of a practice formerly conducted in buildings which they had hired on a quarterly, monthly or even weekly basis. *

The third reason is that all the companies, Elizabethan and Jacobean, were obliged under the terms of their licences when touring the provinces to give at least one performance before the Mayor of every town visited in the Common Hall of that town: and the presumption must be that rather than strike the stage and equipment which they had set up there to go through the whole dreary process of setting up again at other places in the town they gave the other performances permitted by the Mayor in the same hall.†

There is thus a strong presumptive case for thinking that performances in provincial inns were rare, and that in those instances where performances can be proved to have been given in inns, they were presented indoors rather than out. That said, it is time to look at the factual evidence and see to what extent the surviving records confirm or deny these suppositions.

Where the provincial records are concerned the only notice to have come to light so far which links players even indirectly with the yard of an inn is an item from Stourbridge in Worcestershire dated 1610 which states that 'plaiers with ... theire cartes and waggons' were then 'at theire said Inne' [The Crown][59]. This certainly does not establish a performance as having been presented in the yard: only that the Innkeeper's guests have parked their waggons at the inn—possibly in the yard.

The nearest that we get to the yard in the other provincial records [see Table C(2) p. 178] is 'in' or 'within' the house. This phrase can be stretched to incorporate the yard within its meaning: but if performances were given either regularly or even normally in the yard, rather than indoors, this locale would surely have been specified by use of that word. Inns in Tudor England, like hotels today, were built to a design which incorporated both public and private rooms. These public rooms—hall, refectory and gallery— were not large if measured by Victorian or Edwardian standards of theatre building: but such standards of measurement are entirely inappropriate. Rather should we think of the common halls of the

---

* Such an arrangement is strongly suggested by the Churchwardens of St. Botolphs Accounts in respect of Trinity Hall.[58]
† See Ch. IV, note 108, p. 359 below.

Livery Companies, the interiors of town halls, parish churches and private houses of the period, when assessing the stage facilities and seating capacity of these public rooms: nor was the covered tennis court too small to be adapted to meet actors' needs in the Restoration era. A modern standard of comparison is the Studio Theatre of my own University of Bristol which measures only 50' × 28' and yet is large enough to *seat* more than 200 people at a play when the 'musicians' gallery is given over to the audience. Two other points of considerable significance emerge from these records. First, the performances presented in inns at Norwich in 1583 and at Nottingham in 1603 were both given illegally, the latter at night.[60] Secondly, although performances continue to be given in provincial cities until after the accession of Charles I and are often cited up to that time as having been presented in the Town hall, records of performances in inns cease some fifteen to twenty years earlier.

In London, the position is more fully documented but not seriously different. Chambers notes a performance of 1557 at the Saracen's Head, Islington as the earliest on record, but the practice appears to have already been widespread early in Elizabeth's reign.* The Red Bull, Stepney, figures in a legal dispute in 1567†. The Bull in Bishopsgate Street, noticed as a place for fencing prize-fights in 1575 and for plays in 1578, was assigned as we have seen to the Queen's company for the winter of 1583–84. The Bell and the Cross Keys, both in Gracious (or Grace) Street, and the Bel Savage on Ludgate Hill were frequently used after 1576 and possibly before. Worcester's company was using the Boar's Head Tavern (Aldgate? Whitechapel) in conjunction with the Curtain in 1603.[61] James I's action in bringing the acting companies under the direct control of his own family, outlined in Chapters III and IV above, and the licensing of these companies to perform in the houses allocated to them for summer and winter (and by inference *in no other*) accounts in itself for the virtual disappearance of the London inns from theatrical records early in his reign;[62] and the parallel with the provincial records in this respect should be noted.

When we come to examine whereabouts in the precincts of the London Inns these performances were given, the information available to us is found to be derived, with one exception, from sources other than those relating to the named inns just discussed. The exception is Richard Flecknoe's testimony of 1664, where in his *Short Discourse of the English Stage* he reports that the actors,

---

* See pp. 193–195 below: also Fig. 6 (pp. 50–51), and Plate X.

† Between Burbage's later partner, John Brayne and William Sylvester, carpenter, about scaffolds. *ES*, ii, pp. 379–380.

'. . . set up Theaters, first in the City, (as in the Inn-yards of the Cross-Keyes, and Bull in Grace and Bishops-Gate Street at this day is to be seen). . . .'[63]

Flecknoe died *c.* 1678 and there are no grounds for supposing that he saw either of those inns in use as a Playhouse. The Marquis of Newcastle, in a memorandum to Charles II *c.* 1660, includes the Boar's Head in his recollected list of pre-war playhouses, but no other.*

The last notice that we have of an inn used for plays in London comes rather gloomily from the Middlesex Gaol Delivery Register, dated 20th December 1608. It concerns a certain

'William Claiton of Eastsymthfeilde victualler,'

committed to the next Session

'to answer for sufferinge playes to bee played in his house in the night season.[65]

One group of records, all of them prohibiting or restricting performances in London Inns, remains to be considered. Retracing our steps in time from 1608, the first of these occurs in a letter from the Lord Mayor to the Privy Council dated 13th April 1582. In it the Lord Mayor explains that it will be difficult to stop play-acting,

'on holydaies in the afternone, being not the sabbat daye . . . For thoughe they beginne not their playes till after evening prayer, yet all the time of the afternone before they take in hearers and fill the place with such as be therby absent from serving God at Chirch, and attending to serve Gods enemie in an Inne; . . .'[66]

In 1580, the Lord Mayor issued an order for the arrest and committal of players and 'the owners of the houses' in which they had played because of disorders which had arisen either during or after the performances. The plays are said to have been,

'plaied by night . . . begyninge about vij or viij of the clock in the eveninge and contynuinge untill xj or xij of the clock . . .'[67]

This precept is dated 11th January: and while it was clearly possible for the plays to have been performed in the yard of inns by torchlight, it is stretching credulity too far to suppose that either players or spectators would have done this for three or four hours

---

* Chambers thought this Boar's Head had been converted into a permanent theatre and was no longer an Inn, as was the case with Aaron Holland's Red Bull Playhouse in Clerkenwell.[64]

on mid-winter nights. In any case the 'houses' in question may not have been wining and dining places, but private houses.

We have to go back to the year 1577 to come within sighting distance of the yard of a house or inn in a context contemporary with performances. On 23rd July of that year the Court of Aldermen ordered

'that no man(n)er of p(er)son w(i)thin this Cytie or the lyb(er)tyes thereof, shall p(er)mytte or suffer any pleyes or Interludes to be playde wythin any of their dwellynge howses yardes or other places at any tyme hereafter w(i)thoute esp(ec)iall lysence of this Co(u)rte fyrst had and obtayned.'[68]

This completes the list of references to inns and inn-yards in London known to me bearing a date after the building of the Theater. The remainder, all dated between 1553 and 1574, are similar in tone and content to the restraining order of 1577, and supply us with nothing more definite than a series of variants upon the phrase 'dwellynge houses, yardes, or other places'. The similarities however are so striking as to suggest the not unusual bureaucratic procedure of reissuing an original order and adapting it here and there on each occasion to meet new or changed circumstances.

I believe that the original order in this case came into being as a logical sequel to the Act of Parliament of 1543,* and took the form of a City Proclamation dated 6th February 1545. Because of its importance I have included the full text in Appendix B, p. 327 below. Here it can suffice to quote the passage restraining plays.

'his highnes therfore straitlye Chargethe & com(m)aundethe that no maner of p(er)sone or p(er)sones from hensforthe of whatsoever estate degree of Condic(i)on he or they be of presume or take upon hym or them at any tyme hereafter to playe or set foorthe or cause to be played any maner of Enterlude or co(mm)en playe w(i)thin any maner of place or places of this his graces said Citie. Onles it be in the houses of noble men or of the lorde Maire, Shryves or aldermen of the same his highnes Citie for the tyme beinge. Orels [Or else] in the houses of gentelmen or of the substancyall & sad [sic] Co(mm)iners or hed p(ar)issheners of the same Citie or in the open stretes of the said citie as in tyme paste it hathe bene used & accustomed or in the co(mm)en halles of the Companyes felowshipps or brotherheddes of the same Citie.'[69]

This document gives us a remarkably clear picture of the theatrical

* See Chs. II and III, pp. 15–16 and 62–63 above.

scene in London in the middle of the sixteenth century, and goes a long way to confirm the case I have made out for the heavy preponderance of indoor over out-of-door performances.

As a legal document it had the virtue in the eyes of the City Fathers of a royal command and could thus be used as a point of reference when need arose: but as a legal document it is also ambiguous in two important respects. The words 'substancyall & sad [i.e. grave] Commoners' are open to very wide interpretation, and so is the phrase 'in the houses'. It is obvious from the evidence of subsequent documents that many vintners, brewers, publicans, eating-house keepers and hotel keepers assumed themselves to be 'substancial commoners' whose houses came within the law as places where plays could be performed. In this they were no doubt encouraged by the actors who were more interested in controlled gate-money than in the collecting-box of the 'open streets'.

In 1553 the City Fathers adapted the document to forbid plays on Sundays and Calendar holidays 'before the hour of three of the clock in the afternoon', and made this an occasion to define the phrase 'in his house' in clearer terms: and it is here that we first meet the word Yard in the context of plays. No plays are to be 'had made or played w(i)thin eny p(ar)te of his or their howse or howses yarde Gardein or backsyde'.[70]

Two years later the 'vynten(er)s keap(er)s of Taverns Alehouses & other vyttelinge howses were brought sharply to heel with a warning that they would lose their licences if any of them presumed to allow performances of plays 'w(i)thin his or their howse or howses or other what so ev(er) place or places.'[71]

Shortly after Elizabeth's accession, reminders were issued to both private householders and the licensees of public houses. The word house, as far as private persons were concerned, was on that occasion (1564) defined as 'w(i)thin his or theire mansione house yarde gardyn orchard or other whatsoev(er) place or places'. In 1565 performances were specifically forbidden in what is now more amply defined as 'eny Tav(er)ne Inne vyttellynghouse or other place . . . wher any money shalbe demaunded or payd for the syght or hyrynge of the same playes'. One offender against one or other of these injunctions, Robert Fryer, was apprehended in 1566 and recognisances taken that he would not permit performances 'w(i)thin any p(ar)te of his mansion'.[72] The presumption must be, however, that the regulations continued to be more honoured in the breach than in the observance, for in 1569 the City issued a series of further injunctions, both fuller and more vindictive, than any hitherto. Of the four that are extant, two include the word yarde and two do not. The first, dated 3rd January, forbids plays 'in anny house Inne or Brewhouse . . . after the howre of v of the Clocke in the after noenne at annye tyme betwene this and Shrove-tyde nexte'. The dates indicate clearly enough that the purpose of this order was to stop performances after nightfall in the winter months.[73] The next, dated 3rd February, instructs the Aldermen to allow no performances except between 3 and 5 p.m. and then only after taking bonds from the citizens 'in whose houses or other rowmes eny such playes or interludes shalbe made or kepte'. The third, also dated 3rd February, is entitled 'A precept that no p(er)sonne resortyng to anny play shalbe suffered to stand in anny house, Chamb(er) or other close place'. A bond of £40 is to be taken from 'everey such p(er)sone in whose house yard court or gardeyn or other place whatsoever'* performances are given as security for ensuring that the audience will 'remayne & stond in the open (m'ket) place & places where the same enterludes or playes shalbe had played or made duryng all the tyme of the same playes And then honestly to depart'.[74] It could be argued from this last phrase that the Aldermen are thereby instructed to ensure that plays are to be confined to the yard or garden: but I think that this would distort both its meaning and intention. The intention is quite clearly to prevent the use of private in contrast to public parts of the building for immoral or illegal purposes under cover of attending the play: the meaning hinges on the interpretation of the word 'open'. I take it to stand for open in the sense of 'public' and not necessarily as open in the sense of 'open to the sky'. This construction is supported by the fourth of the injunctions of 1569, dated 12th May, which is

'streightly to charge and commaund, that no mannour of parson or parsons [person or persons] . . . being Inkepers, Tablekepers, Tavernours, hall-kepers, or bruers, Do or shall . . . take uppon him or them to set fourth, eyther openly or privatly, anny stage play or interludes, or to permit or suffer to be set fourth or played within his or there mansion howse, yarde, court, garden, orchard, or other place or places whatsover . . .'[75]

Here the word 'open' is clearly contrasted with the word 'private' and is to be applied to all possible parts of an Inn, interior or ex-terior, large enough to accommodate an audience: for 'openly or privately' we can thus substitute 'publicly or privately', that is, by paying for admission or by private invitation. This interpretation receives further support from a letter written by the Lord Mayor

* This phrase is repeated verbatim twice in the same document.

in 1582 to the Earl of Warwick in reply to a complaint received from the Earl about the restraint placed on one of his fencers.

'I did restraine him,' explains the Lord Mayor, 'from playeng in an Inne which was somewhat to [i.e. too] close for infection [i.e. plague], and appointed him to playe in an open place of the leaden hall'[76]

The Leadenhall was a large, roofed building used for the making and storage of the pageants of the civic ridings among other purposes. To describe it as open can only mean that it was spacious and more appropriate in the circumstances for accommodating a public audience than the 'close' or less open inn.

If I am correct in my reading of the preceding list of records, it becomes necessary to scrutinize with a fresh eye the most frequently quoted of all documents relating to London Inns. This is the Act of Common Council, dated 6th December 1574 beginning,

'Whearas hearetofore sondrye greate disorders and inconvenyences have benne found to ensewe to this Cittie by the inordynate hauntyinge of greate multitudes of people, speciallye youthe, to playes, enterludes, and shewes, namelye occasyon of ffrayes & quarrelles, eavell practizes of incontinencye in greate Innes, havinge chambers and secrete places adioyninge to their open stagies and gallyries . . .' etc.[77]

This passage, although the word yard does not occur, seems to depict an inn-yard under the words 'open stagies and gallyries'. Yet here we must be careful not to jump too fast to a deceptive conclusion; for not only is the wording in general suspiciously reminiscent of the Proclamation of 1545 and later adaptations of it, but the word open can as easily mean 'public' in this context as in the Precept of 1569. Indeed the further one advances into the long text of the Act of 1574, the more monotonously familiar does its phrasing become.

'. . . no Inkeper Tavernekeper nor other person whatsoever within the liberties of thys Cittie shall openlye shewe or playe, nor cawse or suffer to be openlye shewed or played, within the hous, yarde or anie other place within the Liberties of this Cyttie anie playe, enterlude, Commodye, Tragidie, matter, or shewe. . . .'etc.

The only novelty in all this is the interesting appearance of the words Comedy and Tragedy as supplements to plays and interludes. The Act goes on to stipulate that,

'no person shall suffer anie plays, enterludes, Comodyes, Tragidies, or shewes to be played or shewed in his hous, yarde, or other place

195

wheareof he then shall have rule or power, but onelye suche persons and in suche places as apon good and reasonable consideracions shewed shalbe thearunto permitted and allowed by the lord maiour and Aldermen for the tyme beinge.'

This Act, therefore, far from being the immediate cause of Burbage's decision to build the Theater in the suburbs, is simply a compendium of all the variants which had been used during the past thirty years in vain attempts to define the words 'substancial commoners' and 'in their houses' and thus enforce the letter of the City Proclamation of 1545.[78]

This lengthy recital of the surviving evidence relating to inns has been necessary to establish two facts which I believe to be cardinal to any understanding of the Elizabethan stage. The first is that we have no justification for assuming from records which associate Inns with stage-plays and actors, that performances automatically took place in the yard or even out of doors. The second, its sequel, is that when trying to dovetail our interpretations of De Witt's drawing of the Swan to fit such knowledge as we can glean from surviving buildings of the period which are visually familiar to us, we are under no obligation—indeed, we have no right—to correlate that drawing with Tudor Inn-yards to the exclusion of all other possibilities. Where the provincial records are concerned, association of actors with inns is explained by any travellers' need —as obvious as it is ordinary—of hotel accommodation. They were no more *obliged* then than they are today to give their performances in the pub where they ate and slept. I do not wish to deny inn-yards their due as occasional places of performance, nor 'other places' in and about the taverns and eating houses: but I do wish to direct the reader's attention to the overwhelming predominance of indoor performances in churches, chapels, private rooms and a variety of halls, as attested in the surviving provincial records, over open-air performances, and to the equally impressive evidence from London to the same effect. In only seven out of some thirty references associating plays and actors with inns is the yard mentioned at all: and of these one is of doubtful veracity while all the others speak of the yard as one of several possible sites including the interior of the 'house' or 'mansion'.

5 Reformation and Renaissance Pressures
i. Tradition and innovation

Where the political fact and implications of the Reformation encouraged the development of debate in dramatic form, the principal spokesmen of the Reformation inhibited rather than fostered the growth of the stage in their public pronouncements. Few of them championed it in any form beyond the early years of Elizabeth's reign, and most of them were bent on the immediate suppression of performances both in churches and on Sundays and Festival days at least, if not altogether. The Renaissance, on the other hand, stimulated interest in the theatre and, by appealing to the precedent of classical antiquity, emphasized aspects of presentation and performance which possessed the fashionable virtue of novelty. Reformation and Renaissance in conjunction combined to snatch pride of place from the popular amateur theatre of church and market-place in the national scene and to hand it instead to the professional players of interludes, thereby placing them squarely within the vision of the commercial speculators.

The principal effect of this change, which was moving towards its crisis during the thirty odd years 1540–1570, was to withdraw interest from the traditions of theatrical organization that had grown up around the amateur, summer stages of the people, and to focus attention upon the indoor, winter theatres of the lords of church, state and commerce. It is in this context that the pageant waggons of the trade guilds, the pageant-stages of the Royal Entries, the arena of *The Castle of Perseverance*, the stages of collegiate courtyards, and of Town hall, inn, church and chamber must be thought of while we are considering the rival models for the professional stages and stagecraft of the public playhouses. The Reformation by first repressing and then suppressing the religious stage did not obliterate the traditional stage-craft associated with the 'mansions' 'houses' and 'devices' of simultaneous settings; but by strangling the parent drama it inevitably impaired the health and vitality of its offspring. Renaissance interest in the theatre on the other hand with its emphasis upon the *scena* and *proscenium* of the Latin stage just as inevitably enhanced the status and possibilities of the screen in church and hall at the expense of 'houses' occupying floor space otherwise available for accommodating paying patrons. Thus a climate was created for humanist preoccupation with the aesthetic problem of unity of place to combine with the professional actors' commercial interest in accommodating as many spectators as possible: and both of these pressures, independently and in conjunction, unwittingly forwarded the Reformers' interest in undermining all traditions associated with the Roman Catholic stage. It is from this strange confluence of independent interests that the nation-wide amateur theatre of mediaeval inspiration met its doom; that the small groups of

Tudor household servants known as *lusores* or 'interluders' were transformed into the royal acting companies of the early Stuart era; and that the theatre of the banquet hall with its roof, raised stage, its screen and candlelight came ultimately to take precedence over all earlier and alternative forms of playhouse.

ii. *Court Revels*

The evolution of the entertainments presented by the mediaeval minstrel troupe in halls and chambers before private audiences for social recreation has already been traced in Volume I (Ch. V–VII). It is only necessary to remind the reader now that during the course of the fifteenth century, if not earlier, stories from both scripture and romance literature came to be dramatized in short mimetic Mummings, Disguisings and Interludes. The Mummings and Disguisings were expensively costumed, and ornamented with elaborate scenic units and explained to the audience by a Presenter: most of the action passed in dumb show and concluded in dancing and the offering of presents. The Interludes, by contrast, allowed the mimes to tell their own story in dialogue form with or without the assistance of the Presenter. It was in this state that the Court of Henry VII bequeathed the moral, farcical, and romantic interlude together with a group of four professional performers to Henry VIII's: by 1512 the Disguising was modified structurally to allow the disguised dancers to take partners from among the spectators in the manner of the Italian *maschere* or mask. The principal advances made during the reign of Henry VIII were the injection of religious and political satire and debate into the interlude, * together with the expansion of the group of performers maintained within the Royal Household from four to eight, and a spectacular increase in the cost of decorating the Disguising or Mask.† It is from this point, historically speaking, that we must resume the study of the auditoriums used and the conditions in which performances were given.

iii. *Hall and Chamber*

Henry VII, as I have argued in Chapter II, and Henry VIII for the first two decades of his reign, deliberately fostered humanist ideals of dramatic display at their Courts, borrowing freely from Italian example and reviving interest in Roman antiquity. To these

* See *EES*, i, pp. 237–243.
† See *EES*, i, pp. 217–222.

PLATE I

No. 1.   Water Show for Queen Elizabeth I at Elvetham, Hants., 1591.

PLATE II

No. 2.   Archbishop Cranmer by G. Flicke.

PLATE III

No. 3.   Thomas Cromwell by an unknown artist.

PLATE IV

Nos. 4 and 5. Emblematic personifications of summer and winter by G. Arcimboldo.

PLATE V

No. 6. Emblematic representation of the life of Sir Henry Unton.

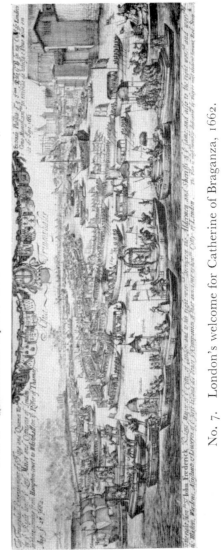

No. 7. London's welcome for Catherine of Braganza, 1662.

PLATE VI

No. 9. The interior of the Guildhall, Exeter.

No. 8. The screen of Exeter Cathedral.

PLATE VII

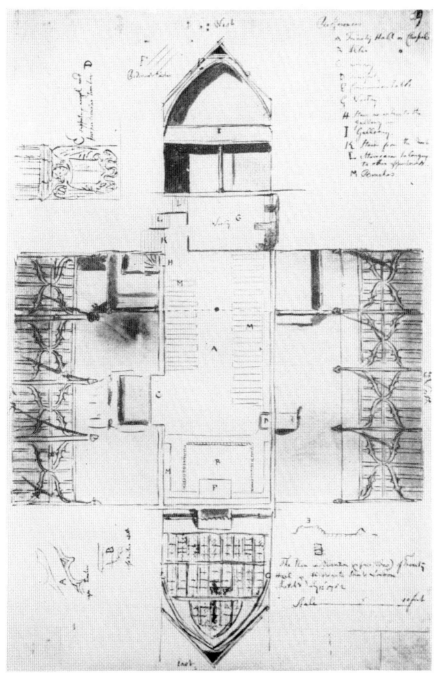

No. 10.   Trinity Hall in Aldersgate Street.

PLATE VIII

tectum

porticus

orchestra

mimorum ades

ingressus

proscenium

planities siue arena

No. 11.   De Witt's sketch of the Swan Theatre, c. 1596.

PLATE IX

No. 12.   Tournament arena, Bologna, 1628.

PLATE X

(a) The front.

(b) The courtyard.

(c) The upper room.

No. 13. The George Inn, Norton St. Philip.

PLATE XI

No. 14. An open stage set up before an inn in the Low Countries, c. 1600.

PLATE XII

Two of the Pageant Arches erected for James I's Coronation, 1603.

No. 16.   The Garden of Plenty.

No. 15.   The City of London.

PLATE XIII

No. 17. Pageant-stage in Flanders marking the cannonization of St. Ignatius Loyola, 1628.

PLATE XIV

No. 18.   Arch of the Faculty of Philosophy. Princess Elizabeth's Entry into
Heidelberg, 1613.

PLATE XV

No. 19.   Arch of the Faculty of Medicine. Princess Elizabeth's Entry into
Heidelberg, 1613.

PLATE XVI

No. 20. Double pageant-stage, Antwerp, 1582. Entry of the Duc d'Alençon
on his return from England.

PLATE XVII

No. 22. The Temple of Janus: one of the arches erected in London for James I's reception, 1603.

No. 21. The Temple of Janus: one of the pageants for Henry IV of France's entry into Avignon, 1601.

PLATE XVIII

No. 23. The Garden of Plenty: pageant-arch erected in Fleet Street for
Charles II's Entry into London, 1661.

PLATE XIX

No. 24.   Charles II's Entry into London 1661: the first arch, Leadenhall
Street.

PLATE XX

No. 25.   Combat at Barriers, Nancy, 1627: the Hall, the Barrier, Pageant-cars and cloud machine.

PLATE XXI

Cet entrée est de Monsieur le Comte de Brionne Grand Chambelan de son Altesse, representant Jason

No. 26. Combat at Barriers, Nancy, 1627: Entry of the Count of Brionne as Jason.

PLATE XXII

No. 28. Entry of the Prince of Lorraine: Garden of the
Hesperides.

No. 29. *Ibid.*: Vulcan and the Cyclops.

Combat at Barriers, Nancy, 1627.

No. 27. Entry of M. de Couuonge and of M. de Chalabre:
Pluto's Palace.

PLATE XXIII

No. 30. Mount Parnassus and the cave called vlas-mert: Entry of the Duc d'Alençon into Antwerp, 1582, on his return from England.

PLATE XXIV

No. 31. The Lord Mayor's Show, London, 1616: the pageant of the Lemon Tree.

No. 32. The Lord Mayor's Show, London, 1616: the pageant of Farringdon's Arbour (Tomb).

PLATE XXV

No. 33. The Lord Mayor's Show, London, 1616: Merman and Mermaid.

No. 34. Fish pageant for the Duc d'Alençon's Entry into Antwerp, 1582, on return from England.

PLATE XXVI

No. 36. Elephant and Castle: the Duc d'Alençon's Entry into Antwerp, 1582.

No. 35. An artificial Leopard: Lord Mayor's Show, London, 1616.

PLATE XXVII

No. 37. Angel on horseback: Lord Mayor's
Show, London, 1616.

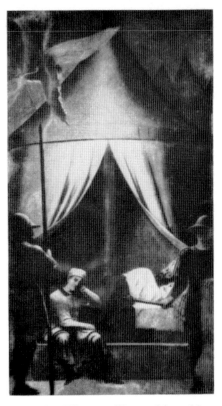

No. 38. The pavilion with a king
sleeping within: from the fresco of
the Dream of Constantine: Piero della
Francesca, Arezzo.

No. 39. Tent on a battlefield: detail from the portrait of Lord Vere by M. J. van
Miereveldt.

PLATE XXVIII

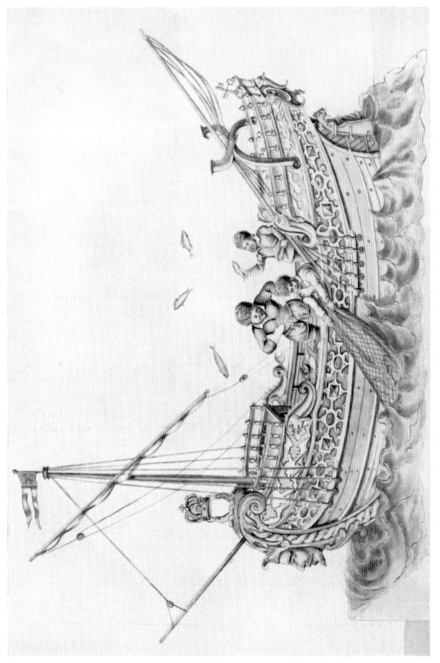

No. 40.   The Fishmongers Ship, Lord Mayor's Show, London, 1616.

PLATE XXIX

No. 41. Pageant-car of King Richard II, Lord Mayor's Show, London, 1616.

No. 42. Triumphal-car: Entry of Henry IV of France into Avignon, 1601.

PLATE XXX

No. 43.   Circular 'Theatre': miniature in the *Térence* of Charles VI
of France, c. 1410.

No. 44.   Serlian comic scene: first page of Horatio Vecchi's
L'Amfiparnasso, Venice, 1597.

PLATE XXXI

No. 45. A 'Palace' inside a 'Mountain': design for a Mask by Inigo Jones, probably for *Oberon*, 1611.

PLATE XXXII

WHITE HALL

No. 46. The Banquet House, Whitehall, built by Inigo Jones for Charles I and used as the 'tiring-house' for the execution of the King. Engraving from *Tragicum Theatrum*, Amsterdam, 1649.

ends, Italian and Flemish artists were encouraged to reside and work in England, while schools situated in or near the capital and the choristers of the Royal Chapels were encouraged to incorporate the performance of Latin plays in their curriculums, which were used subsequently to entertain and edify the Court itself. All these early Tudor evening Revels—Mummeries, Disguisings or Masks, Jousts at Barriers and Interludes—whether traditional in spirit and design or modified by neo-classical precept—were presented to their audiences in one or other of the three rooms spacious enough to contain them, the hall, the chamber or the chapel. In the last of these, the area used for performance was that immediately in front of the rood screen, thus allowing 'seatings' for the socially distinguished spectators on the screen itself or on the stage, and 'standings' for those not entitled to this privilege in the nave, and in the transepts where transepts existed. (See Vol. 1, Figs. 12 and 17.) For a description of conditions in the hall I cannot do better than quote T. W. Craik's summary in *The Tudor Interlude*:

'Most Tudor halls follow a standard pattern, a pattern still to be seen in the halls of Oxford and Cambridge colleges. There are commonly two doors (sometimes three) in the wall nearest the kitchen, when a passage divides the kitchen from the hall; or at other times, particularly when the hall directly adjoins the kitchen, these two doors are in a wooden partition near the kitchen end of the hall. In either case these doors are called the screen doors, and the wall or partition in which they are placed is called the screen. In some halls, but not all, the screen supports a gallery.'[79]

Where Mummeries, Disguisings and Jousts at Barriers were concerned, it was essential to the nature of the entertainment that as much of the floor space as possible should be left clear for the performers and their equipment. Spectators were thus normally accommodated on the dais at the upper end of the hall and along the side walls leaving the screen end clear to admit the performers and their pageant cars.* It is important to remember here that the amateur nature of these performances and the social status of the performers themselves exercised its own influence on the nature of the accommodation provided for spectators: for these revels approximated to those organized at a large private house party, designed for the enjoyment of the guests and not for the benefit of servants and social inferiors. There was thus little need for the 'standings' which consumed a large area of the central floor space

* See *EES*, i, pp. 214, 223 and 245.

at stage plays in the schools and universities: the audience was exclusive, comparatively small, and could be accommodated (either seated or standing) in existing galleries and on scaffolds erected along the side-walls while the musicians could be housed either in the gallery above the screen or on pageant cars of their own. (See Vol. 1, Plate XXVII and Fig. 12.) On occasions when these entertainments followed a banquet, the guests could and often did repair from the meal in the hall to the chamber to view the entertainment: if the revels had taken place in the hall, then the chamber was available for 'the void' or buffet-supper at their close.* Above all, no box-office considerations of 'capacity audiences' exercised any pressure on these arrangements; rather were they determined exclusively by traditional rules of precedence and social etiquette. As the number of people entitled, by virtue of their social rank, to attend these entertainments expanded during the Tudor era, so the problem of accommodation and overcrowding began to embarrass the Lord Chamberlain and his staff of Gentlemen Ushers. This problem had become acute enough in Jacobean times to occasion criticism and complaint,† and it may well have been among the factors occasioning the ultimate substitution of the concentrated scene for that of multiple scenic units spread about the open floor; but it does not appear to have embarrassed Tudor court officials.

Where the staging of interludes and plays was concerned, there is no evidence to prove that the conditions of performance were substantially different, at least initially, from those governing courtly revels. Two factors however of specifically Tudor parenthood began to exercise twin-pressures towards change quite early in the sixteenth century. One of these was the growing humanist interest of schoolmasters and their pupils in classical plays and theatres: the other was the expanding number and professional interest of the adult 'players of interludes' who were maintained as household servants by the nobility.

iv. *Neo-classical Enterprise*

Academic interest in the texts of plays by Plautus, Terence and Seneca, as Miss Campbell made abundantly clear as long ago as 1923, was accompanied by an interest in the manner of their original performance. This interest may be defined, at its simplest, as concern with the two principal characteristics of the classical

---

* See *EES*, i, p. 222.
† See *EES*, i, pp. xl–xli.

stage, the *proscaenium*, or raised platform, and the *scaena*, or screen, dividing the stage from the dressing-rooms. This interest, which in Italy proceeded to develop without interruption throughout the sixteenth century, was frosted in England by the progress of the Reformation for reasons which I have already discussed in Chapter II and which are treated in further detail in the next Chapter.

Nevertheless, in the fifty-odd years of neo-classical enthusiasm which preceded Henry VIII's first divorce and the break with Rome, enough research had been undertaken in Italy and had percolated to England for the notion of a raised platform stage, set up in a hall adjacent to a screen equipped with two or more doors, to have established itself as something approaching a Roman style of theatre, at least in academic and court circles. At St. Paul's School, for instance, Dean Colet was succeeded in 1512 by William Lily who was succeeded in turn by his dramatist son-in-law John Rightwise: and, as Miss Campbell observes,

'Lily came to the school after a sojourn in Rome, where he had gone to perfect himself in Latin under Pomponius Laetus and Sulpitius. It is difficult to conceive of one who had received his Latin training under the first editor of Vitruvius and under the first scholar to arrange Roman plays acted in the Roman fashion in a setting designed according to the precepts of Vitruvius, as returning to England and failing to make use both of the Latin play as a method of teaching Latin and of the Vitruvian principles of scenic representation of the drama.'[80]

We know moreover that plays in Latin were presented by schoolboys at Court during Henry VIII's reign and in English imitations of Latin originals before Elizabeth's accession.*

v. *The Professional Status of Actors*

The other factor which I mentioned as exercising a pressure towards change was the growing professional interest of adult companies. Historians of the theatre, with their attention focused on the pageant-waggons of the Miracle Cycles, the play-fields of the extended Moralities, and the Elizabethan public theatres, have allowed the essentially indoor background and training of the professional acting companies to suffer what seems to me to be an unwarranted neglect. As already demonstrated in Chapter IV, the authority by which they possessed their right to act for private

* See pp. 19–20 above and pp. 251–257 below.

gain was derived from their employment as liveried servants in a nobleman's household. They were servants in the first instance with the special duty of performing plays (usually 'made' for them by the chaplain) in the hall at night during the Christmas season and on other festive occasions. In the course of the fifteenth and early sixteenth centuries, following the precedent of the minstrel troupes, the right of the *lusores* or 'players of interludes' to act in their own homes was extended to include performances in other lords' halls. Anthony Munday in 1580 attributed this practice to the covetousness of the nobility who, he claimed, were anxious to off-load the expense of maintaining these 'servants' from their own pockets on to those of their friends.[81] This may well account in part for the nomadic habits of the Tudor actor; but another reason for this practice is to be found in the advent, after 1530, of the polemical interlude and the deliberate employment of companies in the service of the Reformation: it was clearly in the interest of the sponsors of these plays that they should be toured widely and exhibited to as many audiences as possible.

What is important here is that the professional players of interludes who travelled the country between 1530 and 1576 were not amateurs of the market-place stage, but predominantly professionals of the hall and chamber whose repertoire of plays was devised in the first instance for those halls and not for the street or village green, although they could doubtless be adapted to fit an open-air auditorium if necessary. Moreover, as professionals, the actors' interest in the number of spectators which the hall could contain was governed as much by gate-money as by the ease with which entry to the hall could be controlled. The academic theatre therefore with its raised stage adjacent to the entry doors in the screen and its central floor space available for accommodating spectators had far more to commend it to the professional interluders than either the amateur street theatres of the Miracles and civic ridings or the amateur court theatre of the maskers, dancers and jousters. This then is the explanation which I would offer for the entries in account rolls and other documents relating to the raised wooden stages which make their appearance in churches, in the halls of palaces and castles and in town halls up and down the country from the middle of the sixteenth century onwards.

6 Conclusion

Summarizing my argument therefore, I am asking the reader to reconsider the origin of the professional theatre in this country: to view it in essence not as an outdoor theatre which learnt later how to contain itself indoors, but rather as an indoor theatre, based on the refectory or hall of social recreation, which gradually extended itself as the numbers of its patrons increased to include open-air auditoriums suitably adapted to contain larger numbers but with admission controlled as effectively as in the halls. The *plega-stôw* of *The Castle of Perseverance* and the Cornish Miracles, the Church, Churchyard, the Game-house and the Inns are to be considered as intermediaries between the halls of the landed gentry (and of City Companies and Councils), and the public playhouses of Elizabethan London: and the factors primarily responsible for this transformation are the competition offered by the professional actors of polemical interludes and the school-boy actors of neo-classical interludes to the amateur guild plays, followed by the wholesale suppression of the religious stage between 1559 and 1576.

The explanation of the events which I have offered receives further strong support if we open up the historical context in which they are set still wider to include the very beginnings of drama in this country. As I have argued in Volume I, our theatre of the Middle Ages was a twin-headed phenomenon, a sophisticated theatre of social recreation developing alongside of a popular theatre of worship of much earlier origin. The theatre of worship started life, as one might expect, in the interior of the church; and, with the passage of time, coupled with changes of emphasis and purpose, it extended itself to include open-air productions at appropriate seasons of the year. The theatre of social recreation also started life indoors; but starting life in earnest so much later than the theatre of worship, it borrowed many of the stage-conventions which its popular rival had already formulated for both indoor and outdoor use. When the sophisticated and quasi-professional theatre of social recreation itself came of age, it too moved out of doors at seasonable times of the year, converting gardens, parks, lakes and streams into temporary theatres as occasion warranted. But the eye of the professional actor is ever on the crowd: and when, in England, the government intervened to suppress the theatre of worship, these actors seized upon the opportunity to win for themselves the loyalty which popular audiences had formerly given to its rival. Still an indoor theatre by temperament and upbringing, it was nevertheless strong enough by then to translate whatever auditorium lay to hand, whether indoor or outdoor, to its own use. In doing so the actors provided a point of contact between the highest and the lowest in English society, for they quickly became as much the servants of the people as they were still officially the household servants of noble and even royal masters. Into the game-houses familiar to all sections of society and open to everyone, regardless of rank, who possessed the penny needed to gain admission, the actors brought the scaffold, the screen and the 'houses' of their master's private hall: and as the years passed they integrated the one with the other to form a theatre capable of inspiring and accommodating both Shakespeare's and Jonson's finest plays.

This survey of the architectural precedents for Elizabethan playhouse design has been one of daunting length. It has the advantage in the close however of allowing us now to accept De Witt's sketch of the Swan Theatre at its face value without modification, interpolation or any other unwarranted change. The stage raised on its supports and labelled *proscaenium* stands out in front of the two-doored screen supporting the familiar gallery of rood-screen, refectory and audience chamber. This screen separates the stage from the actor's dressing and property room behind, and is properly labelled *mimorum aedes*. The carefully shaded lines on the floor of the *arena*, in the angles made by the junction of the stage unit and the *orchestra*, indicate clearly that this *mimorum aedes* juts out from the main body of the auditorium and that the screen gallery is in no way integrated with the second tier of that auditorium. The 'heavens' of the civic pageants, the pageant-waggons and the rafters of the banquet chamber are duly incorporated and project over the stage supported on pillars, with the machinery screened from view and protected against the weather by an attic loft. The whole of this stage, with its screen, gallery and dressing-room, indistinguishable from that of the Tudor hall, is set down, put, placed, dumped in the conventional three-tiered Tudor game-house in a manner which will admit the maximum number of spectators consistent with box-office capacity and a reasonable view of the action on the stage. The seating accommodation normally available within the frame of the game-house for bear-baiting (but lost when the stage and tiring-house is positioned in front of it) is amply compensated for by the 'standings' left free in the yard, the lords' rooms in the gallery above the screen and by the provision of stools for use on the stage itself in emergency.

Interpretation of the De Witt drawing in these terms has the additional virtue of resolving at once two other related problems of perennial difficulty to historians: that of reconciling the apparent discrepancy between the ascetic, black and white appearance of surviving inn-yards with references to the theatres as 'gorgeous' and 'painted', and that of reconciling staging conditions in the public theatres with those at Court or on a provincial tour. If our starting point is the stage of the Tudor banqueting hall set down inside a game-house rather than a pageant-waggon or fairground booth set down in the inn-yards, then the columns which De Witt states to have been painted in imitation of marble are credible enough. Moreover, the conditions of performances both at Court and in provincial Town halls were already catered for in principle in the public theatres, no serious change of actors' moves or stage settings being required when exchanging one environment for the other.

I am aware that problems remain concerning both the curious perspective of De Witt's representation of the heavens' loft and the scenic arrangements called for in the stage directions of many Elizabethan plays. These however are subjects which can be more conveniently discussed in Chapter VIII.

VI

THE EMBLEMATIC
TRADITION

1 Picture and Action

'There seems increasingly manifest', wrote G. F. Reynolds in 1940, 'a tendency to let imagination play freely about the indications of staging in the directions and text [of plays] to arrive at interesting results, rather than to determine exactly what the plays demand.'[1]

DESPITE this very clear warning, the processes of reconstructing Elizabethan stages to a recipe of one part fact to as many parts fancy as the writer can muster have forged ahead during the past twenty years. I draw attention to this state of affairs lest my own approach to the problems of stage-conventions be considered ridiculously naïve in its simplicity.

I start from a paradox implicit within the sum total of all descriptions known to me of English public theatres in the period 1576–1642: the fact that people of one frame of mind regarded them as gorgeous palaces, while other people of different disposition regarded them as childishly inadequate to their purpose. Burbage and Alleyn, for instance, still thought well enough of the Globe and the Fortune after the disastrous fires of 1613 and 1621 to go to work at once to find the capital to finance the building of replicas. Jonson and Jasper Mayne on the other hand were quite prepared to ridicule such buildings despite their continuing use and evident popularity. Mention has already been made of Jonson's strictures on the conventions and facilities of these theatres in the Prologue to the 1616 edition of *Every Man in his Humour*: * Jasper Mayne championed these views in his memorial verses for Jonson, published in 1638, in still stronger terms.†

* See *Preface*, pp. ix–x above.
† 'Thy scene was free from monsters; no hard plot
   Call'd down a God t'untie th'unlikely knot:

206

Foreigners, however, who visited these theatres were impressed by what they saw: one even made a sketch of the Swan. Yet no English artist of the period appears to have thought highly enough of them to make any pictorial record for patrons or posterity. Printers, editors and playmakers were extremely casual in the attention given to stage-directions, not troubling in many cases even to be consistent. By marked contrast, not only was every possible care lavished upon the wording of stage directions of the Court Masks so that the settings would be explicit to readers, but the master designer among the artists, Inigo Jones, saved and collected most of his working drawings, bequeathing them to his pupil John Webb.

Before therefore fancy directs us

> 'to plant the music where no ear can reach
> Attire the persons, as no thought can teach
> Sense what they are',[2]

or otherwise to reconstruct the Elizabethan theatre from straws of evidence inflated by imagination into bricks, it behoves us to try to resolve the riddle of this paradox. And as a first step in this direction we may examine the testimony on both sides for evidence of vested interest: having stripped that away we may then have some chance of scrutinizing the paradox in its simplest form.

Prime witnesses to the luxury of the public theatres are the puritan divines. John Stockwood described Burbage's Theater as 'the gorgeous Playing place erected in the fieldes': Gosson comments on 'the beautie of the houses and the Stages', which to Thomas White seemed 'sumptuous Theatre houses'.[3] Since these witnesses were aiming to discredit acting on moral grounds, it is open to us to regard their testimony as prejudiced. We may properly therefore discount at least a portion of the luxury noted by them as having enjoyed a more substantial existence in their mind's eye than in actual fact. As an example of the way in which the puritanical mind distorted by exaggeration what it disliked or feared, it is worth quoting the following indictment of a notable company of Elizabethan boy actors.

'Even in her maiesties chappel do these pretty upstart youthes profane the Lordes Day by the lascivious writhing of their tender

---

The stage was still a stage, two entrances
Were not two parts o' the world, disjoin'd by seas.
Thine were land-tragedies, no prince was found
To swim a whole scene out, then o' the stage drown'd;
Pitch'd fields, as Red-Bull wars, still felt thy doom;
Thou laid'st no sieges to the music room.'

limbs, and gorgeous decking of their apparell, in feigning bawdie fables gathered from the idolatrous heathen poets.'[4]

Nevertheless, before we debase Puritan testimony concerning the luxury of the decoration in the playhouses by making allowance for exaggeration, we must remember that De Witt's statement about the columns painted to resemble marble in the Swan Theatre fits much better with this testimony than with the village architecture of early Tudor yeomen prescribed in most twentieth century reconstructions.

If on the other hand we prefer to start from the other extreme and adopt Jonson's disparaging attitude to the public theatre (as opposed to the ornate Court Theatre of his collaborator Inigo Jones) we must be careful to remember before we strip all vestige of paint and coloured hangings from the interior, that Jonson wrote his best plays for these theatres; that he had second thoughts about the value of Inigo Jones' decorations and that it is the methods of presentation to which he took exception, not the decoration.

In short then, if we confine our attention to the testimony that survives from the period 1576 to approximately 1616, we must admit the strong probability (if we stand by De Witt, the fact) that the interiors of the theatres were ornately and expensively decorated while reserving judgement (temporarily at least) on the nature of the staging conventions. The latter problem, including as it must acting techniques, costume, stage machinery and other aspects of dramatic art, raises a complicated aesthetic question in addition to the simple one of fact. Thus when we take note of Jonson's stricture about the *fact* of the creaking throne coming down from the heavens (a double insult to rational sensibility) we must also take note of his expressed *opinion* that it came down 'the boys to please'. The heavenly storage loft and many other devices of public-theatre stage-craft may well have been simple: but before we equate 'simple' with 'primitive' or 'naïve', we must ask ourselves to whom and in what context? To Jonson and others of his persuasion among the intelligentsia? Or to those whom he dismissed as men of grounded judgement? Who are we to trust? Sydney, Jonson, Jasper Mayne, Pepys and other post-Restoration pundits who were becoming increasingly concerned with the propriety of the classical unities, or the actual owners and managers of the public theatres who invested their box-office takings in this type of theatre in the face of this learned criticism and earned a good living from so doing until civil war ruined both them and their investment?

As I have reiterated constantly throughout these two volumes, I believe we are confronted here with something vastly more important than intellectual snobbery, however much that may be apparent: nothing less in brief than a head-on collision of two fundamentally opposed attitudes to art: the typically mediaeval contentment with emblematic comment on the significance of the visual world versus a new, scientific questing for the photographic image. This search for the technical means to reproduce actuality, as opposed to an almost exclusive concern with extracting the significance behind outward appearances, is obvious enough in the fine arts of renaissance Italy: and, where the art of drama is concerned, nowhere could this conflict of interest become more sharply and swiftly manifest than in methods of scenic presentation. In England there are all the signs that this conflict was developing towards its crisis between 1520 and 1540; but the Reformation, followed by threats of foreign invasion, intervened; and for reasons which I have already treated at length in Chapter II, this crisis was delayed for another sixty years. When it came, it did so within a Protestant England, in the throes of incipient social revolution, where as many individuals were still attached to traditional patterns of thought as were anxious to champion the new. This is not something which we are likely to recognize if we bury our eyes and thoughts in the specifications of a single Elizabethan playhouse: but it is something which we cannot easily ignore if we widen our mental focus to admit the evidence of the continuance of mediaeval traditions of Pageantry into the Stuart era. I have been criticized by some American reviewers, Professor Hardin Craig among them, for confusing my account in Volume I of the religious stage in mediaeval England with Tournaments, Civic Ridings and other aspects of Pageantry.[5] My answer is that Pageantry is itself the quintessence of emblematic art, as anyone acquainted with Heraldry can confirm; to deny it a place in the early history of English drama guarantees failure to understand the subsequent development of both the drama and the methods of performance. In resuming my examination therefore of the emblematic traditions of Pageantry bequeathed by the Middle Ages to the Tudor epoch and of the use made of it, I do so unrepentantly.

2 The Emblems of Pageantry

(a) Civic Occasions

The ornate, costly and skilfully made pageants of the mediaeval Royal Entries survived in England throughout the Shakespearean era, were eclipsed like the public theatres during the years of the Civil War and Commonwealth, only to be triumphantly resurrected again both on land and water at the Restoration. Charles II was welcomed into London with pageant-arches of unexampled splendour in 1661 while water-triumphs of no less magnificence greeted Catherine of Braganza on the Thames in 1662.

If all the material left us to study related exclusively to Royal Entries, perhaps the subject could be allowed to rest at the point where we left off in Volume I—Dekker's, Jonson's and Middleton's show for James I's entry into London. Tudor and Stuart pageantry however is marked by a change of the utmost significance to the history of the theatre: the development in London of pageantry almost as costly and spectacular as that of the traditional Royal Entries, but repeated annually and devoted to the glorification of its chief citizen. The Lord Mayor's Show, engaging as it did the attention of the leading dramatists, actors, musicians and artificers of the day is a neglected source of theatrical history, and as a peripheral influence upon stage spectacle it is at least as important as that of Mask, Ballet and Italian opera. That I am enabled to exploit this source of information instead of dismissing it as so much tedious municipal imagery* is largely due to the recent labours of Professor F. P. Wilson, Professor D. J. Gordon and Miss Jean Robertson in transcribing the dramatic records of the Livery Companies of London for the Malone Society.[6]

My own interest in this and other records of pageantry is threefold: first, in the evidence which it provides of the continued use of emblematic scenic devices; secondly, in the materials employed and the financial outlay; and, thirdly, in the people engaged in constructing them, acting on or in them and enjoying them as spectators. To avoid boring the reader with lists and catalogues I have selected the major scenic devices treated in Volume I—the arbour, the castle, the cave, the fountain, machines, the mountain, the pavilion, the ship, the tomb and the tree—for discussion under separate headings here, before attempting to consider these same devices in the very different contexts first of Tournaments and then of stage-plays.

(i) *The Arbour*

This device, sometimes extended in its meaning to include the garden and the forest-wilderness, we encountered last (Vol. I, p. 91) in its most spectacular form described as a 'summer Arbor'

---

* See *EES*, i, pp. xxxiii–xxxvii.

and conveniently illustrated. Made of trellis work, surmounted by leaves, flowers and fruits and translated into an archway for James I's reception into London entitled *Hortus Euporice* (the Garden of Plenty) it presents a degree of vulgarity in English taste usually regarded as exclusive to buildings and furnishings of the late Victorian era. Two years later it reappeared as 'a very artificiall arboure . . .' in the festivities prepared for Christian IV of Denmark's entry into London. Despite its artificiality it was constructed out of 'greene boughes', and garnished with 'delightfull fruites' and served to conceal a consort of music. The musicians were screened by 'curtains of crimson taffatie', and 'the top of the Arbor [was] made canapie wise and hung round about with [an] inscription'.[7] In construction and appearance this was probably similar to that devised by Anthony Munday for the Lord Mayor's Show of 1616, *The Golden Fishing*, of which a picture exists (Plate XXIV, No. 32). Entitled Sir William Walworth's bower, it represents this knight according to the text as lying on his tomb, but according to the picture as sitting at a table.[8]

Its further reappearances were motivated almost entirely by the need to express the activities of the Livery Companies in emblematic form. The Merchant Taylors had adopted St. John the Baptist in his Wilderness as early as 1392;[*] and the wilderness being represented in terms of a dangerous forest rather than a treeless desert had suggested its use to the Skinners as a setting for the wild beasts whose furs gave them their livelihood. One animal however was particular to the Drapers, the sheep; and they too therefore had a claim on the garden emblem. So, finally, did the Grocers for whom Lydgate in 1432 had prepared a spectacular orchard.[†]

In the seventeenth century these claims continue to be made and met, but inevitably with some overlapping of arbour, garden, tree, field, forest and even hill or mountain in the symbolism. Dekker supplied the Skinners in 1628 with two sumptuous variations on this theme. The first was 'New Troyes Tree of Honor' (i.e. London's), '. . . a queint Arbor, Interwoven with severall Branches of Flowers'. Beside the arbour a tree was placed having twelve branches (one for each of the Livery Companies), and both were enclosed by 'a border of Flowers ...(where lesse Trees also grow)'. The symbolism here is generalized, applying to London itself.[9] The Skinners however are directly figured in the device of the Sun's Bower.

[*] See *EES*, i, pp. 70–71.
[†] See *EES*, i, p. 91.

'The upper part of this, is adorned with severall Flowers, which interwoven together, dresse up a comely *Greene Arbor*, in which the *Sunne* sits, with golden Beames about his Face; an Attire glittering like gold; and a mantle bright as his garment, fringed with gold, his haire curled and yellow. About him are plac'd *Spring, Summer, Autumne,* and *Winter,* in proper Habilments. Beneath these, is a Wildernesse, in which are many sorts of such *Beasts,* whose rich Skinnes serve for *Furres.*'[10]

A year later (1629) Dekker provided the Ironmongers with another arbour 'round about furnished w(i)th trees and 700ers and the upp(er) p(ar)te w(i)th severall fruits . . . *Ver* and *Estas* are seated in this *Tempe*'. 'Tempe' here signified 'The Field of Happinesse'; it again symbolizes London and the arbour is said to be 'supported by foure Great Termes' (i.e. pillars) with pennants flying from them. It cannot have differed much in appearance from Sir William Walworth's Bower (Plate XXIV) of 1616 if Dekker's description is to be trusted: a sketch made by the Dutchman Abram Booth however only shows the tree and the seasons dancing round it. (Fig. 11, p. 216 below.)

Both Middleton and Heywood appear to have shared Dekker's enthusiasm for the Arbour. Middleton provided the Skinners with a thicket-wilderness in 1619, presided over by Orpheus and crowned with 'an artificial cock', often made to crow and flutter his wings. In 1626 he gave the Drapers a 'Beautiful Hill or Fragrant Garden, with flowery banks, near to which lambs and sheep are a-grazing', crowned this time with 'an artificial and curious rain-bow . . . the bow in the clouds'.[12] Heywood supplied the Drapers (twice) and the Clothworkers (once) with arbours. All three are pastoral in design and more directly concerned with sheep than flowers.[13]

John Webster stretches the emblem of the garden as far as is imaginable in a Pageant for the Merchant Taylors (1624), the Monument of Charity and Learning. It was 'fashioned like a beauti-full Garden with all kind of flowers, at the foure Corners foure artificiall Bird Cages, with variety of Birds in them: this for the beauty of the Flowers, and melody of the Birds, to represent a Spring in Winter'. An elm-tree grew in the middle of the garden and a scale model of St. John's College, Oxford, was placed in the background.[14]

Royal Entries and the Lord Mayor's Shows were interrupted by the Civil War and Commonwealth for twenty years.[15] It is the more interesting therefore to notice in what state they returned after the Restoration. Where the arbour is concerned, it survived as a device in both its pre-war form and in a significantly altered shape. In 1662 the Merchant Taylors dressed their barge for the water show welcoming Catherine of Braganza to London, *Aqua Triumphalis*, (1662) as 'a wild Arbour, made in manner of a Wildernesse'. St. John has been translated into a Pilgrim attended by Faith, Hope and Charity who together stand on a stage '12 foot long and 7 foot wide' arched over with the arbour.* The illustration of this pageant which I found in the Huntington Library is published here for the first time (Plate V, No 7).[16]

The other Restoration arbour appeared in the reception which London accorded Charles II in 1661. It is called 'The Garden of Plenty' and took the form of a triumphal arch 'of two Stories, one of the *Dorick* Order, the other of the *Ionick*. The Capitals have not their just Measure, but incline to the Modern Architecture.' Two stages were erected in front of the arch 'divided, planted and adorned like Gardens, each of them eight yards in length, five in breadth'.[17] The arch of this pageant (but not the stages) is conveniently illustrated (Plate XVIII), thus enabling us to compare it directly with the *Hortus Euporice* of 1603 (Plate XII, No. 16). These two pictures provide in themselves the most vivid and the most fitting conclusion to this recital of the fortunes of the arbour as an emblematic scenic device.

(ii) *The Mountain*

Like the arbour, the mountain appears and reappears as a scenic unit with remarkable regularity throughout the Elizabethan and Jacobean era. As a 'Hill' or 'Mount' in the usual entertainments on land, it is augmented by the 'Rock' and the 'Island' in the water triumphs of lake and river: further differentiation between green hill and barren rock allowed too of emblematic contrasts between one part of the world and another, and between desirable and undesirable states of being. Thus, at Elizabeth's Coronation in 1559, the difference between a decayed and a flourishing Commonwealth was figured in terms of two hills,† a device which Heywood adapted in his *Jus Honorarium* of 1636 to denote *Civitas bene Gubernata*.[18] In Heywood's pageant Time, in the course of his speech, picks up 'a leaflesse and withered branch' which he describes as 'A Cities Symbole, ruin'd, and trod downe'. Munday used four hills in his *Metropolis Coronata* (1615) to represent 'strong defensive bulwarkes' as a setting for London.[19] More frequent is the direct

* See p. 211 above.
† See *EES*, i, p. 91, and p. 217 below.

association of the hill with its prime occupant—the Mount of Fame, Britain's Mount, and so on.

The Rock and the Island of the water-shows were similarly treated. Among the devices used in the elaborate water spectacle at Elvetham, Hampshire, in 1591 were the 'Ship Isle' and the 'Snail Mount'.[20] These are illustrated in the engravings accompanying the descriptive pamphlet (Plate I, No. 1). Dekker presented Amphitrite on a rock in 1628 (*Britannia's Honour*), a device used by Munday in the Merchant Taylor's show of 1610 to present Merlin. Merlin's rock was painted and gilded: Amphitrite's was 'queintly contrived' and attended by personified Rivers 'aptly attired according to the quality of such Marine Persons'.[21] Webster decorated his 'Artificiale Rocke' of 1624 (*Monuments of Honour*) 'with mother of Pearle, and such other precious stones': it was also equipped with lamps and candles for better effect at night. Heywood presented Scilla and Charibdis in 1631 as 'two craggy Rockes' elaborately decorated with marine flotsam and vivid evidence of shipwreck.[22]

The prime devotee of the mountain-cum-island however was Thomas Middleton. He used it again and again with remarkable variety of invention. In *The Triumphs of Truth* (1613) he supplied no less than five islands, 'garnished with all manner of Indian fruit-trees, drugs, spiceries, and the like; the middle Island with a faire Castle'. This show was devised for the Grocers Company and the islands bear obvious allusion to their trading activities.[23] He repeated this device when again commissioned by the Grocers in 1617 (*The Triumphs of Honour and Industry*) providing a 'show of dancing Indians in the Island' and a 'Chariot of India'.[24] Working for the Drapers in 1621 he offered 'a mountain, artfully raised and replenished with fine woolly creatures (i.e. *sheep*); Phoebus on the top, shining in a full glory, being circled with the Twelve Celestial Signs'. Aries, as might be expected, had the place of honour and was the speaker.*[25] His masterpiece in this idiom however was the Mount of Truth of 1613, the centrepiece of *The Triumphs of Truth*, a pageant which revived the Old Morality in perambulatory form. It is unquestionably the most ambitious attempt to give the civic riding a fully dramatic form. Truth and Error are the protagonists, both equipped with elaborate pageant-cars, and possessed respectively with an Angel and a Devil (Envy) as an attendant. The two chariots, and their attendants on horseback (together with the five islands used in the water-show), approach the principal edifice which Middleton describes as:

* See *EES*, i, pp. 96–97.

'. . . the true form and fashion of a mount triumphant, but the beauty and glory thereof over-spread with a thick, sulphurous darkness, it being a fog or mist, raised from Error, enviously to blemish that place which bears the title of London's Triumphant Mount, the chief grace and lustre of the whole triumph. At the four corners sit four monsters, Error's disciples, on whom hangs part of the mist for their clothing, holding in their hands little thick clubs, coloured like their garments; the names of these four monsters [are], Barbarism, Ignorance, Impudence, Falsehood: who, at the near approaching of Truth's chariot, are seen a little to tremble . . .'.*

No wonder, for the

'cloud suddenly rises and changes into a bright-spreading canopy, stuck thick with stars, and beams of gold shooting forth round about it, the mount appearing then most rich in beauty and glory, the four monsters falling flat at the foot of the hill'.

An elaborate tableau of civic virtues is then revealed and London speaks. Error, by this time very angry, replies.

'At which the mist falls again and hangs over all the beauty of the mount, not a person of glory seen, only the four monsters gather courage again and take their seats, advancing their clubs above their heads.'

In its own way this mechanical fog gave to humble citizens something of the pleasure latent in a change of scene which Inigo Jones was offering in his decoration of Masks to those courtiers privileged to attend them. No opportunity was lost therefore to repeat the effect as the cortège passed through the city, Error being

'still busy and in action to draw darkness often upon that Mount of Triumph, which by Truth is as often dispersed'.

The moral debate was at length resolved at night when flames, bursting from the head of Zeal, set fire to the chariot of Error leaving it 'only glowing in embers'.

(iii) *The Tree, the Fountain and the Cave*

The fountain as a feature of many gardens, and the cave as the

* This quotation and the four which follow are taken from *Bullen's Middleton*, vii, pp. 227–262.

interior of cliff or hill, were as obviously associated with both the arbour and the mountain in scenic iconography, as was the tree: yet cave, tree and fountain could each on occasion serve an independent function.

Trees, like animals, could particularize a country. * Thus, just as the crocodiles of Heywood's *Londini Status* (1639) appropriately figured the river Nile and Egypt, so the palm tree, 'beautified with leaves as greene as arte could devise', had served to identify Deborah for Queen Elizabeth in 1559.[26] The lemon tree was used somewhat pedestrianly by Anthony Munday to figure a Lord

Fig. 11. The tree, designed and constructed by Garret Christmas for Dekker's *London's Tempe* (1629): from a sketch by Abram Booth.

Mayor of that name in 1616; but the device is redeemed for us by the fortunate survival of an illustration (Plate XXIV, No. 31).[27] Trade symbolism in trees has already been noticed in respect of the Grocers Company.

Mediaeval enthusiasm for the geneaological tree appears to have waned after Elizabeth's accession; I am not myself aware of its having been employed again either in a Royal Entry or in a Civic

* Animals are treated in conjunction with costumes in section (vii), pp. 226–229 below.

Pageant after the very elaborate Jesse-tree of the uniting of the houses of Lancaster and York erected in Gracious Street in 1559.[28] At the Restoration the tree appropriate to the occasion was the Royal Oak, and this did duly find a place in the first of the Pageant Arches in London in 1661: but it is no longer a three-dimensional tree, live or artificial, simply a painting inserted in the arch as a back-cloth for the statue of the monarch himself (Plate XIX).[29]

Use of the fountain was similarly sporadic. George Peele employed it in its traditional form as the habitation of Truth in his *Descensus Astraea* of 1591, giving it a Protestant twist by first letting a priest and a friar (Ignorance and Superstition) attempt to poison it, and then defeating their intention by the timely descent of Astraea, 'Our fair Eliza'.[30] Middleton used the fountain twice, but without elaboration: in 1621 as 'the triple crowned Fountain . . . adorned with the lively figures of all those graces and virtues . . . as Justice, Sincerity, Meekness etc.', and, in 1626, simply as the fountain of Virtue without even bothering to describe it. Munday was more adventurous, adapting it in 1609 into both the form of 'a whale rounded close w(i)thout sight of the boate [*on which it was mounted*] and to row w(i)th ffins, open for ffireworkes at the mouth and water vented at the head', and as one of the furnishings of Bell-Field for the Ironmongers.[31]

The close affinities between the cave and the rock or hill have already been instanced in the case of Merlin in the Rock (1610). An earlier and more elaborate example is to be found among Elizabeth's Coronation pageants where, between the two hills representing the *Ruinosa Respublica* and the *Respublica bene instituta*, 'was made artificiallye one hollow place or cave, with doore and locke enclosed'. This served to house Time and his daughter, Truth: it cannot have differed much from the *Carcer* or prison of the *Laurentius* setting (Fig. 1, p. 5).[32] With the growing popularity of classical mythology the cave was likely to be adapted to provide a home for Vulcan: and, by the same token, it was in association with the Ironmongers Company that this could appropriately be done. Both Munday and Dekker availed themselves of this opportunity. In his *Sidero-Thriambos* of 1618 Munday presented Mulciber attended by the Cyclops in a pageant frame described as an 'Isle or Myne', with persons at the corners representing 'the foure ages of the world and habited according to their true Carracters and natures'.[33] Dekker moved further in the direction of realism with his Lemnian Forge in *London's Tempe* (1629).

'In it are *Vulcan*, the *Smith* of *Lemnos*, with his servants (the

Cyclopes) . . . working at the *Anvile*. Their habits are wast coates, and lether approns: their haire blacke and shaggy, in knotted curles. A fire is seene in the Forge, Bellowes blowing, some filing, some at other workes; Thunder and Lightning on occasion.'[34]

FIG. 12. The forge in a 'cave' designed and constructed by Garret Christmas for Dekker's *London's Tempe* (1629): from a sketch by Abram Booth.

Perhaps the most fascinating of the pageant caves however (at least from the historian's standpoint) is the one figured in the first pageant-arch for Charles II's return to London in 1661. It appears in a painting above the central arch (not as a three-dimensional unit) and marks a complete reversion to the earliest form of all such caverns, Hell's Mouth itself: and the naked figure beating a swift retreat into its gaping jaws bears the head of Oliver Cromwell on its back. John Ogilby's text reads:

'The Painting over the Middle Arch represents the King, mounted in calm Motion, USURPATION flying before him, a figure with many ill-favoured Heads, some bigger, some lesser, and one particularly shooting out of his shoulder, like CROMWELL's; Another Head upon his Rump, or Tayl; Two *Harpies* with a Crown chased by an Angel; Hell's jaws opening.'

Fɪɢ. 13. Detail from Plate XIX.

Hesiod and Vergil are cited as the authorities for including the Harpies in this picture.[35] (See Plates XIX, XXII, Nos. 27 and 29 and XXIII.)

(iv) *Pavilion, Throne, Monument, Castle and City*

Although it is easy enough for us to distinguish a simple tent from a battlemented fort, it is by no means as easy to divide the scenic units in which one or other of these elements (or both in combination) were used, into distinct categories. Both extremes in this idiom appeared at Norwich in 1556 in the celebrations for the installation of the Mayor. The tent is described as

'a Skaffoolld . . . rownnde like a pavillioun':

the fort as

'a greate pageant . . . which was like a greate castell'.

The pavilion was

'Richele adorned, full of targetts [*shields*] with a morien [*a Moor*] on the toppe staunding naked . . .', and inside it, 'stood an auncyente personage who represented Tyme.'

The castle was equipped with

'a greate gate thereunder like a Cytte [*city*] gate, and over the gate a great castell [*?castellation*] with towers'.[36]

Between these two extremes lie a host of variants ranging from a royal Canopy of State' via Neptune's Throne, Virtue's Tower,

219

Farrington's Tomb,* Apollo's Palace, and a Senate House to 'the Castell of the God Mars'. Dekker, Heywood, Middleton, Munday and Webster all batten on this amalgam of a device, elaborating both its function and its embellishments. In treating of it here I only intend to discuss those examples which illustrate the most notable variants on the theme.

Fig. 14. The first scene in the story of Tobit as represented in an Elizabethan wall painting at the White Swan, Stratford-upon-Avon.

The tent found its simplest extension in the throne, being little more than an open pavilion containing a chair mounted on a dais and capped with the invariable cloth of estate. The throne prepared for Queen Elizabeth to view the water-show at Elvetham (1591) may serve as a convenient example for it is both illustrated (Plate I, No. 1) and described in detail. (See also Plate XXVII, Nos. 38 and 39.)

'This canapie was of greene satten, lined with greene taffeta sarcenet: everie seame covered with a broad silver lace; valenced about and fringed with greene silke and silver, more than a handbredth in depth: supported with four silver pillers moveable: and dekt above head with four white plumes, spangled with silver.'[37]

Such changes as could be rung on the throne as a device were confined principally to the fabric and colour of the pavilion. Webster, for instance, devised a Chariot for the Kings of England in 1624 and states that 'over it, there is supported for a Cannopy, a rich and very spatious Pavillion, coloured Crimson'.[38] The basic structure however of pillars overhung with drapery and surmounted by a canopy

* See Sir William Walworth's Bower, *sub* Arbour, p. 211 above.

or cover was clearly capable of extensive variation. The drapery could be translated into curtains that opened and shut or into canvas stretched on frames that could be painted. The pillars, from a basis of flag or tent-poles, could be reinforced and transformed into caryatids, classical columns and even into thick-set towers: and from there it was an easy step to translate the canopied roof into a battlemented terrace. It was this sort of variation in design which had differentiated the houses, temples and palaces of the mediaeval religious stage from one another (see Figs. 2 and 3): and apart from an inevitable change from the gothic towards the classical in architectural style I do not think we have any cause to think that the structures which served the same purposes in these sixteenth and seventeenth century pageant-stages were substantially different either in design or execution. We need not therefore assume that the Temples, Sanctuaries, Palaces and so on were as sharply differentiated in appearance as in name: consistency to general type rather than to particular design is what we should expect. The exception is the Castle which could hardly have been itself without gate and battlements: conversely, their presence normally forbade the structure being given any other name.

The point is illustrated clearly by the treatment accorded to those two perennial ladies of the pageant-stage, Fame and Honour. Fame was presented by Dekker in a 'House' (1612) subsequently referred to as a 'Temple', and by Middleton in both a 'Castle' (1617) and a 'Sanctuary' (1619): Honour was housed by Middleton in a 'Parliament' (1619) (castellated), by Webster in a 'Temple' (1624) and by Heywood in a 'Pallace' (1639). The latter is described as 'a faire and curious structure archt and Tarrest (i.e. *terraced*) above, on the top of which standeth Honour'. Another of Heywood's 'delicate and artificiall composed' structures which is said to be 'built temple-fashion' is nevertheless entitled the Gate of Piety (1638).[39]

This sort of cross-fertilization between elements formerly distinct to particular scenic units is further exemplified in Webster's treatment of his Temple of Honour which is distinguishable only in name from the arbour, the pillars being all 'bound about with Roses, and other beautifull Flowers, which shoot up to the adorning of the Kings Majesties Armes on the top of the Temple'.[40] On occasion however the device was subject to novel treatment unique to itself. Middleton appears to be conscious of this when describing the Temple in his *Triumphs of Integrity* (1623). He calls it,

'an unparalleled masterpiece of art, called the Crystal Sanctuary, styled by the name of the Temple of Integrity, where her immaculate self, with all her glorious and sanctimonious concomitants, sit, transparently seen through the crystal . . . this Crystal Temple is made to open in many parts, at fit and convenient times, and upon occasion of the speech: the columns . . . . of this Crystal Sanctuary are gold, the battlements silver, the whole fabric for the night-triumph adorned and beautified with many lights dispersing their glorious radiances on all sides thorough the crystal'.*[41]

It is Middleton too, who brings us up to date in respect of the 'Council House' of the *Ludus Coventriae* and other mediaeval religious plays by presenting it in its new guise of the 'Parliament' and the 'Senate House'. No less important to our understanding of these devices is Dekker's association of the 'Pallace' with the 'City'. The Parliament is said to be battlemented and decorated with twenty six lights: the Senate house 'reddye for the Children and Players to sytt in' and solid enough to accommodate musicians on the top. No further details are supplied.[42] The Palace or City of Dekker's *London's Tempe* however is better documented.

Fɪɢ. 15. The Palace or Senate-house, designed and constructed by Garret Christmas for Dekker's *London's Tempe* (1629): from a sketch by Abram Booth.

* Heywood took over this device for his pageant of 'London's Mirror' in *Londini Speculum* (1637). See Plates XVII and XXI, No. 26.

'This is called *Apollo's* pallace: because seven persons representing the seven liberall Sciences are richly Inthroned in this Citty.'[43]

They are to be recognized by their costumes.

'Those seven are in loose roabes of severall cullors, with mantles according, and holding in their hands Escutcheons, with Emblemes in them proper to every one quality.'

The Palace or City in which they were 'inthroned' was a two-story building.

'The body of this worke is supported by twelve silver Columnes. At the foure angles of it, foure Pendants play with the Wind; On the top is errected a square Tower, supported by four golden Columnes. In every square is presented the Embosd antique head of an Emperour . . .'.

A sketch, accurate in essentials but fanciful in most details, has survived among those made by Abram Booth of this show (Fig. 14). This structure has affinities with Middleton's Tower of Virtue of 1621 (*The Sun in Aries*) 'which for the strength, safety, and perpetuity, bears the name of the Brazen Tower' the top of which was castellated and gilded.

'. . . the top turrets or pinnacles of this Brazen Tower shine bright like gold; and upon the gilded battlements thereof stand six knights, three in silvered and three in gilt armour . . .'.[44]

With this description the transition to castle proper is all but made. Heywood completes it for us in *Londini Sinus Salutis* (1635), his tribute to the Ironmongers, the armament kings of the day, for he provided 'a Castle munified with sundry Peeces of Ordnance; and Accomodated with all such Persons as are needfull for the defence of such a Citadell'. Mars was the presenter.[45]

Two features about the castle deserve special notice. First it was a two-level structure as Dekker makes explicit in describing the 'Forlorne Castle' of his *Troia Nova Triumphans* (1612).

'There appeare above (on the battlements) Envy, as chiefe Commandresse of that infernall Place.'[46]

This rubric so nearly resembles the stage-directions of countless battle-scenes in Elizabethan and Jacobean plays as to suggest that a battle is imminent. In fact it serves as an excuse for a firework display: and this leads directly to the second point of note about these castles. I think myself that the association of fire and fireworks with these castles is undoubtedly derived from the Castle of the *Pas d'Armes*. Elizabethan examples of its use in that context come from Warwick, Bristol and Elvetham. (See Plates I and XXVI, No. 36 and in Vol. I, Plate VI, No. 8, and Fig. 1, p. 29.)

In Bristol (1574) two castles were built for the Queen to view and battle joined between them: the smaller of the two was called Feble Pollecie, was commanded by Dissension, and was overthrown by the defenders of the 'Main Fort' which, needless to say, represented the loyal city of Bristol.[47] Two years earlier a similar battle had been staged in Warwick where the Earl of Oxford and Sir Fulke Greville commanded 'a fort made of slender tymber coverid with canvas' and, aided by a dragon breathing fire, inadvertently destroyed some neighbouring houses to the great discomfort of the owners.[48] A dragon spouting fire was killed for Prince Henry's amusement in Chester in April 1610, and a castle was blown up on the Thames a month later as a major feature of Munday's *London's Love to the Royal Prince Henry*.[49] The castle could also serve as a prison. In this form the device was a direct extension of the Castle of Hell in the Miracle plays. (See Plate XVI, No. 20).

(v) *Ships, Sea-Chariots and Fishes*

About the ship there is not much to be said beyond the fact that it was amongst the oldest of the scenic symbols,* that it survived the Civil War and Commonwealth in traditional guise, and that it appeared as frequently upon dry land as in aquatic spectacles. It proved irresistible to all the major dramatists who also worked in the pageant idiom; and since an illustration of one of these ships has fortunately survived—that for Munday's *Golden Fishing*, 1616 (see Plate XXVIII)—there is little need to quote from descriptive accounts of the Argoe, the Joel, the Royal Sovereign, and other ships which cropped up so regularly.[50] Brief mention however must be made of the attempt to incorporate the ship into the triumphal arch. This was done in 1661 partly in terms of placing statues and pictures of sea and port figures and nautical scenes on the arch itself, and partly by erecting two stages, one of them 'made like the upper Deck of a ship', in front of the arch. The deck-stage contained a choir of sailors: the other an actor impersonating the River Thames with appropriate attendants. Nowhere perhaps is the contrast between the old emblematic tradition and the new landscape convention of scenic representation dis-

* See *EES*, i, Index, *sub* ship.

played in sharper conflict than within this pageant stage-cum-arch.[51]

If not actually presented in a ship the characters gracing water triumphs were restricted either to the floating rocks and island (see Mountain) or else to shells, whales and dolphins. Pictures survive of both. (Plates XXV and Fig. 5.) Musicians could be concealed inside these large fishes to accompany Proteus, Arion or singing Mermaids.[52] Little else however could be done to rescue these devices from monotony beyond what the painter and wardrobe could jointly achieve by way of visual glamour. If the bills of their expenses are anything to judge by, then they certainly did as much as money and craftsmanship could provide.

(vi) *Machines and Engines*

If the scenic emblems of the Middle Ages lived on, adapting themselves to the changed circumstances of a Protestant England, so too did the devices which caused globes to turn, devils to be fetched out of hell, and angels out of the heavens, and artificial rain or snow to fall on the earth. The Seven Deadly Sins were burnt in effigy on the Thames in the midst of a spectacular firework display when Christian IV of Denmark visited James I in 1606. Dragons flew and breathed flames: fire spurting from Zeal's head set fire to the Chariot of Error as a fitting climax to a long battle with Truth in Middleton's Lord Mayor's Show of 1613, a battle which, as we have seen, was fitly symbolized in a fog that could lift and descend to reveal or obscure the top of a mountain.*

Ascents to heaven appear to have been comparatively rare in the Pageants. For King Christian of Denmark, Divine Concord descended in a cloud from a Pageant in Cheapside to offer a cup and a speech in a manner reminiscent of the angel at Richard II's Coronation in 1377.[53] Heywood presented Sagittarius and fifteen bright stars 'appearing in the Circle hiemall' but does not specify any machinery.[54] In the show in Kenilworth Park (1575) of Gascoigne's authorship a stage direction reads 'Mercurie departeth to heaven' but no indication is given of how this was achieved.[55] Mercurie was presented to Prince Henry by the citizens of Chester in 1610 in a cloud machine. He was 'artifically winged, a wheele of fire burning very cunningly' and descended from a steeple 'upon coardes' to the sound of music.[56] A winged Angel appeared in Middleton's *Triumphs of Truth* (1613), but on horseback not in a machine.[57] Representing London's Genius the angel appeared

---

* See pp. 214–215 above.

again in Munday's *Golden Fishing* of 1616 (see Plate XXVII, No. 37). The Wildemen who annually scattered squibs among the crowd, and the harpy entering Hell Mouth in the painting of 1661 is the nearest approach to devils that I have come across. However, Thomas Churchyarde, among the entertainments which he prepared for Queen Elizabeth when on progress through Suffolk and Norfolk (1578), describes a very ingenious trap mechanism covering a pit which was devised to shroud a consort of music and also twelve water-nymphs.

'Firste, there was measure taken for threescore foote of grounde every way, the hole to be made deepe and foure square, whiche ground was covered with a Canvas paynted greene like the grasse, and at every side on the Canvas, ranne a string through Curtayne rings, whiche string might easily be drawen any kind of way, by reason of two great poales that lay along in the grounde, and aunswered the Curtayne or Canvas on each side so, that drawing a small corde in the middle of the Canvas, the earth woulde seeme to open, and so shut againe, as ye other end of the cord was drawe(n) backward.'[58]

The labour of digging this pit and the ingenuity of the device it was designed to hold are rivalled only by the making of the artificial lake 'cut to the perfect shape of a half moon' at Elvetham (1591) (see Plate I, No. 1) as a compliment to the Queen and to contain the 'Ship Isle' and 'Snail Mount' already cited for the entertainments there.[59]

By far the most popular mechanical device of the pageant-stages was the globe which opened or revolved. Dekker used it in 1603 to welcome James I to London (*Cosmos Neos*);* Webster to present 'seaven of our most famous Navigators'. Middleton and Heywood used the Globe which opened, Heywood's to reveal the four kingdoms united under the Stuarts, 'a round Globe squared', Middleton's 'suddenly opening and flying into eight cants, or distinct parts, discovers in a twinkling eight bright personages most gloriously decked'.[60]

(vii) *Costume and animal disguises*

The symbolism of the scenic units in civic pageantry was carried over into the costumes, head dresses and hand properties of the characters presented; and, clearly, the devisers of the pageants

---

* See *EES*, i. pp. 87 and 96 *et seq.*: Hodges, *The Globe Restored*, Plate 34, p. 147.

made sweeping assumptions about the ability of the beholders to interpret this symbolism for themselves. Personifications of figurative concepts like the Seasons, the Four Elements, the Seven Liberal Sciences, Virtues and Vices, of substantial realities like Cities, Rivers or of conditions like Peace and War were so commonplace that writers often felt able to dispense with detailed description of their costumes in an otherwise full account of a show. (See Plates IV and V, No. 6.)

Dekker provides a list of Virtues presented in an Arbour in *Britannia's Honor* (1628), but does not elaborate upon their costumes, saying simply that they are

'adorned fitting their state and condition, and hold such properties in their hands, as of right belong unto them'.

The Seasons, in another pageant in this same show, are 'in proper Habilments'.[61] Heywood in his *Porta Pietatis* (1638) assembles a similar throng of virtues and equips them with shields bearing mottos, and presents the Seasons in his *Londini Status* (1639) 'everyone habited agreable to his property and condition'.[62] (See Plates XII & XXIX, No. 41.)

On occasion however (perhaps when leisure allowed) very full descriptions are given. Middleton for example, in describing his Castle of Fame (*Honour and Industry*, 1617), lists the persons on the top, and proceeds:

'If you look upon Truth first, you shall find her properly expressed, holding in her right hand a sun, in the other a fan of stars; Antiquity with a scroll in her hand, as keeper of Honour's records; Harmony holding a golden lute, and Fame not without her silver trumpet.'

The long list concludes with Reward and Justice,

'Reward holding a wreath of gold ready for a deserver, and Justice furnished with her sword and balance.'[63]

Great importance was attached to colour; but little liberty was left for fancy within a code of colour symbolism that was at once so formal and so strictly observed. I have quoted some examples of this use of colour in costume from Jonson's and Dekker's descriptions of their shows for James I's reception into London in Volume I (pp. 107–109) and need not labour the point here beyond illustrating that this practice was not confined to these two authors when employed by the City Companies. Middleton thus represents London as

'attired like a reverend mother, a long white hair naturally flowing on either side of her; on her head a model of steeples and turrets; her habit crimson silk, near to the honourable garment of the city; her left hand holding a key of gold'.[64]

Webster and Heywood supply full lists of hand properties and headdresses appropriate to their characters, but only occasional references to colour. That the practice survived however is confirmed in the elaborate description of the costume worn by the River Thames in the second pageant of Charles II's reception into London (1661).[65]

Care was taken to distinguish both these abstract characters from mortals and English mortals from foreigners. This was achieved by close attention to the details of fashionable attire in continental countries and a similar closeness to observed fact in the portrayal of Moors, Indians, Russians and other strangers of exotic dress or facial appearance.[66] A very fair idea of the entire range of costume possibilities may be obtained by looking at the characters presented in Plates XXVI and XXIX. One of these is interesting enough in its own right to merit special notice, the costume provided by Anthony Munday for Richard II in *The Golden Fishing* of 1616 (Plate XXIX). A disguise so complete as to be something more than a costume, in the normal sense of that word, was that of the artificial animal: yet these creatures, like the pantomime horse, took their life from the people under the constructed frames and skins, and are thus better considered in conjunction with the Wardrobe than as machines or scenic devices.* With a long tradition of use in pageantry behind them, animals continued to serve a variety of purposes. Heywood used the peacock, the owl and the dove to identify Juno, Minerva and Venus in his *Londini Sinus Salutis* of 1635: these were probably carved models and no larger than other symbolic hand properties or headdresses.[67] Heraldic beasts, however, within or supporting the arms of the Livery Companies, were taken out of their normal setting and used again and again in life-size or larger re-creations to conceal the men who pulled the pageant-waggons through the streets or rowed them on the water. Sketches survive of Dekker's Ostrich of 1629 and of Munday's Dolphin and mermaids of 1616. (See Plate XXV, Nos. 33 and 34.) Beasts particular to more exotic countries —the rhinoceros, tortoise, camel or crocodile—held their own appeal for the holiday crowd much as they continue to do in Zoos today (See Vol. I, Plate XVIII and Plates XIII and XXVI below),

---

* Historical precedent exists for doing so as early as 1298. See *EES*, i, pp. 53–54.

but even so they rarely if ever appeared without emblematic justification, the tortoise, as an amphibian, for instance, being used as a mount for Proteus, or crocodiles to draw the chariot of the Nile.[68]

FIG. 16. The Ostrich of Dekker's *London's Tempe* (1629): from a sketch by Abram Booth.

(b) *Tournaments*

As both the presenters of civic pageantry and the audiences it was designed to please and impress were commoners, so both participants and spectators at Elizabethan and Jacobean tournaments were predominantly aristocratic. This sharply defined contrast, in the nature and circumstances of the two types of entertainment, made surprisingly little difference however to the sort of spectacle with which each was decorated. Whenever tilts or jousts at barriers were elaborate enough to be dramatized within an allegorical frame, place was identified for the spectators' benefit with the aid of the traditional, three-dimensional emblems of earlier times.

The renaissance exuberance of spirit, which had found perhaps its most magnificent outlet in the many Jousts promoted by Henry VIII, failed to find so powerful a champion in any of his children, for neither Edward, on account of youth and illness, nor his two sisters could easily emulate their father in challenging all comers. Tilting and jousting therefore, although continuing amongst the nobility as a routine pastime, was not accompanied in the middle years of the sixteenth century with either the imagination or the extravagance that had characterized the sport before the Reformation.[69] When therefore towards the end of the century pageantry again became associated with tilting, it had all the marks of an archaic revival attached to it, with first a virgin Queen and then a young Prince of chivalry at its centre: but with Prince Henry's death in 1612, Tournaments in England were doomed. What is interesting here is that the thirty-odd years in which the Tournament flickered into renewed vitality and splendour in the late Elizabethan Accession Tilts and the early Jacobean Masks at Barriers coincided with the period of most vigorous activity in the professional theatre. Moreover, there is that same easy migration of writers and artificers from stage to hall and tiltyard to be reckoned with and vice versa as has been remarked in the preparation of civic pageantry. Just as Sir Philip Sydney, Sir Fulke Greville and other Elizabethan champions of the tiltyard could concern themselves with the literary and dramatic issues of the moment, so Jonson, Shakespeare and Inigo Jones could devote some of their time and energy to the affairs of the Jacobean Tournament.

When Montmorency came to England as a suitor for the Queen in 1582, it was as 'the actors in this triumph' that the challengers and defenders in the elaborate tournaments of the occasion were thought of; and it was the 'princely pompe and qualitie of the actors' which made the occasion one of sufficient note to describe in detail.[70] The principal scenic device was called a 'rolling trench', that is a castle on wheels and described as 'a frame of wood which was covered with canvas and painted outwardly'.[71] In this vehicle 'The four Foster Children of Desire' (Sydney, Fulke Greville, Lord Windsor and the Earl of Arundel) laid siege to the Castle or Fortresse of Perfect Beautie. The latter, it is interesting to note, was nothing more elaborate than the Queen's normal gallery or balcony, overlooking the tiltyard and decorated by her presence in it.[72] It was clearly no great step from laying literal siege to this balcony to laying imitation siege to the music room of a theatre.*

Another tilt accompanied by scenic decoration was that at Westminster in 1590 for which George Peele wrote the verses. The principal scenic unit was 'a Pavillion, made of white Taffeta, containing eight score ells, being in proportion like unto the sacret

* For Jasper Mayne's jibe on this score, see note at foot of pp. 234 and 235.

Temple of the Virgins Vestall'. Five years later Francis Bacon wrote the speeches for another of these Accession Tilts organized on this occasion by the Earl of Essex. The device consisted of a dialogue between a Soldier, a Secretary, a Hermit and a Squire. Some of the speeches have survived, but little indication of what scenic units, if any, were used.[73]

Ben Jonson provided speeches for 'A Challenge at Tilt at a Marriage' in 1613 and Shakespeare was paid 43s. by the Duke of Rutland for providing him with an impressa, while Burbage received a further 43s. for painting it.[74] It is tantalizing that so little has survived by way of description or illustration of the scenic devices used at Elizabethan ceremonial tilts: but there is at least enough evidence to indicate that they were both directly derived from those common to earlier Tudor Tournaments and similar in appearance to those constructed for use in civic pageantry and other open-air entertainments of the Elizabethan era.* We are firmly assured therefore that what I have called the emblematic tradition of scenic decoration, which had developed from the mediaeval religious stage, survived despite the censorship of religious drama at both popular and aristocratic levels of society in the open-air festivities of civic pageantry, tilt and entertainment.

The Joust at Barriers carries us much further: for not only did it transfer this tradition from the open tiltyard into the enclosed hall, but it provides us with one of the most important examples of the transition from the old emblematic to the new landscape methods of representing place. In one sense of course both methods were symbolic rather than photographic to our way of thinking: but the difference between the three-dimensional forest-arbour and castle of Henry VIII's *Les quater Chivalers de la forrest salvigne* at Whitehall in 1511,† and the concentrated scene of mist and clouds which Jonson and Inigo Jones prepared for *The Solemnities of Masque and Barriers at a Marriage*‡ almost a hundred years later, marks a fundamental change of attitude to both the nature of the symbols and the manner of using them.

Comparatively full accounts survive of three Jacobean Barriers, and these are supplemented by a magnificent set of engravings of spectacular Barriers at Nancy in 1627.[75] Curiously the combat at Nancy, although the latest in date, is much nearer in spirit to the *forrest salvigne* than to any of those at James I's court. (See Plates XX to XXII.) Each of the combatants made his entry in a

---

* See *EES*, i, pp. 41–50, and pp. 174–175 above.
† See *EES*, i, p. 217.
‡ See pp. 232–233.

pageant car attended by torchbearers on foot, an orchestra either mounted on an animal's back or in another car, and by a spectacular emblematic pageant appropriate to the mythological character the combatant was himself representing. Thus the Comte de Brionne assumed the disguise of Jason: he entered the hall on board the Argoe, preceded by twenty pages for torchbearers, an orchestra of tritons, the island of Colchos with the golden fleece tied to a tree and guarded by a flame-breathing dragon and Mercury standing on a rock in front of his ethereal palace. This single 'entry' presented no less than five of the traditional scenic emblems, not counting the dragon—Island, tree, rock, palace or temple and ship.[76] Three others—garden, fountain and cave—were used in other entries and are illustrated in Callot's beautiful engravings: so too is the hall itself, showing the seating arrangements, the combat in progress and the large cloud-machine suspended over the entry-cars (Plates XX to XXII). The cloud-machine is described by the author of the text, Sieur Henry Humbert, in great detail.

'At the end of the Hall a sky was presented of the sort that one can see on perfect summer days . . . the sky being opened, light was revealed within it sufficient to distract the most penetrating gaze on account of the subtilty of the lamps . . . and out of it descended the seven planets richly adorned who spoke some verses.'[77]

There is no hint of a raised stage or a proscenium arch either in the text or in the engraving.

It is the more remarkable therefore that Ben Jonson in his Barriers for the Earl of Essex's wedding twenty years earlier should have used the raised stage and concentrated scene to much the same purpose.

'On the next night, whose solemnity was of BARRIERS (all mention of the former [the Mask of Hymen] being utterly removed and taken away) there appeared, at the lower end of the hall, a mist made of delicate perfumes; out of which (a battle being sounded under the stage) did seem to break forth two ladies, the one representing TRUTH, the other OPINION . . . These after the mist was vanished, began to examine each other curiously with their eyes, and approaching the State, the one expostulated the other . . .'.[78]

After a long debate about marriage and virginity, the ladies 'descended the hall', i.e. returned to the stage, where to drums and fifes the combatants made their entries on foot and without pageant-cars. They descended from the stage and marched to positions on either side of the hall facing each other across the Bar. The combats followed until,

'. . . on a sudden . . . a striking light seemed to fill all the hall, and out of it an ANGEL or messenger of glory appearing'.

The angel announced the return of TRUTH in a cloud-machine: and since what the angel says provides us with the source of Middleton's spectacular Pageant of Truth and Error of 1613 (see pp. 214–215 above) the speech merits quotation in full.

> 'Princes, attend a tale of height, and wonder.
> Truth is descended in a second thunder,
> And now will greet you, with judicial state,
> To grace the nuptial part in this debate;
> And end with reconciled hands these wars.
> Upon her head she wears a crown of stars,
> Through which her orient hair waves to her waist,
> By which believing mortals hold her fast,
> And in those golden cords are carried even,
> Till with her breath she blows them up to heaven.
> She wears a robe enchas'd with eagles eyes,
> To signify her sight in mysteries:
> Upon each shoulder sits a milk-white dove,
> And at her feet do witty serpents move:
> Her spacious arms do reach from East to West,
> And you may see her heart shine through her breast.
> Her right hand holds a sun with burning rays,
> Her left a curious bunch of golden keys,
> With which heaven's gates she locketh, and displays.
> A crystal mirror hangeth at her breast,
> By which men's consciences are search'd, and drest:
> On her coach-wheels Hypocrisy lies rack'd;
> And squint-ey'd Slander, with Vain-glory back'd.
> Her bright eyes burn to dust, in which shines Fate:
> An Angel ushers her triumphant gait,
> Whilst with her fingers fans of stars she twists,
> And with them beats back Error, clad in mists.
> Eternal Unity behind her shines,
> That fire and water, earth and air combines.
> Her voice is like a trumpet loud, and shrill,
> Which bids all sounds in earth, and heaven be still.
> And see! descended from her chariot now,
> In this related pomp she visits you.

Jonson was also responsible for the Speeches at the Barriers arranged in 1610 when Prince Henry was created Prince of Wales.[79] Unfortunately the stage directions are meagre. The Lady of the Lake is 'discovered': Arthur is 'discovered as a star above'. To 'thunder and lightening, etc.' Merlin rises 'out of the tomb'. Meliadus is then 'discovered' with six companions in 'St. George's Portico'. Meliadus (Prince Henry) is led to 'his tent' and a shield descends from heaven. There he is addressed by Merlin at astonishing length until Chivalry is spotted 'in yon cave'. This is the cue for the combats to start. Remembering that these Barriers were presented five days after the performance of *The Mask of Oberon*, I would suggest somewhat hesitantly the following approximate reconstruction of the arrangement of the hall.*

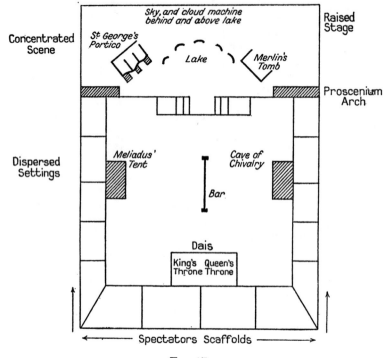

FIG. 17

Once Prince Henry and his companions had moved from the stage to their 'tent', Merlin could conveniently address his two hundred and five line oration from off the small forward platform directly at 'Meliadus' and at the same time retain command of his whole audience including the King and Queen.

Within two years of these festivities of the banquet hall and

* The dates were Jan. 1st and 6th respectively, 1610–11. Inigo Jones worked with Jonson on the Mask and probably on the Barriers (see Plate XX).

those in Chester and on the Thames, Prince Henry was dead, and in 1616 Prince Charles succeeded to the title of Prince of Wales. The Inns of Court were called upon to prepare a Barriers for this occasion. The text has survived and has been admirably edited by D. S. Bland for *The Guildhall Miscellany*.[80] Stage directions are virtually non-existent, but the scene appears to have consisted of a triumphal arch, an obelisk and four pavilions.

The Inscription of the Triumphal Arch.

Honori perpetuo. S.
Carolo, serenissimo, Wall. Princ. invictiss. F. R. Jacob.
Augustiss. et potentiss. mag. Britan. Fran. Hib. et Insul
adiacent. Imp. Princ. iuvent[.] religion. Justic. clemen.
fortitudin. aliaecumque patern. virtu. imitatori immutabili.

The Obiliske

Lex. pax. protectio. Securitas.
The Sheildes of the Pages
The Britane Knights. A goulden fleece.
The Word
Alter mittatur Jason
The Cicilians Aetna flaminge
The Word
Poena Gigantum
The Craetans. The Character of Jup. with a thunderbolt
The Word
Jovis incunabula magni
The Ciprians. An alter with harts offered.
The Word
Deae Paphiae[81]

The four groups of knights, British, Sicilian, Cretan and Cypriot were the disguises assumed by the groups of ten contestants from each of the four Inns. After a satirical debate between Truth and Occasion, the knights 'issue from under the triumphal arch', the Britons and Cypriots aligning themselves against the Cretans and Sicilians.

Whether the pavilions were simply tents, identifiable by symbolic escutcheons superimposed upon them, or fully developed scenic units is hard to tell: I suspect the former as they play no part in the action. It is clear at least that there was no raised stage or concentrated scene and that the staging of this Barriers marked as sharp a reversion to the pre-Jonsonian principles of textual construction as had Daniel's *Tethys Festival* of 1610 in respect of the Mask proper.[82] Certainly the audience were not impressed, for William Beeches writing to Dudley Carlton afterwards remarked that despite 'a grate deale of braverie' the show was 'contemptibly censured after the performance.'[83]

What might have happened to the Barriers (and the tilt) had Prince Charles displayed the same fanatical devotion to these martial exercises as his unlucky brother can only be imagined: for the fact is that Charles did not, and the promise of Ben Jonson's two essays in the genre was given no further opportunity to fulfil itself.

3 The Costs of Pageantry

Flickering through the pages of this chapter, like objects seen through a mist no sooner descried than obscured again, are hints of intimate associations between Tudor and Stuart Pageantry and the stage. Whether it is a Barriers devised as a sequel to a Mask, like Jonson's *Hymenaei*, or an author like Peele preparing texts for a ceremonial tilt, a civic pageant and a company of professional actors, or an actor like Richard Burbage lending his skill to all three, or whether it is a group of dramatists like Middleton, Webster and Heywood using descriptive phrases in pageant texts which resemble the stage directions of their own plays, the connection provokes a desire for more exact knowledge of its nature.

A start at least can be made towards obtaining it by examining both the surviving expense accounts of the varied forms of pageantry (which are remarkably full) and the statements made there and elsewhere about the craftsmen and the audiences for whose benefit this money was spent. The account books of the Livery Companies, for instance, supply us with an extensive source of information about the carpenters, carvers and painters who, working in association with the dramatists, realized the scenic effects at which they aimed and which they describe in the printed editions of their texts. Dekker, Jonson and Heywood make as many interesting comments about their employers and their audiences in these published texts describing their 'Triumphs' as may be gleaned from any other first-hand witness.

The Elizabethan and Jacobean Courts took over from the early Tudors the household arrangements for organizing tilts and jousts.* Permission was obtained from the sovereign to issue a challenge; and, when that was granted, it was duly advertised sufficiently far in advance of the occasion for elaborate preparations to be made. Having issued his challenge, the defender was responsible for meeting the costs involved, but not necessarily for providing the decorative equipment. The Revels Office, after 1573, served as a channel between the defenders and the Offices of the

* See *EES*, i, pp. 31–41.

Works and Wardrobe from whence scenic units and costumes could be obtained. The staff of carpenters, joiners, carvers, painters and tailors under the Surveyor of the Works and the Master of the Wardrobe could build scaffolds and make or hire from stock the costumes and properties required, while the Armoury could supply the ordnance and other necessary equipment for Tilt or Barriers. The services of the professional acting companies could also be called upon if required, at first as the personal servants of the defenders and challengers themselves and later as servants of the respective Royal Household. When it came therefore to presenting Tournaments on the public stage in plays like *Richard II* or *The White Devil*, we may safely assume that both text and action were drawn from life. In short, the arrangements were so similar to those made for the staging of plays and masks at Court that the matter can be dealt with under that heading and is accordingly relegated to the next Chapter.

A very different situation prevailed in respect of civic pageantry: for the City Government in London owned neither its own theatres nor its own acting companies and was at loggerheads with the Court about the total suppression of both. Nevertheless, where pageantry was concerned, it used the facilities at its disposal in a manner curiously similar to the Court. Indeed it is by no means far-fetched to regard the swelling splendour of the Lord Mayor's shows in Jacobean and Caroline times as deliberately rivalling the opulent masks of the Court at Westminster: for in the underlying basis of flattery and inflated self-esteem, in the extravagance of the expenditure, and in the spectacular quality of both types of entertainment, there is a similarity so remarkable as to be more than coincidence. As great powers among nations in our own times use military parades to impress the strength of their resources upon their rivals as tension mounts between them, so it is possible to sense in the ostentatious Masks of Twelfth Night and Shrovetide on the one hand and the elaborate land and water triumphs of St. Simon and Jude's Day a similarly dangerous and aggressive spirit beneath the theatrical cloak of these festivities at Court and in the City. Middleton, as we have seen, adapted for the City in 1613 the image of Truth, screened from view by a fog of Error, to which Jonson had treated the Court in 1606. This may not be a case of direct plagiary but, rather, an instance of borrowing from a common source: nevertheless the point is made either way that the image itself served both the mask of the banquet hall and the pageant of the street equally well. The connection had become explicit in Heywood's mind when preparing his *Londini Emporia* for the Cloth-workers Company in 1633. Describing the third show by land, he says that it

'is a modell devised to humour the throng, who come rather to see than to heare: and without some such intruded anti-maske, many who carry their ears in their eyes, will not sticke to say, *I will not give a pinne for the Show*'.[84]

If Heywood's use of the word 'throng' seems here to be as contemptuous of the groundlings as Jonson's 'men of grounded judgement' of 1603 yet the burden of his comment exactly parallels Jonson's bitter 'Get with your peddling poetry to the stage' in respect of Court Masks *c.* 1618.

It is Heywood too who makes the most significant of remarks about his merchant employers. Summing up his account of his show of 1631 for the Haberdashers, he wrote:

'Nothing here devised or expressed was any way forraigne unto them [i.e. the Master and Committees of management] but of all these my conceptions, they were as able to Judge, as ready to Heare, and to direct as well as to Censure; neither was there any difficulty which needed a comment, but as soone known as showne, and apprehended as read: which makes me now confident of the best ranke of the Cittisens: That as to the Honour and strength both of the Citty and Kingdome in generall, they exercise Armes in publicke, so to the benefit of their Judgements, and inriching of their knowledge, they neglect not the studdy of arts, and practise of literature in private, so that of them it may be truly said they are, *Tam Mercurio quam Marte periti*.'[85]

When too we compare the spectacle of Charles I and Henrietta Maria presented to an adoring court as the chief personages in Masks at Court with that of the Mayor and Sheriffs presented to the public gaze as the chief figures in the pageantry of Cheapside, it is not difficult to understand how Heywood could come to use the horrors of the Thirty Years War as subject matter for a pageant in his *Londini Status* for the Drapers in 1639: and in accepting it, the Committees of the Company showed a degree of common-sense realism entirely lacking among the courtiers responsible for the production of Davenant's *Salmacida Spoila* in the same year.[86]

It is reasonable therefore to regard both the Lord Mayor's Show and the Court Masks of the Caroline period as two faces of a coin which had parted company. This coin was minted in Mediaeval and Tudor times as the Royal Entry and in it both faces, sovereign and subjects, had been united in a shared experience. Charles I dispensed with a triumphal entry into London at his accession, giving instructions that the pageants which had been prepared should be taken down. Instead both he and his consort presented themselves frequently to the charmed circle of their friends and servants at Whitehall in the allegorical disguises of Masks, while the chief citizen of London took his place in the city two miles away, making an annual journey to Westminster the excuse for a Praetor's triumphal progress among the people. *

The cost to the City of James I's reception in 1603 was £784: the cost of the last Lord Mayor's Show before the Civil War was £787 3s. 4d.[87] The former bill was met by taxes levied on all the wards of the City: the latter by the Drapers Company alone. The Drapers had already spent £747 2s. 0d. for their show in the preceding year; the Ironmongers had spent £550 10s. 9d. in 1635; London's Tempe (1629) cost £537 11s. 0d.[88] These amounts are not large compared to the four-figure sums spent on the Court Masks: but as an indication of the City's wealth they tell their own tale, and when compared with the expenditure on James I's entry they point a moral as well.

The normal method of organizing these Mayoral Shows (at least by the end of the sixteenth century) was for the company concerned to appoint committees under the Master and Wardens to invite tenders, to judge between those submitted and to contract directly with the poet and artificers chosen for the provision of the whole show. Partnerships between dramatists and artificers became as regular as that between Jonson and Inigo Jones on the Court Masks. Anthony Munday partnered John Grinkin; Dekker and Middleton preferred Garret Christmas, a choice seconded by Heywood who also collaborated regularly with the two sons John and Mathias after the father's death in 1637. Poet and artificer together prepared their scenario or 'plot', costed it and submitted it to the company. [89]

Dekker and Garret Christmas for example presented the Ironmongers in 1629

'w(i)th a plott [i.e. of London's Tempe] wherein was contayned 6 severall Pageants

Namely   A Sea Lyon } for the **Water**
            2 Sea Horses:
            An Estridge
            Lemnions forge
            Tempe or the ffeild of hapines
            7 Liberall Sciences

* The word Praetor is used frequently in the descriptive pamphlets as a form of address for the Lord Mayor.

ffor the accomplishing whereof they demaunded £200, w(hi)ch theis present conceived to be an overvalue, and thereupon offerred them £180 w(hi)ch they accepted of for the making and finishing of the said Pageants to be furnished w(i)th Children and Speakers and their apparell and necessaries thereunto belonging . . .'.[90]

Included in the estimate are land and water carriage, 'green-men with their ffireworks', the music and 500 copies of the 'declara(ti)on of the said Shewe'. Unless I am seriously mistaken the document entitled 'The explana(ti)on of the Shewe on the Lo(rd) Maio(r's) day' preserved among the Ironmongers' records is this very 'plott'.[91] Thus, with the exception of Christmas' working drawings we possess every document of consequence relating to this pageant: the agreement with the Company, the plot, the total cost (£530 11s. 10d.) and many of the itemized expenses, Dekker's 'declaration' of the show itself and a set of sketches, albeit drawn by a foreigner and from memory at that (Figs. 5, 11, 12, 15 and 16).

Once the poet and artificer had secured the contract, it was usual for them to subcontract with carvers, painters, gunsmiths and other specialists, or to nominate them for employment by the company. Anthony Munday thus calls in a man called Clay, who is described as a carver and shipwright, to design the ship in his show of 1616 (Plate XXVIII).[92] Both in these directions, and in the vital matters of 'apparell' and music, the scope of patronage was large. I suspect myself that it was primarily for this reason that the City Companies usually appointed a man directly associated with the public playhouses to devise their shows, since his connections with actors (adult and child) and technicians of all kinds were closer and more reliable than those of other authors.

One group of people to whom this recurrent patronage must have been particularly welcome were the 'green-men with their fireworks' (close relations of the devils of the religious stage) and the performers of 'feats of activity' including drolls and fencers. Their part in the Lord Mayor's shows was often important enough to warrant separate contracts. John Bradshaw and Thomas Jones, Masters of Defence, were paid year after year during the early part of the seventeenth century for providing fencers; Hugh Watts for attending to the fireworks and the brothers(?) Robert and Thomas Legg for supervising the waterworks also received very large sums.[93]

Enough references to actors occur in the records to whet one's appetite for more knowledge of them and their duties: but the temptation to speculate on this account must be resisted as the references to specific individuals and groups are too widely scattered to allow it. I leave the reader to draw his own conclusions therefore from the following table of those references which I have encountered.

Date and type of show	Notable participants	References
1556 Ld Mayor's Show	Children of St. Anthony's school under Mr. Leese	MSC III, p. 40
1561 Ld Mayor's Show	Children of Westminster school under Mr. Tailor	EP, ii, 18
1566 Ld Mayor's Show	Children of Westminster school under Mr. Tailor (Quiristers)	MSC III, p. 46
1610 Prince Henry's Entry (London)	John Rice and Richard Burbage engaged to play 'The Queen of Cornwall' and 'Amphion' respectively in Thames water-triumph	EP, i, p. 231
1611 Ld Mayor's Show	John Lowen of the King's Men engaged to play 'Lepstone'	MSC III, pp. 81 and 167
1612 Ld Mayor's Show	Heminges, one of the King's Men and joint editor with Condell of the Shakespeare 1st Folio, worked with Dekker on the text and trained some of the speakers	MSC, p. 85 EP, ii, pp. 31–32
1613 Challenge at Tilt	Text by Jonson Duke of Rutland's impressa by Shakespeare and Burbage	ES, i, 148
1613 Ld Mayor's Show	A pageant said to be '. . . reddye for the Children and Players to sytt in'	
1616 Barriers (Inns of Court)	Burbage, Heminges, Field and Condell said to be gainers financially	Poem in Bodleian MS. Eng. poet c. 11, f. 72
1639 Ld Mayor's Show	Standings for ye Players William Hall	MSC III, p. 69

A complete list of the authors of the Lord Mayor's Shows between 1535 and 1639 is printed in Malone Society *Collections III* (pp. xliv–xlvi): from this it can be seen that of the thirty-nine texts of which the author is known, twenty-five were written by leading dramatists and only fourteen (including seven by Anthony Munday) by other poets. A list of the painters, carvers and other artificers who built and decorated the scenic units is provided in Appendix F. Considering how full this list is, it is unfortunate that we have no corresponding knowledge at present of the artist-craftsmen whose skill fashioned the scenic decorations for plays and masks at Court.

A factor of obvious importance in all these civic appointments was membership of the company most immediately concerned. Of the men listed above, Anthony Munday was admitted to the Freedom List of the Drapers Company in 1585, and by 1588 was employed by the City as a Messenger of the Chamber.[94] The actor John Lowen was admitted a freeman of the Goldsmiths Company in 1593; John Webster was made freeman of the Merchant Taylors in 1617; Middleton was appointed City Chronologer in 1620.[95] A charge of nepotism however against the Companies would be unjustified: the fact that the commission for the show was put out to tender and a choice made refutes that. Connections clearly counted for something, but so did the best value offered for the money demanded. *

Just as hard to determine is the exact relationship between the men commissioned to supply the text and those commissioned to provide the spectacle. Miss Jean Robertson has argued convincingly that the relationship changed: that where at the outset in 1540 the poet set the whole drift and tone of the show which the artist-craftsmen had then only to realize in three-dimensional form, the artificers gradually came to be regarded first as the poets' equals and finally as their masters.† She sees a measure of balance established during the first decade of the seventeenth century, and in a manner which avoided conflict on matters of aesthetic principle. By then the show had developed in scale to a point where each of the component items needed to be considered as part of a single artistic scheme, and not only in its own particular terms of reference. The scheme of the whole show and the writing of the verses were the poet's responsibility: the actual design (and much of the detail) of the individual pageants was the responsibility of the artificer. I believe myself that the poet was also what we would call the producer of the show, and that his fee (usually larger than the artificer's) was reckoned to cover this executive aspect of his

---

* See p. 239 above.

† 'Rapports du poète et de l'artiste dans les cortèges du Lord Maire,' *Les Fêtes de la Renaissance I*, ed. J. Jacquot, Paris, 1956.

duties as well as the 'invention of the devices'. Anyone who has worked in the theatre knows how the material facts of rehearsal can modify both a producer's initial ideas about the settings and a designer's first impressions of his producer's intentions. In a good working partnership each sparks ideas out of the other from first to last. Trouble arises from a direct conflict of personality or from a conflict of aesthetic concepts in respect of the relative value of text and spectacle. This latter difficulty (possibly aggravated by the former) transformed the early working partnership of Ben Jonson and Inigo Jones into a discordant feud of personal rivalry and bitter recrimination. No such conflict appears to have marred the relationship between the city poets and artificers. Heywood, acknowledging the contribution of John and Mathias Christmas to *Londini Speculum* (1639), carried compliment as far as it could go.

'For the Artists, and directors of these Pageants and showes . . . I can say no more but thus, that proportioning their Workes according to the limits of the gates [i.e. the City Gates] through which they were to passe, being ty'de not to exceede one Inch either in height, or breadth: My opinion is, that few Workmen about the Towne can paralell them, much lesse exceede them . . .'.[96]

The elevation of the artificer to the status of 'director' gives some indication of the change of balance effected between 1600 and 1640. Heywood's equally fulsome tribute to John and Mathias' father, Garret Christmas, in *Londini Artium* for the Haberdashers Company of 1632 provides some reasons for it.

'Scaturigo or Fountaine of Vertue

I come last to the Artist, the Moddellor and Composer of these severall Peeces, Maister *Gerard Christmas*, of whom (*si paruis componere, magna licet*) as *Augustus Caesar*, speaking of *Rome*, boasted, that hee found it of Bricke, but . . . left it of . . . Marble: So he who found these Pageants and Showes of Wicker and Paper, rather appearing monstrous and prodigious Births, then any Beast (presented in them) in the least kind imitating Nature: hath reduc't them to that sollidity and substance for the Materialls, that they are so farre from one dayes washing to deface them, that the weathering of many Winters can not impeach them: and for their excellent Figures and well-proportioned lineaments, (by none preceding him) that could be sayd to bee paralleld: In regard therefore there bee so many strangers of all Countries, and such as can iudge of Workemanship, come to be spectators of these Annuall Triumphs,

I could wish that the undertaking thereof might be hereafter con-
ferd (for the Honour of the Citty) upon men like able and sufficient.
For his owne particular I conclude: *Hunc aliquis vix imitando
superare potest*!'[97]

Interestingly enough William Davenant and Inigo Jones conclude
the printed text of *Salmacida Spolia* with a similar description of
their respective contributions.

'The invention, ornament, scenes and apparitions, with their de-
scriptions, were made by Inigo Jones, Surveyor General of His
Majesty's works. What was spoken or sung, by William Davenant,
Her Majesty's servant. The subject was set down by them both.'[98]

If, for what Davenant calls 'the subject', we substitute what
Dekker, Middleton and Heywood called 'the device' or 'the invention', the division of labour in the making of the Caroline masks
and the devising of the civic pageants of the same period can be
seen to be the same. Moreover, the amity within the partnerships
between poet and artificer in both genres displays a mutual understanding and acceptance of the respective scenic conventions in
which they were working. The style of the pageants, as we have
seen, remained consistently emblematic until the Civil War. It will
be my purpose in the next chapter to show that the style of the
masks did not: for we are confronted there under James I and
Charles I not only with a self-conscious substitution of landscape
scenic techniques for the old emblematic ones, but a conflict of
aesthetic principle between poet and artificer concerning which of
the two conventions best fitted the verbal exposition of 'the
subject'.

The regular public and private theatres of Elizabethan and
Jacobean times represent a middle point between the extremes depicted in these two forms of occasional entertainment, the one civic
and popular, the other courtly and sophisticated. If we can determine with any precision the differences separating the two
extremes, then we are in a fair way to learning what lay between,
and thus to determining with some measure of accuracy what
stage conventions and what production techniques governed the
staging of plays by the professional acting companies in their own
theatres.

VII

THE QUEST FOR THE IMAGE

1 *A Renaissance by Fits and Starts*

WHEN the political and social uncertainties of the Wars of the Roses at last gave place under Tudor rule to conditions of comparative stability, the arts in England had lost so much ground to continental thought and practice that Henry VII and Henry VIII found themselves obliged to import foreigners if the balance was to be redressed. The commissions extended to Pietro Torrigiano to work on the new chapel at Westminster (Henry VII's), to Polydore Vergil to write the official history of England and to Hans Holbein to paint the portraits of the new dynasty and its officials, form one aspect of this determination to place the English Court on a level with its continental rivals. The contacts established in ecclesiastical and academic life between English and foreign philosophers and teachers resulting in friendships like those between Erasmus and Dean Colet and Sir Thomas More were based on a similar desire to recover lost ground and prepared the way for far-reaching reforms. Another example—outwardly perhaps the most spectacular—was a change in both the scale and cost of Court Revels. From Italy came the new masking costumes (not without fears of scandal), and from France a growing interest in the literary and scenic possibilities of Tournaments.[1] The marriage first of Prince Arthur and then of Prince Henry to Katherine of Aragon brought England into Europe again and restored a diplomatic prestige unknown since the days of Agincourt. The Emperor Charles V was welcomed to London in 1522 with spectacular Festivities.[2] Even at popular level foreign example did not go unnoticed, the stages of the Flemish Chambers of Rhetoric having as marked an effect upon the elaboration of civic pageantry in Tudor England as French and Italian example had on the affairs of the Court and its offshoots in ecclesiastical and scholastic life.[3]

The speed of the recovery achieved by this courtship of foreign example during the first fifty years of the Tudor era is astounding. Unfortunately, for reasons fully explained in Chapter II, the headway gained was almost as swiftly lost following Henry VIII's divorce, his break with Rome, his subsequent excommunication and the reaction which followed against all things Latin or Italian.

Where the theatre was concerned, much of the 'new look' which had been given to the drama and to the technical means of presenting it between 1485 and 1530 had become deeply enough entrenched to stay put despite the reaction: but the reaction effectively prevented any further large-scale importation of Italian experiments either in dramatic writing or theatrical practice for another fifty years. The excommunication first of Edward VI and then of Elizabeth, followed by the mounting threat of invasion from an alliance of Catholic powers, frosted the first fruits of the renaissance in English artistic life, and injected a new and unexpected vitality into traditional forms of expression.* When therefore the political climate in England admitted a rapprochement with Italy after the defeat of the Armada, theatre practice in the two countries was again as seriously out of step as it had been a hundred years earlier when the uniting of the houses of Lancaster and York brought the Wars of the Roses to their end.

2 *The Classical Scene in Italy, 1485–1530*

In the years when England, under the leadership of Henry VII and Henry VIII, was attempting to catch up with her continental rivals, Italian thinking did not stand still. Indeed, the years 1486–1518 embraced a revolution in attitude to dramatic theory and practice which was destined in the course of time to transform the traditional emblematic theatre of all Europe into one of scenic realism, and to open the way to the motion picture and television dramas of our own time.

The seeds of this revolution were sown in Rome and had borne their first fruits before the fifteenth century had ended. The general interest among aristocratic society in classical antiquity found its principal theatrical exponent in Pomponius Laetus (1425–98) whose Roman Academy survived suppression by Pope Paul II to be championed by Sixtus IV, Leo X and Cardinal Rafael Riario. It was this Academy which sponsored the publication of Vitruvius' *De Architectura* in 1486, and it was to Cardinal Riario that the work was dedicated.[4] The books devoted by this Roman

* See Ch. II, pp. 25–34 above.

military engineer of the second century A.D. to theatre architecture and scenic decoration (Nos. 5 and 10) thus came to form the basis of all thinking about the staging of classical plays which, at that time, were everywhere attracting scholarly attention on their own account. Where however the critical study of the texts of plays and of treatises about the writing of them could be carried on in a reasonably exact manner, the study of stagecraft (like that of classical painting) was handicapped by vagueness. This vagueness was due in part to the fact that Vitruvius' work described only the late Hellenistic theatres known to him, and in part to the fact that the only tangible remains of the scenic arrangements in question to which reference could be made were ruins. The consequences were paradoxical: on the one hand to encourage (for lack of detailed evidence) a quite unwarranted generalized dogmatism, and on the other to provide architects and painters with considerable scope for personal initiative and invention in filling in the gaps on the practical front.

Roman enthusiasm proved contagious, spreading rapidly to Ferrara, Florence, Mantua and Milan: and by the end of the fifteenth century banqueting halls arranged for dramatic perform-ances in these and other cities had become the scene of active and competitive experiment in the staging of plays according to sup-posed classical principles. 5 These principles were clearly defined in at least three respects, all revolutionary. The first governed the relationship of the *proscaenium* or stage to the *scena* or setting; the second suggested the changing of the setting in the course of the dramatic action; and the third made the architect responsible for the planning of both. The idea of a raised stage was nothing new, nor was the idea of concentrating the scenic units which comprised the setting on or around that raised stage: neither, for that matter, was the idea of changing the locale of dramatic action within the time-span of the play's duration. * The novelty lay in the notion that stage and setting in classical times had formed a single archi-tectural concept deriving its artistic unity, and thus its validity, from the design and invention of the architect who built it.6 Formality in the overall visual appearance of the stage picture, and the appropriateness of this picture to the action represented, thus came to assume an importance in the art of drama which was al-together new: and it was precisely here that both the theorists and the practising artists found themselves in acute difficulties. The theorists, sensitive to the proprieties of unity in classical litera-ture, were anxious to see the stylistic unity of the text matched in

* See *EES*, i, pp. 151 *et seq.*

its stage presentation. This was an objective which architects and painters had no difficulty in accepting as an aesthetic principle, busy as they were themselves in the pursuit of the same objective in the fine arts. Where both theorists and artists found themselves in trouble, was in interpreting Vitruvius' rather hazy directions about implementing this objective in the theatre.

The multiple scene of mediaeval inspiration, however objectionable it became to neo-classical enthusiasts when judged in Vitruvian terms of reference, had nevertheless possessed many functional advantages which, let it be clearly said, the Roman theatre (and possibly the Greek) had never possessed. Chief among these was the ease with which actors and audience could move from one place to another in accordance with the demands made by the playmaker in his narrative: in short, for all Renaissance thinking to the contrary, the 'barbarous' Middle Ages had succeeded in giving practical expression to Aristotelian precept concerning the place of spectacle in relation to the drama.* In rejecting mediaeval standards and established methods of identifying place on the stage, neo-classical enthusiasts were themselves unwittingly opening the way to the subjection of the drama to the claims of spectacle.

The problem confronting the Italian academicians at the close of the fifteenth century and at the start of the sixteenth was how to combine the multiplicity of setting demanded by most plays (ancient as well as 'modern') with the formal unity of visual appearance demanded by Vitruvius in his description of the single classical 'scena'. Liberty was granted them in three very important respects: authority from Vitruvius to differentiate one genre of play from another in terms of the setting (tragic, comic and satiric, or pastoral scene); to change small areas within the surface of the *frons scenae* to accord with differences of setting prescribed by dramatic poets; and thirdly to employ perspective painting to achieve these ends.[7] The result was to encourage the development of an arched façade in the style of a basilica, designed to integrate the 'houses' of the multiple setting within a single stylistically coherent frame suitable to the genre of the play. Yet the more intensively this objective was pursued the more obviously did all semblance of genuine differences of locality disappear. The labelled arches of the woodcuts illustrating the plays of Terence are as ridiculous, considered as representations of neighbouring houses in a street, as the emblematic castles, palaces and temples of the mediaeval religious stage, considered as copies of actual castles etc.; both are symbols, differently ordered and disposed (see

* See *EES*, i, pp. 153–6 and 309–19.

Plate XXX and Figs. 1, 2 and 10). If the formality of the unified scene was to be preserved and yet continue to admit a diversity of stage-locality corresponding with that required by dramatic narrative, only two courses of action were possible. Either, means must be found to change the identity of the scene *during the progress of the play*, or plays must be written the whole action of which passed in a single place. The inevitability of this painful choice was probably not appreciated immediately either by the archaeologically-minded antiquarians and literary theorists or by the practising artists, architects and dramatists of the fifteenth century: yet this choice was the inescapable watershed destined to split the poet from the painter, the painter from the poet, 'dumbe poesie' from 'speaking pictures', the emblem from the image and to stir up a conflict of opinion concerning 'unity of place' that was to divide everyone interested in letters and the theatre throughout Europe. [8] Only the slightest hints of the likely trouble to come are discernible in the account of the staging of Plautus' *Menaechmi* at Ferrara either in 1486, or again in 1491, when Niccolo del Cogo was commissioned to provide the settings:[9] but when in 1514 Raphael succeeded Bramante as overseer of the fine arts and entertainments of the Papal Court, signs of trouble are discernible.[10] When, in 1518, the first play in the vernacular imitated from antiquity was performed in Rome with settings by Peruzzi entailing elaborate use of perspective painting, and when, in 1521, the *De Architectura* was published in the Italian vernacular, the battle had begun: for given artists on the one hand of the creative ability of Peruzzi, Leonardo, Raphael and their immediate successors, and dramatists restrained by pedants to imitating Latin plays on the other, there could be little doubt concerning which group was more likely to catch the imagination of the spectators, and, at their insistence, to win the financial support of princely patrons.[11]

The paucity of models left for the dramatists to imitate has not I think engaged sufficient critical attention. Plautus, Terence and Seneca were regarded at the time as adequate models on which to build the new drama because they were Roman. This is an attitude which has lingered, at least in academic circles, without serious question ever since. If however we were to suppose that all records of English drama were to disappear in the course of an atomic war with the exception of certain comedies by Oscar Wilde and Pinero and Byron's verse tragedies, we might legitimately wonder how firm a basis this repertoire of plays would offer to posterity for initiating a revival of 'ancient' European culture. Yet the situation confronting the would-be playmakers and poets of renaissance

Italy was not seriously different: for the comedies of Plautus and Terence were as far removed in time and spirit from their roots in Greek New Comedy as those of Wilde and Pinero are from their roots in the manners comedy of Restoration England, while Byron's tragedies could at least claim to have been performed, as Seneca's could not. Once we have understood therefore how ridiculously restricted the Italian dramatists were in being forced by the antiquarian zeal of their patrons to subordinate creative initiative to the imitation of so small a repertoire of plays by so unrepresentative a group of authors, it is easy enough to see why the architect-painters quickly took control of the situation.

The shape of things to come is clearly manifested in the success attending Barberini's *La Calandria*, which received its first performance in Urbino in 1513 and was then revived in Rome in 1518.[12] Descriptions of both performances have survived to us and indicate clearly that the opulence and the *natural* look of the settings provoked at least as much wonder and comment as either the play or the acting: no less significant is the interjection of *intermezzi* between the acts of the comedy.[13]

Descriptions of these early essays in scenic perspective are difficult to interpret accurately because of ambiguities in the wording. However, I think we can safely assume that by the time the Reformation began in England the architect painters in Italy had already won for themselves three crucial points which were likely to give them an advantage in any future dispute with the dramatists and critics. By fair means—that is to say with Vitruvian authority behind them—they had, like Jacob, deprived Esau of his birthright, by taking over for themselves the poet's erstwhile responsibility for the provision of princely entertainments. In discharging the newly acquired responsibility, they secured two further rights. First they could use their authority to deploy the 'mansions' or 'houses' of former days to organize a co-ordinated stage picture as nearly approaching an actual landscape as their individual mastery of perspective allowed. And secondly, they gained the right to give their handiwork an element of surprise by concealing it behind a painted curtain which allowed them to display their skill as landscape artists without competition from the playmaker.[14] By 1530, granted patrons encouraged by Vitruvian precept to finance ever more grandiose scenic display, and artists capable of exploiting the opportunity which that provided for creative enterprise, there was nothing left to stop the playmaker from dwindling into the insignificance of a mule that owes its keep to its ability to carry its rider.

3 *The Classical Revival in England, 1485–1585*

By the time that the trial of Katherine of Aragon had reduced the gaiety of the English Court to such an ebb that the Christmas season passed without plays,* these Renaissance theories of ancient drama and its performance had made considerable incursions upon theatrical life in England. From no source however is there the slightest indication either that painters had assumed the authority of their Italian counterparts in respect of Court Revels or that the concentrated Vitruvian scene was offering any serious challenge to the traditional dispersed and wholly emblematic scenes of pageant, play and disguising. Miss L. B. Campbell, in *Scenes and Machines on the English Stage during the Renaissance*, has argued cogently that many Italian precepts in respect of classical plays and their staging had percolated into England during the early years of the sixteenth century. Nevertheless, the haphazard nature of their entry forbade any immediate and widespread understanding of their implications: and, in my view, it was largely on this account that no attempt had been made in England, in either academic or artistic circles, to emulate Italian example in the systematic study of Vitruvius before Henry VIII started his divorce proceedings.

The only records of productions of classical plays at Court concern performances in 1527 and 1528 of Plautus' *Menaechmi* and Terence's *Phormio*, the latter presented by the boys of St. Paul's School at the invitation of Cardinal Wolsey:[15] but this does not mean that no other classical plays were performed either by boys or by adults. At Cambridge a play by Terence was performed in King's Hall (not King's College) in 1510, and a play by Plautus was performed in the Christmas season of 1522–23 in the hall of Queens' College. The latter was provided with 'houses' as we learn from this curious item of expenditure:

'pro clavis dictis Teynternayles, quibus firmabantur ornamenta edium in eadem comedia. j^d ob'.[16]

I would doubt myself whether this performance, or any other in England up to this time, was more advanced in its scenic techniques than the Italian revival of the *Menaechmi* at Ferrara in 1486. Records are so scanty as to advise caution on this point: but certainly after 1530 the vocabulary of English records becomes both fuller and more specific, while the expense accounts of Magdalen College Oxford indicate in a positive manner that a predominantly amateur

* See *EES*, i, p. 238.

repertoire of exclusively religious plays gave place at exactly that
time to a sequence of entertainments that is recognizably different
in kind. Indeed after 1530 the words *proscaenium, scena* and
theatrum as well as the terms 'comedy' and 'tragedy', come into
regular use in the expense accounts of most Colleges at both
Oxford and Cambridge.

At Magdalen, Oxford, one Hammons is paid 1s. 6d. (1538–39)
for three days work *circa proscaenium*: at Christ's, Cambridge 1s. is
spent in 1532–33 'for settyng up yᵉ stage for yᵉ play & for naylles':
at Trinity, mention is made in 1546–47 of 'the stage in the hall' and
a year later of *Expensae circa theatru(m) et ludos.*[17] These words
and phrases become increasingly frequent in all the records.

Of one thing we can be reasonably certain: the conscientious use
of classical Latin words to describe the work done or works made in
the course of preparing college halls for plays after 1530 displays a
growing awareness of Italian thought and practice in the matter. I
would go further myself in adding that the presence of a raised
stage in the hall (which had to be built and then removed) was
both a novelty in itself and directly attributable either to continental example or to an acquaintance with the text of the *De
Architectura*. Both sources of information are to be expected in a
University environment. Where however we must be careful in
our interpretation of these records is in translating the words
scena and *aedes* into English, for we have to remember that the
university clerks of the period could just as easily be dubbing traditional parts of the stage and methods of staging plays with the
most appropriate Latin name as be describing an exact replica of a
theatre or stage in the classical style. Eye-witness descriptions of
performances written in classical Latin must be approached with
similar caution and for the same reasons: a notable case in point is
John Bereblock's account of the plays prepared for Queen Elizabeth's visit to Oxford in 1566 and fully discussed in Volume I
(Appendix H).

Here a study of the emblematic tradition of scenic spectacle can
be particularly helpful, since the knowledge which we can derive
from it concerning scaffolds, scenic 'houses' and machines etc., at
once warns us against mistaking the presence of these production
items in school and college halls as being necessarily Italian im-
ports of renaissance inspiration. There is no question but that the
Latin titles given to these items are of renaissance origin; but the
items themselves can just as easily be traditional products of
native design and origin,* even when they carry in their decora-

* See Ch. V, pp. 163–172 above.

tion vestiges of a classical cornice here or of a capital there, or other echoes of a time when things Roman were welcomed into England and not frowned upon as evidence of Popery. Only when we are confronted with a raised stage at one end of the hall on which the 'houses' are so ordered in relation to one another as to provide the spectators at the other end of the hall with an impression of receding perspective can we be quite sure that the true Italian scene was in use.

One easy check enabling us to judge at a glance whether the stagecraft of a given performance conformed to traditional English concepts or to the new Italian ones of the Renaissance is the seating plan for the audience. If spectators were permitted to sit on the stage, more especially the sovereign or other important guests, then the scene employed was not Vitruvian: for the whole aesthetic of the Vitruvian scene as interpreted in the Renaissance was based on the ideal of providing the audience with a picture conforming as nearly as was mechanically possible to the landscape scene of real life, and this necessitated viewing the fabricated reproduction from a distance. If the scene itself was geometrically designed and laid out to conform with the 'vanishing point' of receding perspective, it followed that the vantage point for the best view of that scene must be as inexorably (because geometrically) fixed at a given height and distance from the scene.[18]

If points C and D in the diagram on p. 254 represent the extreme edges of a stage, then any movement from B towards A, or to either side of B, will result in a correspondingly reduced or distorted view of the scene as a whole.

I have myself found no single instance of a seating plan in England which demonstrably accords with this arrangement (outside the Court Disguising) prior to 1605: and until such a seating plan can be proved to exist in connection with an entertainment I would assert that the full implications of the Vitruvian stage scene, far from being mastered, were not even understood. In other words, the image had not replaced the emblem as the prime quest of the scenic artificer. His job was still essentially to make the stage action prescribed by the dramatist intelligible to the spectator in terms of the exits, entrances, ascents and descents and other comings and goings spoken of by the actors. He had the liberty, proportional to the money awarded for the purpose, to decorate these exits and entrances and supposed localities—house, palace, temple, sky, hell, etc.—as he pleased: but he was not required to impose any order upon them other than those of function and practicability. (See Figs. 1, 2 and 3.)

The chief advantage of emblematic stage conventions, as I have already explained, was the ready way in which they could be expanded or contracted in scale to accord with resources available to the company concerned. Two doors in the screen of a hall or church could serve to indicate two 'houses' as easily as two constructed

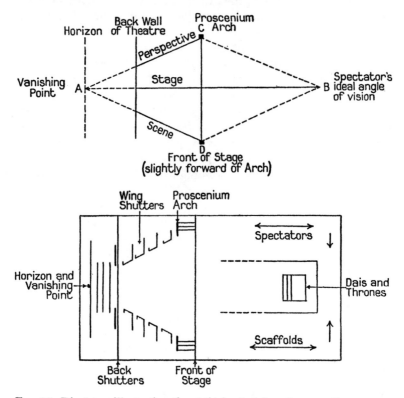

FIG. 18. Diagrams illustrating the optical principles of perspective scenes.
a) Serlian sight-lines.
b) Simplified outline of Inigo Jones' arrangement of the stage and auditorium for the *Mask of Florimène*, 1635: from B.M. MS. Landsowne, 1171, ff. 15b–16.

scenic units on a stage in the open air: constructed 'houses' however could clearly be more easily given an appearance of luxury than the doors of an existing screen, by virtue of the materials used and the skill of the carpenter and painter employed on their construction.* The identifying of the houses, whether simple doors or splendid three-dimensional units, was established for the

* Compare Plates VI and VII with Plate XIV and Fig. 10.

audience by the actors both within their dialogue and assisted by their mime, and in some instances by 'scriptures' or labels.[19] All this had been common practice for generations in the theatres of both worship and social recreation; and no Italian theorists or engineers were needed to instruct English artificers in how to make 'houses' or to teach dramatists how to provide for them in their dialogue. It is even possible that the use of a raised stage was suggested by the need to conceal trap-mechanism of the kind familiar on the religious stage rather than by neo-classical precept. This however I incline to doubt; for if this were so, then it should have made its appearance at indoor performances much earlier than the fifteen-thirties. As it is (and if the records are to be trusted), the raised stage is peculiar to the open-air theatre prior to 1530 or thereabouts. After that we find it present with increasing regularity in Oxford and Cambridge halls and, by 1541, in the Town Hall at Norwich.[20] By 1546, also from Norwich, we have a clear statement concerning the positioning of the stage—'the skaffold at the [far] ende of the halle'.[21] The first notice which places a University stage definitively at the end of the hall comes from Queens' College, Cambridge, and is dated 1547.[22] A raised stage was provided at Court in 1528 for a performance of Plautus' *Menaechmi* which the Venetian Ambassador saw and described as 'very well designed'; and although it is not specifically stated to be at the end of the hall, I think it unlikely that anyone as knowledgeable about Italian stage-craft at that date as the Venetian ambassador would have paid it this compliment had it been placed anywhere else.[23]

I think we can safely conclude therefore that the innovation of the raised stage indoors situated at one end of the hall had been made in England before Rome became a nasty word. Its acceptance became general within the next twenty years; and, by Elizabeth's accession, we have evidence enough from schools, universities, provincial halls and from the Court itself to state with assurance that this was the normal form of stage employed by all companies of actors whose claim to professional status was vested in the wearing of a nobleman's livery. This at least was a product of the Renaissance in the English theatre, and one moreover which was not seriously retarded by the Reformation. I suspect however that the reasons for its adoption by the professional acting companies were as much practical as theoretical if not more so. In the first place, concentrating the play's action both within the confines of the scaffold and at the end of the hall adjacent to the screen (i.e. the 'far' or 'lower' end as viewed from the dais) assisted the professional actor to admit more paying customers within the restricting walls of a small hall than the old *platea* of the central floor space. Secondly the screen possessed its own advantages both scenically in its emblematic possibilities and functionally in masking the dressing-room from public view.*

No such practical returns were likely to accompany any substitution of the Vitruvian perspective scene for the traditional emblematic 'houses'. The Vitruvian scene, because of its formal unity, was both rigid in itself and costly to construct. Moreover, it was clumsy to handle and difficult to transport. No professional company, with its eye on the margin of financial profit to be derived from its gate money, could be expected to take kindly to the financial outlay required for building the sort of settings with which Raphael had equipped *La Calandria*: nor was it thinkable to travel a setting of those proportions on provincial circuits with no certainty that the setting, even if it arrived intact, would fit the various halls available to the company in the towns and cities visited. By contrast, the emblematic 'house' was ideally suited to the needs of a nomadic professional company. Many of the simpler interludes could be performed with no more than two of them, and the two doors in the normal hall-screen could serve in themselves to differentiate the one from the other. From that point onward elaboration could vary according to local taste and to the resources of the moment. The doors could be dressed with hangings and supplemented with three-dimensional 'houses' set on the stage. An arbour, a rock with sliding panel combining the symbolic properties of cave and mountain, a couple of trees, a bed and a tent with variable trimmings to serve as palace, castle, throne, tomb or temple, could between them meet all terrestrial needs when the objective of both playmaker and artificer was simply to identify the locality of the stage action for the spectators. Many Tudor plays demanded, in addition, a practicable heaven and hell, and possibly a ship: but even when these items are included the total stock of scenic gear which an ambitious company required if it was to be equipped against all eventualities was neither large nor financially onerous. Canvas cloths with these objects painted on them could, in many instances, serve their purpose just as well as the more cumbersome three-dimensional units. In different circumstances the units could be ornately decorated and hold all the fascination of the most expensive kind of modern industrial models or Victorian children's toys.

* See n. 22, p. 371. The dressing-room or tiring-house is described as *vestium scenicarum* in the Accounts of Queens' College, Cambridge for 1540–41 (*MSC II*, p. 183).

If it is objected that the simultaneous display of two or more of these objects on the stage was likely to prove artistically offensive, the reply must be: to whom? Certainly not to the popular audience brought up to respect precisely this mixture both in religious plays and on the tableau-stages of the Royal Entries which co-existed with the new polemical fare of the professional interluders. Nor is there the least sign in the mummeries, disguisings, barriers and masks of the Tudor Court that aristocratic opinion was troubled on this account before Sydney's famous *Apologie* was published in 1595.[24] This cannot be said of Italian opinion in the period 1530–88: and it is to that subject that we must now return our attention.

4 *The Italian Landscape Scene, 1520–1588*

With the painters and architects firmly in the saddle from 1520 onwards, or thereabouts, Italian efforts to rationalise the ambiguities in the Vitruvian text progressed by leaps and bounds during the next thirty years. By 1585 the *Teatro Olimpico* had been built at Vicenza as a permanent monument to the degree of progress made. By 1588 (the year of the Armada in England) a further significant advance had been made in another theatre that can still be inspected, the ducal theatre of Sabbionetta near Mantua.[25]

Essential supplements to Vitruvius' *De Architectura*, if his precepts were to be translated from debatable theories into practical fact, were two other works by ancient authors which became widely available at much the same time. Euclid's *Principles of Geometry* was published in Latin translation in 1482, and the *Onomasticon* of Pollux (which contained descriptions of the machinery used in Greek theatres of the second century B.C.) followed in 1502.[26] These two works provided architects and painters with the tools needed to interpret Vitruvius' ambiguous instructions about scenery and how to change it. Euclid offered the essential introduction to the acquisition of skill in perspective painting: Pollux, the authoritative methods of changing stage pictures during the course of the stage action. By the time that Leonardo da Vinci died (1514) the art of reproducing a likeness of a three-dimensional landscape upon a two-dimensional surface had already been mastered by the painters.[27] This achievement could be taken over by the scenic artist in terms of the stage cloth or painted curtain. This provided the designer with his first essay in a change of scene: for one landscape painted on a front curtain screening the whole stage could be removed to reveal a second composite scene of three-dimensional 'houses' placed in front of a second painted landscape, or back-cloth. It was this technique which, as far as one may judge, Raphael employed for the staging of *La Calandria* in 1518.*

Further advances in this direction of landscape realism depended upon the development of techniques which would integrate three-dimensional 'houses' and painted back-cloth into a single composite picture, and which would allow the picture thus achieved to transform itself by mechanical means from the depicting of one locality into depicting another. Yet, within this dual objective, there existed a conflict of principle which had still to be resolved; for where Vitruvius had sanctioned perspective paintings placed on the *frons scenae*, or behind the openings in it, and had stated that these pictures could be changed by machinery, he did not so much as contemplate the perspective paintings being magnified to the size where they virtually banished the *frons scenae* from the audience's vision. In other words, the stage to which he and Pollux referred was still an author's and an actor's stage where pictures, whether painted in perspective or not, were admitted on sufferance to identify place. The stage which the Renaissance architect of the mid sixteenth century was contemplating was, by contrast, one on which play and actor existed as vehicles for a display of the architect's own mastery of geometrical and optical sciences, the manipulation of pigment and of his own ingenuity in the technical skills of mechanical engineering.

The spate of commentaries resulting from the study of Vitruvius, Euclid and Pollux, together with the constant stream of practical experiments in princes' halls, culminated in the publication between 1537 and 1547 of two works which were generally acknowledged to form the starting point of all future endeavour: Philander's notes on Vitruvius (1544) and Serlio's *Architettura*, the fifth book of which appeared in 1547.[28] A pupil of Peruzzi, Serlio devoted the second book of this monumental work to painting in perspective, principally in terms of theatrical scene-painting, or *scenographia*. Chambers, Campbell and Nicoll and others have described this book in sufficient detail for it to be unnecessary for me to outline its contents here.[29] Two comments, however, must be made on the general tone of the text and on its illustrations. Let us take the illustrations first. Three of them, the 'Comicall', 'Tragicall' and 'Satiricall' scenes have been reproduced time without number, but seldom does it seem to have been noticed that in the brilliance of the three-dimensional perspective which they

* See p. 249 above, and n. 10 to this Chapter below.

represent, all sight of the Vitruvian *frons scenae* has been lost. The 'houses' of the mediaeval religious stage are all there, disposed around the acting area in a manner resembling the lay-out of Fouquet's familiar miniature of the martyrdom of St. Appolonia, and with steps leading down from the stage which would have enabled Herod to 'rage' in the hall as conveniently as in the street had he been called upon to do so. Yet not only are the houses recognizably different in architectural style: they are subordinated in relation both to the acting area and to one another by the geometrical and optical requirements of the painter's 'vanishing point' on the 'horizon'. The consequences of this change are twofold. In the first place the 'houses', by bordering upon a single city square (or woodland clearing in the 'Satiricall' scene) restrict the stage action to that square and its immediate environment. No longer can two 'houses' represent places geographically as far apart as Bethlehem and Egypt,* or spiritually as distant from each other as Heaven and Hell. This is a clear infringement of the dramatist's authority in the theatre. The second consequence infringes upon the actors' authority: for no longer can they walk where they may want to on the stage, but only within those parts of it where their own physical height will not make the painter's receding perspective look ridiculous by dwarfing it.[30]

The impression which Serlio's illustrations of the three 'scenes' so strongly suggests of an endeavour to capture an image of the landscapes of everyday life in town and country is reinforced by his text. The realistic detail in which the 'satiricall' scene is described with its flowers, snails and other minutiae of woodland life, the mechanical devices prescribed for obtaining lighting effects, and the instructions given in how to employ puppets to supply an illusion of continuing activity at moments when no actor is on-stage, all indicate a striving to present 'the appearance of the real and natural' in terms of the artificial.[31] Nor, since these shows were the entertainments of princes and sponsored (again on Vitruvian authority) to impress, was the cost of the artifice of any account. Moreover, since they were designed to celebrate festive occasions and since the actors were largely court amateurs, nobody questioned the propriety of the cost or of the time needed to prepare these settings in the manner that professional actors giving regular performances would immediately have done.

Serlio defined the three types of classical scene in a manner which his contemporaries accepted as authoritative. His pronouncements on the nature of machines and of their uses were

* *EES*, i, p. 154. Also Plate XXX, No. 44 below.

regarded as equally oracular. What however neither he nor any of his fellows were able to achieve at that point in time was to relate the two, the scenes and the machines, so as to effect a complete transformation of landscape within the action of the play. Stimulus nevertheless had been given to the idea of attempting to link the use of machines to effecting changes of scene by Philander's notes on Vitruvius: but Philander, as a theorist rather than as an artist, was still thinking of both scenes and machines as objects seen through the openings in the *frons scenae* and not as applied to the individual scenic elements of the Serlian perspective landscapes.[32] This approach to the problems of reconstructing the ancient Roman theatre, involving a rationalizing of the Vitruvian text along lines suggested by the supplementary knowledge gleaned from Euclid and Pollux, was matched by the archaeological research of Daniel Barbaro and Andrea Palladio in the ruins of the ancient theatre at Berga, near Vicenza.[33] By 1556, when Barbaro published his own annotated edition of Vitruvius, he was able to couple the *periaktoi* or revolving prisms discussed by Philander with his own discoveries concerning the *frons scenae* derived from practical research.

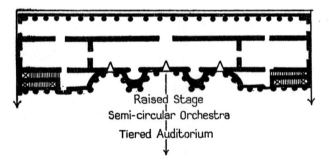

Fig. 19. Daniel Barbaro's reconstruction of the *frons scenae* of the ancient Roman theatre with *periaktoi*.

When therefore in 1580 Palladio started to build the *Teatro Olimpico* at Vicenza his work was at once reactionary and revolutionary. This theatre, built specifically for the Olimpic Academicians of Vicenza, was the first in Italy to have been designed as a permanent edifice and was thus revolutionary: but by its wholehearted adherence to the Vitruvian *frons scenae* defined by Barbaro, and by its rejection of the open Serlian perspective scene it was also reactionary.[34] Whether or not Palladio intended to place *periaktoi* behind the open arches in his *frons scenae* is an open question, for he died before the work was finished and left no record of his intentions. The building was completed in 1585 by Scamozzi, and in the event he chose to dispense with *periaktoi*, and to compromise instead with the Serlian perspective scene. Behind each of the five arches he placed rows of 'houses' made of wood and constructed in heavy relief, providing the spectator with several views of streets seen through the arches. Actors could walk up these streets as far as the division between the second and third house without destroying the illusion, but no further.[35]

This precarious balance between the findings of archaeological research and the creative inspiration of artists of genius, which the *Teatro Olimpico* mirrors so faithfully, was not long lived. It was Scamozzi himself who took the next and crucial step which was to settle the matter in the painters' favour. Commissioned in 1588 by the Duke of Sabbionetta to design and build another theatre, he seized upon the central arch of the *frons scenae* which, in the *Teatro Olimpico*, Palladio had already made so much larger and taller than its four flanking companions, and opened it up laterally to absorb its neighbours into itself.[36]

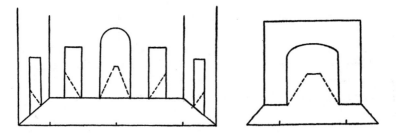

FIG. 20. Diagrammatic outlines of the *frons scenae* as reconstructed and adapted by Palladio and Scamozzi in:

a) The *Teatro Olimpico*, Vicenza.   b) The Ducal theatre at Sabbionetta.

As a result, he was able to offer the spectators a view of a whole city square instead of a street. He did not abandon the *frons scenae*; but what audiences at Sabbionetta saw through the arch that pierced it was neither an emblematic *periaktoi* nor a series of token streets but the full Serlian landscape scene. This scene could not be changed in the course of a play's action except by the removal of the front curtain. But given this technique and a working knowledge of *periaktoi*, it was only a matter of time before the comic, tragic and satiric scenes could be made, not only interchangeable

with one another to suit the nature of the play in hand, but interchangeable with alternative scenes of original design—even during
a play's action.

During those summer months that Scamozzi was designing this
building, England was at grips with the Invincible Armada.

5 The Italian Landscape Scene in England, 1530–1660

What then had the Italians achieved before news reached them
of the defeat of the Spanish Armada? Briefly, they had rediscovered
by patient research and costly experiment the lost art of perspective painting together with a knowledge of the approximate appearance of the Roman theatre and its methods of play-production:
but in their experiments they had also gone beyond the strict limits
of historical research. Partly on account of the meagre stock of
surviving plays which they had had to work from, partly on account
of the creative genius of the architects and painters principally
concerned, and partly on account of the personal vanity and
extravagance of many of their patrons, they had succeeded in sub-
ordinating both the dramatist and the actor to the architect in their
theatres; and, in the theatre at Sabbionetta, they were on the point
of making the architect the master of the antiquarian, the scholar
and the critic as well. Houses, heaven, hell, thunder, lightning,
machinery—in short, the whole scenic alphabet of the mediaeval
stage—were still present in the neo-classical theatre of their
making: but all of them had undergone or were undergoing a
change of name, and all of them had been reorganized in point of
placement on the stage to accord with the rigorous and constricting
demands of receding perspective. The auditorium too had been
formalized and rearranged to accord with these changes on the
stage.

At first glance, therefore, it seems extraordinary that in England
where, seemingly, there had been no comparable antiquarian or
architectural revolution, a group of young dramatists should at this
same moment have been ready to startle the world with the most
remarkable repertoire of plays written since Athens was the centre
of the Western world. By 1588 England, like Italy, had lost its
religious drama: but the reasons explaining this loss in the two
countries could not have been more different. In Italy, the *sacre
rappresentazioni* were a lost cause among patrons with the money to
sponsor them before the fifteenth century was out: in England they
survived, even if mutilated here and there, till 1570, when the

dangers to the State heralded by the Northern Rebellion and the ex-communication of the Queen obliged the government to suppress them. Thus, paradoxically, the Reformation concluded in England the chapter of theatre history that the Renaissance had ended in Italy. This knowledge is more important than it might appear to be, for it largely explains why English dramatic literature of the late sixteenth century is qualitatively so much better than the Italian, and why no scenic revolution occurred in England equivalent to that which we have just traced in Italy, before the execution of Mary Queen of Scots and the defeat of the Armada. The Renaissance spirit, held in check in England by the political and social perils which followed Henry VIII's break with Rome, burst out with fifty years of pent-up vigour into a theatre still dominated by its playmakers and its actors, when national security permitted it to do so.

Up to 1570 there is only one document among the surviving dramatic records which remotely suggests a fundamental shift of attitude towards the mid sixteenth century products of Italian experiment in theatre architecture and stage design. This is John Bereblock's account of the preparations at Oxford for the Queen's visit in 1566. His report is written in high-flown renaissance Latin and is given a prominent place by Miss Campbell in *Scenes and Machines on the English Stage during the Renaissance* as an example of the progress made in this country towards imitating the staging methods propounded by Serlio, Philander, Barbaro and Palladio. Her suggestion is important enough to warrant comment here; for, if it is correct, then the neo-Vitruvian scene must be taken into serious account as one of the precedents informing the design of the Elizabethan public theatres. That her suggestion is groundless, I am myself certain. I have supplied the reader with a reprint of Bereblock's original Latin text, together with a literal translation, a detailed commentary and two sketches in Volume I (Appendix H, pp. 355–59). To this I need only add two further comments now. First, the fact that the Queen's throne was placed on the stage automatically precluded the use of the neo-Vitruvian scene as interpreted by Serlio, i.e. the open, 'comicall', 'tragicall' or 'satiricall' scene. Secondly, the fact that the 'houses' were built *ex utroque scenae latere* (on *both* sides of the stage) just as automatically precludes our assuming the presence of Barbaro's *frons scenae* with either *periaktoi*, or streets in bas-relief, behind its openings.

Miss Campbell cites, as further evidence of neo-classical staging methods at Oxford, the machinery used in 1583 in the plays performed to celebrate the Palatine of Siradia's visit,

'Mercurie and Iris descending and ascending from and to an high place, the tempest wherein it hailed small comfects, rained rose water and snewd [*snowed*] an artificial kind of snew, all strange, marvellous and abundant.'[37]

Mercury and Iris may have been comparatively new inhabitants of cloud-machines, but the machine itself had been in use on the English stage for over two hundred years. And 'marvellous' as the hail, rain and snow may have seemed, this does not alter the fact that all three had been employed by the citizens of York to welcome Henry VII nearly a hundred years earlier. *

More pertinent is the evidence which Miss Campbell produces of a knowledge of perspective painting in the Revels Office post-1570.

'The connynge of the office resteth in skill of devise, in understanding of historyes, in iudgement of commedies, tragedyes and shewes, in sight of perspective and architecture, some smacke of geometrye and other thinges wherefore the best helpe is for the officers to make good choyce of cunynge artificers . . .'.[38]

As Miss Campbell observes, the document also specifies that a plot is to be made and that it is

'to be drawen and sett fourthe in payntinge by some connynge Artificer in that Arte and to be considered of by all the officers'.

These plots however do not prove the use of Serlian scenes, for as we have seen, they were being demanded of artificers working on the Lord Mayor's shows as early as 1556:[39] nor do I think that the requirements 'in sight and perspective and architecture' and of 'some smacke of geometrye and other thinges' amounts to more than what would be needed to design and paint a cloth, or to build a banquet hall equipped with a raised stage and tiered scaffold round its walls.

The implications of the raised stage have already been considered:† perspective cloths remain to be discussed. Two examples of such cloths in stage use, but in simultaneous settings, are illustrated for us. The first is to be seen in the French *Ballet Comique* of 1582, employed as a backing to Circe's Garden (see Vol. I, Plate XXVII). The second serves a similar purpose in the sea battle presented in the Cortile of the Pitti Palace at Florence in

---

* See *EES*, i, pp. 95–96.
† See pp. 255–256 above.

1589 (see Vol. I, Plate XXIV).* Both cloths represent cities, but in both instances the cloth is clearly used as an emblem of a landscape and not as a component item in an artificially constructed landscape. This is the crucial difference. In Florence the knowledge of how to construct a Serlian landscape scene undoubtedly existed: in France this is more doubtful.[40] That scenic cloths were provided at the English Court is proved by entries in the Revels Office Accounts between 1580 and 1585: and the probability is that the knowledge of perspective painting possessed by the Master or Yeoman was employed in the painting of these emblematic cloths.[41]

It is reasonable therefore for us to regard the process noticed in the period 1485–1530 of absorbing superficial details of Italian stage techniques into English theatre practice to have continued through the next fifty years, if at a slower pace on account of Reformation prejudice. A knowledge of Euclid and Italian thinking on the subject of architecture can be assumed in England after 1563 when John Shute published his *First and Chief Grounds of Architecture*, if not before, since he acknowledges his debt to Vitruvius, Serlio and Philander in introducing his work, despite confining his actual text to a discussion of the five orders of architecture. The crucial factors in England however continued to be the restraining influences of the professional actors, and of Protestant antipathy to Rome, Latin, and by extension to things Italian. The nomadic actors, given their normal equipment of a raised stage backed by a two-door screen supporting a gallery, and a stock of scenic emblems, had nothing to gain from costly experiments with the neo-

* In Vol. I, I published two engravings illustrating 'a typical Renaissance *Banqueting Hall* arranged for a Disguising of the traditional mediaeval kind, probably Italian or French, *c.* 1500' (Plate XXIV, Nos. 35 and 36: note p. 398). I had myself failed to identify these engravings, but simultaneously with the publication of Volume I, Professor A. M. Nagler published an article 'Theater Der Medici', *Maske und Kothurn*, IV (1958) No. 2/3, pp. 168–98, from which it becomes clear that they represent the Cortile of the Pitti Palace in Florence in 1589, roofed over with red satin and prepared for an aquatic tournament in masquerade as part of the marriage festivities arranged for Christine de Lorraine and the Grand Duke of Tuscany.

Shortly afterwards, the pictures were independently identified for me by Mr. Christopher Marsden of Newton Hall, Cambridge. I am further indebted to him for a microfilm copy of the text describing these events: Giuseppe Pavoni, *Diario descritto da Giuseppe Pavoni Delle Feste celebrate nella solenissime Nozze dell Serenissimi Sposi, il Sig. Gran Duchi di Toscanna,* Bologna (Giovanni Rossi, 1589), pp. 35 *et seq.*, taken from the unique copy in the Bibliothèque de l'Arsenal—C 93.830 [Arsenal Ra 5.148] together with a long critical note of his own.

A transcript of the text and a translation, together with Mr. Marsden's note, are printed in Appendix H, pp. 341–348 below.

classical stage which was difficult to handle and transport. Protestant opinion however, much as the more moderate section of it
may have wished for a swift rapprochement with Italy and Italian
achievement, could not regard the excommunication of the Queen
as anything but a threat to national security and international
peace. Active and overt flirtation with the literature and *mores* of
classical Rome became identified, by association, with missals,
friars, vestments and other 'rags of Rome', and laid the sponsor
open to charges of idolatry: and, as the dual threat from Scotland
and from Spain increased, these could quickly be translated into
charges of high-treason. The more fanatical spirits, while concentrating their attack on the theatre—doubly vulnerable as Roman
Catholic in origin and neo-classical in pretension—did not hesitate
to include poetry within their criticism. When Stephen Gosson in
1579 went so far as to dedicate a work in this vein to Sydney (*The
School of Abuse*), it provoked a reply which marked a turning of the
tide.[42] Sydney's retort (*The Defence of Poesie*) was written in 1581,
was highly critical of contemporary literary methods and dramatic
art, as practised in England, and was unreserved in its praise of
classical precept. The work was written in the spirit of the editors
of Vitruvius, but it is significant that Sydney elected not to publish
it. The first edition appeared in 1595, six years after his death,
under the title of *An Apologie for Poetry*, by which time the dangers
from Scotland, Spain and Rome had largely passed. Earlier Elizabethan critics, notably Ascham and Puttenham (like Udall and
Bucer before them), had commended the plays of the ancient
authors to the attention of schoolboys and statesmen alike, but on
grounds of the purity of the Latin in which they were written: on
the subject of the morality professed in them they were more reserved.[43] Sydney's *Apologie* was the first critical work in English
that took the question of play production into any serious account:
and even that brief excursion into the subject was concerned with
unity of place and not Serlian 'scenography'.[44] In other words,
Sydney's concern was with propriety, not with the provision of
artificial landscapes. Had he been aware of the uses to which this
classical concern for propriety was being put in the Italian intermezzi of that time, I can scarcely think it would have received his
approval any more than it was to appeal to Ben Jonson, once the
first fine careless rapture of his partnership with Inigo Jones had
worn off.

Summing up then, I can find no more evidence to suggest that
the strictly Elizabethan public theatres owed their design to
Vitruvian, Serlian or Palladian precept than exists in fact to prove

that the design was developed either from the inn-yards of Tudor London or the pageant-waggons of the religious stage. If one must indulge in the dangerous guessing-game of attributing borrowings, then I think one may fairly attribute the design of the 'frame' to the earlier game-houses and tournament arenas. The raised stage, two-doored screen, gallery and painted woodwork of the De Witt sketch can legitimately be looked on as indirect borrowing from neo-Vitruvian precept embodied in the staging facilities of the banquet-chamber and town-hall as rearranged by Tudor Chamberlains. With similar caution, I would attribute the emblematic nature of the stage-directions in Elizabethan plays to a borrowing from the conventions of the religious stage preserved, after the suppression of the latter, in all forms of pageantry. To the inn-yards I can attribute nothing unless it be the ground-plan of the Fortune Theatre.

By far the most important evidence however to prove that all strictly Elizabethan staging—whether in the public theatres, the private theatres, the banquet chambers of the Court or the town-halls of provincial cities—corresponded more nearly to the emblematic methods of the Lord Mayor's Shows than to the landscape scenes of the Italian intermezzi comes from the printed texts of the Masks staged at court after 1605. These texts, embellished with stage directions in language more appropriate to modern photography than ancient Heraldry, bring us into touch with a self-conscious quest to reproduce in the theatre the images of actual life. Aurelian Townshend and William Davenant describe the Masks for which they wrote songs and verses at the Court of Charles I in a language that is immediately identifiable with that used by Serlio and his successors in Italy. Ben Jonson, before he was displaced by Davenant and others as an author of masks, grasped the implications of such language firmly enough to heap the derision of his satire upon it: but he, like them, came to this understanding of it by the hard practical road of a working partnership with 'Vitruvius Britannicus' or, as Ben styled him, Inigo, Marquis Would-be.

The partnership started with Queen Anne's Mask for Twelfth Night 1604/5, *The Mask of Blackness*.[45] Jonson was in full control, devising the subject of the Mask (what he calls 'the invention') writing the text and providing readers after the event with copious footnotes to justify his every step. Jones, freshly returned after two years of study in Italy, provided a single setting and a front curtain. Whether Jones had visited Vicenza or Sabbionetta on this first journey abroad is at present not known: what is certain is that he had acquired the skill to do what Peruzzi had achieved in decorating the Rome production of *La Calandria* in 1518, for it is just this kind of a setting that Jonson describes as the 'bodily part' of the *Mask of Blackness* and which, as he remarks, 'was of master Inigo Jones's design and act'.[46]

This relationship of poet and artificer in the preparation of Masks is as crucial to their development as that which we have traced in the very different context of the Royal Entries and the Lord Mayor's shows. Where the *Mask of Blackness* was concerned, Jonson enjoyed authority enough as the man responsible for subject and text to allow Jones a free hand, the more especially since Jones' ideas *appeared* to reinforce his own expressed views about the desirability of imitating Italian example. Yet the very language which Jonson uses to describe Jones' contribution conceals, ironically enough, the *causa bellandi* that was in due time to shatter the seeming amity of the partnership. I have quoted the opening stage direction (p. 4 above) in which the word 'Landscape' occurs, printed strikingly in black-letter type; another passage in this long direction merits quotation here. Having described the front curtain and the setting revealed when that curtain fell, he passes to the backcloth.

'... the scene behind seemed a vast sea (and united with this that flowed forth) from the termination, or horizon of which (being the level of the State [i.e. *the King's throne*] which was placed in the upper end of the hall) was drawn by the lines of perspective, the whole work shooting downwards from the eye'.[47]

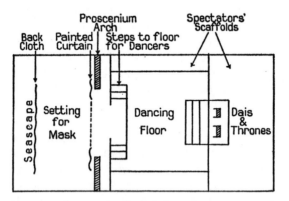

FIG. 21 a). Conjectural reconstruction of the arrangements in the hall for the *Mask of Blackness* (1604/5).

Compare this with the scenic arrangements for Samuel Daniel's

Vision of Twelve Goddesses of the preceding year and the degree of change wrought by Jones, even as the inferior partner, is at once apparent.[48]

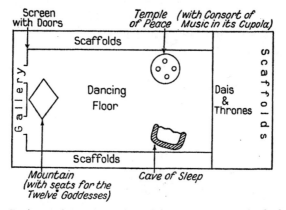

FIG. 21. b) Conjectural reconstruction of the arrangements in the hall for the *Vision of Twelve Goddesses* (1603/4).

Jonson does not appear to have recognized the challenge implicit in Jones' redistribution of the scene in accordance with the principles of optical science. Year after year the partnership proceeded on its way with only such interruptions as circumstance made inevitable. One of these was the death of Prince Henry. Jones, temporarily out of a job, took the occasion to renew his acquaintance with Italy. This time he undoubtedly visited Vicenza, for he annotated his copy of Palladio's works with detailed observations of his own about the *Teatro Olimpico*. He also became acquainted with Giulio Parigi's many spectacular designs for the Florentine Festival of 1608.[49]

Before this visit he had collaborated with Jonson on *Hymenaei* and the subsequent Barriers (1606), *The Hue and Cry after Cupid* (1608), the *Mask of Queens* (1609) and *Oberon*, and Prince Henry's Barriers, in 1612.[50] In none of these masks did he attempt anything more drastic in general concept than Jonson had already sanctioned in respect of *The Mask of Blackness*. In each he made some minor experiment or other, none of them however sufficiently significant *in itself* to give Jonson any cause for alarm.[51] Indeed, in one sense, this sequence of masks is surprisingly reminiscent of Daniel's *Twelve Goddesses* and of the Lord Mayor's Shows in that the principal scenic device is one or other of the familiar emblematic units—the sea-chariot of Oceanus (*Blackness*), the revolving globe which opened (*Hymenaei*), the Throne of Beauty, the Rock which opened, the House of Fame, and so on. Moreover, Jonson himself in setting the seal of his approval upon the anti-mask in 1609, provided Jones with an open invitation to extend his own contribution to the entertainment. The consequences however of all these minor experiments, innovations and changes, allied to Jones' researches in Italy, found its collective expression in the Christmas season of 1617 with the production of *The Vision of Delight*. The stage directions, which are very brief, tell their own story.

1. The SCENE,—A Street in Perspective of fair building discovered.

> DELIGHT
>
> Is seen to come as afar off, accompanied with GRACE, LOVE, HARMONY, REVEL, SPORT, LAUGHTER. WONDER following.

> Stilo recitativo

2. 'Here the first ANTIMASK entered.
   A She-monster delivered of six BURRATINES, that dance with six PANTALOONS:'

. . . .

3. 'Here the NIGHT rises [slowly], and takes her chariot bespangled with stars.'

. . . .

4. 'By this time the Night and Moon being both risen: NIGHT hovering over the place, sung.'

. . . .

5. 'The Scene here changed to cloud, and PHANT'SIE breaking forth, spake.'

. . . .

6. 'Here the second Antimask of Phantasms came forth which danced.'

. . . .

7. 'Here one of the HOURS descending, the whole scene changed to the bower of ZEPHYRUS, whilst PEACE sung as followeth.'

. . . .

8. 'Here (to a loud music), the Bower opens, and the MASKERS are discovered as the Glories of the Spring.'

. . . .

9. 'Here they danced their ENTRY, after which they sung again.'

. . . .

10. 'They danced their Main Dance, after which they sung.'

. . . .

11. 'They danced with LADIES, and the whole REVELS followed; after which AURORA appeared, (the Night and Moon [being] descended,) and this Epilogue followed.'

. . . .

12. 'Here they danced their going off and ENDED.'[52]

In all of this only the 'bower of Zephyrus' remains to remind us of the emblematic tradition of identifying place on the stage. The street, the night sky and the coming of dawn are all essays in the new landscape techniques, and even the bower is so treated as to form a further landscape which, by providing variety and contrast, avoided the risk of the closed scene becoming monotonous to watch.

Scarcely less important is Jones' obvious concern with the extremes of light and shade obtainable within his pictures, or 'chiaroscuro'. The great masters of this art in painting were Tintoretto, Caravaggio and Rembrandt, all of them contemporaries of Jones; and it is scarcely necessary to observe that nothing is more obviously dramatic in painting than the effects obtainable from mysterious shadows, sharp silhouettes and the illumination of particular features by some particular source of light like a candle or a ray of sunshine. Serlio had spoken with all the force of dogmatic pronouncement on the possibilities which skilled illumination added to the landscape scene.[53] The visitor to the Teatro Olimpico may still see the little coloured-glass lamps suspended in iron brackets behind the up-stage edges of the wooden houses in the street perspectives behind the arches in the *frons scenae*. The glow of hundreds of these oil lamps and the candles, flickering iridescently, provides a form of illumination infinitely more subtle than anything that can be achieved by the harder and more brilliant effect of gas or electric light.[54] Jones' use of the pictorial contrasts obtainable by means of concentrations of lamps was frequent and calculated. On occasions however the device could be used emblematically, as in Jonson's *Mask of Augurs*, where, after the second Antimask,

'which was a perplexed DANCE of straying and deformed PILGRIMS taking several paths, till with the opening of the light above, and breaking forth of APOLLO, they were all frighted away . . .'.[55]

Light had been used for its spectacular quality in open-air pageantry and in Court Disguisings of an earlier time. But nothing approaching the aesthetic novelty of chiaroscuro effects within a landscape

271

or used to contrast one landscape with another could be provided within the perambulatory spectacle of the Lord Mayor's Shows. Even Middleton's 'mount of Truth' screened by its dispersable 'fog of Error' appears tame by comparison: for Jones had proved it possible not only to reproduce the landscapes familiar in life by artificial means upon the stage, but to change these pictures at will and on the spot, and even to impose sufficient order upon artificial light to reproduce the contrast between day and night realistically. The price of this achievement, apart from the financial one, was the same curtailment of the dramatist's and the actor's freedom of action as we have noticed in Italian drama. A lesser man than Jonson might still not have recognized the challenge implicit in this situation; but not for nothing was he esteemed the greatest scholar of his day. As so often happens when matters of great moment are at stake, enlightenment was triggered off by an incident that was in itself childish, and unworthy of both men.

Jones, having mastered the crafts (arts as he claimed) of the landscape scenes invented by his Italian mentors, had himself invented means of changing them in the course of dramatic action. He felt entitled therefore to some share in the credit for the 'invention' which Jonson had hitherto reserved to himself. Jonson, already acknowledged as the best writer of masks, had duly awarded Jones the credit for 'the bodily part' of the masks on which they had worked together: but the invention, or devising of them, and the responsibility for its general treatment, had become disputed territory, since Jones could now achieve more than Jonson necessarily wished to contemplate, and saw no reason why his patrons should be denied the spectacle he could offer them for no better reason than Jonson's literary scruples. This is the essence of that conflict of principle which underlay the trivial dispute about whose name should take precedence on the title page of the *Mask of Augurs* in 1618.[56]

It is difficult to be dispassionate about this quarrel and to avoid taking the part of one or other of the protagonists. When however as sensitive and authoritative a critic as Miss C. V. Wedgwood, for example, in fact does this, however unwittingly, the falsification of judgement which results is serious. Writing of Jonson in *Seventeenth-Century English Literature* she states,

'Tired of the quarrelsome stage, he devoted himself to the masque, arranging elaborate Court entertainments to be set with all the mechanical ingenuity of Inigo Jones. It was a contemptible form of the dramatist's art.'[57]

Miss Wedgwood, in my view, is here gravely unjust both to Jonson and Jones. Some masks, from a literary standpoint, were contemptible; but so were some others from the scenic viewpoint. The Barriers of 1616 as we have seen was severely censured on this score, and so was Jonson's *Pleasure reconciled to Virtue* of 1618, as a result of which Jones was said to have 'lost in his reputac(i)on'.[58] Human failings and errors were responsible for these occasional misadventures, literary and spectacular, not the genre itself. From a literary and dramatic standpoint, none of Jonson's early masks are contemptible, nor are many of Shirley's. Where spectacle is concerned, Jones' designs for costumes and settings have stood the test of comparison with those by continental artists of the period successfully enough for him to enjoy as wide an international reputation as a painter and architect today as he earned at the time. Miss Welsford, in her assessment of the Jones–Jonson quarrel, has probed to the heart of the matter.

'Unfortunately,' she writes, 'their artistic ideals were incompatible, and it was their very devotion to their respective arts that made peace between them impossible.'[59]

In this verdict she avoids the mistake of dismissing those masks which were artistically successful along with those which were not, and also does justice to Jonson and to Jones, both of whom were men of integrity, but who were victims too of their time and circumstance. I number myself among those who regard the subjection of dramatist and actor to the dictates of the architect and painter—to which the Mask opened the door in England—as a serious distortion of the nature of dramatic art, and one from which we in this century are only now beginning to recover: but I can also admit that the scenic spectacle of the Mask was a means through which artists and spectators could both experiment with and accustom themselves to a new vision of life expressed in landscape art, in *chiaroscuro* painting and in architecture. To dismiss Inigo Jones as plagiarist, mechanic, snob and as the artistic inferior Jonson represented him as being is to dismiss Rembrandt, Vandyke, Tiepolo and Wren as similar charlatans. Jones was as much a man of his time as Jonson, and in giving of his best with single-minded devotion revolutionized English architecture before surrendering his person and his fortune to Cromwell's soldiers at the siege of Basing House. It is hardly surprising therefore that a man of this calibre should have held views on points of artistic principle with which he was not prepared to compromise. Nor should he be blamed if the Jacobean and Caroline Court took a lively enough interest in the new visions of life, which he was offering them, to encourage him to stand by these views, even when challenged by men of such literary stature as Jonson and Shirley. His only fault was to have been a man of his time.

Shirley, like Jonson, appreciated the nature of the challenge; and, in his *The Bird in the Cage* (1633) and in *The Royal Master* (1638), wrote of masks and their artificers in the same sharp satirical tone as Jonson did in his *Expostulation*. Jones, however, by the time that Charles I succeeded to his father's throne, had come to possess a degree of power at Court derived from his official appointment as Surveyor of the Kings Works stronger than any author other than the Poet Laureate. By then, too, neo-Vitruvian theory concerning the architect's responsibility for Court entertainments had become widely enough accepted in England for him to exercise some say about whom he worked with. From being the inferior artificer, whose humble origins Jonson stigmatized as one 'who first began with thirty pound in pipkins' favoured by the poet who chose to call upon his services, Jones had emerged as the Master Surveyor, the Justice of the Peace and Member of Parliament who could offer patronage in his own right to such poets as cared to write at his direction, and deny it to those who would not.[60]

The consequences of this change of personal status are made obvious enough in the wording of the printed preambles to Aurelian Townshend's *Albion's Triumph* and *Tempe Restored*, both of 1632.

'The King and Queenes Majesty having signified their pleasure to have a new Maske this New yeare', wrote Townshend, 'Master *Inigo Jones* and I were employed in the Invention. And we agreed the subie(ct) of it should be a Triumphe in *Albipolis* the chiefe City of *Albion*.'[61]

Granted the freedom to order the development of the narrative in accordance with scenic possibilities and requirements implicit in this shared responsibility for 'the invention', Jones had virtually gained the point of artistic principle which he demanded and which Jonson, for all his theoretical attachment to neo-classical precept, denied him. *Tempe Restored*, which followed at Shrovetide, ought properly to be described as *by* Inigo Jones with songs and verses by Townshend.

'The subject and Allegory of the Masque, with the descriptions, and Apparatus of the Sceanes were invented by *Inigo Jones*, Surveyor of His Majestie's worke.'[62]

In other words, Jones, commanded by the Queen to prepare a mask for her to present to the King, worked out the scenario on his own, gave it to Townshend and commissioned him to supply the songs and verses where needed. Within a few months of this mask, Jonson died: and in this context one may remark that Shakespeare was fortunate not to have lived so long as his great rival, for it is hard to see how he could have adapted his interpretation of dramatic art to conform with the new Italian tenets of landscape art which Jones had successfully championed into the life of the English theatre.

The last decade before the Civil War served to consolidate the architect-painter's newly acquired dominance over the poet. Despite Shirley's firm stand, Carew and Davenant were ready to work with Jones on his terms.[63] The Twelfth Night Mask for 1638, Davenant's *Britannia Triumphans*, contains a description of a Palace which might just as easily be an emblematic scenic unit lifted from or placed in the account of a Lord Mayor's Show: but it concludes with a description of a sea-scape in a language quite new to the English theatre and impossible to parallel in Civic Pageantry.

'After this, some ships were discern'd sailing afar off several ways, and in the end a great fleet was discovered, which, passing by with a side wind, tackt about, and with a prosperous gale entered into the haven, this continuing to entertain the sight whilst the dancing lasted.'[64]

Short of using film, it would be hard to approach closer than this to complete verisimilitude. That this quest was in fact being actively and self-consciously pursued is made explicit in the stage directions of the last Court Mask, *Salmacida Spolia*.

'The Antimasques being past, all the Scene was changed into craggy rocks and inaccessible mountains, in the upper parts where any earth could fasten, were some trees, but of strange forms, such as only grow in remote parts of the Alps, and in desolate places.'[65]

The quest for the image having reached a successful conclusion in terms of visual spectacle, landscaped scenery had come to stay; but the price to be paid in the theatre for this achievement was the ultimate eclipse of poetic drama. Only with the advent of Sound Broadcasting was the mind of the spectator set free again to conjure settings imaginatively out of the dramatist's poetic emblems.

VIII

STAGE FURNITURE

N OBODY, confronted with the evidence presented in this
volume, its predecessor and the sources from which both
have been compiled, can doubt any longer that scenic decoration
figured largely and colourfully in most dramatic entertainments of
the sixteenth century. It can still be objected however that Masks
(or Disguisings) were not plays, that Pageants and Tournaments
were not plays and that mediaeval religious plays were not
Elizabethan secular plays. Evidence therefore has still to be offered
to prove that scenic decoration normally accompanied all stage-
plays throughout the Tudor era and that the stage furnishings in
question were similar in kind to those already revealed to us by the
records of Masks, Pageantry and the religious stage.

The two preceding chapters have gone a long way to supplying
answers to both problems: for the evidence presented in them has
served to illustrate the two extremes of purpose aimed at by the
painters and artificers of the period when working in association
with dramatists and actors for the entertainment and edification of
their audiences. On the one hand we have had to reckon with
skilled craftsmen whose function was to reinforce with their 'dumb
poesie' the speaking pictures supplied by the playmakers and actors
whom they served. On the other hand we have been confronted
with architects and landscape painters seeking to borrow the
breath of life from the stage in order to instil a lively, three-
dimensional existence into the inanimate, two-dimensional crea-
tions of their studios. There is the third possibility that neither
journeyman-artificer nor architect-painter found any place on the
pay-roll of Elizabethan theatre managements. Unfortunately it is
not possible to eliminate any two of these possibilities and thus
leave the third as the undisputed subject of our concern since all
three have been postulated by one author or another as possible or
probable.* Each therefore must be considered in turn.

* See p. 156 above and p. 278, n. 3 below.

Anyone who seeks to argue, as I do, that scenic decoration played as large a part in the Elizabethan theatre as it had previously done on the mediaeval religious stage and as colourful a part as it was later to do in theatres built after the Civil War, is well advised to admit that no evidence exists of regular payments made by Elizabethan acting companies or theatre owners to painters and artificers. Evidence does exist to prove however that painters, carvers and joiners were paid by the Master of the Revels for making settings for plays presented at Court by professional acting companies. 2s. 4d., for example, was paid in 1574 for

'Cariage of iiij Lodes of Tymber for the Rock [w(hi)ch Mr. Rosse made for my L(or)d of Leicesters menns playe] & for other frames for players howses.'[1]

John Rose (Rosse) was in the regular employ of the Revels Office, and the play which James Burbage and his fellows performed on that occasion was 'matter of Panecia'. This was two years before they built the Theater. In December 1576 (within a few months, that is, of its erection) 5s. was paid by the Revels Office,

'ffor Cariadge by water of a paynted cloth and two frames for the Earle of Leicesters to the Court'.[2]

These two examples serve to illustrate the historian's dilemma very neatly. Is the 'Rock' of 1574 one of those emblematic devices familiar to us from the records of Pageantry and the religious stage? Are the 'frames for players howses' of that year and the 'paynted cloth' of 1576 component items of Serlian décors? And does the Revels Office expenditure on any or all of these items indicate that the builder-leaseholders of the Theater lacked both? Chambers and Lawrence took the reasonable view that if the public playhouses had been equipped with scenic decoration of either sort it would have been unnecessary for the Revels Office to go to the expense of fitting them out, and that in consequence two different forms of stage-craft must be postulated for performances given at Court and those given in the theatres. Chambers and Reynolds interpreted the Revels Office accounts to prove the continuance of simultaneous 'mansion' stage-craft—the dispersed scene—at Court, while Reynolds felt obliged to challenge Chambers in arguing its probable continuance in the public theatres too: but Miss Campbell has argued that the painted cloths, great cloths, curtains, ropes, pulleys, clouds and frames for houses of the Revels accounts bespeak an extensive knowledge of Italian landscape techniques within a concentrated scene. Mr. Hotson has been bold enough to state that 'mansions' of a quasi permanent kind were in constant view on the stages of the public theatres despite the conspicuous absence of them in De Witt's sketch of the Swan. An inner stage with running curtains (also lacking in De Witt's sketch) has been assumed by most historians, and latterly the suggestion has been made that the front of the tiring-house in the public theatres was hinged below the gallery to lift up or swing down as required.[3]

The great temptation has always been, and still is, to presuppose a measure of compromise between the scenic conventions of the past on the one hand, as represented in the lists of stage properties and other furnishings supplied to the acting companies by the Revels Office for performances at Court, and the scenic conventions of the future on the other hand, as represented in the early Jacobean Masks. It is the concept of progress with its insistence upon continuous development expressed in logical terms of neatly progressive steps from alpha towards omega which puts this temptation in our path. If we yield to it, we are almost bound to invent an inner-stage as a basis for a subsequent proscenium arch; we become reluctant to contemplate the existence of 'mansions' on the public stage because their disappearance becomes difficult to explain if the demise of the religious drama is forfeited as the reason; perspective scenes and machines by contrast can be admitted to English academic and court stages as parallels in the sixteenth century to the Italian antecedents of the seventeenth century which also found acceptance in England. Either way the provincial stage comes to be dismissed as of no consequence. How then are we to cut this Gordian knot? If not by force or by evasion, then I believe the surest approach is in terms of the two extremes already traced and documented in Chapters VI and VII, for by this means we can at least work from a basis of fact rather than from one of convenient hypothesis.

For a start therefore, let us take the landscape stage-techniques of Inigo Jones in his partnerships with Carew, Davenant and Townshend. These belong to the 1630's, and the language of the stage-directions through which they are revealed to us has no precedent in England. The architect painter is there in the saddle with a firm hold upon the reins of 'invention' as well as being the wielder of the whip of control over the 'bodily part' of that 'invention': no spectators are permitted any place on the stage. This state of affairs is unexampled in the stage directions of Elizabethan plays, in either the Revels Office accounts or those of the Office of Works in the period 1558–1603. Nor is anything remotely like it suggested in documents relating to pageantry or to the acting

companies and their playhouses during that period. I think therefore that it may safely be eliminated from our calculations. In other
words, whether we be concerned with productions at Court, or in
the public theatres or in provincial playhouses, we are dealing not
with an architect's theatre or a painter's theatre, but with a
dramatist's and actor's theatre. And, if this be true, we are thus
still dealing with a theatre similar in its aesthetic fundamentals to
those of the theatres of worship and of recreation inherited from
the mediaeval past.

Approached from this standpoint, the public playhouses divide
themselves into two categories at least, and possibly three. There
are those built during Elizabeth's reign, and those built after the
introduction to England of the proscenium arch and perspective
settings of the early Jonson-Jones Masks—the second Globe
(1613), the Hope (1614) and the second Fortune (1621).* These
three theatres, in terms of historical period, may be aligned with
the Private Theatres allocated by Patent to the Jacobean and
Caroline Royal companies: and among these private theatres all
bar one were planned and built before Inigo Jones secured his
victory over the poet playmakers. The exception is the Cockpit in
Whitehall built by Jones for William Davenant on the site of the
Royal game-house, c. 1632.[4] If then we exclude this latest of the
London theatres to be built before the Civil War, we may fairly
say that, in terms of the known facts, all theatres of the Jacobean
and Caroline period were derived from their Elizabethan antecedents and modified in both their seating arrangements and their
stage-equipment in accordance with practical experience gained
over the years, rather than by neo-classical concepts of academic
theory or research. We are then left with the group of playhouses
built during Elizabeth's reign, and with these we may legitimately
align the Red Bull of 1605. Subdivision of this group into two
categories is strongly suggested by what we know of the policies
of Tudor government towards the theatre in London. In 1597 the
Privy Council were at last prevailed upon to order the destruction
of the existing playhouses, that is the Theater, the Curtain, the
Rose, the Swan and the theatre in Newington Butts. This order
was not carried out. We do not know why the Privy Council
allowed its instructions to be flouted so glaringly, but we must
suspect that the threat of demolition sufficed to bring the owners
sharply enough to heel to reassure the government and admit of its
entering upon a new agreement with the acting companies:[5] for, a
year later, the Theater was pulled down by the company that

* See Table D, p. 281 below.

occupied it, and another playhouse erected by this same company on the south bank, and a lease secured of the large chamber in the Blackfriars in the heart of the City itself. Faced with these extra-ordinary facts, the historian must, I think, allow for some dif-ferences both of architectural design and stage-practice between theatres built in London before and after 1597. This implies divid-ing the first Globe (1598), the first Fortune (1601/2) and the Red Bull (1605) from the earlier Elizabethan theatres and aligning them more or less closely with the Burbage family's intentions in respect of the Blackfriars. The whole matter is possibly simplified and made more intelligible when tabulated as shown in Table D opposite. Such tabulation has the advantage of revealing the degree of continuity that existed throughout the whole period, no matter how many subdivisions we create to allow for possible modifica-tions and improvements with the passage of time. Thus the building of the first Globe and first Fortune, for example, did not invalidate the Curtain or the Swan: the Hope was largely modelled on the Swan yet could be built to that plan despite the increasing use of the roofed chambers in the Blackfriars and Whitefriars as theatres: the Red Bull, regarded in Caroline times as dingy and vulgar, was nevertheless built after both the first Globe and the first Fortune and could hardly have been seriously different or inferior to either of them. If, further, we add to this knowledge all the evidence we possess of production conditions in the provinces, then I think that an *a priori* case exists for concentrating our attention upon an emblematic manner of stage presentation broadly aligned with the conditions familiar to us on the religious stage up to the time of its suppression, with Court production up to 1604/5, and with civic pageantry up to the Civil War and beyond. Put another way, it becomes well-nigh impossible to consider the stage-craft practised in the theatres built between 1576 and 1596 in any other context, since that is the only one which looks all the immediate *and* the related facts squarely in the face.

2 Emblematic Devices and Stage-plays at Court

Henry VIII died within two years of making responsibility for Court Revels an independent office within his own Household under the general supervision of the Lord Chamberlain. From 1547 onwards however, until some fifteen years after the building of the Theater, we possess a remarkably detailed series of documents re-cording the annual payments made by the Revels Office for the purchase of stage furnishings and in wages to the men employed on

TABLE D—LONDON THEATRES

Date of Construction	Name of House	Roofed or Unroofed	Analysis

GROUP I, 1576–1596

1576	Theater	Unroofed	Pleg-stówe or Pleg-hús derivatives: multi-purpose recreation houses
1577	Curtain	Unroofed	
1579?	Newington Butts	Unroofed	
1587–94	Rose	Unroofed	
1594–96	Swan	Unroofed	

GROUP II, 1596–1608

1598	1st Globe	Unroofed	Houses built exclusively for performances of stage plays
1601/2	1st Fortune	Unroofed	
1605	Red Bull	Unroofed	
	Curtain	Unroofed	Survivals from Group I, probably modified after 1600
	Swan	Unroofed	
(c. 1583)†	The Bull	Roofed	Indoor theatres in use at these dates by professional companies in the winter months
(c. 1594)†	The Cross Keys	Roofed	
(c. 1596)†	The Bell Savage	Roofed	
(c. 1599)†	The Boar's Head	Roofed	

GROUP III, 1608–1642 and after

(1608)*	Blackfriars	Roofed	Indoor playhouses used by adult Royal Companies
(1609)*	Whitefriars	Roofed	
1629	Salisbury Court	Roofed	
1613	Hope	Unroofed	Reversion to Group I
1614	2nd Globe	Unroofed	Revisions of Group II-style playhouses
1621	2nd Fortune	Unroofed	
	Curtain	Unroofed	Survivals from Groups I and II respectively
	Red Bull	Unroofed	
1616	The Cockpit, destroyed, rebuilt and known later as The Phoenix	Unroofed / Roofed	The first name suggests a reversion to Group I, but the date of building and the second name suggest the style of Group III

* Used before this by boy companies (?exclusively), and occasionally rather than regularly.

† The date given is that of the first reference to use of the building as a theatre. See Fig. 6, pp. 50–51 above.

making them. These documents are supplemented by the fragmentary records of the Office of Works during the Elizabethan and Jacobean period.[6] The materials bought and the uses made of them may be divided conveniently into what we might reasonably call 'hard' and 'soft' furnishings. The most casual of glances at any of the Revels Office documents reveals at once that far more money and time was expended upon soft furnishings than upon hard. There are two reasons for this. In the first place the majority of the soft-furnishing fabrics purchased were converted into costumes: in the second, many of the materials and much of the labour used in preparing the stages and auditoriums for Court performances were supplied and paid for by the Office of Works and not by the Revels Office.

More careful examination of the documents however reveals quite clearly that the division between hard and soft furnishings in respect of stage equipment is a real one. Under 'soft furnishings' may be grouped '*Hangings*', *Cloths* and *Curtains*, while 'hard furnishings' remains an appropriate label for *Rocks, Mounts, Battlements, Trees, Clouds* and *Houses*. Care however has to be taken to distinguish between these items and the long lists of equipment which relate to the lighting of the stage and auditorium. Similar care has to be taken where soft furnishings are concerned, to distinguish between hangings used on or about the stage and hangings used to decorate the auditorium, or, on special occasions, in the actual construction of a banqueting hall for plays or masks. Two examples may serve to establish this point; and, although both have been printed by Chambers in footnotes, they are important enough to my argument to merit elevation here to the body of the text.

1. 'The Banketting House made at Whitehall for thentertaynement of the seide duke did drawe the charges ensving for the covering therof with canvasse: the decking therof with birche & ivie: and the ffretting, and garnishing therof, with fflowers, and compartementes, with pendentes & armes paynted & gilded for the purpose. The ffloore therof being all strewed with rose leaves pickt & sweetned with sweete waters &c.'*

2. 'A banketting house was begun at Westminster, on the south west side of hir maiesties palace of White hall, made in maner

* Details not included by Chambers in his note, but supplied in the Revels Office Accounts (p. 167), include,
    Lynen Draper
        Mistris Dane for xx[ti] peeces of Vandelas to cover the Banketting-howse conteyning in the whole 1006 ells . . . Item more for xvij ells of the same rate . . . And for 130 ells Canvas . . .
    Wages of Taillers
        Robert Welton . . . by him paid for workmanshipp doone upon the same Canvas to Coover the howse
        Thomas Hales for cutting owte of the Canvas & fitting the same for the howse . . .

and forme of a long square, three hundred thirtie and two foot
in measure about; thirtie principals made of great masts, being
fortie foot in length a peece, standing vpright; betweene euerie
one of these masts ten foot asunder and more. The walles of
this house were closed with canuas, and painted all the outsides
of the same most artificiallie with a worke called rustike, much
like to stone. This house had two hundred ninetie and two
lights of glasse. The sides within the same house was made with
ten heights of degrees for people to stand upon: and in the top
of this house was wrought most cunninglie upon canuas, works
of iuie and hollie, with pendents made of wicker rods, and
garnished with baie, rue, and all maner of strange flowers garnished with spangles of gold, as also beautified with hanging
toseans made of hollie and iuie, with all maner of strange
fruits, as pomegranats, orenges, pompions, cucumbers, grapes,
carrets, with such other like, spangled with gold, and most
richlie hanged. Betwixt these works of baies and iuie, were
great spaces of canuas, which was most cunninglie painted, the
clouds with starres, the sunne and sunne beames, with diuerse
other cotes of sundrie sortes belonging to the queenes maiestie,
most richlie garnished with gold.'[7]

These descriptions provide us with a vivid picture of the
spectacle within which a mask or play at Court proceeded on its
appointed course; and since no blacking out of the auditorium was
contemplated, this spectacle, enriched by the actors' costumes, was
a constant factor. These descriptions also explain several of the
most puzzling features of the Revels Office records. Not only can
we begin to understand why the Master and his assistants needed
some knowledge of perspective and 'some smacke of geometrye' as
a qualification for appointment, but it also becomes evident what
purpose the 'greate cloths' and 'great painted cloths' of the expense
accounts were required to serve. *

If 'cloths' were needed to decorate the walls of the hall, and even
to serve as walls in their own right on occasions, they were also
needed to drape over the hand rails on the 'degrees', or spectators'
scaffolds, round the sides of the hall and as backings for thrones
and chairs of state. A long list of these 'coverynges' as they are
called is given in a Revels Office Inventory of 1554 together with a
list of the 'Hanginges some tymes Belonginge to Tymberhowses',
one of which may serve as an example.

'Item xvj paynes of a hanginge wherof viij of blewe velvat and

* See Ch. VII, pp. 263–265 above.

viij of greene velvatt enbrodred upo(n) w(i)th crownes and Roses
con(teyning) in the hole in lengthe viij yardes, di, and one nayle
in depth ij yardes q(uar)t(er) & iij nayles makinge in the hole xxᵗˡ
yardes iij q(uar)t(e)rs and twoe nayles.' (See Vol. I, Plate IX.)

This set of hangings, with its many panels of different shapes and
sizes, of which this is merely one, was probably designed and executed to dress the timber galleries of a tiltyard; but coverings as
well as hangings were required for dressing the dais and cloth of
estate of the throne; also for scaffolds erected indoors to accommodate humbler spectators. In most instances these cloths were
heavily embroidered with heraldic devices. * Such are the Crownes
and Roses in the example quoted above. Another is the

'Cov(er)ing of clothe of golde & Russett vellett p(ur)lyd Em-
broderyd w(i)th a ffawcon [*falcon*] and Oystriche ffethers of
Sylver imbossid.'⁸

of an earlier inventory, these being Ann Boleyn's and Henry
VIII's personal cyphers.† Sometimes however the decoration of
the spectators' scaffolds could be varied with paintings on canvas.
Thus Richard Bosum, painter, was paid 55s. in 1559, 'for makinge
of pyctures upon clothe in the frunte and the gallerye'. These
pictures can scarcely have differed much in appearance from the
painted panels familiar to us as ornamentation on the tiered circles
of eighteenth- and nineteenth-century theatres. Windows too had to
be covered in palace halls, and for this purpose great 'hangings' or
curtains were required. These habits were by no means new innovations brought about by the creation of the Revels Office; and,
where painted cloths are concerned, it is especially important to be
aware of this. Pavilions provided by the Office of the Tents for important ceremonial occasions like Henry VIII's meeting with
Francis I at the Field of the Cloth of Gold (that phrase is itself
suggestive) were not simply tents, but large timber frames roofed
over and covered round the sides by canvas cloths ornately painted
and decorated inside and out. The methods used in the construction of these temporary homes were identical to those used on the
construction of triumphal arches for Royal Entries, although the
finished product differed somewhat in its appearance.⁹ In short,
when we encounter references in the Revels Office Accounts to
very large canvas cloths, painted or embroidered, and to hangings

* On occasions, heraldic cloths of this sort formed an integral part of a
scenic unit: See *EES*, i, p. 244.
† See *EES*, i, p. 105.

and curtains big enough to be described as 'greate', there is good reason to accept these items as part of the furnishings of the auditorium rather than as part of the furnishings of the stage, unless they are specifically related by the notary to scenic devices. I arrive at this conclusion because of the careful way in which the clerks of the Office noted the use to which materials were put when scenic structures were in question. Not only did they usually trouble to record what play or mask any particular scenic device was constructed for, but also what company was going to use it or had made use of it. References to painted cloths and curtains, when they do occur in the context of materials used or monies expended on scenic devices, are unquestionably stage furnishings, as may be judged from the example already quoted on p. 277.

What purposes then did curtains and cloths serve when used as an integral part of the scenic devices? One answer at least may be obtained from considering the uses to which they had been put on stages of a date earlier than those to which the Revels Office records refer. Curtains were used in 1501 to dress the windows of a great lantern on wheels 'w(i)th many p(ro)pre and godly wyndowes' and to shroud the twelve ladies concealed inside it.* They were used again in 1528 to screen a mountain from view while an interlude was performed prior to the disguising in which the 'rich mount' was to figure.[10] It is precisely within these terms of reference that we find curtains being employed on the stage settings of Elizabethan Court revels. Thus, John Rosse, painter and property maker, was paid 2s. in 1573 'for poles & shyvers for draft of the Curtins before the senat howse', 8d. for 'Curtyn Ringes', 1s. for 'Edging the Curtins with ffrenge' and 10d. for 'Tape and Corde for the same'.[11] In 1580, Thomas Skiner, Mercer, provided the Revels Office with ten yards of orange taffeta sarcenet for making up into 'Curtyns' which were 'implowid aboute Storie of pompay plaid by the Childring of powles', that is, as curtains for the 'senate howse' which, together with 'one great citty', formed the setting for the play 'enacted in the hall on twelf nighte'.[12] For a pastoral in 1584, a mountain was required together with 'one greate curteyne' and 'one great cloth of canvas'.[13] Assuming that all three were used in conjunction, I do not see that we need regard this curtain as anything more than a repetition of the screening device used in 1528 to give temporary concealment to the mountain. The great cloth of canvas may or may not have been used to provide the mountain with a backing, arboreal or celestial. Cloths were certainly used in this way in conjunction with another scenic

* *EES*, i, 225.

unit, the battlement. The Twelfth Night play for 1585 was *Five Plays in One*, and for this the Office provided 'a greate cloth and a battlement of canvas and canvas for a well and a mounte'.[14] On only one other occasion is this popular property, the battlement, specifically associated with a 'greate cloth'.* Elsewhere it either figures on its own or is coupled with a City. This gives us a clear hint as to the nature of the cloth: for an artificial battlement would at once assume the character of a fortified town-wall, if set squarely in front of a picture of the roofs, spires and domes of a town, and allow passage for the defenders behind it as well as room for the attackers in front of it. Exactly this arrangement is pictured for us in the naval battle of 1589 in the Cortile of the Pitti Palace, Florence. (See *EES*, i, Plate XXIV and footnote* p. 265 above.) I know of no picture of the mountain in relation to its cloth, but a parallel arrangement exists in the representation of Circe's Garden as an arbour backed by a view of a town in the French Court Ballet of 1582 (*EES*, i, Plate XXVII).[15]

Not all 'Cities' were represented in terms of paintings. Some took the form of a more than usually ornate three-dimensional castle. Again, precedent existed for this technique from the earliest times: it was in this way that the City of Troy was presented to Charles V of France in 1378. This edifice was no less than twenty foot square and forty foot high, with a bower on each corner and a larger tower in the centre.† That these techniques had not been forgotten is proved by our knowledge that 'Cities' of precisely this sort had accompanied the production in Lincoln of the play of *Old Tobit* in 1564. Included in the inventory of stage furnishings are,

'Item, the city of Jerusalem, with towers and pinacles
Item, the city of Rages, with towers and pinacles.'

These cities and a third, however, were in addition to sundry palaces and houses, and even a room—Sarah's chamber.‡ These castles-cum-cities were constructed out of wooden frames, covered with canvas and ornately decorated. The technique was identical to that described for us in respect of one of the pageant arches for Katherine of Aragon's reception into London in 1501— 'batilments of tymber cov(e)red and leyed ov(e)r w(i)t(h) canvas empeynted like frestone and whight lyme, so that the semys of the stone were p(er)ceyved like as mortur or sement had been betwene'.§

* 1582.
† See *EES*, i, pp. 213–215.
‡ See *EES*, i, p. 246.
§ See *EES*, i, pp. 100–101.

I am of the opinion that the canvas walls of these elaborate structures were first cut out of the bulk cloth, stretched by means of 'teynter-nayles' on the wooden frames and then sized and painted in position: after the paint had dried I think the canvas was removed, rolled and carried independently of the frames from the hall where it had been painted to the hall where it was to be used. Once both frames and canvas had arrived, they were put together again immediately before use, and were then dismantled again after the performance, and returned to their place of origin as independent units for storage.[16] If I am correct, then it would be

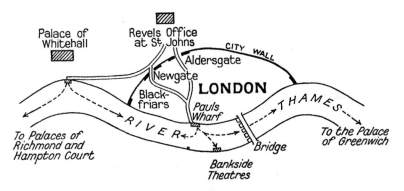

FIG. 22. Map illustrating the transport routes between the Revels Office (St John's) and the royal palaces to the East and West of the City of London.

more accurate to describe the canvas as painted cloth than as canvas from the moment that the paint on it had dried sufficiently to allow it to be separated from the frames. My reasons for adopting this view are these. First, although the canvas-covered frames of Tudor times bore a superficial resemblance to the 'flats' of our own theatres, these frames, whether required for pageant arches or scenic units in a banquet chamber, had to carry roofs and support the strain of heavy weights and much activity on and around them (see *EES*, i, Plates XV, XVI and XVII). No modern-style 'flat' is expected to withstand this sort of direct stress from above. If we regard the 'frames' as more nearly resembling those of the 'timber-houses' for spectators at Tournaments than those of modern theatre flats, we shall not be far from the mark (see *EES*, i, Frontispiece and Plates VI, VIII, IX and XVII).[17] Secondly, whereas our flats are usually made and painted in or near the theatre in which they are going to be used, the Elizabethan frames were made in the Revels Office in Clerkenwell and then had to be transported by road and river to and from Whitehall, Greenwich, Richmond or

Hampton Court. Charges for the hire of horses, waggons and boats are frequent and extensive. No artist or craftsman in his right mind would attempt to carry frames of the size of 'timberhouses', complete with painted cloths (especially in winter) from the workshops at St. John's through the City to Paul's Wharf, off-load them there from waggons onto barges, then sail up or down river with them for several miles only to have to take them off the barges again and load them on to waggons before reaching their final destination in the palace banquet chamber.[18]

A third reason for separating the painted cloths from the frames (as also for making the frames themselves collapsible) was the problem of storage at both ends of these tedious journeys. A 'Rock' big enough to seat Apollo and nine muses, or a mountain with Twelve Goddesses on its slopes is no mean structure: nor is a 'senate house' of sufficient size to hold six or more senators, or a 'battlement' or castle strong enough to support scaling-ladders from in front and a posse of defenders on its top. Moreover, the Revels Accounts make it plain that what the master and his servants normally had to cope with was furniture, not for a single play, but for a season of six or more plays and masks.[19] The 'arbour' of the *Ballet Comique* (France, 1582: *EES*, i, Plates XXVII and XXVIII, No. 41) cannot have measured less than 15 feet high by 4 feet in diameter: the fountain (*ibid.*, Plate XXVIII, No. 42) not less than 20 feet by 12 feet. The same approximate proportions are indicated by the Callot engravings of the Combat at Barriers at Nancy of 1627 (Plates XX, XXI & XXII).* In England for the Christmas and Shrovetide Revels of 1582–83, the Office furnished six plays with no less than

3 Cloths (one new)	5 Battlements (four new)
4 Cities (three new)	4 Pavilions

If we take 10 foot square as the approximate mean average of the area occupied by each of these structures (excluding the cloths) we find that, when set out side by side, this collection would have covered an area of ground 130 foot square—or more than twice the total floor space available in any Tudor banquet hall. In this same year (1582) two separate purchases of canvas were made totalling 385 yards at a cost of £17 10s. 0d.[20] If we remove the pavilions from our calculations since they were made at least in part of sarcenet (25 yards) and add the cloths, then the total of scenic devices to be made from it becomes one cloth, three cities and four battlements (eight in all), and 40 yards of canvas can be allotted to each

* See Ch. VI, pp. 231–232 above.

structure with 60 yards in hand for the pavilions and other minor items. Forty yards is sufficient to cover all four sides of a structure measuring 10 foot square up to a height of four or five feet from the ground, supposing that the canvas was not woven to any greater width.

I conclude therefore that the frames were solidly built, designed and constructed to be fastened to one another by means of cramps (gripping appliances tightened by a screw: the 'vices' of the accounts),[21] nuts and bolts, and that the canvas was cut as a single piece for each device. The canvas could be 'wrapped round' and nailed to the frames thus enclosing all the frames belonging to one device once they had been set up and cramped in position. The roofs, 'fringes', cornices, and other decorations already pre-fabricated were then superimposed upon the assembled units and the completed item touched up with glue, paint and such additional mouldings as the Lord Chamberlain demanded. The touching up would have been just as extensive had the devices been transported whole, for no amount of care could have safeguarded them against damage in transit. Such a method of construction would at once resolve the transportation difficulties and the problems of storage both in the palace and in the workshops at Clerkenwell. In short we are comparing four stackable frames, a bag of cramps, nuts and bolts and a roll of painted canvas with a solid structure measuring some hundred cubic feet in its fully erected state, and deciding that where the former method would have offered the Revels Office few problems the latter would have been almost impossible of fulfilment.*

Thus, where soft furnishings are concerned, we may be fairly certain that the majority of the materials bought by the Revels Office were used for making costumes and for decorating the auditorium, while some, notably canvas and sarcenet, were employed, either on their own account or in conjunction with hard furnishings, to fashion scenic devices. And always we must try to bear in mind the fact that as a visual spectacle, stage and auditorium formed a single picture for the spectator. This fact must be accorded just as important a place in our thinking about the hard furnishings

* Having myself had to arrange transport for stage-scenery between England and Italy by rail, boat and rail, and between England and Austria and Germany by lorry, I am here not speaking speculatively but from experience. For a recent production of *Love's Labour's Lost* taken to Italy, the canvas for the setting was painted in Bristol, taken off the frame when dry and rolled into bales of a size convenient to handle in transit. Arrived in the theatre in Italy, it was attached to rostrums and frames provided locally, and cut to shape and trimmed on the spot.

listed in the Revels Accounts: for many items which we might be tempted to associate with the stage were prepared for more general use. Chief among these were the timber planks for stages and scaffolds, and the metal, wire and wood for chandeliers and lighting brackets, together with special beams and winches for their suspension.[22] Additional stages had occasionally to be built for musicians and dancers.[23] Not all of this work came under the aegis of the Office of Works, although much of it did. In 1578–79, for example, the Office of Works was responsible for repairs to the fabric of the Banquet Chamber Hall at Whitehall and

'also for makinge of p(ar)ti(t)ions, Skaffoldes and other nec(essar)ies for playes, Tragedies and Bearebayting at Shrovetyde', and 'for makinge certan peces that were wantinge in the Judges house in the Tilte, settinge upp the same House in the Tilteyarde'.[24]

At Richmond, in the same year, the Works were responsible

'for settinge up degrees and skaffoldes, making p(ar)ti(ti)ons and barryers for playes, Tragidies and Revels there'.[25]

Again at Richmond, but ten years later, the works met the bill for

'fframynge postes and Railes for plaies(,) setting up degrees in the greate Chamber(,) Nayllinge one [on] brackettes and boordes for the people to sitt one [on](,) making new halpaces (daises) there for the Queenes Ma(jes)tes use(,) and a new stage of xiiij foote square for the plaiers to plaie on(,) and Halpaces for the lordes and ladies to sitt on and iij other Halepaces for the people to stande on, and after the plaies eanded for taking downe and removinge the provisions'.[26]

Against these items supplied by the Office of Works we may set those provided by the Revels Office. In 1578–79 three plays were given at Shrovetide in Whitehall, two by adult companies (Warwick's and Hunsdon's) and one by children (Chapel). For these the Revels Office paid out in wages and for materials:

	Wages	*Materials*
Carpenters:	£2	£4 13s. 4d.
Joiners:	£2 5s. 8d.	
Wyredrawers:	£1 8s. 4d.	£8 11s. 3d.
Painters:	£4 7s. 0d.	£5 15s. 4d.
Property Makers:	£2 8s. 0d.	£4 7s. 11d.
Ironmongers:		£2 7s. 1d.
Drapers (for canvas, etc.):		£4 11s. 0d.[27]

The settings on this occasion included a cloud-machine, a Rock, a scaling-ladder and a chair for Warwick's Company, a waggon for the Chapel play, a painted chest for Hunsdon's men, and two frames. Five plays were presented at Richmond ten years later, but it is not possible to isolate the expenses incurred there from those at Greenwich and Whitehall in the months before and after. * From these two sets of accounts one gains the impression that the Revels Office was primarily concerned with the tailoring of the costumes and the painting and illumination of the stage and auditorium while the Works were responsible for the repairs to the building, the stage and the seating arrangements. That this conclusion may be an oversimplification however is made very clear from the Revels Accounts for other years. In 1579–80, 2s. 6d. was spent on 'single Quarters to enlardge the Scaffolde in the hall one [on] Twelfe night . . . (and) doble quarters for the same Cause'. Five years earlier a carpenter's bill for £6 13s. 9d. had been presented for elm and oak boards and also oak and beech 'Rafters', some of the oak rafters being 'xiiij foote long'. In the preceding year (1573) a similar bill for planks, poles and rafters was met by the Office, while a year earlier still 6d. was spent on 'Boordes to brace the skaffoldes'.[28] Nevertheless, the finding of such items as these among lists predominantly given over to costumes, painting, lighting and scenic decorations takes so keen a search as to suggest that they were abnormal: as exceptions, they can be accounted for easily enough in terms of some particular emergency. The 'Boordes to brace the skaffoldes' is an item entered against the 'Propertymaker & his parcells', suggesting that the skaffoldes in question were scenic structures: the 'rafters' of 1573–75 were almost as certainly required for mounting and operating the cloud-machine and for hanging the painted cloth for which 'pynnes styf and greate' were needed. I suggest that the enlargement of *the* scaffolde in the hall' in 1579–80—the only entry of its kind in all the records—was necessitated by a miscalculation somewhere in the initial measuring up of the stage, or in the 'plot' or ground plan of the 'houses' on the stage drawn up in the office: such mistakes are not unknown today.

Two items however in a document in the standard edition of the Revels Accounts, which still remain to be considered, cannot be explained in this way. The first of these is an entry which reads,

'Carpenters occupied not onelye in repayring of the old frame and

* Where payments to Carpenters totalled £6 15s. 6d. 'for timber bordes and workemanshipp in mending and setting up of the houses by greate in the saide twoe yeares', those to the wiredrawers amounted to £28 19s. 3d. within the same period.

Settinge of it upp But alsoe in makinge of Certayne particions and Dore(?s) with diuerse other necessaries, &c.'

The second records payment for,

'Cartes by the daye occupied in caringe of the frame into the hall as alsoe in caringe of the saide fram from the Hall to the storeyarde againe with diverse other necessaries &c.'[29]

The document is BM. MS. Lansdowne 9, no. 58; and it is dated 19th February–March 1567–68 and is printed by Feuillerat on pages 120–123 of his *Documents Relating to the Office of the Revels in the time of Elizabeth*. In a note (p. 449) he adds, 'I have a pretty strong suspicion that this *Liber* belongs to the Office of the Works, and not to the Revels.' The element of doubt can, I think, confidently be removed. Not only is the initial entry 'Chardges Done for the Revells . . .' (repeated in the final entry) unlike any other, but the John Colbrande who heads the list of Carpenters who received payment is undoubtedly John Colbrande, Master Carpenter in the Office of the Works under Thomas Graves, Surveyor, and Thomas Fowler, Comptroler.[30] Except for the two items relating to the frame which I have quoted, most of the entries in the document relate to the fabric of the building—windows, paving stones, brickwork and roof.

Granting that this document is one of the Works account books, what was this frame which was 'old', which needed to be 'set up', and which had to be 'carried from the hall to the storeyard'? Was it a 'house' like the frames of later Revels Office entries? Was it the stage? Or was it some sort of screen employed as a scenic backing to the stage and, if so, was it of the neo-Terentian kind with door (doors?) and curtained partitions? Before we jump to any of these conclusions—and all of them are inviting—it is as well to recognize that there is no similarly worded entry in the Works Accounts surviving for the years 1578–1603. Any conclusion we may reach will thus inevitably be speculative and hypothetical. The nearest approach to an equivalent that I have found is an entry for the year 1580–81:

'Makinge up of degres & partitions in the greate Chamber, and in the Hall againste the playes and Revels at Xrmas and Shrovetide . . . Mendinge of ye Tilte in sundrie places, with framinge and settinge up of postes and railes on both sides thereof, and erecting of a Skaffolde there under her Highnes Windowe . . .'.[31]

I myself incline to the belief that 'the frame' of 1567–68 was that of the auditorium; that is, the tiered rostrums over which boards were laid to form 'degrees' on which spectators could sit or stand, but excluding those special platforms or scaffolds erected to accommodate the sovereign, ambassadors, the Lord Chamberlain and other persons with special functions like musicians. (See Plate XX.) Although the 'certayne particions and Dore(?s)' are not necessarily to be read here as meaning integral parts of 'the old frame', both features were normally associated with other indoor auditoriums in an intimate way: the degrees could not be allowed to block the entrance doors, and were themselves divided by partitions to provide a sequence of semi-private rooms or boxes. Just as relevant, the word frame is the term used by Elizabethans to describe the auditorium, as opposed to the stage, of their later, public theatres.[32]

There is one further point to be noticed in respect of the Works Accounts for 1567–68. This document records payments to men identified as Carpenters, an item which corresponds with what we might expect of an Office charged with responsibility for the construction of stages and auditoriums. What is unusual is that Carpenters are not listed among the tradesmen to whom payments are made by the Revels Office prior to that date; nor do they begin until 1573, the year, that is, after the reorganization of the Office.[33] Before 1573 the Revels Office employed 'joiners', 'carvers' and 'propertymen' who bought wood and worked in it: in 1573, when Thomas Blagrave entered upon his acting-Mastership, and regularly thereafter, carpenters were employed in addition. I would suggest that one of the results therefore of the reorganization of the Office was that thereafter the Revels took over responsibility for providing the frames for scenic units, notably 'houses', that had previously been made for them by the Office of Works.

Summarising the analysis of the Revels Accounts made thus far, it seems reasonably clear to me that the Office of Works assumed responsibility throughout the sixteenth century for everything in the banquet chamber that might reasonably be described as hard furnishings, with two exceptions—frames for scenic units after 1573, and last-minute adjustments to the stage. It seems equally clear that the Revels Office was required to provide all items that could be listed as soft furnishings (including stage properties) and assumed the further responsibility of superintending the lighting of the hall. The lighting involved not only the supply of candles, lamps and torches, but the holders (brackets and branches) and the suspension gear.[34] In trying to visualize the appearance of all this equipment as set up for the benefit of the professional acting companies when they were summoned by the Master of the Revels to perform at Court, it would be as well if we substituted for the vague phrase 'at Court' a clear image of a lofty hall measuring approximately 100 feet in length by some 35 to 45 feet in width.* These dimensions are approximately twice the size of those prescribing the floor space of the normal provincial Guildhall or Company Hall.† In addition the Court could and frequently did use a second hall, the Great Chamber, in association with the hall itself. These halls were not designed as theatres: for the greater part of every year they stood empty of all theatrical furnishings. At the two great Calendar Festivals, the Christmas and Shrovetide seasons, and on sundry other special occasions, they were fitted up with tiered seats, a stage for the acting of plays, stages for seating dignitaries of the court, and sometimes with further stages for musicians and dancers. All this equipment, together with the soft furnishings with which it was draped and decorated, was promptly removed afterwards and stored in the respective London depositories of the Revels Office and the Office of Works.

The Revels Office was expected to take an annual inventory of all the 'caparisons, hanginges, garmentes, vestures, properties and other stuff, store, and Implements of the revells'.[35] This catalogue of materials embraced all the furnishings appropriate to masks, masks at barriers, tilting, bear-baiting and the Lord of Misrule as well as stage-plays: and since the materials were of the very best, they were guarded with care against pillage, theft and the depredations of moth and damp. As the years passed, items were duly depreciated, marked as 'not serviceable', and either disposed of or cut up for the 'new-fashioning' of something else. Thus, in the first year of Elizabeth's reign, we find expenditure sanctioned against

'Translatinge new makinge garnysshinge furnysshinge and fynysshinge of dyvers and sundrye garmentes Apparell vestures and propertyes aswell of Maskes as for playes and other pastymes.'[36]

Many detailed instances are supplied of which one can serve for illustration. Six gowns, sleeves, under sleeves and capes having been

'translated into a Maske of Astronomers and againe into a Maske of Barbarians'

come to be described as

* The Hall at Hampton Court, for example, was fifteen foot larger than that at Whitehall, whereas the Hall at Windsor was twelve feet narrower than that at Whitehall.
† See note 31.

'so aften translated and shewen forworne and knowen as no more serviceable nor chargeable'.[37]

This logic, while applicable to the Court, would not apply to plays performed in public or in the provinces. There is thus strong reason to suggest that once a garment was 'no more serviceable' to the Revels Office, and not 'chargeable' in the inventory, it could pass either as a gift or at some small charge into the wardrobe of a professional acting company where for another year or two at least it could continue to be both 'serviceable' and 'chargeable'. *

Much the same procedure was adopted in respect of scenic units and properties. Thus in 1558–59 Robert Trunckwell, Joiner, and his man were paid 24s. for

'alteringe of to modells by them before made and nowe ageane turnede to Another purpose . . .'.[38]

A careful library-collection was maintained within the Revels Office of designs and working drawings.

'Soe sone as anye Maske or other devise ys finished the patterne and platte of the same shalbe Drawne and putt in collers by A painter aswell for witnes of the worcke, as for presidente to the office, to induse, Devise, and shewe, Difference, of that is to come frome that ys paste.'[39]

The importance of this regulation is obvious enough in relation to a system of scenic decoration based on a code of emblematic devices rather than on one of pictorial landscape: lack of variety in the emblems had to be compensated for by the variety of treatment accorded to them. We have already seen this principle in action, in respect of the Lord Mayors' Shows: not only were 'paterns', 'plots' and 'models' prepared in advance, scrutinized, costed and authorized by responsible committees, but many of the devices were taken into the Company's Hall after the Riding where they were then exhibited and stored. Thus both in the Revels Office and the city a device existed, where scenic emblems were concerned, of 'new-making', of 'translating' and 'turning to another purpose', or of disposal. When an object was no longer deemed to be 'serviceable' the readiest market, as with costumes, was likely to be found among the professional acting companies.

The scenic units designed and made in the Tudor Revels Office,

* It may have been from this source that Anthony Munday collected the private wardrobe from which he furnished the Lord Mayors' shows.

like those of the Lord Mayors' Shows, were exclusively emblematic. Between 1547 and 1558 the Clerks of the Office record payments for making a mountain, a tower, a chariot, and a dragon: between 1558 and 1576 it provided a rock with a fountain, an arbour, a castle, 'divers Cities and Townes', palaces, houses, clouds, a chariot, a prison, trees (including 'trees for a wilderness' and 'great hollow trees'), a senate house with curtains, a hell mouth: between 1576 and 1603 this list was augmented by pavilions, battlements, a village and a wood. It is not possible to associate the scenic devices listed between 1547 and 1558 directly with plays. The 'mounte' however was used twice, once for a Mask and then for the story of Orpheus:[40] the tower, resembling 'the Tower of babylon' is associated with 'maskyng garmentes' and also, under a separate entry, with 'pleyers garmentes'.[41] All the Elizabethan devices however can be related directly to stageplays. I have set out in Appendix G (pp. 339–340 below) a list of professional acting companies and the scenic emblems which were made for their use. Two general observations may be made about the facts revealed in this Appendix. First, the professional acting companies were quite as accustomed to using 'mansions', 'houses' or 'devices' in their productions of 'secular' plays prior to the building of the Theater as their predominantly amateur predecessors, the companies of Church and schools and trade guilds, had been in London and in provincial cities. Secondly, the play involving battlements, scaling-ladders and cities or towns was evidently much more popular after 1576 than before. There would seem to me therefore to be strong *a priori* grounds for supposing that professional actors would not deny themselves equipment in their own theatres of a sort demanded at Court and to which provincial audiences were accustomed to being treated at the hands of amateurs. On the other hand, three cogent practical factors must be taken into account militating against the use of 'houses' in the professional theatres—construction costs, storage and transportation.

As staged, it would have been unnecessary for the Revels Office to equip the acting companies with scenic devices of the sort required at Court had they been possessed of their own. We must assume therefore that either they did not possess their own, or that those which they owned and used for public performances were too small and too shop-soiled to be acceptable to court audiences. Reasons for such a situation are not hard to discern. Elaborate scenic units had been required during the fifteenth and early sixteenth centuries for Court Disguisings, for Tournaments, for Royal Entries and other civic ridings and for the grandiose but occasional religious dramas of church and city. All of the entertainments were predominantly amateur and sponsored by patrons who could afford to pay for their construction and storage. The professional acting companies of this period were small, rarely numbering more than four players in their ranks. Henry VIII increased his personal troupe of 'players of interludes' from four to eight, but this must be regarded as the maximum, and abnormal even in the middle decades of the sixteenth century. A troupe of four to eight players, dependent for their livelihood on a nomadic existence in the countryside, is a very different proposition from a troupe of twelve to sixteen players permitted to perform regularly on weekdays in London. Thus the professional acting companies of the period 1530–80—an era, bounded at one end by the first attacks on the amateur religious stage and at the other by the final suppression of the religious stage—should not be discussed in the same terms of reference as the early Tudor amateurs or the Jacobean Royal Companies. Rather were they unlike the Tudor amateurs, in that their numbers were small and not large and because they depended on receipts from their performances for their livelihood, and unlike the Jacobean companies, in that they lacked both the personal security and the financial backing of companies possessed of Royal Patents. It would be unrealistic of us therefore to expect that during this period of transition professional acting companies would have put plays into their repertoires which demanded much by way of scenic equipment: for they had neither the number of actors to warrant extensive use of it, nor the capital backing to finance its purchase, nor workshops or house room of their own in which to store it. The survival of the religious stage however until the fifteen-seventies, together with the example set by the court and academic amateurs in respect of scenic decoration, can only have been regarded by the professional companies as something which they must strive to emulate if they were to capture for themselves a truly representative national audience.

As a first step in this direction they took over the raised stage of the Italian neo-classical theorists, and placed it against the screen of hall and church, and used both in conjunction with such hand properties and furniture as could be made inexpensively and could be transported over long distances with reasonable care. Wherever they went they expected to find the stage and screen provided for them; and if, on occasion, the screen was lacking, they could adapt their performance to fit the churchyard, private house or other alternative site which was offered to them by reverting to earlier precedents. The properties and furniture were their own concern.

Equipping themselves with tents, trees, an artificial rock and a wall presented no great difficulty: and given a tent or tents, everything from a simple throne or pavilion to house, palace, temple, castle or city could be presented emblematically by means of varying the basic proportions of the tent with vanes, shields and other decorative devices. The trees and the rock, either singly or in combination, could similarly serve to suggest (and thus present) a wide variety of landscape ranging from the domestic garden to the forest, wilderness or desert. Ships are notably lacking from early Tudor plays. It is very much this state of affairs that is represented by the company of 'Athenian' town-players whom Shakespeare calls upon to perform at Duke Theseus' Court, and also by the players of Wittenberg who visit the Danish Court at Elsinore in *Hamlet*. The Athenian mechanicals needed a wall (a painted cloth made ridiculous by being held in position by one of the actors): the players of Wittenberg needed two trees with a bench set between them to reproduce the scene of the murder in the orchard arbour. The moral and polemical interludes of the period 1530–70 rarely demanded much more than this of the acting companies who owned the scripts: indeed one may reasonably infer from the stage directions that as much care was taken by the playmakers to see that the scenic demands did not over-tax the companies' resources as was taken to see that the acting roles of a play's cast list could be doubled or trebled within the limits of a company of four or eight players.[42] As I have argued elsewhere, when the Revels Office came to be established by Henry VIII in 1545 its concern with plays was as much political (even if indirectly through the Lord Chamberlain and the Privy Council) as it was practical.* Under Edward VI and Queen Mary, the Master's responsibilities in practical matters had not come to extend much beyond the furnishing of Masks, Tilts, Barriers and the entertainments presided over by the Lord of Misrule. The choir-boy companies and the royal company of interluders could reasonably expect to be kitted-out with costumes, properties and stage furnishings from the appropriate offices of the Royal Household in remuneration for services rendered. Few of the country-gentlemen's companies however, recruited from dissolved religious houses or from the ranks of talented mechanicals had any grounds to anticipate subsidies of this sort. The fabrics for their costumes had to be acquired from churches that had no further use for vestments, cloths and hangings or from merchants and private individuals: their properties and furnishings had to be made and paid for out of their own earnings.

* See *EES*, i, p. 283, and p. 64 above.

Only during Elizabeth's reign, with many years of touring experience and ensemble playing behind them, did these genuinely professional companies of actors begin to compete with the children of the royal chapels and the adult players of the royal household for the distinction of command performances: and only then could they expect to be equipped on a scale worthy of this distinction. If the Revels Office Accounts represent the situation accurately, only three companies had in fact earned this distinction before 1576, the Earl of Leicester's, the Earl of Lincoln's and the Lord Chamberlain's.

Thus, when the Theater came to be built in that year, we have no grounds for thinking that Leicester's company owned any substantial store of scenic equipment or was in the habit of using 'houses' or 'devices' as elaborate as those with which the Revels Office fitted it out when it came to Court in 1572, 1573, 1574 and 1575. What then did its members ask for as minimal requirements for stage-plays when they approached their grocer-financier John Brayne for the loan of the capital needed to build their playhouse or gamehouse in Shoreditch? Did they ask for as much as the provincial amateurs had been in the habit of receiving from their town councils and trade guilds? Did they demand for themselves what they had come to expect from the Master of the Revels when appearing at Court?

3 Actors' Needs in a Public Playhouse or Gamehouse, 1576–1596

The least those professional actors could have asked for at that point in time was the equivalent of those conditions which had previously been available to them in provincial guildhalls, in London halls and taverns, and in the private halls of the noble masters from whose livery they derived their right to act. This included a raised stage, a changing-room, two entrances from the changing-room giving direct access to the stage and, if possible, both a gallery above the changing-room and sufficient space in which to store their tents, trees, rocks, furniture and properties when not in use on the stage. Mindful of conditions prevailing up to that time on the amateur religious stage, as well as in the universities and at court, they would have presented their financiers with a further list of highly desirable features. This second list would have included provision for the installation of simple machinery both above and below the stage itself and facilities for music. Faced with these demands, the financiers had the option of installing within the 'frame' of the game-house either a movable structure built to a very simple design or a more complicated structure which could not easily be removed. The probability is that in the first instance, that is to say in the case of the Theater (1576) and the Curtain (1577), they opted for a simple structure which could easily be removed to allow for as many other forms of popular recreation as possible to be conducted within the arena prescribed by the permanent frame: once the initial gamble on the citizens' willingness to support stage-plays in a game-house in the north-eastern suburbs had begun to pay good dividends, a more permanent and complicated structure could readily be considered, and admitted when the chance offered to construct a third and fourth playhouse. It was to this second, more developed pattern, as I believe, that Henslowe's Rose (1594) and Langley's Swan (1596) were built on the South Bank.

This thesis does not eliminate the possibility that both the Theater and the Curtain were modified in the course of time, and proportionately with the earnings derived from the stage-plays presented by the companies which used them: but such modifications as may have been made can hardly have affected the frame, only the stage and changing-room area. In the very nature of the evidence however we cannot advance much beyond probability in any of these matters, since we have neither sketches of the interiors of the theatres, nor builders' contracts, nor descriptive word-pictures. Yet we know much more than is generally supposed concerning the inherited traditions of play performance in the general context of which the professional companies set about their task of designing public playhouses: and on this account, as has been demonstrated in Chapter V, it may be stated with near certainty that the auditorium and the playing area were thought about, discussed and in the event designed as separate units linked together for commercial expediency rather than conceived in the first instance as a single entity, functional and aesthetic. That the stage and auditorium of the Theater were built as units having a life independent of one another is hinted at by several facts. We know that its frame or auditorium was transported across the Thames in 1598 for use in the construction of the Globe whereas the stage and changing-room apparently were not. We know that Henslowe used the stage of the Globe as the model for his stage in the Fortune, a fact which would suggest that it was different and better suited to production needs than its predecessors, including both Henslowe's own Rose and Langley's Swan. In Henslowe's contract with John

Cholmley for the purchase of the land on which they were to erect the Rose, it is stated that the carpenter, John Grygges, is to build 'the saide play house w(i)th all furniture therunto belonginge or appartayninge', a phrase which is more clearly defined in the subsequent Fortune contract. There, instructions are given to the Carpenter, Peter Street, in two distinct sections, those for the frame, followed by those for 'a Stadge and Tyreinge howse to be made, erected & settupp w(i)thin the saide fframe w(i)th a shadowe or cover over the saide Stadge'.[43] This wording is made still more specific in the Hope contract of 1613, where the carpenter is instructed to rebuild the Bear Garden, that is, the amphitheatrical auditorium,

'And also A fitt and convenient Tyre house and a stage to be carryed or taken awaie, and to stande uppon tressells.'[44]

Thus, even as late as 1613, at least one capitalist-manager, in partnership with one of London's star actors, still regarded the multi-purpose auditorium as worth an investment of £360 in builder's fees alone, and conceived of the stage and tiring-house in different terms of reference from those of the frame.

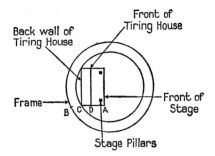

FIG. 23. Ground plan illustrating the relationship of the stage and tiring-house to the frame of the Swan Theatre.

If then we adopt the premise that in the earliest of the public theatres the frame on the one hand and the stage and changing-room on the other were independent of one another, what impression may we glean of the physical appearance and construction of the stage unit? Here, I think, we have no choice but to accept the sketch of the Swan as our starting-point and modify its features slightly in respect of other theatres built either before or after.

Looking at the sketch (Plate VIII) and accompanying words of description, the object nearest to us is the *proscaenium* or raised

stage. This is shown to be lifted above ground level by large supports and to be open at the sides. From other and earlier sources
we know that the normal way of doing this was for long heavy
planks of wood to be braced together and laid on trestles, barrels
or tables.[45] From the sketch it appears that the changing-room or
mimorum aedes is set squarely on this stage: certainly its flat façade
projects well clear of the inner circumference of the frame.

It is possible however that the *proscaenium* or raised stage ter-
minated at the point in the sketch where it joins the *mimorum
aedes*, and that the whole of the *mimorum aedes*—façade with doors,
gallery with partitions and hut above—was as independent of the
proscaenium as it was of the frame. In other words, the *mimorum
aedes*, together with its superstructure, could have risen directly
from the ground and not off the stage.

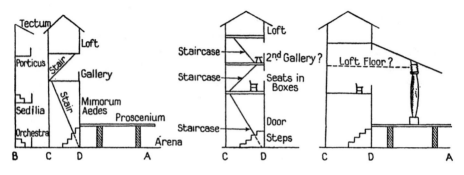

FIG. 24. Cross-section of Fig. 23 in elevation showing:
a) Tiring-house and stage in relation to the frame.
b) Detail of tiring-house.
c) Tiring-house linked to stage by penthouse 'heavens' and pillar supports.

An arrangement such as is suggested in these sketches is no more
than a natural extension of and improvement upon a simple platform stage set down in the arena adjacent to a single-story
'timberhouse' designed as a changing-room.

This 'timberhouse' can be thought of in terms of the single 'scaffold' of the Chevalier Délibéré (see Vol. I, Frontispiece, and Fig. 3)
or of the more elaborate scaffolds of the tiltyard as depicted for us
by Roi René (Vol. I, Plate VIII). Either sort could be set up and
dismantled without much time or effort, and stored in its component parts when not required, or it could be lightly roofed but
otherwise left transparent, or it could be covered round about with
hangings or painted canvas. This very simple structure, erected
within the confines of the gamehouse, was ideally suited to a

variety of needs—the scaffold or gallery as a judges' platform for fencing-matches and other athletic games, as private 'boxes' for the owners of the gamehouse, or as a music room; and the area beneath the scaffold or gallery as a tiring-house and property room

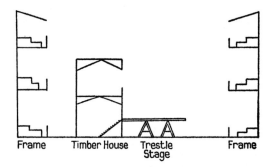

Frame   Timber House   Trestle   Frame
                          Stage

FIG. 25. Timber-house and trestle stage in the arena of a Game-house. (See Fig. 10, p. 180 above.)

for actors. In other words, I have here arbitrarily amalgamated the judges' platform of the combat arena in Tuthill Fields to meet needs specific to actors, with the tents provided on that occasion for the arming of the combatants in imitation of the screen-gallery-changing-room arrangement of College halls and Guildhalls.* Actors' exits, on this assumption, would perforce involve descending from stage level to yard level within the tiring-house, and stage entrances would similarly involve ascending a short flight of steps. Direct access however would be available on a single level from the tiring-house to any trap in the stage floor and no machinery necessary to hoist a man up from below or to lower him through it from above. Chariots could enter the yard from behind the tiring-house (as could ships on wheels) and approach the stage from either side or from the front. A bed could not be 'thrust out' from anywhere but a tent or canopy already set on the stage.†

The addition of a further storey to the timberhouse would permit the installation of the winch-machinery required for ascents to heaven and provide a measure of storage equipment: the addition of two stories would allow a second gallery to be inserted between the gallery over the screen below and the loft above. Turning again to the sketch of the Swan we are assured of the existence of the loft above, but we may only insert the second gallery hypothetically, as there is nothing to suggest its existence in the sketch.

* See Ch. V, p. 164 and Ch. VII, p. 256 above.
† See pp. 310 *et seq.* below for more detailed discussion of these questions.

Interpretation of the sketch is made additionally difficult by the curiously inadequate perspective of the drawing in the area where the loft, with its flag and trumpeter, coincides with both the roof of the frame and the roof over the rear part of the stage. I think myself that De Witt deliberately distorted the perspective in order to illustrate a feature of the playhouse which struck him forcefully but which optically could not have figured in the drawing without a measure of distortion. In what other playhouse of the world did a trumpeter appear against the skyline to sound the start of a performance? This was surely something worth recording, even if it involved drawing the loft as seen from a point well to the right of centre in the auditorium in a sketch otherwise drawn from dead centre?* It is pertinent to observe that there are three separate roofs represented in the sketch—frame, loft, and roof over the stage; and all three are depicted not as flat but sloping. The primary reason for sloping roofs is simply to prevent rain water collecting on them; but the matter cannot rest there. We must surely ask why this third roof, that over the stage, supported at its downstage extremities by classical columns, was needed at all? Clearly *not* to protect the actors, since those depicted at work on the stage are well forward of it. Nor, according to the strict lines of the sketch, can it possibly be there to contain machinery and 'creaking thrones' or any other stage property. Nor can it have existed as a 'shadow' in the sense of keeping the sun out of the eyes of people in the gallery, for in all the London maps representing the bankside theatres the loft projects above the roof in the South-western quadrant of the amphitheatres.† It is plainly ridiculous to argue that it existed to carry paintings of the zodiac in representation of the heavens, since the whole arena was open to the sky itself, whether blue and cloudless or overcast. If De Witt had drawn the Swan in section for us, he must have represented this roof in one of two ways. (See Fig. 26, opposite.)

If we take Fig. (a) to represent the truth, then the roof can only serve one possible purpose—to protect something of value set below it on the rear half of the stage. If we admit Fig. (b) instead, then that purpose still holds but allows, in addition, the presence of a trap in the roof, together with winch-mechanism for hauling people and properties up and down through it. Either way its

* Further evidence for diagrammatic illustration is to be seen in the fact that the trumpeter is shown blowing his trumpet to open the play while the play's action is already proceeding on the *proscaenium* below.

† In this position they would have been sitting with their backs to the sun in any case.

existence went a long way towards making the *mimorum aedes*, if not the *proscaenium*, immovable. Henslowe's insistence in the Hope contract of 1613 that 'the Heavens all over the saide stage' are 'to be borne or carryed w(i)thout any postes or supporters to be fixed or sett uppon the saide stage' indicates clearly enough that 'postes' or 'supporters' were deemed a nuisance in a playhouse to be shared by actors and bears.[46]

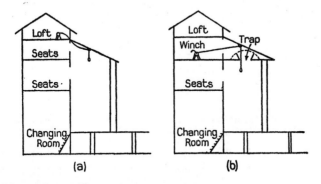

FIG. 26. Modifications of the timber-house to incorporate the 'heavens'.

I arrive at the conclusion therefore that experience at the Theater and the Curtain had convinced Langley when he came to build the Swan (and Henslowe too in respect of the Rose*) that some sacrifice of mobility was worth making. I suggest that one of the reasons behind this decision was to ensure that the rear-half of the stage should be protected against rain, particularly rain driving in from the South-west, which, in England, is the prevailing wind direction; that a second reason was to admit of descents from above, forward of the screen-gallery; and that both were directly related to changes in the economy of the acting companies between 1576 and 1596 and in the increasing scenic demands of the plays added to their repertoires during those two decades. The Revels Accounts testify to the growing popularity during the fifteen-eighties of 'histories' with the battlements and cities required for their staging.[47] Other documents testify to a corresponding increase in the numbers of sharer and hireling members of the acting companies.[48] It seems to me only realistic to anticipate then that these companies gradually came to regard their former stage furniture as inadequate both to their plays and for their audiences, at least in London. Provincial audiences could be regarded in this respect as

* See pp. 308–309 below.

the inferiors of the London audiences in the same way that London public audiences were deemed inferior to those of the Court. The actors who performed regularly in the public theatres were not simply the servants of gentlemen, but of the highest noblemen in the land. Their masters therefore were well enough connected

  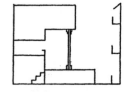

a) Playhouse or Gamehouse in the manner of the Theater or the Curtain

b) Playhouse in the manner of the Rose or the Swan

c) Playhouse in the manner of the 1st Globe

FIG. 27. From Game-house to house for stage-plays in diagrammatic silhouette.

with the Privy Council and with the Royal Household to have first-refusal on scenic items and playing gear which had served its turn in the Revels Office. These costly and ornate emblems having been designed for display in a roofed auditorium deserved protection from the weather in an open-air theatre. The problem of storing them would be no less acute there however than in their original environment. Answers existed in the enlargement of the *mimorum aedes* upwards and the addition, in conjunction with it, of a protective covering for a portion of the stage. The roof or shadow could serve to protect the scenic emblems set out on the back of the stage: the problem of their storage when not in use could be met, in part by the addition of the loft, and in part by the installation of a winch and pulley set in the loft and extending under the 'shadow' with which to raise and lower them from and to the stage below. What I am suggesting here amounts to a compromise between the 'timberhouse' of the original Theater and Curtain lacking both loft and 'shadow', and the first Globe and Fortune in which loft and shadow had become integrated into a single permanent unit.

In other words, the shadow of the Swan was a penthouse lean-to, not unlike a car-port, designed to shelter scenic emblems in use on the stage during performance, and to screen the creaking throne, and possibly other emblems, from public view when hoisted up under the roof by the winch inside the loft. I think it unlikely that there was a second gallery 'above' in the *mimorum aedes* at the Swan.

The tall, semi-permanent *mimorum aedes* of the Swan brought

306

advantages to the actors, but only at the price of sacrificing something between a fifth and a quarter of the seating capacity of the
frame. This might well be regarded as too heavy a price to pay;
but nearly twenty years had passed since the building of the
Theater, and were this old argument to be used now by the
financiers, the actors could well reply that the seating space lost in
the galleries of the frame was more than compensated for by the
number of spectators they admitted to places on and near the stage
itself. The loss of the *orchestra* seats was compensated for by stools
set on the stage; that of *sedilia* seating was made good by the
gallery of the *mimorum aedes*; the indifferent accommodation lost in
the *porticus* was amply recompensed by the standings available in
the *planities sive arena*. This logic is hard to refute once both sides,
financiers and actors, can agree that the building is to be used predominantly for stage-plays and only occasionally for 'feats of
activity'. In the event of stage-plays being suppressed by order of
the Surrey Magistrates (unlikely) or of the Privy Council (quite
possible), both stage and *mimorum aedes* could quickly be de-
molished with small financial loss, leaving the frame intact for
fencing, cock-fighting, bear-baiting and other games. Either way
the major investment was secure. In the event, the Privy Council
signed the order for the suppression of the London playhouses
within a year of the completion of the Swan. The Lord Chamberlain's men, having taken a lease of the Blackfriars, reacted by pull-
ing down the Theater and transporting the woodwork of the frame
across the Thames for use in the construction of the Globe.
Henslowe and Alleyn, either independently or in imitation of the
Burbage management, obtained permission to build the Fortune
for the Admiral's men. The Curtain, mysteriously, survived. So did
the Swan, but whether in its original condition as a fully equipped
playhouse for stage-plays or whether in a modified state for prize-
fights in the first instance and stage-plays only on occasion is open
to question.[49] On a ground plan of the Manor of Paris Garden,
based on a survey of 1st November 1624, but dated 1627, it appears, significantly, as an amphitheatre lacking either stage or
mimorum aedes.[50] (See Fig. 28.)

The details that I have offered by way of supplement to De
Witt's sketch and the justification for the whole have been arrived
at by an imaginative marriage between the data provided in the
sketch and that which can be drawn from the historical context in
which the theatre came to be built. The validity of the resulting
(and largely hypothetical) reconstruction can however be tested if
we switch our attention from a theatre of which we have a sketch

but with which we cannot connect a single play with any certainty, to a theatre which we can positively identify with many plays, but of which we possess no picture. Langley's Swan was opened some few years after its near-neighbour on the Bankside, Henslowe's Rose.[51] Henslowe made many notes concerning his expenses in the building of the Rose, and of the equipment purchased for it both before and after the opening of the Swan.

From these notes we learn that the Rose was thatched, that both the frame and the stage were painted, that it was equipped with

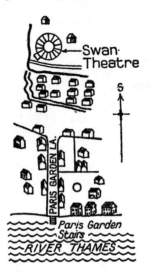

Fig. 28. Detail from a map of the Manor of Paris Garden, 1627.

'heavens' and that it contained storage space enough for a large wardrobe together with several substantial scenic emblems. The Rose was closed in 1595 during Lent, which gave the management the chance to execute repairs. Henslowe noted down what he had

'layd owt abowt my playhowsse ffor payntynge & doinge it abowt w(i)th ealme bordes & other Repracyones . . .'.[52]

The list of items includes nine payments to 'the paynter' amounting in all to 96s. In June of that year a throne was either installed in the heavens or refurbished. The entry reads,

'It(e)m p(ai)d for carpenters worke & mackinge the throne In the heuenes the 4 of June 1595 £7–2–0.'[53]

Two months later in the same year this acquisitive financier bought an Inn in Southwark, the James' Head, and furnished it, among

308

other things, with painted cloths in both 'the halle' and 'the parler'.[54]

From an earlier set of notes (dated 1592) we learn that thatchers were paid for work on the roof of the playhouse, that painters received 26s. for their services, and that ceilings were installed in both his Lords' Room and 'the Rome over the tyerhowsse'. A further 11s. was incurred 'for payntinge my stage'.[55]

Fragmentary though these items are, they become of great value when considered in conjunction with De Witt's sketch of the Swan. Henslowe's payments to thatchers confirm the impression we get from the picture that the roof of the loft at least was thatched. De Witt's draughtsmanship suggests to me that both the *tectum* of the frame and the 'shadow' of the Swan were tiled, an improvement which Henslowe himself incorporated into the Fortune five years later. The ceiling of the room *over* the tiring-house at the Rose indicated beyond dispute that the tiring-house was situated where De Witt placed it in the Swan, and not under the stage as the most recent reconstructor of the Globe has fancied. It also goes some way to confirm my contention that the tiring-house of the earliest theatres was an open timberhouse, since this ceiling was clearly an addition to the fabric of the Rose and not a repair. The payments to painters confirm both the strictures of the Puritan preachers on the luxurious appearance of the London playhouses and De Witt's notes about the imitation marble on the pillars of the Swan. Finally, Henslowe's expenditure on his throne in the heavens makes it almost certain that the Swan was similarly equipped in imitation. It also suggests that this feature was not an integral part of the furnishings of either the Rose when it first opened or of its predecessors in the North Bank suburbs, the Theater and the Curtain. The original contract between Henslowe and John Cholmley, grocer, for the purchase of the land on which the Rose was built however suggests strongly that the playhouse was intended to be used primarily for the production of stage-plays if not to the total exclusion of other 'use' or 'exercise'.* Yet we must be careful about this, for even in the Fortune theatre, in a lease dated 1608, it is 'stage playing or other exercise, Com(m)oditye or use whatsoever' which Henslowe specified as the activities 'to be used or exercised within the playhowse'.†

* Dated 10th January 1586/7.

† This phrase, which occurs in the draft of a lease of 1/32nd part of the playhouse to Thomas Dowton, is paralleled a few lines later by a clause covering the collection of money when 'any play or other exercise shalbe acted or exercised in the play howse'.[56]

4 Scenic Emblems in Elizabethan Public Playhouses

If Henslowe's notes provide us with information which cor-
roborates many features of De Witt's version of the Swan, they
also supply us with enough information to prove beyond dispute
that 'mansions' or 'houses' were used on the stage of the Rose.
This knowledge is derived not only from the well-known '*Booke of
the Inventory of the goods of my* Lord Admeralles men' (1598/99)
but also from scattered entries in the so-called Diary. The scenic
devices in question are all directly paralleled among the scenic
emblems listed in the Revels Office Accounts and described in
surviving records of the Lord Mayors' Shows.

The Inventory reveals that one company owned,

3 Trees	2 Tombs
3 Rocks	2 Frames
3 Animals	2 Steeples (with chime of bells)

together with one of each of the following,

Cage	Bedstead
Hellmouth	City
Chariot	Stable
Pair of stairs	Wooden Canopy
Rainbow	Cloth
Picture	Sign

and one Cauldron.[57]

This list confronts us with a striking paradox: we can ask 'why so
many?' or 'why so few?' with equal justification. Even a full-scale
mediaeval Miracle Cycle could hardly demand as many scenic emblems: yet, if this list represents the company's whole stock, it is
notably short of the arbours, castles, palaces, temples, ships and
cloud-machines which, as we have seen, figured among the normal
emblematic devices of disguisings, masks, tournaments and civic
ridings.

Some light is shed on this mystery by the association of some of
the stage furniture in the list with particular plays. The 'sign', for
example, is specifically stated to belong to *Mother Redcap* by
Anthony Munday and Michael Drayton. This play was new in
1597, the authors receiving 55s. from Henslowe for 'the laste
payment' on 5th January. So too was the play of *Dido and Eneus*,

which received its first performance on 8th January.*[58] One of the
two tombs in the inventory belonged to this play: the other belonged to a play called *Guido* presumably named after the title
role.† This play had received its first performance a year earlier
than *Dido*. Dido's tomb therefore must have differed substantially
from that made for Guido, at least in its decorative appearance.
Thus, just as the arbours or the palaces of the Lord Mayors' Shows
and the Revels Office differed from each other in order that variety
might be provided within a restricted convention, so too were the
emblems of a public theatre varied in their external appearance
from play to play within the limitations imposed upon them by
their function. This point is reinforced by what we know of the
other items recorded in duplicate and triplicate in the inventory. Of
the three trees listed, for instance, one is specified as being a bay
tree, another as a tree of golden apples and a third as Tantalus'
tree.[60] Of the three rocks, two are listed as 'moss banks' and one as
a rock, but all three are simply variants of the 'mountain', 'mount'
or 'rock' so familiar to us in the context of masks and tiltings.[61]

It is difficult to arrive at any certain knowledge of how or when
these emblems came into the possession of the Admiral's men. Since
some of them are identified in the list with particular plays, we may
reasonably assume that they were acquired, bought or made for
those plays and that the name of the original play stuck as a descriptive epithet as tends to happen in theatres today. On the other
hand, Henslowe seems to have been content to let his property-men
adapt existing stock, or make new purchases, without accounting
for every individual item purchased. Frequently he records the
loan of money 'to buy divers things for' a new play or to refurbish
an old one. The sums in question are usually in the range of
£3 to £6, but sometimes amount to much more.[62] On 14th April
1599, for example, £15 was advanced 'to macke divers thinges for
the playe of the spencers' followed by a further £5 a mere two
days later.[63] The production costs for *The Seven Wise Masters*
totalled £38, of which £20 was allocated to the purchase of
fabrics.[64] Sometimes, but very rarely, a particular scenic purchase
is entered by name. Thus, in October 1602,

'p(ai)d for poleyes & worckmanshipp for to hange absolome . . .
xiiij^d',

* This knowledge is of greater importance than it seems, for it indicates
clearly enough that the play was not Marlowe's *Dido Queen of Carthage*, but
either a redaction of it or a new play on the same subject. Nor was Marlowe's
the first: see Table A, p. 175 above.
    † The inventory includes 'Guydoes' cloak and also Dido's 'robe'.[59]

while on the 23rd of the month 20s. was lent to John Thare,

'to paye unto the paynter of the propertyes for the playe of the iij brothers'.[65]

The purchase of particular costumes, by contrast, is recorded frequently and in detail. I would hazard the guess myself that the reason for this was the need to keep a closer watch on costumes and fabrics than on stage properties and furnishings. The extensive use of contemporary costume offered an obvious temptation to the more penurious and less scrupulous members of the companies. No such ready use or market could be found for arbours, rocks or artificial animals.

As I have remarked earlier in this chapter, there is strong reason to think that the leading companies obtained some of their scenic equipment gratis from the Revels Office, once it had been marked down on the Master's inventories as no longer serviceable or chargeable. These more or less fortuitous acquisitions, however, would not remove the need to provide certain items of equipment demanded by a particular new play, but which were not easily obtainable ready made. One such item was the 'frame for the heading in Black Jone', listed in the Admiral's inventory. This play belonged to Henslowe in 1598, but nothing is known of it beyond the fact that an executioner's scaffold was among the stage furniture used for its production.[66] Four years later however Henslow spent 13s.

'Layd owt at the apoyntmente of the companye to macke a scafowld & bare [bar] for the playe of berowne & carpenters wages.'[67]

These items appear in the text and stage directions as requirements for the trial and execution of Byron in Chapman's *Tragedy of Charles, Duke of Byron* (Act v, Scene 1).* The trial takes place

---

* It cannot be proved that Henslowe's 'playe of burone', 'berowne' was Chapman's *The Conspiracie, And Tragedy of Charles Duke of Byron, Marshall of France*. Chapman's play was printed in 1608 and said to have been 'acted lately in two plays, at the Black-Friers'. Chambers (*ES*, iii, pp. 257–8) thinks that Henslowe's play and Chapman's are not related: Greg (*Henslowe's Diary*, ii, 231) admits the possibility, but thinks it unlikely. It is dangerous indeed to plead a case against two such authorities. However, since it can be proved that Chapman was writing for Henslowe in 1597 (Admiral's: see *Diary*, i, ff. 25b–27b and ii, 184) and since neither Chambers nor Greg seem to have taken any notice of the fact that the properties bought by Henslowe for his 'playe of berowne' are precisely those demanded in the text of Chapman's play, I think the contrary view is at least worth stating.

The date of the first payment towards production expenses (which in the Diary almost always precede the first performance by several weeks) for this play is 25th Sept. 1602. The Duke of Biron was executed between two and

in 'the golden chamber' that is on the open stage before the king's throne canopied about with cloth of gold embroidered with 'flower-de-luce'. Byron's escort, Vitry, points this out to the prisoner and then says

'To the bar, my lord'.

The trial over, the characters disperse in groups and a long conversation follows in an unspecified place, which we must assume to be the guard-chamber or prison where Byron is held prisoner since Byron is himself the principal speaker. He makes his exit on the line,

'Come, I'll go where ye will, ye shall not lead me.'

A second conversation follows of sixty-seven lines, before Byron is led in again for execution. The sentence is read out, concluding

'. . . for reparation of which crimes they [the judges] deprived him of all his estates, honours, and dignities, and condemned him to lose his head upon a scaffold at the Greave.†

Byron expostulates on this indignity until at length Vitry intervenes.

'My lord, 'tis late; will't please you to go up?
BYRON: Up? 'tis a fair preferment . . .'

---

three months earlier. Essex had met his death on Tower Hill eighteen months earlier still in similar circumstances. Thus there seems to me to be good reason to suppose that Henslowe's play was Chapman's first draft of a play about the Essex rebellion under the convenient disguise of a topical, French *cause célèbre* which, by 1608, had served its actors well enough to admit of publication complete with such redactions as actors and author had made in the six years since it was first performed.

Chambers states that Chapman's source was Grimeston, *General Inventorie of the History of France*, 1607; but this was a cumulative work, an edition of the earlier material being offered twice to Ponsonby for printing (1597 and 1600).

I do not deny that Chapman may have used the 1607 edition of this work when preparing his text for the printers; but this does not mean that he used it in the first draft which he prepared for the actors. It seems to me in the highest degree unlikely that any company of actors at that time would have agreed to release their copyright in the play to the printer within a few months of its first performance: yet that is precisely what Chambers is postulating. A play on the other hand which had been in repertory for six years might well have been released, the more especially if revival in 1607 or 1608 had involved the company in trouble with the censorship as Chambers argues that it had. I think therefore that there is still as strong a case for the two plays being related as not. Either way however my argument about the staging of the last act is unaffected, since the printed text is of later date than Henslowe's reference. See Marion Jones and Glynne Wickham, 'The Stage Furnishings of George Chapman's *The Tragedy of Charles, Duke of Biron*' in *Theatre Notebook*, Vol. XVI (1962) No. 4, pp. 113–117.

† The place of public execution in Paris, La Place de Grève.

Act V of this play thus demonstrates for us with the utmost clarity how scenic devices were deployed on the Elizabethan public stage. The throne is brought down from 'the heavens' and backed with an 'estate' of fleur-de-lys to identify it as the French king's. The bar is placed before it, the prisoner called to it, and the trial proceeds. The prisoner is led off while the judges sum up and prepare the verdict. As they leave the stage, the throne is hoisted up again into the heavens and the bar is removed. Byron then re-enters from the tiring-house and the stage assumes the aspect of his prison. His exit, and the seventy-odd lines of dialogue which follow, allow the frame of the scaffold to be brought in from the tiring-house and set up behind the speakers for use in the final scene. The only possible alternative to this sequence of events in production is for throne, bar and scaffold to be established simultaneously upon the stage throughout the entire action.

Is there any means of knowing which alternative was in fact adopted? I incline myself to believe that both methods were used, the device depending on the play and the discretion of the property man or stage manager. My argument in support of settings on view throughout the action is almost wholly subjective. It is suggested by the tradition of the religious stage, more precisely those plays which were given stationary performance, like *The Castle of Perseverance* or the *Ludus Coventriae*: the presence of Hell-mouth, both in Henslowe's property-list and in Charles II's London Entry of 1661, suggests that to ignore this tradition would be unwise. Secondly, there is the evidence of the English Wagner Book. The stage which it describes (whether real or imaginary) is mediaeval in character but adapted to Elizabethan conditions of performance: it postulates 'mansions' set on the stage and implies that, with the exception of the throne, they remained in position throughout the play's action.*

'They might distinctly perceiue a goodlye Stage to be reard (shining to sight like the bright burnish golde) uppon many a faire Pillar of clearest Cristall, whose feete rested uppon the Arch of the broad Raynebow, therein was the high Throne wherein the King should sit, and that prowdly placed with two and twenty degrees to the top, and round about curious wrought chaires for diverse other Potentates, there might you see the ground-worke at the one end of the Stage whereout the personated divels should enter in their fiery ornaments, made like the broad wide mouth of an huge Dragon . . . the teeth of this Hels-mouth far out stretching...

* The following extract is reproduced from *ES*, iii, 72.

At the other end in opposition was seene the place where in the bloudlesse skirmishes are so often perfourmed on the Stage, the Wals . . . of . . . Iron attempered with the most firme steele . . . environed with high and stately Turrets of the like metall and beautye, and hereat many in-gates and out-gates: out of each side lay the bended Ordinaunces, showing at their wide hollowes the crueltye of death: out of sundry loopes many large Banners and Streamers were pendant, brieflye nothing was there wanting that might make it a faire Castle. There might you see to be short the Gibbet, the Posts, the Ladders, the tiring house, there everything which in the like houses either use or necessity makes common.'

Thirdly, there is the curious fact that, of all the stage properties, the throne alone was suspended in the heavens. Why, we should ask, were other substantial emblems like arbours and senate-houses not similarly 'flown'? I would answer that while most scenic units could be disposed upon the stage according to convenience, the throne as the seat of judgement could only occupy the centre-stage position. In an actor's theatre, as opposed to a decorator's theatre, this emblematic necessity can conflict directly with practical convenience. In other words, sacrifice of the centre-stage position as an acting area to the claims of spectacle is something which cannot be contemplated. Thus, granted the necessity on both symbolic and aesthetic grounds for presenting the throne in a centre-stage position, and the force of the actor's claim upon this same area on both aesthetic and practical grounds, some compromise must be found to meet both. The solution adopted, as I believe, was the 'flying' of the throne whenever it was not required in the stage action.* No such compulsion operated in respect of those areas of the stage backing or flanking the position reserved for the throne: there is accordingly no reason why the furniture of Henslowe's inventory— be it rock, moss banks, stable or city of Rome—could not occupy these areas throughout the action of a play provided that there was space enough between them to provide the actors with easy access between the tiring-house and the front half of the stage.

Two further advantages of a strictly practical kind follow from placing all the houses and devices required for a play simultaneously upon the stage before the start. First, both visually and aurally, authors and actors stand to gain in audience concentration more than they may lose in scenic surprise or variety, since any shifting of large stage furniture behind the actors must result in

---

* A further reason for suspending the throne may have been clearance of the area near the central stage-trap.

deflecting the audience's attention from the play to the scene-change. Even in the landscape-artist's theatre of the Court Masks, elaborate precautions were taken to prevent this happening. Secondly, the prior placement of the furniture would permit larger scenic units to be used on the stage than could conveniently be brought in and out through the tiring-house doors, particularly if access to the stage from the tiring-house was up steps as I have suggested.* Reasonable protection against rain was offered to all furnishings by the shadow or heavens.

The purchase and storage of the scaffold frames for *Black Joan* and *Byron* have an important additional significance. Why, we should ask, was it necessary to go to the trouble of constructing an executioner's raised scaffold, when the scene could be played on the gallery of the *mimorum aedes*? The answer, as anyone who has had any experience of actors or of stage-production has long suspected, is that the scene could *not* be played on the gallery. This scene in *Byron* is the climax of the play, providing the leading actor with his best speeches and his finest moment. No actor worthy of the part would contemplate playing the scene in so remote and dark a corner of the stage: and, indeed, Alleyn was not expected to. The company built him a scaffold, set it forward of the *mimorum aedes* and allowed him to play the scene from a position on the stage where he could be both seen and heard by everybody present. This advantage applies with equal force to other scenic emblems. By this means Henslowe's bedstead could be concealed behind its curtain-pavilion until required and literally thrust forward to the centre-stage area for the scene in which it figured.[68] The simple opening and shutting of a running curtain could similarly bring a tomb or senate-house into the action of a play and out again. 'Discoveries' present no difficulties. Again, a City or battlements, as at Court, could be built sturdily enough with 'wheel and frame' to withstand the weight of scaling-ladders and actors on the top in *The Siege of London*, just as the headsman's scaffold and the stairs which gave access to it were practicable.† Given the example of the Lord Mayors' Shows, I think that chariots, like Tamburlaine's, did not appear *on* the stage, but made their entry at yard level from behind the tiring house and were driven by 'pampered jades', horses or heraldic beasts as the text demanded, alongside of the stage.‡ At

---

* See pp. 302–303 above.

† If the description of the battlement in the Wagner book is to be trusted, the frame was made of iron, not wood. See p. 387 above.

‡ The inventory lists a dragon, a 'lyon' and a large horse (possibly Trojan).[69]

the Swan, the driver could pass from his seat to the stage and vice versa with ease, since seat and stage were aligned at approximately the same height. Phaeton's chariot, listed by Henslowe, more probably descended from the heavens (substituted in Dekker's play for the throne), and possibly crashed on the two steeples which figure without identity in the inventory.[70] Integral to this form of production is the hanging of the stage itself (floor to yard) and the timberhouse behind it with curtains, painted cloths, arras and other draperies, appropriate to the play and in advance of the performance. The drapery around the edge of the stage corresponds to the cloths hung round the base of pageant-waggons to conceal wheels or porters from public view.[71] Those on the timberhouse resemble just as closely the hangings of the booth-stages of fair-ground and market square.[72] The incorporation of both of these devices in the design of the public theatre needed no originality since they enhanced the functional facilities of the stage and gave an added finish and glamour to the appearance of the playhouse as a whole. 'Tasso's picture' and 'the clothe of the Sone & Mone' of the inventory come within this category: significantly, they also have their counterparts in the Revels Office Accounts.*

Evidence to support the supposition that scenic emblems were shifted during performance is scanty. Clearly, furniture in our own strict sense—like the bench on the fore-stage depicted by De Witt—could be moved during a play's action. Tables and chairs were certainly carried on and off by servants, set for a banquet, as in *Titus Andronicus* (V. iii), or prepared for games of cards and chess as in *The Tragedy of Byron* (IV, i).

> KING HENRY IV: Madam, y'are honour'd much that Duke Byron
> Is so observant: some to cards with him;
> You four, as now you come, sit to Primero;
> And I will fight a battle at chess.

The card game at least proceeds in view of the audience: the king leaves the room, re-enters, and breaks up the game.

> 'Enough, 'tis late, and time to end our play.
> On all hands; all forbear the room.
> (*To Byron*) My Lord
> Stay you with me.'[73]

Whether similar mobility applied to larger furnishings is an open question. The initial stage direction of Robert Greene's *King James*

* See pp. 282–285 above. Also Plates XIII, XXVI and Fig. 10.

the Fourth* (*c.* 1591) although quoted already merits repetition here. It reads:

> '*Music playing within, enter* ASTER OBERON, *King of Fairies; and* ANTICS, *who dance about a tomb placed conveniently on the stage; out of which suddenly starts up, as they dance,* BOHAN, *a Scot, attired like a ridsall man, from whom the* ANTICS *fly.* OBERON *manet.*'[75]

It is possible that the Antics carried this tomb with them from the tiring-house, put it down on the stage and danced round it, but the wording actually used suggests that the tomb had been placed in a convenient position by the stage management before the action began. The tomb contains, besides Bohun the Scot, his two sons Nano and Slipper who make their entry upon the stage later in the scene. Thus, although the Antics could have carried the tomb, it would have been a clumsy object to handle: moreover, if it was carried on to the stage, we should expect to find a line in the text, or a stage direction, instructing the Antics to carry it off again. There is no such instruction: Slipper and Nano leave the stage and Bohun says to Oberon,

> 'Gang with me to the gallery, and I'll
> show thee the same [story] in action by
> guid fellows of our countreymen . . .'

To which Oberon replies,

> 'That I will see: lead, and I'll follow thee.'[76]

As this place of concealment is later referred to by Bohun as 'our arbour', it is permissible to suppose that this tomb, like Farrington's in the Lord Mayor's Show of 1616, was constructed in the style of an arbour and that the 'gallery' was the balustraded, upper-storey of the tomb.† However, as a tomb figures in the second dumb-show—Cyrus of Persia 'laid in a marble tomb'—I incline to think that the gallery in question was one of the rooms depicted by De Witt above the *mimorum aedes*. Cyrus' tomb is said to carry an inscription the text of which is quoted in the dialogue.[77] This gives us some indication of the purpose of the 'sign' for the play of *Mother Redcap* listed in Henslowe's inventory: for the 'sign' or inscription serves to inform the spectators that the tomb has changed its identity from Bohun's home to Cyrus' monument. The text of *James IV* becomes so hopelessly corrupt at this point that it is useless to try to follow the stage action in further detail; but it is

---

* This play was possibly bought by Henslowe who certainly (with Alleyn) owned Greene's other plays.[74]

† See p. 211 above.

worth noting that Act V, scene iii is set on the walls of the city of Dunbar, and that the defendants descend from the walls and open the gates to the besiegers. I take this scene to involve the use of a 'battlement' of the kind which figures so frequently in the Revels Accounts of the fifteen-eighties. This emblem is also required in the 'plot' or scenario of *Frederick and Basilea* (1597) and again in that of *Troilus and Cressida,** both of which survive among the Henslowe-Alleyn papers.[78]

> 'To them Pedro Basilea upon the walls.
> come downe Pedro Basilea.'

> 'Alaru(m). [En]ter Antenor pursued by Diomede
> to them Aiax to the[m] on the
> walls Hector Paris [&] Deiphobus
> & m⟨r⟩ Hunt.   exeunt
> 'Alaru(m). Enter D[io]med . & Troylus . to them
> Achillis [t]o them Hector and Deiphobus
> to them on the walls Priam Paris
> Helen Polixina & Cassandra to them
> ulisses Aiax . menalay & Hea[ralds]
> Priam & they on the wall descend
> to them.'

The Troilus plot also provides evidence of the pavilion in use as an emblem.

> 'Enter Diomede to Achillis [   ]
> to them menalay, to them Ulisses
> to them Achillis in his Tent to
> them. Aiax w(i)th patroclus on his
> back. exeunt.

Two tents are prescribed for Act V, scene iii of Shakespeare's *King Richard the Third*. Both have to be open to allow interior action and dialogue, and they are set to flank the stage-trap through which the Ghost of Prince Edward rises, followed in turn by other Ghosts. In a scene of exceptional formality the Ghosts each address Richard and Richmond in turn sleeping and dreaming in their respective tents. Like the tomb in *James IV* these tents were almost certainly pre-set, as is indicated clearly enough in the plot of *The Second Part of the Seven Deadly Sins* (1592) which starts,

> 'A tent being plast one the stage
> for Henry the sixt . he in it A sleepe
> to him The Leutena(n)t' . . . etc.[79]

(See Plate XXVII, No. 38.)

---

* A play about the Trojan War—not Shakespeare's or Heywood's—possibly Dekker's.

Further use of scenic emblems is illustrated in the 'plots' of *Dead Man's Fortune* (1593?) and *The Battle of Alcazar* (1598?), which demand, respectively, a prison and a chariot.[80] The latter also requires a two-level structure with curtains for a discovery in the lower part. A prison figures as one of the scenic emblems in the inventory of the play of *Tobit* performed in Lincoln in 1564.* That prison was provided with 'a covering' (? a roof) as was the tomb in the same play.[81] On the other hand, it must be remembered that a prison, as in *The Tragedy of Byron*, could be represented without recourse to a mansion-emblem, and that *The Battle of Alcazar* may not have been written for any of the early playhouses. Just as important is the fact that the plot of *The First Part of Tamar Cam*, which is complete, requires no scenic units for its production: other Elizabethan plays are no more exacting, and in this respect parallel the simpler Interludes of early Tudor times.[82] In this fact moreover may lie the explanation of why no scenic units are depicted by De Witt on the stage of the Swan. Alternatively, if the sketch was made during a rehearsal, as the lack of an audience would suggest and as most scholars now agree, the absence of 'mansions' may be explained on that account alone: for a rehearsal in a theatre presenting a repertoire of plays more often consists of running lines and refreshing actors' memories about exits and entrances than of full-scale dress-rehearsal. For this purpose only seats and hand properties are normally required.

Two questions raised earlier in this chapter remain to be answered. What was the relationship of the gallery above the *mimorum aedes* to the stage below and in front of it, and what provision was made within the playhouse for storing the scenic emblems not being used in a performance?

In the early playhouses at least I see no reason to suppose that the gallery above the tiring-house (which at the Rose was equipped with a ceiling) was anything other than a scaffold for spectators as De Witt represents it at the Swan. Of the 84 loggias provided with a lock and key at Romans (in Provence) in 1509 for the *Mystère des Trois Doms*, five were reserved for the private use of the organizers and their friends (see *EES*, i, p. 164): at the Swan the gallery is depicted for us as divided into six compartments of a similarly exclusive and advantageous kind. I therefore take them to be what we would call house-seats, disposable at the discretion of the management. One such loggia, and possibly more, could at any time be held in reserve to seat musicians or actors cast as Presenters or inductors. For Oberon and his dancing Antics in

* See *EES*, i, p. 244 and Plate XVI, No. 20.

Greene's *James IV*, musicians as we have seen, were placed 'within', that is inside the tiring house. For *The Tragedy of Byron* however they are placed 'above', together with a singer. The king is already on the stage. A group of lords enter and from among them Epernon speaks.

> EPERNON: 'Will't please your Majesty to take your place?
> The Mask is coming.
> HENRY: Room my lords; stand close.

With the centre-stage area thus neatly cleared, the mask enters and occupies it.

> '*Music and a song above, and Cupid enters with table(t)*
> *written hung about his neck; after him two torch bearers;*
> *after them* MARIE D'ENTRAGUES, *and four ladies more with*
> *their torch bearers, &c.* Cupid *speaks.*

The familiar picture of Sir Henry Unton's wedding Mask provides us with an illustration of the appearance of these maskers:* indeed, if in our mind's eye we remove the musicians to one of the rooms in the gallery over the tiring-house in the Swan, we have an illustration of the scene as a whole.[83] Actors like Oberon and Bohun in *James IV* or Christopher Sly in *The Taming of The Shrew*, could retire to one of these rooms in the stage-gallery once they had served their function as Presenters in launching the play. From there they could appropriately comment on the action, or descend to the stage and merge themselves with the play again as the text demanded. Actors and friends of the management in these seats were provided with an exceptionally intimate view of the stage action and of the audience; but since this view included the tops of the scenic emblems, it was not as good a view as that provided in the lords' rooms flanking the front of the stage on either side, or from the stools on the stage itself.

Evidence of a factual kind to substantiate the idea that the galleries of the early playhouses ever accommodated bedroom scenes or battle scenes is non-existent; and as a theory it has to be balanced against our knowledge of stage-practice in respect of executioners' scaffolds and roofed tombs and prisons. As an assumption it would be easier to accept if the gallery were depicted in the Swan sketch as,

(a) an open terrace,
(b) a terrace projecting outwards from the *mimorum aedes*.

* See Plate V, No. 6.

Neither of these conditions is fulfilled in the sketch. One pressure however which may well have exercised the actors to consider bringing the tiring-house gallery into use during performance was the problem of storing scenic units of any size on the premises. That storage is a major problem, even in modern times and when confined to costumes, furniture and hand properties, is vouched for by the management of the reconstructed Globe at Ashland, Oregon. There it is only usual to present four plays in repertoire over two months, but, as the years pass, the stock built up over previous seasons becomes steadily more difficult to accommodate. Much of it has to be disposed of or broken up to make room for the wardrobe and furnishings of the current season.[84] What arrangements the Admiral's men, or any other company for that matter, were able to make to meet this problem we do not know. Limited storage accommodation was available within the *mimorum aedes*, both in the dressing-room area at ground level and in the loft above the stage gallery and adjoining the 'heavens'. Just as relevant, an emblematic convention for the identification of place on the stage allowed many scenic devices to be used again and again after slight modification in decorative detail or with the aid of 'scriptures' to meet the demands of a wide range of plays.[85] The economy in storage space effected by means of ringing the changes on basic stock is considerable; but on occasion, as with the tombs for Guido and Dido and with the three trees (bay, golden apple and Tantalus) in the inventory of 1598, duplication was deemed essential. The use of hangings and painted cloths in conjunction with collapsible frames effected a similar economy in storage space, both in the Revels Office and on the public stage. Even so, any move which could be made towards using the *mimorum aedes* itself for establishing locale in stage action and thereby economizing upon the number of scenic emblems which had to be constructed, paid for, set on the stage and subsequently stored was to be welcomed. Responsibility for effecting changes of this order, however, rested as much with the financier-owners of the playhouses as with the actor-tenants. With the Swan closed in 1597, and the Rose, the Curtain and the Theater threatened with demolition on Privy Council instructions, both owners and tenants had strong cause to re-think the future in terms of past experience. Were they to sit tight and hope for a change of heart in Whitehall? Or were they to take the initiative and confront Whitehall with proposals for a new deal? If the latter course were to be adopted, was not this the occasion for the actors to insist that many features of the former multi-purpose gamehouse be dropped, and that new houses be designed in which the proven needs of stage-plays took priority over those of any other speculative 'use' or 'exercises'. It was against this background of political pressure and practical expediency, as I think, that the Theater was translated in 1598 into the first Globe, and that the Fortune Theatre was started in 1601 to replace the Rose.

The design of these two theatres and of those which followed them, together with a discussion of the manner in which plays were acted in them, remain to be considered in Volume III.

APPENDIX A

PAGEANT SETTINGS OF THE
LONDON LIVERY COMPANIES

Midsummer Shows and Lord Mayors' Shows
1504–1603

Date	Company	Devices	Page reference in MSC III
I Midsummer Shows, 1504–1545			
1512	Drapers	Achilles. The Assumption	p. 2
		The Castell of Sm^a	
1519	Skinners	Martyrdom of St. Thomas Becket	pp. 3–4
		Prison. The Maundy. Other pageants *	
1520	Drapers	The Assumption: Cloudes Incarnac(i)ons	pp. 4–5
1521	Drapers	The Castyll of Werr'†	p. 5
		The Story of Iesse	
		Saynt Iohn Eu(a)ngelist	
		The Kyng of the Moores pavillion	pp. 6–11
1522	Drapers	The Assumption	p. 11
		The Golden Fleece ‡	
1523	Drapers	The Assumption	p. 13
		St. Ursula	
1529	Drapers	St. John Evangelist (uppon a mounte)	p. 18
		St. Ursula (uppon a castull)	
		The Story of Jesse	
		The Assumption	
1530	Drapers	xij p(rop)hettes	p. 20
		j castell	
1532	Drapers	j castell	p. 21
		a mounte	
1534	Drapers	St. Christopher	pp. 21–24
		Lady M.	
1535	Skinners	King Solomon	pp. 25–26
		St. John Evangelist (with dragon)	

* Performances on two nights appears to have been a regular feature of these shows.
† Costume item.
‡ Specially made for Emperor Charles V's visit to London.

APPENDIX A

Date	Company	Devices	Page reference in MSC III
		The King (? William the Conqueror)	
		Corpus Christi (6 children and portative organ)	
		The Visitation (St. Elizabeth and Mary)	
1536	Drapers	The Assumption	pp. 27–28
		Castell of Monmouth*	
		King of the Moors Pavillion	
1539	Grocers	? Great Gate	p. 31
1541	Drapers	The Assumption	pp. 32–34
		Christ in the Temple	
		Rock	
		St. Margaret†	

II Lord Mayors' Shows, 1540–1603

Date	Company	Devices	Page reference
1540	Drapers	The Assumption	p. 37
1551	Skinners	Ship	p. 38
		? Professional players	
1553	Merchant Taylors	St. John Evangelist	*EP*, ii, pp. 13–14
1561	Merchant Taylors	David, Orpheus, Amphion Arion and Topas: for details of the setting see *EP*, ii, p. 18, n. 2	pp. 41–44
1568	Merchant Taylors	The City on 4 wheels	p. 47
		St. John Evangelist	p. 48
1585	Skinners	?Monument or Throne of London ‡	*EP*, ii, pp. 23–24
1602	Merchant Taylors	Ship§	pp. 58–60

This list would be much fuller than it is if as many records of other companies were available to us as have survived from the Drapers Company in the early half of the century and from the Merchant Taylors Company in the latter half. Even so, the records that we possess suffice to illustrate three important, and I think hitherto unsuspected, points.

First, the Drapers' pageant of the Assumption in London outlasted the York and Chester Pageants on that subject by some ten to twenty years. Secondly this pageant and several others including the Skinners' pageant of St. Thomas Becket, and the Drapers' pageants of St. John, Jesse and St. Margaret were not simply tableaux, but short plays involving speech, song and action. This prompts an important question: were these pageants the survivors of a London guild cycle or cycles? The heavy preponderance of religious subjects, the mixture of biblical themes and stories of saints,

* The name of one of the Sheriffs was Humfrey Monmouth, Draper.
† Aqua-vitae for fire in the dragon's mouth.
‡ Deduced from George Peele's verses.
§ Taken into the Company's Hall.

and the carrying of banners depicting the same subjects as those represented in the pageants,* suggests to me a distribution of plays from several cyclic groups similar to that which we know existed in York and Beverley. I do not wish to press this point further than the scanty evidence warrants; but the fact that the Drapers could bring out their pageant of the Assumption with impunity as late as 1540 destroys such cause as one might otherwise have for supposing that cyclic religious plays in London disappeared from the city's life much earlier than in provincial cities.†

The third point of interest is the regularity with which the traditional scenic emblems—castle, mountain, tree, pavilion etc.—appeared in London streets and halls throughout the sixteenth century. Thus although descriptions of them are not as full as those which follow in the seventeenth century, it is evident that they would at once be recognizable to all ranks of society when making their appearance in any interlude or stage-play whether presented to private or public audiences.

* See *EES*, i, pp. 147–149.
† See p. 70 above.

APPENDIX B

London: City Proclamation of 6th February, 1545

A p(ro)clamac(i)on for the Abolyshem(en)t of Int(er)ludes. fforasmoche as by reason and Occasyon of the manyfold and sundrye Enterludes and co(mm)en Playes that nowe of late dayes have been by dyvers and sondrye p(er)sones more co(m)monly and besylye [*busily*] set foorthe and played [*than*] heretofore hathe bene accustomed in dyvers & many suspycyous darke & inconvenyent plac(e)s of this our most drad & most Beninge soveraign lorde the king(e)s Citie & chamber of london wherein no suche playes ought to be played And that namelye & cheiffelye upon the Sondaye & other hallydayes in the tyme of Evensonge & other devyne s(er)vice Celebrate & said in the said citie to whiche places a greate p(ar)te of the youthe of the same Citie & manye other light Idle and evyll disposed p(er)sones daylye and Contynuallye frequentynge hauntynge & followyinge the same playes have not onelye bene the Rather moved & provoked therebye to all provytye p(ro)clyvytye & Redynes of dyvers & sondrye kyndes of vyce & synne. And the said youthe by that Occasyon not onely provoked to the unjuste wastynge and Consumynge of theire maisters good(e)s the neglectinge and Omyssyon of theyre faithefull s(er)vice & due Obedyence to there said maisters. But also to the no little losse and hynderaunce of gods hono(u)r & the devyne s(er)vice aforesaid and to the Augmentynge of many other inconvenyenc(e)s mo[*re*] whiche daylye sprynge & ensue thereof to the highe displeasure of Almyghtye god the great norysshement & Encrease off moche vyce synne & Idelnes & to the greate decaye & hurt of the co(m)mon welthe of the said Citie as of Archerye & other laufull & laudable exercyses as o(u)r said most gracious soveraign lorde is Credeblye enformed. his highnes therfore straitlye Chargethe & co(m)maundethe that no maner of p(er)son or p(er)sones from hensforthe of what soever estate degree or Condi(i)on he or they be of presume or take upon hym or them at any tyme hereafter to playe or set foorthe or cause to be played any maner of Enterlude or co(mm)en playe w(i)thin any maner of place or places of this his grace(e)s said Citie. Onles it be in the houses of noble men or of the lorde Maire Shryves or aldermen of the same his highnes Citie for the tyme beinge Orels in the houses of gentelmen or of the substancyall & sad Co(mm)iners or hed p(ar)issheners of the same Citie or in the open stret(e)s of the said citie as in tyme paste it hathe bene used & accustomed or in the co(mm)en hall(e)s of the Companyes felowshipps or brotherhedd(e)s of the same Citie. And that at the Request & desyre of the same Companyes felowships and Brotherhedd(e)s and in theire co(mm)en assembles & presence at tymes mete

& convenyent for the same and in none otherwise And further that no maner of p(er)son or p(er)sones of what estate degree or condic(i)on soever he or thei be of presume at any tyme hereafter or take upon hym or them to set up or affixe . . .

The text breaks off short at this point and is obviously incomplete. The word following 'affixe' was probably 'bills', and the sense of the sentence as a whole that no plays were to be publicly advertised whether by bill-posting or by any other means within the city.

APPENDIX C

An Extract from *De Honestis Ludis* of Martin Bucer, 1551

The young (i.e. *schoolboys and others undergoing instruction*) will be able to take part in acting comedies and tragedies and thus provide their public with wholesome entertainment which is not without value in increasing piety: but religious men will be needed to compose these comedies and tragedies, men schooled in the knowledge of Christ's Kingdom and also endowed with discrimination. Doubtless in plays of this kind a representation would be shown of human thoughts, actions and fortunes, both those of everyday, ordinary people, as happens in comedies, and of unusual characters such as excite greater wonder, which is the mark of tragedy, likely to unite the principles of a religious life to a sure amendment of character.

For example, let us suppose that the quarrel between Abraham's and Lot's shepherds and their mutual departure in different directions were represented as a comedy. . . . In comedy of this kind subject matter could be treated and presented in the form of an entertainment that was valuable to the religious life. . . . Similarly, the story of Rebecca, sought, won and brought as wife to Isaac would undoubtedly provide abundant material both for religious comedy and for the building of moral character: because from this story the dutiful care of parents to seek religious marriages for their children could be well depicted, as also could the loyalty and the devotion of honest servants. A similar theme could be extracted from that part of the story of Jacob which describes how through fear of his brother he left his parents and went away to his uncle Laban.

For the making of tragedies the Scriptures constantly offer an abundance of material in almost all the stories of the Holy Fathers, the kings, the prophets and Apostles, continuously from Adam, the first parent of the human race. For these stories are thickly packed with godlike and heroic people, with emotion, with character, with actions and with unforeseen events moreover which happen contrary to expectation and which Aristotle calls 'reversals of fortune'. Since all these qualities have wonderful power to strengthen faith in God, to arouse love and desire of God and to create and increase not only admiration of piety and justice, but also the horror of impiety and of the sowing and fostering of every kind of evil, how much more fitting it would be were Christians to take their poems from sources which can depict great and famous human thoughts, struggles and inborn talents, changes of feeling and of fortune, than from the profane plays and stories of the pagans! Furthermore, these qualities must be handled in either kind of poetry, comic or tragic, in such a way that when the faults and sins of men are being described and shown in action as though before our eyes, even the crimes of the most abandoned of men, yet some dread of divine judgement and of a horror of sin should appear in them: no exultant delight in crime or shameless insolence should be displayed. Therefore it is more important to modify the poetic style than to subtract anything from the duty of edifying the audience; this demands that in every representation of sin the condemnation of the individual conscience should be perceived together with fearful respect for the judgement of God.

While, however, good and honourable actions are presented, a joyful sense of divine mercy should be expressed as clearly as possible within them, certain and confident, yet controlled and self-distrustful, glorying in God in the assurance of the promises of God with holy and spiritual joy in welldoing. For in this way the inborn talents, the characters and emotions of the good are represented in exact imitation in order to renew all forms of piety and virtue among the people. So that Christ's people, however, may profit from religious comedies and tragedies, men will have to be appointed to the task of preventing the performance of any comedy or tragedy which they have not seen beforehand and decided should be acted. They must be men both outstanding in their knowledge of this kind of literature and also of established and constant zeal for Christ's kingdom.

These men will also take care that nothing frivolous or theatrical be allowed in the performance but that everything be directed in a style that is religious and serious yet pleasing, at any rate to the pious: in this kind of production the characters and natures of the men represented will be depicted more carefully than their actions, emotions and passions: and they will be acted in such a way as to arouse in the audience both a longing to imitate them and a hatred of bad ways and deeds, thus stimulating a more watchful state of mind against evil.

These precautions observed, it will certainly be possible to make available to the young much useful subject-matter for plays both in the vernacular and in Latin and Greek; and these plays, when enthusiasm and interest in this kind of comedy and tragedy has been aroused, will be a valuable means of nourishing and increasing virtue. There already exist some comedies and tragedies of this kind which are not to be despised: and even if the learned of this world look in vain in such comedies for that wit, that charm and grace of language, which they admire in the plays of Aristophanes, Terence and Plautus, and miss in such tragedies the dignity, the subtlety and the polished style of Sophocles, Euripides and Seneca, yet those who are learned in the kingdom of God and who are eager to learn the wisdom of living to God do not look in vain in modern plays (*lit:* in the poems of our men) for heavenly teaching, emotion, character, language and events worthy of sons of God. It is to be desired, however, that those to whom God has granted it to excel in these matters, should choose to employ their gift to his glory rather than to hinder the good desires of others by untimely criticisms; and that they should prefer moreover to present comedies and tragedies in which knowledge of eternal life is manifestly clear (even if some literary niceties are lacking), rather than plays in which both spirit and character are defiled by impious and disgusting interchanges of buffoonery, even if some pleasure is given by refinements of wit and language.

The Latin text is printed in ES, iv, pp. 188–190

The *De Regno Christi*, of which the *De honestis ludis* forms a section, was presented by Bucer to Edward VI as a Christmas gift in 1551. Bucer was at that time Regius Professor of Divinity at Cambridge: he died later that year. Thomas Whythorne writes in his autobiography,

> 'He, being dead and buried, the Papists in Queen Mary's days took up his cask or coffin, and also the cask or coffin of one named Paulus Fagius . . . and burned them both at a stake as the relics of two arch-heretics.'

Whythorne goes on to relate how in Elizabeth's days Bucer's remains were again dug up and reconsecrated. (*Autobiography, ed. cit.*, pp. xxxv–xxxvi and 120–124.)

APPENDIX D

The Chamberlains' Accounts at Norwich, 1534 to 1550

Michaelmas 26. Hen. VIII. to Michaelmas 27. Hen. VIII. (1534–35)

And payd to the Kyngs pleyers (*the words* 'at Saynt Olaves gild' *follow, but are deleted*) vi s. viii d.

27–28. Hen. VIII (1535–36)

And payd to the Duke of Norfolks players at Mr Maiers com-andem(en)t vi s. viii d.

33–34. Hen. VIII (1541–42)

It(e)m payd for sedge to strowe the Halle ther when the prynces players playd an enterlude ther, ii d. drynke for the players— ii d. to ii laborers that fechyd barrells and tymber and made a scaffold then—ii d. vi d. wytson weke.

34–35. Hen. VIII (1542–43)

It(e)m p(ai)d to the Erle of Arnedells (*Arundel's*) players who playd on myhelmes day in the begynnyng of this accompt an en-terlude in the sembly chambyr of ye guldhall vi s. viii d. wherof was gathered amongst the Aldermen iii s. viii d. and so was p(ai)d by the accomptante ii s.

It(e)m p(ai)d for p(er)fume for the chambyr whyche savord sore —ii d. and to a laborer (tha)t swept ye chambyr and made a skafold upon the fourmes ther ii d. iiii d.

Notebook jotting:

And p(ai)d at the comandement of Mr Mayer to c(er)ten game players pleyenge in the asemble chamber & beside iiii s. viii d. gathered amonge the compenye w(i)th ii d. p(ai)d for p(re)-paryng a stage ffor them and ii d. for p(er)fume spent in the counsell chamb(er) ffor to avoide the stronge savor ther by reason of a chymney in the pr(i)son whereoff the Swote (*refuse*) was brent (*burned*) ii s. iiii d.

35–36. Hen. VIII (1543–44)

Item p(ai)d on the Sonday aft(e)r Twelfth day to vi laborers that caryed xii long popill (*poplar*) planks from the comon . . . to the como(n) Halle to make a skaffold for an Interlude to be playd ther by my lord of Sussex men vi d.

It(e)m to a sergente (tha)t made ye skaffold w(i)t(h) brede and drynke as well for the players as for the laborers & sargent viii d.

It(e)m ther was gevyn to the sayd players in reward—x s. of the which was gatherd of Mr Mayor and his brethern ii s. x d. and so was p(ai)d by the accomptant vii s. ii d.

It(e)m gaf to the prynces players the xviii day of novembyr in reward bycause (tha)t mr Mayor hade no leyser to se them playe

iii s. iiii d.

36–37. Hen. VIII (1544–45)

It(e)m gof in reward the xi day of January to my lord of sussex players bycause Mr Mayer and his brethern was at no leyser to se them playe and also the comon halle at (tha)t tyme occupyed w(i)t(h) the Kyngs Greyne   £2. v s.

It(e)m gaf in reward to my lord prynces players playeng an Interlude upon ye assencon Day in Mr Castyldens place byfore Mr Mayer & his brethern and other comyns   vi s. vi d.

38. Hen. VIII–I. Edward VI (1546–47)

Impr(i)mis gaf in reward to the qwenys players who playd an Interlude at the comon Halle on the tewysday in the vi^th weke after myhelmas whose matter was the m(a)rket of myscheffe—x s. of the whyche was gatherd amonge the pepyll ther—vi s. iiii d. and so was payd by the accomptant   iii s. viii d.

It(e)m p(ai)d for fechyng of tymber & makyng the skaffold at the ⌈far⌉ ende of the halle   ii d.

It(e)m gaff in reward to my lord prynces players who playd an Interlude at ye Comon Halle on Seynt Katheryns day

xiii s. iiii d.

It(e)m for makyng of the skaffold and for drynke for the players

v d.

It(e)m gaf in reward to mr byrde scolemaster of the gram(ar) scole for his scolers playeng an Interlude in the chappell of the comon halle the sonday aft(e)r Twelth Day   x s.

It(e)m gof in reward on the Sonday beyng sent Jamys Evyn to certen Spanyards and Ytalyans who dawnsyd antycks & played dyv(e)rse other feets at the Comon Halle before Mr Mayor and the co(m)i(n)al(i)te   xiii s. iiii d.

It(e)m for a fferkyn of bere for them &c   ix d.

It(e)m to dyv(e)rs men (tha)t removyd the tabyles trustylls & fforymes (*tables, trestles and forms*) & set them agayne when all thyngs was don   iiii d.

2 & 3 Edward VI (1548–49)

It(e)m the xi day of Decembyr to ye Kyngs players playeng an Interlude in the Comon Halle on the Sonday monday & tewysday

xx s.

It(e)m to a carpente(r) (tha)t made certen skaffolds   iiii d.

It(e)m p(ai)d to my lord p(ro)tectors players who playd an Interlude at the Comon Halle the xiii day of Decembyr x s. whereof Re(?*ceived*) of mr Rogers then mayer v s. and so paid by the accomptant   v s.

It(e)m for charcole / candyll / drynke and menys labores (tha)t made ye skaffold & kept the dore   xiiii d.

It(e)m payd for a skaffold makyng at ye Como(n) Halle for an

APPENDIX D

2 & 3 Edward VI (1548–49)—*continued*

enterlude playd ther ye Sonday byfore Candylmas & for drynks & charcole   iiii d.

It(e)m the reward was payd by master mayer but payd to ii men (tha)t kept the dores   iiii d.

3 & 4 Edward VI (1549–50)

It(e)m p(ai)d ther by the sayd comandment to mr Thomas Todde Mayer to gyf reward to the Kyngs players for (tha)t it was thought good not meet for them to playe at the tyme then reques(t)yd by reason of the late comoc(i)on*   x s.

* In all probability the Kett rebellion: see Ch. III, p. 65 above.

APPENDIX E

Statutes IV, ii, 1024

1 James I c. 7

'An Acte for the Continuance and Explanation of the Statute
made in the 39 yeere of the Raigne of our late Queene Elizabeth, intituled An Acte for Punishmente of Rogues, Vagabondes
and Sturdie Beggers.

Sec. 1 Whereas by a Statute made in the nine and thirtieth yeere of the
Raigne of the late Queene Elizabeth, there was an Acte made, intituled An Acte for Punishment of Rogues, Vagabondes and
Sturdie Beggers, it was enacted, That all p(er)sons callinge themselves Scholers goinge aboute begginge, all Seafaringe men
p(re)tending losse of their Shippes or Goods on the Sea, goinge
aboute the Countrie begginge, all idle p(er)sons goinge aboute in
any Countrie, either begginge, or usinge any subtile Crafte or unlawfull Games or* Playes, or fayninge themselves to have knowledge in Phisiognomie Palmestry or other like craftye Science, or
p(re)tendinge that they can tell Destinies Fortunes or such other
like fantasticall Imaginations; all p(er)sons that be, or utter
themselves to be Proctors Procurors Patent Gatherers or
Collectors for Gaoles Prisons or Hospitals; all Fencers Bear-
wardes com(m)on Players of Enterludes, and Minstrels wand-
ringe abroad, (other then Players of Enterludes belonginge to any
Baron of this Realme, or any other honourable P(er)sonage of
greater Degree, to be authorized to play under the Hande and
Seale of Armes of such Baron or P(er)sonage) shalbe taken
adjudged and deemed as Rogues Vagabondes and Sturdie Beggers,
and shall suffer such Paine and Punishment as in the saide Acte is
in that behalfe appointed, as by the same Acte more at large is
declared; Sithence the makinge of which Acte divers Doubtes and
Questions have bene moved and growen by diversitie of Opinions
taken in and upon the letter of the saide Acte: For a plaine Declaration whereof be it declared and enacted, That from henceforthe no Authoritie to be given or made by any Baron of this
Realme or any other honourable Personage of greater Degree,
unto any other person or p(er)sons, shall be availeable to free and
discharge the saide p(er)sons, or any of them, from the Paines
and Punishmentes in the saide Statute mentioned, but that they
shall be taken within the Offence and Punishment of the same
Statute.

* For 'or', 1604, read 'and' 1572.

APPENDIX E

Marginal Notes: 1 Recital of Stat. 39 Eliz. c. 4 s. 2 declaring
Players, &c to be Vagabonds:
2 No licence by any Nobleman shall exempt Players.

Statutes IV, ii, 899: 39 Eliz. C. 4 § 2

Identical wording to: (. . . Baron or Personage); then seven-line
list of additional types of offender, 'all Juglers, Tynkers,
Pedlers . . . wandering in the Habit Forme or Attyre of
counterfayte Egipcians'.
Then identical to '. . . is in that Acte appointed'.

APPENDIX F

A LIST OF JACOBEAN & CAROLINE LORD MAYORS' SHOWS

in London, giving the Company of which the Lord Mayor was a member and the poets and principal artificers and painters employed on each occasion

Date	Company	Author	Principal Artificer and Painter	Title of Show
1604	Haberdashers	Ben Jonson	John Grinkin	Not known
1605	Merchant Taylors	Anthony Munday	Mr. Hearne	Triumphs of Reunited Britannia
1606	Clothworkers	Not known	Not known	Not known
1607	Mercers	Not known	Not known	Not known
1608	? No Show			
1609	Ironmongers	Anthony Munday	John Grinkin	Camp-bell: the Ironmongers Faire Field
1610	Merchant Taylors	Anthony Munday	John Grinkin	Not known
1611	Goldsmiths	Anthony Munday	John Grinkin	Chryso-Thriambos
1612	Merchant Taylors	Thomas Dekker	Nicholas Sotherne and George Jackson	Troia-Nova Triumphans
1613	Grocers	Thomas Middleton	John Grinkin	Triumphs of Truth
1614	Drapers	Anthony Munday	Not known	Himatia-Poleos
1615	Drapers	Anthony Munday	Not known	Metropolis Coronata
1616	Fishmongers	Anthony Munday	Mr. Clay and Mr. Kemby	Chrysanaleia: the Golden Fishing
1617	Grocers	Thomas Middleton	Not known	Triumphs of Honour and Industry
1618	Ironmongers	Anthony Munday	John Grinkin	Sidero-Thriambos
1619	Skinners	Thomas Middleton	Not known	Triumphs of Love and Antiquity
1620	Haberdashers	John Squire	? Francis Tipslie	τῆς Εἰρήνης Τροπαῖα
1621	Drapers	Thomas Middleton	Garret Christmas	The Sun in Aries
1622	Grocers	Thomas Middleton	Garret Christmas	Triumphs of Honour and Virtue
1623	Drapers	Munday and Middleton	Garret Christmas	Triumphs of the Golden Fleece (Water) Triumphs of Integrity (Land)
1624	Merchant Taylors	John Webster	John Terry William Patten George Lovett	Monuments of Honour
1625	No Show			
1626	Drapers	Thomas Middleton	Garret Christmas	Triumphs of Health and Prosperity
1627	Haberdashers	Thomas Dekker	Garret Christmas	Not known
1628	Skinners	Thomas Dekker	Garret Christmas and Mr. Norman	Britannia's Honour
1629	Ironmongers	Thomas Dekker	Garret Christmas	London's Tempe
1630	Merchant Taylors	Thomas Dekker	Not known	Not known

Date	Company	Author	Principal Artificer and Painter	Title of Show
1631	Haberdashers	Thomas Heywood	Garret Christmas	*London's Jus Honorarium*
1632	Haberdashers	Thomas Heywood	Garret Christmas	*Londini Artium and Scientiarum Scaturigo*
1633	Clothworkers	Thomas Heywood	Garret Christmas	*Londini Emporia*
1634	Clothworkers	John Taylor	Robert Norman Zachery Taylor	*Triumphs of Fame and Honour*
1635	Ironmongers	Thomas Heywood	John Christmas	*Londini Sinus Salutis*
1636	Fishmongers	Not known	Not known	Not known
1637	Haberdashers	Thomas Heywood	John and Mathias Christmas	*Londini Speculum*
1638	Drapers	Thomas Heywood	John and Mathias Christmas	*Porta Pietatis*
1639	Haberdashers	Thomas Heywood	John and Mathias Christmas	*Londini Status Pacatus*
1640	Grocers	No Show		

APPENDIX G

Professional acting companies, plays and the scenic units prepared for them by the Revels Office, 1564–1576, extracted from *Documents relating to the Office of the Revels*, ed. cit.

Date	Company	Scenic units	Play
1564	Children of the Chapel	Cities and Townes	Edwardes Tragedy
	Sir Percival Harte's Son's men	Cities and Townes and the Emperors pallace	

Westminster grammar school boys gave performances of Terence's *Heautontimorumenos* and Plautus' *Miles Gloriosus* that year, but no scenic devices are listed.

Date	Company	Scenic units	Play
1567	Not known	Stratoes house, Gobbyns howse, Orestioes howse, Rome, the Pallace of prosperitie, Scotland, a Castle	Seven Plays: As playne as Canne be, The paynfull pillgrimage, Jacke and Jyll, Sixe fooles, Witte and Will, Prodigalitie, Orestes, and a Tragedie of the Kinge of Scottes
1571/72 Christmas	Sir Robert Lane's men* Children of Pauls Children of Windsor Children of the Chapel	apte howses: made of Canvasse, fframed, ffashioned & paynted	Lady Barbara Effiginia Ajax and Ulisses Narcissus
Shrovetide	Sir Robert Lane's men* Children of Westminster		Cloridon & Radiamanta Paris & Vienna
1572 Christmas	Children af Paul's Dutton's men* Earl of Leciester's men Earl of Leicester's men Children of Windsor	An altar, a desk, Holly Tree, and holly for a forest, trees for a wilderness, players houses,	Not known
Shrovetide	Children of Eaton Merchant Taylor's School	a picture of Andromeda, an image of canvas stuft	
1573 Christmas	Earl of Leicester's Children of Pauls Earl of Leicesters Children of Westminster Lord Clinton's Children of Windsor	Houses, great hollow trees, senate house with curtains, holly and ivy, counterfeit fishes, an arbour ? great painted cloths	Predor: & Lucia Alkmeon Mamillia Truth, ffaythfullnesse & Mercye Herpetulus the blew knighte & perobia Quintus ffabius

Holly and ivy is specified for 'the play of predor': armour for 'the play of Quintus ffabius'

* *i.e.* The Earl of Lincoln's Company

APPENDIX G

Date	Company	Scenic units	Play
Candlemas	Merchant Taylors	Houses and painted cloths	Timoclia at the sege of Thebes
Shrovetide	Earl of Leicester's men		Philemon & philecia
	Merchant Taylor's men		Percius & Anthomiris
1574–5	Earl of Leicester's boys	An elaborate Rock for Leicester's men. Houses and a cloud-machine for the others, not defined	Not known
	Lord Clinton's men		Pretestus
Christmas	Earl of Leicester's men		Panecia
	Lord Clinton's men		Two plays
	Children of Windsor		Not known
			Not known
Candlemas	Children of Pauls		
Shrovetide	Children of the Chapel		Not known
?	Lord Chamberlain's men		Phedrastus, & Phigon & Lucia
1576	Earl of Warwick's		The Paynters daughter
	Lord Howard's		Toolie
	Earl of Leicester's	Painted cloth and two frames	The historie of the Collyer
1576–7	Children of Paul's		The historie of Error
	Children of Windsor & Chapel	Two frames	The hystorie of Mutius Sceuola
	Lord Chamberlain's		The historye of the Cenofalles
	Lord Howard's		
	Earl of Warwick's		
	Children of Paul's		

APPENDIX H

Guiseppe Pavoni's description of the festivities in Florence, 1589, marking the wedding of Christine de Lorraine and the Grand Duke of Tuscany, transcribed from the unique printed copy of Pavoni's *Diario* (Bologna, 1589) in the Bibliothèque de l'Arsenal, Paris

(See Ch. VII, footnote to p. 265 above.)

ITALIAN TEXT

'IL GIOVEDI, che fu alli II. nel Palazzo de' Pitti si fece quel bellissimo Torneo tanto desiderato dalle genti. Era tutto il cortile vacuo, ma coper- [36] to di tela rossa. Sotto le loggie vi erano i palchi: & dinanti à detti palchi vi erano li gradi, un più alto dell'altro, ove non vi sedeva altri, che le donne; & davanti à detti palchi vi era una serraglia alta tre braccia, che circondava tutto il Cortile, quale era bittumata in modo, che non havea nessun spiraglio; fatta così à posta, per farvi una battaglia navale.

Verso il Giardino vi era un Castello, finto à modo d'una inespugnabil fortezza, nel quale per guardia di esso stavano di molti Turchi.

Nel mezo del Cortile vi era la Sbarra pel traverso, che teneva divisi li Cavalieri quando combattevano: ma era tutta ripiena di fuochi artificiati. Et d'intorno à detto Cortile apparve un numero infinito di lumi, che facevano apparire l'oscura notte un chiaro, & rilucente giorno.

Et à detta festa non vi poteva entrar persona alcuna, se prima non mostrava il segno di Porcellana, che per tale effetto erano stati dispensati, & si passava per tre corpi di guardie, stando nella terza, & ultima il Sereniss. Gran Duca in persona, & in sua compagnia vi era l'Eccellentissimo Sig. Don Pietro suo fratello, & altri Signori, ma alle Gentildonne Francesi, & Fiorentine, & anco alli Signori Francesi era libera l'entrata.

Assettati che furono tutti à' suoi luochi, fu dato il segno con dui tiri di bombarda, ch'entrassero in capo i cavalieri con le lor belle inventioni: & così il [37] primo che comparve, fù un carro trionfale, sopra del quale vi era un Negromante, che mentre andave attorno il steccato, andava scongiurando: & in un tratto comparve un'altro carro trionfale, tirato da un Drago grandissimo, con dentro due Cavalieri, & una rara musica: & si fermarono à cantare dinanti ove stava la Serenissima Sposa; si come fecero anco tutte le altre inventioni.

I Cavalieri, che furono i primi à entrare in cápo, furono il Sereniss. Duca di Mantova, & l'Eccellentissimo Signor Don Pietro de' Medici, che

341

erano li Mantenitori, qual gionti dinanti al Castello, smonta rono in terra;
& il lor carro trionfale si partì, dando céno al Castello con un tiro d'artiglieria, che erano gionti li Mantenitori, & subito fece l'entrata la seconda
inventione, che fù una montagna grandissima, con la sua musica, & non si
vedeva chi la menasse. Così fermatasi davanti la Sereniss. Sposa s'aperse,
e ne uscì di quella due Cavalieri, quali s'andarono à porre da l'altra banda
della sbarra. Venuta l'hora del combattere, il Mastro di Campo diede il
segno à i Cavalieri: i quali ruppero l'un contra l'altro tre picche per uno:
poi mettendo mano allo stocco si tirarono cinque colpi per uno: il che
successo, si tiravano da banda, dando luoco all'altre inventioni, che di
mano in mano arrivavano in Campo: le quali furono al numero di dodici,
una più bella dell'altra, e vi erano di strane bizarrie, come Fonti, Nu[38]-
vole, Boschi, Nicchie, Anotomie d'animali su carri, Navi, Scogli, Sirene,
Uccelli grandissimi, Elefanti; & ultimamente comparve Don Virginio
cóla sua inventione, che era una gran Montagna, & un Cocodrillo, su'l
quale gli era à cavallo uno Incantatore; dopò questi sequìra un carro
trionfale, nel quale era detto Don Virginio con otto Ninfe, cicè quattro
per banda, che con belle panierine di fiori, con i suoi Sonetti, gli andavano
compartendo nel grembo di quelle Principesse, & altre Signore; & esso
Don Virginio stava di dietro del carro in alta Sedia tutto armato, che
pareva un Marte. Dopo lui seguiva un Giardino, il quale, mentre che
entrava nel steccato si andò distendendo per ordine attorno, attorno, che
faceva con la sua bella, & improvisa vista, maravigliare tutti li circon-
stanti, ne si vedeva da chi fosse condotto, parendo, che caminasse per in-
canto; & in detto giardino si vedeva tessuto, e da maestrevole mano
fabricato diverse sorti di capricci, come nave, fuste, torri, castelli,
huomini à cavallo, piramidi, boschetti, uno Elefante, & altri animali
quadrupedi, et il tutto era fatto di verdura; dentro de i quali si sentiva
diverse sorti di uccelletti, che con la diversità de i lor canti, faceano
un'harmonia dolce, & suave. Et perche detto giardino come hò detto di
sopra, faceva spaliera intorno al Campo, volse la sorte, che arrivasse un
boschetto pieno di uccelli dinanti alla Serenissima Sposa, i quali pi[39]-
gliarono il volo chi quà, & chi là, cercando salvarsi, & uno di essi si andò à
coricare nel suo grembo, che ben meritava la vita: la qual volse, che fosse
conservato, & custodito vivo per memoria. Così smontato detto Don
Virginio, andò ad assaltar l'adversario, rompendo le sue picche con molta
destrezza, & leggiadria, facendo gli assalti, & le ritirate con tanta attitu-
dine, che fece stupire ogn'uno; & fatti li colpi delli stocchi, s'andò à porre
con gli altri. I qua li poi tutti si divisero in due parti, & fecero la folla, e
piglíado in mano una picca per uno, si vennero ad incontrare, & quella con
molta destrezza ruppero, & tirandosi indietro dui passi, misero mano à
gli stocchi, & con quegli percotendosi l'un contra l'altro, che pareva
rovinasse il cielo: & seguivano tuttavia la tresca, se non erano interrotti
dalli fuochi artificiati posti nella sbarra, che scoppiò in due parti, uscendo
fuori raggi, soppioni, scoppij, & altre girandole, che durò per un gran
pezzo, & con questo si finì quel gratioso Torneo; che per le maraviglio se
inventioni, che comparvero nello steccato, per la dispostezza delli

Signori combattenti, & per il bell'ordine posto nell'armeggiare, fù giudicato non vi si poter trovar menda alcuna.

Vicino alle quattro hore di notte, il Gran Duca, Gran Duchessa, & tutti gli altri Principi, & Principesse, & così Gentilhuomini, & Gentildonne andarono à cena, che fù battezzata per collatione: le [40] cerimonie, & sorti de'rinfrescamenti, che vi erano, non mi estenderò in narrargli; ne meno vi starò à dire, che si siano viste in queste Serenissime Nozze due superbissime Credenze, una delle quali era tutta d'Oro, & l'altra d'Argento, degne veramente d'un così gran Principe, come elle sono; l'artifitio, e la manifattura, con che sono state lavorate, non mi basta l'animo à esplicarlo; perche fa di bisogno passiamo al veder la battaglia navale, che ancor'io hò bisogno di cena, e di riposo; & per questo non si maraviglino i Lettori, se sarò breve nel divisare i particolari, con qualche strettezza.

Mentre, che si faceva la collatione, per certi sotterranei, aquedotti, che sorgevano, si riempì lo steccato d'acqua, in altezza di forse cinque piedi: & per certe bocche, ò porti entrò l'armata, al numero di diciotto vasselli tra grandi, & piccoli, tra i quali vi era un Galeoncino con tre farò, quattro Galere grosse, & il restante Galere sottili, con altri vasselli, & una fregata, che serviva per portar l'ambasciate; & in detta armata vi era della ciurma propria, che serve sopra le Galere del Gran Duca, quale và in corso con il suo Generale, havendone il detto Gran Duca fatto venire da Pisa gran numero per tale effetto. Cosi sendo detta armata all'ordine, dettero nelle trombe, tamburri, pive, gnacchare, & altri instrumenti da guerra maritima, & consparar molti pez[41]zi d'artigliaria: perilche li Prencipi udito questo nuovo strepito, abbandonarono la collatione, ritiràdosi ogn'uno alli suoi luochi, che come viddero quel mare, e quella armata, con il Castello, che era posto da un capo del mare verso il Giardino, restarono tutti attoniti, & stupefatti, come fosse possibile, che in si poco spatio di tempo si fossero fatte táte gran cose.

Assettati li Principi alli suoi luochi, furon date alle ciurme alquante paniere di pane, & da bere per rinfrescamento; & in questo mentre una fregata si cacciò sotto il Castello, sì per spiar gli andamenti de'nemici, come per torre il saggio dell'altezza delle mura: la quale essendo scoperta dalle sentinelle, gli spararono dui pezzi d'artiglieria, di maniera, che la fregata hebbe fatica à salvarsi.

Fatto questo, li Turchi mandarono fuori quattro delle loro Galere à pigliar lingua, le quali diedero in sei delle nostre: & nel primo impeto spararono tutte le artigliarie l'una contra l'altra, & attaccarono la battaglia, sendo accostate l'una con l'altra armata. Quivi si vedeva animosamente un menar di mani; perche ogn'uno cercava di guadagnar la Galera nemica, & giuocavano di fuochi artificiati, che abbruciavano fino nell'acqua. Si sentiva gridare in Turchesco quelli, che erano feriti, & quelli, che cascavano in acqua: i quali anco nell'acqua combattevano con Christiani, che anco loro erano caduti: & tra il romore delle strida, & fuochi, le trombe, i tam[42]burri, & altri simili strepiti, pareva, che'l mondo rovinasse. Finalmente l'armata Christiana superò la Turchesca, dissipando di mala maniera i lor vasselli: talche si vedevano per il mare diverse reliquie; come timoni, antenne, pavesi, remi, & altri simili instrumenti, con de gli huomini attaccati per non affogarsi, che nuotavano, ritirandosi ogn'uno verso i suoi.

Vedendo i Turchi la perdita de'suoi, mandarono fuori altri tre vasselli, forse con pensiero di superare i Christiani, per essere di già stanchi, e mal trattati, se ben vincitori della prima battaglia: & quivi di nuovo si attaccarono insieme con maggior'ardore di prima: ma in fatti sendo sopragionto nuovo soccorso alli Christiani, attaccarono il fuoco in una Galea Turchesca, che non si puote difendere; il che veduto da li Turchi di quella, per campar la vita, si gettarono in mare, & con il nuoto fuggivano alla volta del Castello. Il restante de loro vaselli vennero tutti in poter de'Christiani, & cosi fu dissipata tutta quell'armata nimica, & si fece molte allegrezze, & suoni, & canti in segno di vittoria, ritirando i Christiani la loro armata per risarcirla, & munirla, & rinfrescar le genti, per far poi l'espugnatione del Castello.

Rinfrescate le ciurme, cavato fuori de'vasselli i feriti, & messovi de'Soldati freschi, & veterani, s'inviò l'armata Christiani posta in due file verso il Castello per dargli l'assalto, & quivi si senti un romore [43] d'artiglerie tanto grande, che pareva il ciel cadesse, enpiendosi il mare, & l'aria di fumo, che più non si scorgeva cosa alcuna: & fù giudicato che tra una parte, & l'altra in questo assalto fosse sparrato più di tre milatiri. Finalmente con l'opportunità del fumo, fu attaccate le scale di corda con gli uncini alle mura, & da certi valenti Greci, che vi montarono sopra fu inalborata l'insegna de'Christiani: & allhora si cominciò nuova battaglia, & con più ardore che prima, sforzandosi li Turchi di ributtar gli assalitori con fuochi, con soffioni, & altre machine, de'quali molti cadevano in acqua: ove per questo i Christiani tralasciarono l'impresa, anzi attaccandovi nuove scale, crebbe tanto la moltitudine de gli assalitori, che s'impadronirono delle mura, & del Castello. Et quì con far molti segni d'allegrezza, con canti, e suoni, & balli sul Castello finirono la festa, ch'era vicino le otto hore di notte.'

ENGLISH TRANSLATION

On Thursday at 11.0 that magnificent tournament so desired by all people was held in Palazzo de'Pitti. The courtyard was completely empty, but covered [36] with red cloth; under the galleries were the stands for spectators, and before the said stands the tiers where sat none but the ladies; also before the said stands a barricade three arms length high which surrounded the courtyard and was reinforced in such a way as to leave no opening; so constructed as to be fitting for a naval battle.

Towards the gardens stood a dummy castle in the shape of an impregnable fortress and filled with a number of Turks (i.e. *people dressed to represent Turks*) to defend it.

In the centre of the courtyard was the dividing barrier which kept the knights separated one from another when they fought and which was filled with a quantity of fireworks. Around the said courtyard could be seen an infinite number of lights, which made the obscure night like to a clear and shining day.

None could enter the said festivity but he first needs show the insignia of Porcelain, which granted him dispensation, and then one passed through three companies of soldiers, in the third and last of which was the most Serene Grand Duke in person, and in his company the most Excellent Signor Don Pietro his brother and other knights; the French and Florentine ladies and also the French knights were allowed free entry.

All being seated in their places, the signal was given, with two firings from the mortar, for the knights to lead the entry with their fine inventions, and so the first [37] appeared; a triumphal chariot in which was a Magician, who, as he went round the barricade, made his incantations: suddenly another triumphal chariot appeared, led by an exceeding great dragon and containing two knights, together with a rare music, and they halted before the most Serene Bride and sang, as did all following inventions.

The knights who were the first to enter were the most Serene Duke of Mantua and the most Excellent Signor Don Pietro de'Medici, the challengers, who, having come before the castle, dismounted, and their triumphal chariot departed, announcing to the castle with a burst of artillery that the challengers had arrived; there then immediately entered the second device, which was an exceeding great mountain together with music, nor could it be seen who was leading it. Having halted in front of the most Serene Bride, it opened, and there came forth two knights, who went and took up position on the other side of the dividing barrier. The hour of combat having come, the Master of the Field gave the sign to the knights, who broke each of them three lances one against the other, after which they drew their rapiers and made each five thrusts one at another, and, this accomplished, drew to one side, giving place to the other, which little by little came into the Field (i.e. *the Courtyard*). These were of the number of twelve, each more wondrous than the other, and there were among them strange and bizarre things, such as Fountains, Clouds, Woods, Arbours, Shapes of Animals in chariots, Ships, Rocks, Sirens, exceeding great Birds, Elephants; lastly there appeared Don Virginio with his device, which was a great Mountain, and a Crocodile, on the back of which sat an Enchanter; after these came a triumphal chariot in which sat the said Don Virginio with eight Nymphs, four on each side, and these had pretty baskets of flowers and Sonnets of his, the which they scattered in the lap of the Princesses and other ladies present; the said Don Virginio was behind the chariot seated on high and clad in full armour, like Mars himself. After him there came a Garden, which, while entering the arena, spread out in an ordered fashion all around, and caused all those present to marvel at its beautiful and sudden appearance, nor did it appear who was leading it, but 'twas as if it proceeded by enchantment; in the said garden could be seen woven and fabricated by a masterful hand divers sorts of amusements, such as a ship, pirate galleys, towers, castles, men on horseback, pyramids, woods, an Elephant, and other quadruped animals, the whole being made out of greenery, and inside the which could be heard divers sorts of small birds who with the variety of their song made a sweet and pleasing harmony. And as the said garden stretched round the Field, as I have said, Fortune willed that there should arrive in front of the most Serene Bride a wood full of birds, the which took [39] flight here and there in an attempt to escape, and one of them went to lay itself in her lap, most worthy of life, which she willed should be kept and maintained alive as a souvenir. The said Don Virginio having dismounted, he proceeded to attack his adversary, breaking his lances with much ability and grace, making his sallies and withdrawals with such excellence that all were amazed; and having made his thrusts with the rapier, he went to take up position with the others. These then divided into two groups and made a throng, and having each one taken up a pike, they confronted each other and broke pikes with great dexterity; then withdrawing two paces they drew their rapiers and beat each other with them till it seemed that the sky would come down; indeed, they would have continued the engagement if they had not been interrupted by the fireworks placed in the dividing barrier, which broke into two pieces, putting forth rays of fire, explosions large and small, and other catherine wheels, and this lasted for some time; with this finished, this gracious Tournament, which, for the wonder of its inventions appearing in the arena, the willingness of the knights in combat, and the fair discipline in the show of arms, was judged to be lacking in nothing whatsoever.

Towards the fourth hour of the night the Grand Duke, the Grand Duchess, and all the other Princes and Princesses, and in like fashion the Courtiers and Gentlewomen, went to dinner, which was called breakfast; I will not [40] go to any lengths to describe the ceremonies and various types of refreshments there available, nor will I stay to relate how in these most Serene Wedding Festivities were seen two superb Sideboards, one of which was all in Gold, and the other of Silver, truly worthy, as they are, of such a great Prince; the workmanship and design with which they were constructed I have not the patience to relate; since it is necessary, let us pass to a description of the naval battle—I have need of food and rest, and let my readers therefore not marvel if I recount its various parts briefly and in no great detail.

While the food was being consumed, the arena was filled with water to a height of about five feet by means of certain subterranean aqueducts there leading; and through certain openings or ports there entered the armada, comprising eighteen vessels, large and small, among which were a small Galley with three lamps, four large Galleys, and the rest light Galleys, with other vessels and a frigate, which served to carry messages. In the said armada there was an authentic crew, which serves on the Galleys of the Grand Duke, under its own General, the Grand Duke having ordered a great number of them from Pisa for this show. The said armada being drawn up, trumpets, drums, pipes, castanets, and other instruments of marine warfare were sounded, and many pieces of artillery were sounded at once [41], whereupon the Princes, hearing this new sound, left their food, and each one returned to his place. When they saw that sea and that armada, with the Castle placed at one end of the sea, towards the Garden, they were all struck with amazement and wonder that it should have been possible to do so many great things in such a short time.

The Princes having taken up their positions, the crew were given several baskets of bread and drink for refreshment; meanwhile the frigate made its way under the Castle, both to spy out the workings of the enemy and to determine the height of the walls; it was sighted by the sentinels, who shot off two salvoes of artillery, so that the frigate escaped with difficulty.

The Turks then sent out four of their Galleys to attempt a landing (?), and these met with six of our own; in the first clash all the pieces of artillery fired one against the other, and battle was joined, both armies being close to each other. Here was seen a valiant striking of blows, as each tried to capture the enemy's Galley, and fireworks were all around, burning even in the water. Cries in Turkish were heard from the wounded and from those who had fallen in the water, these last fighting with the Christians who had also fallen in; what with the noise of the shouts and the fireworks, the trumpets, the drums, [42] and other such noises, it seemed the end of the world were at hand. At last the Christian army overcame the Turkish one, scattering their vessels in all directions, so that various remnants became visible on the sea, such as rudders, yards, shields, oars, and other similar things, with men clinging on to them to avoid drowning, and swimming, each one towards his own side.

The Turks, seeing their losses, sent forth three other vessels, perhaps with the intention of overcoming the Christians, who were already weary and hard put, although they had won the first battle; and so they joined battle again, with greater ardour than before, but the Christians had received new reinforcements, and set fire to a Turkish Galley, which was unable to defend itself. When the Turks on it saw this, they threw themselves into the sea to save their lives, and fled swimming in the direction of the Castle. The remainder of their vessels was seized by the Christians, and so the enemy armada was entirely dispersed; there was much rejoicing, with sounds and music in sign of victory, the Christians withdrawing their army to replenish and refurbish it, and refresh its members with a view to taking the Castle.

The crew being refreshed, the wounded having been removed from the vessels, and new and fresh soldiers having been put there, together with some veterans, the Christian army was sent forward in two columns towards the Castle with a view to attacking it, and here was heard a burst of artillery [43] so great that it seemed that the sky were falling in; the sea and the air were filled with smoke, and nothing more could be seen. It was estimated that on one side and the other more than three thousand shots had been fired in all. At last, with the help of the smoke, rope ladders were attached to the walls by means of hooks, and the Christian flag was placed there by certain valiant Greeks, whereupon battle began

347

anew, with greater ardour than before, the Turks attempting to throw their assailants back with fire, bellows, and other contrivances; and indeed many fell into the water, for which reason the Christians abandoned the venture, and attached other ladders to the walls, so increasing the multitude of the assailants that they gained possession of the walls and of the Castle. And here, with many signs of joy, songs, and dancing, on the Castle, did they finish the festivities, it being near the eighth hour of the night.

I am indebted to Mr. Christopher Marsden of Newton Hall, Cambridge, for the following critical note.

'The courtyard of the Pitti Palace was that done by Ammanti and was roofed over for the occasion. This was also done however for the Marriage of Don Francesco de Medici in 1579. The illustrated book by R. Gualterolti has an engraving which can be compared to Plate XXIV, No. 35 of *EES*, i. It is entitled,

Della descrizione del regale apparatu fatto nella città di Firenze, per la venuta, e per le nozze di Christina di Loreno, Firenze, 1589. fol.

On pp. 9–12 Gualterolti describes the cortile with its cloth roof.

'Al pari dell' ultimo tetto era tirata una tela, che facera cielo contra il cielo sopra il cortile, per che il sereno della notte non offendese i rinivanti.'

At the level of the roof top an awning was stretched across the courtyard acting as a sky below the sky above, so that the night light should not disturb those returning.

There is also a description of the method used to illuminate the courtyard, and the precautions taken to let the smoke out, etc.

M. Zerner of the Bibliothèque Nationale is of the opinion that the prints illustrated in Plate XXIV of *EES*, i, are by two different artists. That of the empty cortile with the *Sbarra*, or Barrier, in the centre is by an artist unknown, but who may be Cherubino Alberti who signed one of a series of twelve small engravings (not printed in *EES*, i) depicting the triumphal cars used in connection with the Barriers.

After the Barriers, the Lords and Ladies went to dine. During their absence the cortile was flooded with water in preparation for the 'naval combat' which greeted the Court on its return to the Cortile. This is depicted in the second of the two prints in Plate XXIV, which M. Zerner attributes to Scarabelli. Apart from the Pavoni text there is a slight mention of the change from *Sbarra*, or Barriers, to the *Naumachia*, or Naval Combat, in P. N. Cardi, *Venuta della Serenissima Christina di Loreno* (Firenze, Marescotti, 1590); also in *LE ULTIME FESTE et apparati fatti Firenza nelle nozze . . . gran duca di Toscana*, Bologna, 1589. Copies of both are in the Library of the Warburg Institute.

NOTES AND SOURCES

Chapter I, pages 3–12. New Stages for Old

1. Johnson, *Works, ed. cit.*, vii, pp. 169–170.
2. *Ibid.*, viii, pp. 402 *et seq.*
3. *Ibid.*, viii, 404.
4. See B. Hunningher, 'A Baroque Architect Among Painters and Poets', in *Theatre Research* Vol. III (1961), pp. 23–31.

Chapter II, pages 13–53. Reformation and Renaissance

1. Statute 34, 35, Hen. VIII, cap. i. *Statutes of the Realm*, III, 894. §vii.
2. See H. H. Adams, *English Domestic or Homiletic Tragedy, 1575 to 1642*, Columbia U.P., 1942. It may be added that with the decline of learning among the clergy immediately following the dissolution of the religious houses, these Homilies served to provide clerics who could not write a sermon for themselves with a safe substitute. See Warton, *HEP*, pp. 625 *et seq.*

   On New Year's Day, 1561, Queen Elizabeth attended service at St. Paul's Cathedral. The Dean had obtained some wood-cuts from a foreigner 'representing the stories and passions of the saints and martyrs', and inserted them in a specially bound copy of the Common Prayer Book which he intended as a New Year's Gift for the Queen 'against the Epistles and Gospels of their festivals'.

   The Queen, far from being pleased, summoned the Dean to her presence after the service and cross-examined him herself. His explanation that his intention had been to please drew the retort, 'You know I have an aversion to idolatry, to images and pictures of this kind.' See *PQE*, i, 'Remarkable Public Events' (1561), pp. 64–67.
3. See B. R. Joseph, *Elizabethan Acting*, 1951. For rebellions attributed to plays, see pp. 62–63 and 65–66 below.
4. John Bale, *Three Laws*, 1538, Sig. G. ib: reprinted by J. S. Farmer in Tudor Facsimile Texts, 1908. On the subject of emblematic stage costume in general see T. W. Craik, *The Tudor Interlude*, 1958, Ch. III.
5. *The English Renaissance: fact or fiction?*, 1952, p. 23.
6. *Robert of Brunne's 'Handlyng of Synne,'* ed. F. J. Furnivall for E.E.T.S., 1901, pp. 154–155, lines 4656–4662. Prynne uses almost these words in his *Histrio-Mastix*; see Ch. III, p. 95, n. 67.
7. 'A sermon against Miracle-Plays', printed by W. C. Hazlett in *English Drama*, pp. 73–79: see p. 77. On this subject see also H. C. Gardiner, *Mysteries End*, pp. 11 *et seq.*
8. L. Tyerman, *The Life & Times of the Reverend John Wesley, M.A.*, 5th ed., 1890, p. 54. See also P. T. Underdown, 'Religious opposition to licensing the Bristol & Birmingham Theatres' in *University of Birmingham Historical Journal*, Vol. VI, No. 2 (1958), who cites this example and many others just as pertinent.

9. *Works*, vi, 27.

10. *Ibid.*, pp. 62–63.

11. *Ibid.*, p. 64.

12. *Ibid.*, p. 84: see also in the same scene (III, iv) lines 70–75, and in *The Silent Woman*, V, i, throughout the debate on possible grounds for Morose's divorce.

13. *Works*, vi, pp. 109 *et seq.*

14. *Ibid.*, p. 110.

15. *Ibid.*, p. 83.

16. *Ibid.*, p. 110. See also Ch. IV, p. 110.

17. *HEP*, p. 622.

18. Ed. J. S. Farmer in '*Lost*' *Tudor Plays*, 1907; III, vi, p. 225

19. *HEP*, p. 620.

20. *Ibid.*, p. 615.

21. E. A. Greenlaw, *Studies in Spenser's Historical Allegory* (Johns Hopkins Monographs in Literary History, Vol. 2) Baltimore, 1932.

22. Ben Jonson, *Epigrams XIV*, 'To William Camden'; *Works*, viii, 31.

23. Greenlaw, *op. cit.*, p. 23.

24. *The Dramatic Writings of John Bale*, ed. J. S. Farmer, 1908, p. 272.

25. On the Italian Academies see L. B. Campbell, *Scenes & Machines on the English Stage*, 1927; also H. Leclerc, *Les Origines Italiennes de l'Architecture Théâtrale Moderne*, 1946.

26. John Bale, 'A Tragedye or enterlude manyfestyng the chefe promyses of God unto man by all ages in the olde lawe, from the fall of Adam to the incarnacyon of the lorde Jesus Christ. Compyled by John Bale, An. Do. 1538, and now fyrst imprynted, 1577.' ed. J. S. Farmer, in 'Tudor Facsimile Texts', 1908. See Chambers, *Med. Stage*, ii, pp. 448–449.

27. Denys Hay, *Polydore Vergil, Renaissance historian and man of letters*, 1952, pp. 131–132.

28. *Ibid.*, *pp.* 162–163.

29. *Works*, iii, 437.

30. See especially the 1598 and 1601 editions of *Every Man in his Humour*. The first version of this play is set in Italy and the characters have Italian names. In the revised version Jonson anglicized both. See *Works*, i, pp. 333 *et seq.*, and iii, p. 303.

31. *Works*, vi, pp. 133 *et seq.*

32. *Ibid.*, p. 135.

33. Duo autem angeli induti erunt Gabriel et Raphael cum amictibus albis cincti desuper cum stola ad collum et in cruce ante pectus. Super capud uero portabunt quasdam barretas adiacentes in capite super aures, et in circulo capitis desuper habebunt formam triangularem aut quadrangularem non nimis latas, cum duabus fanis retro uelud in mitra episcopi . . . Habebunt etiam duo angeli quilibet duas alas, et portabunt in manu dextra quilibet unam uirgam rubeam.

BN. MS. Latin 17330, transcribed and edited by Karl Young in P.M.L.A. XXVI (1911), pp. 181–234. The quotation above is taken from this transcript, pp. 205–206 (fol. 18b). The translation is that made by A. B. Weiner, *Phillippe de Mézières' description of the FESTUM PRAESENTATIONIS BEATAE MARIAE*, Yale, 1958, p. 45.

34. B.M. *MS. Harl* 2177: 'of the Godis (*goods*) now beyng in Trentye Church of Chester 1532'. ff. 19–32b. The quotation is taken from f. 27b. See Salter, *MDC*, pp. 19–22.

35. *Ibid.*, f. 28b.

36. *Med. Stage*, ii, 347.

37. *Ibid.*, p. 398.

38. *Ant. & Cleopatra*, IV, xv, lines 7–9. Dover Wilson (*NS*, 230) suggests this manner of staging. For other suggestions, see *The London Shakespeare*, ed. J. Munro, vi, p. 1342.

39. Malone Society, *Collections III*, p. xxv. The editors (D. J. Gordon & Jean Robertson) in their long 'Introduction' also discuss the Midsummer Show which included spectacular Pageantry in the early sixteenth century, but which was eclipsed by the Lord Mayor's Show in the latter half of the century.

40. *Hen. VIII*, I, i, lines 12 *et seq.* See A. S. Venezky, *Pageantry on the Shakespearean Stage*, 1951.

41. T. F. Ordish, *Early London Theatres*, 1894, pp. 29–30.

42. Chambers, *ES*, iv, 257.

Chapter III, pages 54–97, State Control of British Drama, 1530–1642

1. I have to thank Miss P. Morgan, the Cathedral Librarian at Hereford, for bringing this information to my notice. The passage quoted occurs on fol. 92 of the Register. The translation is that made by J. H. Parry in his edition of the Register, for Cantilupe Soc., Hereford, 1910.

2. Bodl. *MSS Vernon*, f. 299: also B.M. *MS.Harl.*, 525, 2, f. 35.

3. *Annals of the Stage*, 1831, 3 vols., i, pp. 114–116. See *HEP*, pp. 128–130; *Med. Stage*, ii, pp. 151, 205 and 356.

4. See *EES*, i, pp. 224 and 352.

5. Gardiner, *Mysteries End*, pp. 102 *et seq.*; pp. 107 *et seq.*

6. *Med. Stage*, ii, pp. 372 and 386. In York, plays on the life of the Virgin were dropped from the Corpus Christi Cycle earlier still. On the other hand, a Pageant of the Assumption was frequently presented by the Drapers Company in the streets of London until as late as 1541. See Appendix A.

7. Ed. E. Arber, English Reprints, 1870, p. 84.

8. N. Bacon, *Annals of Ipswich*, Ipswich, 1884, pp. 190–195 and 205. Gardiner, *op. cit.*, p. 49.

9. *Med. Stage*, ii, p. 220: V. C. Gildersleeve, *Govt. Reg.*, p. 6. See also J. Lamb, Collection of Documents from C.C.C.C., 1839, p. 49.

10. Gardiner, *op. cit.*, p. 49: *Govt. Reg.*, p. 7. For a similar prohibition in Suffolk in 1537, see *Letters & Papers of Henry VIII*, XII, pp. 557, 585.

11. Gardiner, *op. cit.*, p. 53: Collier, *English Dramatic Poetry*, i, p. 123.

12. Gardiner, *op. cit.*, p. 54, n. 32. See also R. W. Dixon, *History of the Church of England*, 6 vols. (3rd ed. 1895–1902), iii, p. 123.

13. Statutes of the Realm, 34, 35 Henry VIII, c. 1: W. C. Hazlitt, *English Drama*, 1869, pp. 3–6. The Act specifies that action is necessary on account of the 'diversitie of opinions, sayinges, varyannces, argumentes, tumultes, and scisms (which) have been sprong and arysen amonges his sayd subiectes, within this his realme . . .'. It goes on to provide that 'it shall be lawfull to all and every persone and personnes, to sette forth songes playes and enterludes, to be used and exercised within this realme, & other the Kynges dominions, for the rebukyng and reproching of vices, etc. . . .'. See p. 14 above.

14. *Op. cit.*, p. 53.

15. *Med. Stage*, ii, pp. 217–224, and 446–447: Gardiner, *op. cit.*, pp. 48 *et seq.* Cromwell's personal company of actors performed in King's College, Cambridge, in 1536/37 and at New College, Oxford, in the following year. See *MSC, II*, p. 151 and *V*, p. 41. For Cranmer's interest see Ch. IV n. 13 and *EES*, i, p. 116.

16. *The Dramatic Writings of John Bale*, ed. J. Farmer, 1908, pp. 228–229.

17. Holinshed, *Chronicle*, London 1586/87, iii. 1028. See also Gardiner, *op. cit.*, p. 50.

18. *Med. Stage*, ii, pp. 222–223.

19. *Ibid.*, p. 221.

20. W. C. Hazlitt, *English Drama*, p. 8: cited by Gildersleeve, *Govt. Reg.*, pp. 8–9.

21. *Statutes*, IV, pt. i, p. 38.

22. Hazlitt, *op. cit.*, pp. 9–14.

23. B.M. *MS. Cot. Vit. F. V.* f. 73. *Henry Machyn's Diary*, ed. for Camden Soc. by J. G. Nichols, 1848 (Vol. 42), p. 138.

24. *Henry Machyn's Diary, ed. cit.*, p. 145.

25. Act I, scene iv. See also V, iii. Ed. J. S. Farmer *'Lost' Tudor Plays*, 1907.

26. *Govt. Reg.*, p. 11, citing *Acts of the Privy Council*, v, pp. 234, 237.

27. *Henry Machyn's Diary, ed. cit.*, pp. 160, 161.

28. *English Drama*, pp. 15–18.

29. *Govt. Reg.*, pp. 11 and 25. See also *ES*, i, 270, n. 1.

30. *Govt. Reg.*, p. 12. See also *ES*, i, p. 275.

31. *Govt. Reg.*, p. 12, citing *Acts of the Privy Council*, pp. 110 and 148.

32. *Govt. Reg.*, p. 12. See also *ES*, ii, p. 444.

33. *Govt. Reg.*, pp. 12–13.

34. See *Statute cit.*, in n. 13 above: see also *Govt. Reg.*, pp. 18 and 54.

35. See *EES*, i, pp. 114–116.

36. *ES,* iv, pp. 263–266: also *ES,* i, p. 276. See also *Govt. Reg.,* pp. 13 *et seq.*

37. Quoted in *ES,* iv, pp. 269–271. Printed in *Statutes,* iv, 590. For the revisions, see *Statutes,* iv, pp. 610, 718, 899. See also Gildersleeve, *Govt. Reg.,* pp. 27 *et seq.*

38. *Govt. Reg.,* pp. 153–154. Leicester's Patent of 10th May 1574 is given in *ES,* ii, pp. 87–88: the City Edict of 6th Dec. 1574 in *ES,* iv, pp. 273–276.

39. Quoted in full in *ES,* iv, pp. 285–287.

40. *Ibid.,* p. 286.

41. *Govt. Reg.,* p. 154.

42. *ES,* iv, p. 272.

43. See J. M. Neale, *Queen Elizabeth,* pp. 175–190.

44. *A Forme of Christian Pollicie gathered out of French,* 1574. BK. iii, Ch. 7, cited in *ES,* iv, pp. 195–196.

45. *ES,* iv, pp. 198–199 and 203–205. See also *Govt. Reg.,* p. 159.

46. *ES,* iv, p. 287. See also the Orders of the Court of Aldermen of 29th March 1582 and 17th January 1583, printed in *MSC. II,* pp. 312 and 313.

47. *ES,* iv, p. 291. Chambers adds a note of his own on the dating of this Order.

48. See *Govt. Reg.,* pp. 158, 163–164 and 172.

49. The letters are printed in *ES,* iv, p. 292. *Govt. Reg.,* pp. 165–6.

50. It is on the grounds of 'sondrye greate disorders and inconvenyences' that the Act of Common Council of 6th December 1574 was issued. This is printed, *ES,* iv, pp. 273 *et seq.* See also Ch. V, p. 195. For specific instances of riots see *ES,* i, pp. 264–5 and 287.

51. *ES,* iv, pp. 283–284.

52. The Star Chamber Decree of 12th November 1589 is given in *ES,* iv, pp. 306–307. It should be read in conjunction with the equally important Star Chamber Decree concerning the printing of books and plays of 23rd June 1586, given in *ES,* iv, p. 303. See *Govt Reg.,* pp. 18 and 54; also *ES,* i, pp. 294–295.

53. W. W. Greg, *Henslowe's Diary,* Pt. II, pp. 116–118.

54. The correspondence between the Lord Mayor and the Archbishop, together with the instructions to Aldermen to interview Tilney, and the deliberations of the Merchant Taylors Company on the subject, are printed in *ES,* iv, pp. 307–309. The Mercers Company were similarly approached and similarly cautious in their response: see *MSC. III,* p. 166.

55. On the subject of *Ric. II* and the Essex Rebellion, see L. B. Campbell, *Shakespeare's 'Histories'—mirrors of Elizabethan policy,* 1947. See also pp. 312–313.

56. Full details concerning the Patents awarded to all these Companies are given by Bentley, Chambers and Murray. See also *Govt. Reg.,* pp. 231–234.

57. *ES,* iv, p. 336.

58. See Bentley, *J & CS*, vol. 1.

59. See *Govt. Reg.*, pp. 61 *et seq.*

60. *Ibid.*, p. 214.

61. For the history of the Companies cited see Murray, *EDC*, i, and Bentley *J & CS*, i.

62. *ES*, iv, p. 335.

63. Gardiner, *Mysteries End*, p. 58, n. 52.

64. *Govt. Reg.*, p. 223.

65. *Ibid.*, p. 226.

66. On the conduct of actors during the Civil War see L. Hotson, *Commonwealth & Restoration Stage*, 1928, pp. 3–70. The player known to have taken the Parliament's side was Elliard Swanston: Hotson, *op. cit.*, pp. 14 and 15.

67. 1st ed. London, 1633. Title Page.

68. For post-Restoration strolling players in the Provinces, see Hotson, *op. cit.*, pp. 167 *et seq.*, and Sybil Rosenfeld, *Strolling Players & Drama in the Provinces, 1660–1795*, 1939.

69. Hotson, *op. cit.*, pp. 202 *et seq.*, and Murray *EDC*, ii, pp. 329–331. On Herbert's conduct of the censorship see *Govt. Reg.*, pp. 118–132 and Bentley *J & CS*, i, pp. 2 *et seq.*

Chapter IV, pages 98–149. Actors, Playmakers and Theatres under State Control

1. Chambers, *ES*, i, pp. 304 *et seq.*, especially p. 304, n. 1. See Ward Williamson, 'Notes on the Decline of Provincial Drama in England, 1530–1642', *American Educational Theatre Journal*, Vol. XIII (1961), No. 4, pp. 280–287: also W. Ringler, 'The First Phase of the Elizabethan Attack on the Stage, 1558–1579', *Huntington Library Quarterly*, Vol. V (1942), pp. 391–418.

2. *ES*, i, p. 309.

3. *Ibid.*, iv, p. 300.

4. See T. H. Vail Motter, *The School Drama in England*, 1929; F. S. Boas, *University Drama in the Tudor Age*, 1914; and *ES*, ii, pp. 8–76.

5. See R. Withington, *EP*, i, Chs. I and II, and Chambers, *ES*, i, pp. 106–148: also Welsford *CM*, pp. 75 *et seq.*, and especially pp. 116–148.

6. See N. D. Shergold, *The Staging of the Secular Drama in Spain, 1550–1700*, Ph.D. Thesis, Cambridge, 1953, especially pp. 35 and 65–66.

7. *Govt. Reg.*, p. 151. For other inhibitions of particular companies at this time, see *MSC. II*, pp. 289–291.

8. *ES*, iv, pp. 261, 262.

9. *Govt. Reg.*, p. 26: also *ES*, i, p. 270.

10. Printed by Chambers, *ES*, iv, pp. 260, 261.

11. *Govt. Reg.*, p. 27.

12. *Statutes*, IV, ii, p. 1024. See Appendix E, p. 335 above.

13. *The Autobiography of Thomas Whythorne*, ed. J. M. Osborn, 1961, pp. 243–245. Whythorne was a lute player and a teacher of music who served his apprenticeship under John Heywood. 'At the request of doctor Thomas Cranmer, late archbishop of Canterbury, he [i.e. Heywood] made a certain interlude or play, the which was devised upon the parts of Man, at the end whereof he likeneth and applieth the circumstances thereof to the universal estate of Christ's church all the which aforesaid [*plays*], before they were published, I did write out for him, or had the use of them to read them. And I have the copies of most of them in a book at this present of mine own writing.' *Ibid.*, pp. 13–14; an extract from the play is given on p. 74. See Ch. III, n. 15, p. 352 above and Plates II and III.

14. See *EES*, i, p. 143; *Med. Stage*, ii, p. 379. In App. C. of *EES*, i, I have printed a long list of payments to players who entertained the clergy of Selby Abbey. It is interesting to note therefore, in the present context, that this Abbey could also supply its own company of players: 'Et clericis de Selby (*Abbey*) Indentibus coram domino abbate ad idem tempus (June 24th, 1398) xij d'. York: Arch: Journal, XV (1900), pp. 408–419; see p. 413.

15. *HEP*, p. 567.

16. This would appear to have been the status of the unfortunate 'Ruffe, the Scott' executed in 1557 for his part in an abortive attempt to present a Protestant interlude in London: see Ch. III, p. 71 above. A similar relationship existed between the Chaplain and those servants employed as players in noble households: see p. 125 above.

17. *The Anatomie of Abuses*, 1583, p. 146, *cit.* in *ES*, iv, p. 224.

18. *Sermon preached at the Crosse, Feb. xiiij, 1607*; *cit.* in *ES*, iv, p. 249. Similar sentiments are expressed in another sermon preached in 1610; see *ES*, iv, p. 254.

19. *ES*, iv, p. 217.

20. Malone Society Reprints, 1957. Sig. A. ij. See also the Chorus concluding Act I of *Gorboduc*. For general discussion see L. Schrade, *La Representation d'Edipo Tiranno au Teatro Olimpico*, 1960, pp. 11–32.

21. *ES*, i, p. 254. The academic debate on the ethics of acting reaches its height in the exchanges at the University of Oxford between John Rainolds and William Gager, 1591–92. See Boas, *University Drama*; also, K. Young, *An Elizabethan Defence of the Stage* (Wisconsin Shakespeare Studies, 103) 1916; W. P. Holden, *Anti-Puritan Satire, 1572–1642*, Yale Studies in English, 1954, Ch. II, 'The Puritans and the Stage', pp. 94–154 and Chambers, *ES*, i, pp. 251 *et seq.*

22. *ES*, iv, p. 205.

23. *Ibid.*, p. 200.

24. *Ibid.*, p. 210.

25. See *ES*, ii, pp. 78 *et seq.*: also S. Angelo, 'The Court Festivals of Henry VII', in *Bulletin of the John Rylands Library* (Oct. 1960), Vol. 3, No. 1, pp. 12–45.

26. See Collier, *op. cit.*, i, pp. 45 *et seq.*

27. *MSC. III*, p. 137: *ES*, ii, p. 81. For Durham see *Med. Stage*, ii, p. 244; for Selby Abbey see *EES*, i, pp. 334–339.

28. See *ES*, ii, p. 81 and *Med. Stage*, i, p. 183 n. 2.

29. *ES*, ii, p. 80.

30. Murray, *EDC*, i, p. 117.

31. *ES*, ii, 387.

32. *ES*, iv, 197.

33. *Ibid.*, p. 204.

34. *Ibid.*, p. 241.

35. See *ES*, i, pp. 352–358. Details of those actors who were sharers in Elizabethan Companies and those who held a lesser status are given by Murray, *EDC*, i, and by Chambers *ES*, ii, pp. 77–240. For the famous law-suit on shares in the King's Company, see *J & CS*, i, pp. 43 *et seq.*

36. See *ES*, i, pp. 286–197 and iv, pp. 291, 292.

37. *ES*, iv, p. 244.

38. *J & CS*, i, p. 164, citing 1st Quarto of Middleton's Inner Temple Masque, 1618–19, HN, B3b. See also the London properties owned by Henslowe, *ES*, i, 359. It was badly damaged by an angry crowd in 1618.

39. *J & CS*, i, pp. 31 *et seq.*

40. *EDC*, ii, pp. 400–401.

41. *Ibid.*, p. 235.

42. In respect of forged licences see *EDC*, ii, pp. 339 and 351: in respect of plague, p. 347 under 24th May, and p. 336 under 7th June.

43. *ES*, iv, pp. 256–257.

44. *English Drama*, pp. 64–65; *Govt. Reg.*, pp. 224–225.

45. *Works*, v, pp. 16 and 18.

46. *Ibid.*, v, pp. 19–20.

47. *Ibid.*, iii, p. 421 and iv, p. 33.

48. *Ibid.*, iii, p. 301 (Folio text: the Quarto has no dedication): v, p. 431 and vii, p. 280.

49. D. Nichol Smith, 'Authors & Patrons' in *Shakespeare's England*, 2 vols., 1916, ii, p. 211.

50. See Jonson, *Works*, i, p. 73 and *ES*, i, pp. 349 and 370.

51. *Henslowe's Diary, Greg*, i, p. 47; Chambers *ES*, i, p. 363, and Nichol Smith, *op. cit.*, p. 202.

52. *Works*, i, pp. 231–232.

53. *Ibid.*, p. 240.

54. See *Works*, i, pp. 114 *et seq.*

55. *HEP*, p. 478. Medwall was himself chaplain to Cardinal Morton.

56. R. B. McKerrow, 'Booksellers, Printers, and the Stationers Trade,' in *Shakespeare's England*, ii, p. 215.

57. *Ibid.*, pp. 216 and 217. See also *ES*, iii, pp. 160 *et seq.*

58. R. B. McKerrow, *op. cit.*, pp. 217–218.

59. *ES*, iv, p. 241.

60. *2 Return from Parnassus*, V, lines 1920–21, ed. J. B. Leishman, 1949.

61. See *ES*, iii, pp. 184 *et seq.*

62. *EDC*, i, p. 164: see also *J & CS*, i, pp. 22, 54 and 65–66.

63. *J & CS*, i, pp. 141 *et seq.*

64. See R. A. Foakes, 'The Significance of Henslowe's Diary' in *Philologica Progensia*, III (1960), pp. 214–222.

65. See C. J. Sisson, *Lost Plays of Shakespeare's Age* (1936), pp. 80–124. *J & CS*, iii, pp. 252–256.

66. Sisson, *op. cit.*, p. 110; *J & CS*, iii, p. 254.

67. *J & CS*, iii, pp. 269–272.

68. See W. Greg, *Henslowe's Diary*, Pt. 1, under payments for plays for the years 1597 and 1598.

69. *J & CS*, i, pp. 43 *et seq.*

70. *Ibid.*, iii and iv, *sub* plays and playwrights.

71. *Ibid.*, i, pp. 10 *et seq.*

72. *Ibid.*, i, pp. 38–39.

73. *Ibid.*, i, p. 37.

74. *Ibid.*, i, pp. 106–107.

75. *Ibid.*, i, pp. 60–61.

76. *ES*, ii, *sub.* Public Theatres, 'Theater', 'Curtain', etc.: also Reynolds, *op. cit.*, p. 6. For a gamehouse or playhouse built in Great Yarmouth in 1538, see Ch. V above, pp. 166–167.

77. *ES*, ii, pp. 411–414.

78. See *ES*, i, pp. 359–368. Henslowe notes the marriage of his daughter to Alleyn in his diary (Fol. 2): see *Henslowe's Diary, Greg,* i, p. 3, and ii, pp. 4–7.

79. *ES*, ii, p. 417.

80. For Davenant's plays and bibliography see *J & CS*, iii, pp. 193–225: for Thomas Killigrew, *ibid.*, iv, pp. 694–710. The unedifying story of the securing of Royal Patents for the Duke's Company and the King's Company by Davenant and Killigrew respectively is admirably narrated in great detail by Leslie Hotson, *Commonwealth and Restoration Stage,* pp. 197 *et seq.*

81. On Davenant's collaboration with Inigo Jones, see Ch. VII above, pp. 274–275. On John Webb's settings for *The Siege of Rhodes,* see L. B. Campbell, *Scenes & Machines,* pp. 221–226, and Hotson, *Commonwealth and Restoration Stage,* pp. 153–154. Also note 92, p. 358.

82. On Herbert's struggle to reassert his authority over plays, players and playhouses at the Restoration, see *Govt. Reg.*, pp. 68–69 and 70–73: also Hotson, *op. cit.*, pp. 202–206 and 210–213.

83. See W. J. Lawrence, 'The origin of the English Picture-Stage', in *The Elizabethan Playhouse*, Second Series, pp. 121 *et seq.*: also *Scenes & Machines*, pp. 210–211 and *Govt. Reg.*, pp. 205–206. On the siting of the original cockpit in Whitehall and of the theatre taking its name designed *c.* 1632 by Inigo Jones see *ES*, i, pp. 216, n. 2, and p. 234. On the history of the Cockpit in Drury Lane see Hotson, *op. cit.*, pp. 88–100, and *J & CS*, i, pp. 160–164.

84. For the history of these theatres during the Civil War and Commonwealth, see Hotson *op. cit.*, pp. 82–114, and p. 208. Beeston, Mohun and Rhodes were the men primarily responsible for preserving the continuity of acting traditions.

85. The Disguising of the fifteenth century, as I have argued in Volume I (pp. 179–228), provided the common stock for the Mask in England, Opera in Italy and Ballet in France in the seventeenth century. The first theatre to be designed and built for opera was the *Teatro di San Casiano* in Venice, erected in 1637: Cardinal Mazarin introduced Italian opera to the French Court in 1645. Davenant clearly had it in mind to combine opera with ballet in the repertoire of the theatre he was to build in 1639, but abandoned (see note 83 above).

86. The Duke's Theatre in Dorset Gardens was not opened until 9th November 1671: before that date Davenant's company used Lisle's Tennis Court in Lincoln's Inn Fields of which Davenant obtained the lease in 1660. The Theatre Royal in Bridges Street opened on 7th May 1663; before that date Killigrew's company acted at Gibbon's Tennis Court which was situated near Lisle's in Clement's Inn Fields. After the fire at the Theatre Royal in Bridges Street, Killigrew's Company moved to Lisle's Tennis Court and played there for two years, For the siting of these early Restoration Theatres, see Hotson, *op. cit.*, pp. 114–127.

87. On this subject see Hotson, *op. cit.*, Ch. I, 'Players & Parliament: surreptitious drama, 1642–1655', and *The Dramatic Works of Sir William Davenant*, ed. J. Maidment and W. H. Logan (5 vols., 1872), i, pp. xlix *et seq.*

88. Maidment and Logan, *Davenant*, i, p. lxviii.

89. *Ibid.*, lxvii. See also the Prologue to the 2nd Part of *The Siege of Rhodes*.

90. Cited by Hotson, *op. cit.*, p. 207; see also Maidment and Logan, *Davenant*, i, pp. lxiv–lxix.

91. Hotson, *op. cit.*, pp. 242–243. See H. W. Lanier, *The First English Actresses*, N.Y., 1930.

92. Concerning John Webb's designs for *The Siege of Rhodes*, now in the Duke of Devonshire's Collection at Chatsworth, see W. G. Keith, 'The Designs for the First Moveable Scenery on the English Public Stage', *Burlington Magazine*, vol. xxv, pp. 29 *et seq.* and 85 *et seq.* The designs are reproduced by Keith and, on a smaller scale, by Richard Southern in *Changeable Scenery*, 1952. The designs should be carefully compared with the stage directions; it then becomes clear at once that the landscape scenes are themselves emblems. On this subject see Davenant's *Love and Honour* and *The Siege of Rhodes*, ed. J. W. Tupper, 1909, pp. xl *et seq.*

93. *The Works of Sr. William Davenant*, printed for Henry Herringman, 1673 in fol., pt. 2, p. 87.

94. See 'An Expostulation with Inigo Jones', *Works*, viii, pp. 402–407, and compare this with Dryden's remarks on unity of place in his *Essay of Dramatic Poesy*.

95. Hotson, *op. cit.*, pp. 208, and 240, n. 29.

96. See *Govt. Reg.*, p. 233. The Patent is printed in *ES*, ii, pp. 68–69; for provincial notices see *EDC*, ii, pp. 5–6 and 14–15.

97. *ES*, ii, 69; *EDC*, ii, p. 6.

98. *EDC*, ii, p. 8.

99. *Ibid.*, ii, p. 347.

100. *Ibid.*, ii, pp. 347–348.

101. *Ibid.*, ii, p. 359–360. The two following quotations in the text are taken from the same source, pp. 348–9.

102. *Ibid.*, ii, p. 349.

103. *Ibid.*, ii, p. 350.

104. *Ibid.*, ii, p. 355.

105. *Ibid.*, ii, pp. 400–401.

106. *Ibid.*, ii, p. 409.

107. *Ibid.*, ii, p. 410.

108. *Ibid.*, ii, p. 322. See also p. 319 for action on this account in 1582, quoted below.

> Nov. 17. 'It is agreed that frome henceforthe there shall not bee anye ffees or Rewards gevon by the Chamber of this Towne, nor anye of the xxiiii^{ti} or xlviii^{ti} to be charged w(i)th anye payments ffor or towards anye Bearewards, Beearbaytings, Players, Playes, Ent(er)ludes or Games, or anye of theym Except the Quenes Maiest(ie)s or the Lords of the Pryve Counsall, nor that anye Players bee suffred to play att the Towne Hall (Except before except) & then butt onlye before the Mayor & his bretherne, uppon peyne of xl s. to be lost by the Mayor that shall suffer or doe to the cont(ra)rye, to be Levyed by his successo(r), upon peyne of £v if he make default therein, &c.'

A description of conditions in Gloucester, taken from R. Willis' treatise, *Mount Tabor*, 1639, is quoted by Chambers, *Med. Stage*, ii, p. 189, n. 5 and *ES*, i, p. 333.

> 'In the City of *Gloucester*, the manner is (as I think it is in other like corporations) that when Players of Enterludes come to towne, they first attend the Mayor, to enforme him what noble-mans servants they are, and so to get licence for their publike playing; and if the Mayor like the Actors, or would shew respect to their Lord and Master, he appoints them to play their first play before himselfe, and the Aldermen and common Counsell ; and that is called the Mayors play, where every one that will comes in without money, the Mayor giving the players a reward as hee thinks fit, to shew respect unto them.'

N.B. The conditions described are those prevailing in the writer's youth, not those in 1639.

109. *EDC*, ii, pp. 219 (Bristol), 232 (Canterbury), 272 (Exeter), 399 (Southampton), and 410 (Worcester): *c.f.* Middleton, *Mayor of Quinborough*, V, i:

> FIRST PLAYER: Sir, we have play'd before a lord ere now
> Though we be country actors.
> SIMON: A lord? ha, ha!
> Thou'lt find it a harder thing to please a mayor.

110. See *ES*, i, pp. 331–332, iv. pp. 345–351, and *EDC*, ii, pp. 170 *et seq.*, and i, p. 163; also *J & CS*, i, pp. 20, 26, and 49 *et seq.*

111. See *EDC*, ii, pp. 329–331.

112. For Jolly's career on the continent during the Civil War and Commonwealth, see Hotson, *op. cit.*, pp. 167–176.

113. *Ibid.*, p. 177. His own Patent and his agreement with Davenant and Killigrew are printed by Hotson, pp. 177–178 and pp. 179–182.

114. *Ibid.*, p. 182.

115. Hotson gives a clear account of the way in which Davenant and Killigrew contrived to take advantage of Jolly's absence in the provinces to cheat him of his Patent and thereby to secure their own monopoly; see pp. 182–188.

116. See R. Southern, *Changeable Scenery*, 1952, pp. 124–162.

117. See S. Rosenfeld, *Strolling Players and Drama in the Provinces, 1660–1765*, pp. 2 *et seq.*

Chapter V, pages 153–205. Playhouses

1. *ES*, ii, p. 384.

2. The contracts for the Fortune and the Hope are printed in *ES*, ii, pp. 436–439 and 466–468 respectively, and in Hodges, *The Globe Restored*, App. F & App. G. Both follow W. W. Greg, *Henslowe Papers*, 1907, pp. 4 and 19. On the accuracy of Greg's transcript, see Note 25 of this Chapter.

3. For full discussion of this subject see L. B. Campbell, *Scenes and Machines on the English Stage during the Renaissance*, 1923, reprinted 1960; also Hélène Leclerc, *Les Origines Italiennes de l'Architecture Théâtrale Moderne*, Paris, 1946.

4. Reynolds, *op. cit.*, p. 1.

5. *ES*, iii, p. 144 and ii, pp. 8 *et seq.*

6. *ES*, ii, pp. 475 *et seq.*

7. *ES*, ii, p. 516. The Greyfriars became a Foundling Hospital: see Stow's *Survey*, i, 319.

8. *ES*, ii, pp. 383 *et seq.*

9. See J. Lees-Milne, *The Age of Inigo Jones*, 1953; especially p. 144.

10. *ES*, ii, p. 525.

11. *ES*, ii, p. 538 and p. 528.

12. *Ant. Rep.*, i, pp. 181–183; also *PQE*, i, pp. 133–137, and *EES*, i, pp. 34–38. Tuthill Fields was situated near the Palace of Westminster.

13. See *EES*, i, p. 194; also Richard Southern, *The Medieval Theatre in the Round*, 1957; and Plate XXX, No. 43.

14. *ES*, ii, p. 449. On London maps of the period see *ES*, ii, pp. 353–355 and 376–379: also I. A. Shapiro, 'The Bankside Theatres: Early Engravings,' *Shakespeare Survey, I*, 1948.

15. *Ed. cit.*, p. 324.

16. It is known that wherever the Romans went as colonizers they deemed it necessary to provide themselves with the theatres and amphitheatres to which they were accustomed in their native Italy. In Britain there still survive today the theatre at St. Albans, and the superb amphitheatre at Caerleon which the archaeological excavations of 1935 opened to view once more after centuries of neglect, if not of total oblivion. Others are thought to have existed at Banbury, Cirencester, Colchester and Dorchester. Caerleon was merely a grass-covered mound when Chambers wrote his *Elizabethan Stage*, although significantly called 'King Arthur's Round Table' by local inhabitants.

    Could local tradition harbour an important truth? May the origin of *Round Tables*, both in Arthurian Romance and in the annals of Chivalry, lie in table-land (*platea*) rather than in the meal-table or council-table (*mensa*)? If we allow ourselves to suppose that the theatres and amphitheatres of Roman Britain were subsequently fortified, defended and used against Saxon invaders (like earlier Celtic earthworks), not only does a possible association with Arthur suggest itself, but a source is provided for the origin of the pleg-stów, or recreation ground, of Saxon England; and this in its turn might help to explain how circular lists came to be used for certain kinds of Tournament in the Middle Ages. See *EES*, i, pp. 16 *et seq.*, and Figs. 2 and 3.

17. See T. N. Toller, Anglo-Saxon Dictionary, Oxford, 1882, *sub Plega-* II (athletic) sport, game; often in poetry applied to fighting: see compounds.

18. *Georgics*, ii, line 381.

19. See Toller, *op. cit.*, and Du Cange, *sub Hastiludium* and *Torneamentum*.

20. Toller, *op. cit.*, *sub Pleg-stów*; see also Ordish, *Early London Theatres*, 1894, pp. 13 *et seq.*, and 43 *et seq.*

21. I am indebted to Mr. A. A. C. Hedges, Borough Librarian and Curator of the Central Library, Great Yarmouth, for this transcript from the first volume of the MS. *Books of Entries* in the town archives. The town's assembly books grew out of these *Books of Entries*. The transcript given by W. J. Palmer in *Perlustration of Great Yarmouth*, 3 vols., 1872–75, i, pp. 351–352 and cited by Murray (*EDC*, ii, 286) and Chambers (*ES*, i, 336) is not accurate.

    The word 'game' was evidently used for a dramatic entertainment in 1493 as the churchwardens of St. Nicholas' Church received 15/10d. for a 'game' played on Christmas Day in that year. This would indicate a direct translation of the word *ludus*, as used in liturgical Latin, into the vernacular. In 1558 the Churchwardens' Accounts for Holy Trinity, Bungay, contain the entry,

'P(ai)d to Will(ia)m Holbruck for ryding to Yarmouth for ye game gere, xijd.'

In 1577, ironically enough, a churchwarden records a receipt given to 'game Players' who had bought costumes made out of church vestments. See *Med. Stage*, ii, p. 343.

Game players are recorded in Norwich in 1534/35 when they performed before the Mayor on a raised stage in the Council Chamber. See Appendix D, p. 332 above.

22. Stow's *Survey*, ii, pp. 368–369, n. 73. The word 'activities' is dropped in the printed edition of 1598, but there is the note in the margin, 'Theater and Curtine for Comedies and other shewes'. cf. Ordish, *op. cit.*, p. 45. Howes' continuation of Stow's *Annales*, p. 926; cf. *ES*, ii, p. 419.

23. For a fencing prize at the Theater see p. 195 above. It is interesting to note that in two Orders of the Court of Aldermen, issued on 17th October and 9th November 1581, forbidding cockfighting and football, these recreations are described as 'cockepytt playe' and 'footeball playe': see *Collections II*, p. 312; also n. 24 above.

24. *ES*, iv, pp. 199–200.

25. A comparison between the 'G' of Gilbert Katheren's name on the one hand with the 'S' in St. Saviour's or 'Sett' (line 16) on the other is conclusive. The G's differ slightly from one another but the S's do not.

Game place is confirmed later in the contract (and Greg reads it correctly in his transcript) and also occurs in Muniment 51, the subcontract for brickwork on the Hope: 'one Game place or plaie house' (Warner, *Catalogue*, p. 241).

I am indebted to Mr. Remington Patterson, Lecturer in English at Barnard College, Columbia University, N.Y., for drawing my attention to the extract from a legal dispute over the boundaries of Crown land and Episcopal land on the Bankside. The Bishop of Winchester exhibited a bill against Edward Alleyn and Jacob Meade, to which Alleyn answered on 5th Feburary 1622. He said in reviewing the history of the two properties, which Henslowe had held:

'. . . hee the said Phillipp Henslowe intendinge to alter the game place standinge vppon the Landes belonginge to the Bishoppricke of Winchester . . . had made a beginninge of a ffoundacōn for a newe game place to bee sett in a more Convenient place, but the said Phillipp Henslowe takinge consideracōn and advise thearof, Caused the ffoundacōn to bee made thearof vppon the Landes belonginge to the Crowne . . . and uppon that newe ffoundation [*sic*] did erect and build the house Called the Hope nowe imployed and vsed for a game place for baitinge his Ma^tes Beares and Bulles and for a playehouse, to wch vse it is imployed and vsed att this daye . . .'

26. See Welsford, *CM*, pp. 173 *et seq.*

27. See H. Leclerc, *Origines Italiennes de l'Architecture Théâtrale Moderne*, pp. 190–195. On illustrations to renaissance editions of Terence, see *ES*, iii, pp. 6–8, and M. Herrmann, *Forschungen sur deutschen Theatergeschicte des Mittelalters und der Renaissance*, 1914, pp. 280 *et seq.* The

best modern authority is E. W. Robbins, *Dramatic Characterization in Printed Commentaries on Terence 1473–1600*, Urbana (Ill.), 1951.

28. For details of the building of the Curtain, the Rose and the Swan, see *ES*, ii, pp. 400–414.

29. *ES*, ii, 466.

30. On the suppression of the religious stage, 1570–80, see pp. 79–83 above; on Leicester's Patent, see p. 80 above.

31. Table A: for sources see *ES*, iv, pp. 60–74, and *EP*, i, Chs. IV and V.

32. Table C(1): this list is compiled from references in *EDC*, ii, and *Med. Stage*, ii.

33. Table C(2): this list is an expanded version of column 4 in Table C(1).

34. *MSC. II*, pp. 258–284: see especially pp. 262–263.

35. *EDC*, ii, p. 383.

36. *Ibid.*, ii, p. 284. For a performance in 1566 in the churchyard of the Suffolk village of Bungay see *Med. Stage*, ii, p. 343.

37. *EDC*, ii, 337.

38. *Ibid.*, ii, 341.

39. *Ibid.*, ii, 402 and accompanying note.

40. *Ibid.*, ii, 277.

41. *Ibid.*, ii, 278.

42. *Ibid.*, ii, 279.

43. *Ibid.*, ii, 327.

44. *Ibid.*, ii, pp. 361–364.

45. *Ibid.*, ii, 409.

46. *Ibid.*, ii, pp. 214–215. See *EES*, i, p. 386, notes 24 and 25.

47. *Ibid.*, ii, pp. 309–310.

48. *Ibid.*, ii, pp. 233, 235 and 400–401 respectively.

49. *Ibid.*, ii, 410. See also Ch. V, p. 167 above, for action at Great Yarmouth.

50. 'An Early Elizabethan Playhouse', *Shakespeare Survey 6*, (1953), pp. 64–74.

51. *MSC. II, III & V*: For performances in the Halls of the Livery Companies see *III*, pp. xviii, 132 *et seq.*, and 183–184; for performances in Cambridge Halls, see *II*, pp. 150–230; for performances in Oxford, see *V*, pp. 30–95. See also L. B. Campbell, *Scenes and Machines*, p. 19; F. S. Boas, *University Drama in the Tudor Age*, 1914; and T. H. Vail Motter, *The School Drama in England*, 1929.

52. *MSC. III*, p. 136.

53. *MSC. II*, p. 291, citing Rep., xi, f. 135.

54. *Ibid.*, p. 288, citing *Journal*, xiv, f. 319; *Letter Book Q*, f. 51b.

55. *ES*, ii, p. 527.

56. *ES*, ii, pp. 380–383 and pp. 443–445.

57. *ES*, i, p. 284.

58. See *Shakespeare Survey 6*, p. 66; also *EDC* ii, p. 408.

59. P.R.O. Sta. Cha. 8/307/14 quoted by Hotson, *Shakespeare's Wooden 'O'*, p. 70 and used by him to illustrate his thesis of performances on wagon stages in the yard.

60. *EDC*, ii, pp. 336 and 377 respectively; also p. 235 & *ES*, ii, pp. 222–223.

61. See n. 56 above and Fig. 6, pp. 50–51 above.

62. See Gildersleeve, *Govt. Reg.*, pp. 28–42; also *ES*, ii, pp. 208–209, 229–231, 234–235 and pp. 242–243.

63. *ES*, iv, p. 369. The phrase 'at this day is to be seen' is ambiguous and can as easily refer to the Inns as to theatres in their yards.

64. *ES*, ii, pp. 444–445.

65. *ES*, iv, p. 340.

66. *ES*, iv, pp. 288–289. This recital scarcely accords with Chambers' own view that Innyards proved popular as places in which 'an audience could quickly gather'.

67. *MSC. II*, p. 310, citing *Journal*, xxi, f. 7; *Letter Book Z*, f. 15b.

68. *Ibid.*, p. 310, citing *Rep.*, xix, f. 224b.

69. *Ibid.*, p. 292, citing *Journal*, xv, f. 242; *Letter Book Q*, f. 169. For the full text see pp. 327–328 above.

70. 2nd March. *MSC. II*, pp. 294–295, citing *Journal*, xvi, f. 254; *Letter Book R*, f. 245.

71. 7th March, *ibid.*, pp. 296–297, citing *Journal*, xvi, f. 328; *Letter Book S*, f. 20b.

72. 1564, 12th February. *Ibid.*, pp. 299–300, citing *Journal*, xviii, f. 184; *Letter Book T*, f. 189.
1565, 29th November. *Ibid.*, p. 300, citing *Rep.*, xv. f. 500b, and cf. *Journal*, xviii, f. 362.
1566, 30th April. *Ibid.*, p. 301, citing *Rep.*, xvi, f. 42b; *Letter Book V*, f. 21b.

73. *Ibid.*, p. 303, citing *Journal*, xix, f. 138b; *Letter Book V*, f. 209b.
In this connection it is worth remarking that most of the prosecutions of inn-keepers of which we have record are for permitting plays at night. See pp. 190 and 191 above.

74. *Ibid.*, pp. 303–305, citing *Rep.*, xvi., f. 442b; *Journal*, xix, f. 143b; *Letter Book V*, ff. 222 and 215.

75. *ES*, iv, p. 267, citing *Journal*, xix, f. 167b. See also p. 240 above for use of the word 'open' in this sense in Gloucester.

76. *ES*, iv, p. 290, citing *Remembrancia*, i, p. 384. The fencer apparently did not take advantage of this offer. The result was that he missed his opportunity (or so the Lord Mayor claims), for the plague got so much worse than even the Leadenhall was not deemed 'open' enough and the fencer was accordingly instructed to hold his prize-fight 'in the open feilds'. He can still go to the Theater if he can reach agreement with the owners, and he can advertise the match in the City on any day except a Sunday.

77. *ES*, iv, p. 273; *MSC. I.*, p. 175. The following two quoted extracts are taken from the same source.

78. For the text of the Proclamation see Appendix B, pp. 327–328 above. See also pp. 192–193 above.

79. *Op. cit.*, p. 9

80. *Scenes and Machines*, pp. 83–84. Yet Lily was nevertheless the man chosen to write the verses for the pageants prepared for the reception of the Emperor Charles V into London, 1522: see *EP*, i, p. 175, citing *Rep.* iv, f. 134b; also *EES*, i, pp. 80, 81 and 84.

81. See p. 116 above and *ES*, iv, p. 209.

Chapter VI, pages 206–244. The Emblematic Tradition

1. *Op. cit.*, p. 93.

2. *Works*, viii, p. 404 (spelling modernized).

3. See *ES*, iv, pp. 200, 217 and 197 respectively.

4. *ES*, ii, pp. 34–35: *HEP*, ed. cit., p. 812, n. 4.

5. See *Speculum*, XXXIV (1959), No. 4, pp. 702–705. In this same review Professor Craig states, '. . . the author (i.e. *myself*) does not think there is much virtue in the familiar theory of the origin of Easter *ordines* and *ludi* from the *Quem quaeritis* trope'. (p. 702). This is sheer invention. Nowhere in Vol. I do I disclaim this theory: in fact I have stated no less than three times that I accept it; see *EES*, i, pp. 124, 230, 310–312.

6. *MSC. III*, 1954; *MSC. V*, 1959.

7. *PJI*, ii, pp. 54–69; see especially p. 68. Also *EP*, i, p. 227, n. 2.

8. J. Nichols, *The Fishmongers Pageant*, 1616; ed. 1844.

9. 'Britannia's Honour, *Bowers' Dekker*, iv, pp. 81–95; see especially p. 86.

10. *Ibid.*, pp. 93–94.

11. 'London's Tempe', *Bowers' Dekker*, iv, pp. 98–112; see pp. 109–110.

12. 'Triumphs of Love and Antiquity', *Bullen's Middleton*, vii, p. 318; 'Triumphs of Health and Prosperity', *ibid.*, p. 404

13. 'Porta Pietatis' (Drapers) 1638, *Works*, v, p. 267; 'Londini Status', (Drapers) 1639, *Works*, v, p. 365; 'Londini Emporia' (Cloth-workers) 1633, *Works*, iv, p. 324. The latter included a trade-pageant of sheep (2nd tableau) and 'The Bower of Blisse' (4th tableau).

14. *Lucas' Webster*, iii, p. 323, lines 244–248.

15. See *EP*, ii, pp. 43–48; also i, pp. 238–239.

16. John Tatham, *Aqua Triumphalis*, London, 1662. The copy from which these quotations are taken is that in Guildhall.

17. John Ogilby, *The Relation of His Majestie's Entertainment*, London, 1661. The text from which these quotations are taken is that of the expanded and illustrated edition of 1662, *The Entertainment of . . . Charles II*, a copy of which is in Guildhall.

18. *Works*, iv, pp. 262–281; see especially pp. 272–273. For Elizabeth's Coronation Shows see *PQE*, i, Sig. B. The pamphlet which Nichols reprints is that by Richard Tothill, *The Royal Passage of her Majesty from the Tower of London*, etc. London, 1558, copies of which are in the British Museum and at Guildhall. See *EP*, i, pp. 199–202.

19. A copy of the descriptive pamphlet is in the British Museum. It is reprinted in *PJI*, iii, pp. 107 *et seq.*

20. Printed in *PQE*, ii.

21. For Munday's Show see *MSC, III*, pp. 78 and 79; for Dekker's Show, *Bowers' Dekker*, iv, p. 83 and *MSC, III*, pp. 112–114.

22. See *Lucas' Webster*, iii, p. 325 and *MSC, III*, pp. 106–108. *Heywood's Works*, iv, p. 270 and *MSC, III*, pp. 120–121.

23. *Bullen's Middleton*, vii, p. 239 and *PJI*, ii, p. 684.

24. *Bullen's Middleton*, vii, p. 298.

25. *Ibid.*, p. 346. See also *EES*, i, p. 97.

26. *PQE*, i, Sig. D[2]2b.; Heywood, *Works*, v, pp. 361–362.

27. See Fishmongers Pageant, and Jean Robertson, 'Rapports du Poète et de l'Artiste dans la Préparation des Cortèges du Lord Maire' in *Les Fêtes de la Renaissance, I*, ed. J. Jacquot, Paris, 1956, pp. 270 *et seq.*

28. *PQE*, i, Sig. B[2]4, and *EES*, i, p. 72.

29. A late example of the Jesse Tree (1594) is illustrated and discussed by G. R. Kernodle in 'The Medieval Pageant Waggons of Louvain', p. 73 and Plate 4, in *The Theatre Annual*, 1952 (Vol. X), New York, 1952.

30. George Peele, *Descensus Astraeae*, 1585. Copies of this pamphlet are in the Bodleian and at Guildhall. It is reprinted in Bullen's *Peele*, ed. 1829, i, pp. 361 *et seq.* See also D. H. Horne, *The Life & Minor Works of George Peele*, New Haven, 1952, pp. 65–109.

31. 'The Sun in Aries', *Bullen's Middleton*, vii, p. 348 and *MSC, III*, p. 101; 'The Triumphs of Health and Prosperity', *MSC, III*, p. 110; for Munday's 'Campbell, or the Ironmongers' Fair Field', see *MSC, III*, pp. 73–75 and *EP*, ii, pp. 29–30.

32. *PQE*, i, Sig. C[2]4.

33. This pamphlet is in the British Museum (C. 33, e. 7 (20)). Mulciber appeared as a character in what seems like a similar setting in the pageants for King Christian of Denmark's reception in London, 1606. See *EP*, i, p. 228, n. 1.

34. *Bowers' Dekker*, iv, p. 106; see also *MSC, III*, pp. 115 and 118.

35. J. Ogilby, *The Entertainment of . . . Charles II*, London, 1662, p. 28.

36. *EP*, ii, pp. 16–17, citing the MS. *Mayor's Book of Norwich*, pp. 139–143.

37. *PQE*, ii, 12; cf. *EES*, i, Fig. 11, p. 154 and G. F. Reynolds, *op. cit.*, p. 44.

38. See *Lucas' Webster*, iii, p. 321, lines 162–3.

39. See Dekker's 'Troia Nova Triumphans'; Middleton's 'Triumphs of Honour and Industry', 'Triumphs of Love and Antiquity'; Webster's 'The Monuments of Honour'; Heywood's 'Porta Pietatis' and 'Londini Status'. Good pictorial examples of the *Sanctuary* or *Temple* are provided from a Flemish source in the *Omgang de Louvain*, edited by Edward van

Even, Brussels and Louvain, 1863; see G. R. Kernodle, 'The Mediaeval Pageant Waggons of Louvain', *ed. cit.*, Plates 5, 9 and 10. See n. 29 above.

40. *Lucas' Webster*, iii, p. 319, lines 92–94.

41. *Bullen's Middleton*, vii, p. 391. For a much earlier example of the use of windows and light in a pageant see the Disguisings at the wedding of Prince Arthur and Catherine of Aragon 1501, quoted in *EES*, i, p. 252. For a later example, see Heywood's 'Londini Speculum' of 1637; London's Mirror is said to be 'decored with glasses of all sorts'. *Works*, iv, p. 315. On lights in Masks see Ch. VII, n. 54 below.

42. *MSC, III*, pp. 87–88; *Bullen's Middleton*, vii, p. 234.

43. For this and the next two quotations see *Bowers' Dekker*, iv, p. 111.

44. *Bullen's Middleton*, vii, pp. 341–342. This pageant warrants comparison with Jonson's Temple of Janus for James I's entry into London, 1603. 'The scene carried the frontispiece of a temple, the walls of which and gates were of brass; their pillars silver, their capitals and bases gold; in the highest point of all was erected a Janus' head . . .' *Works*, viii, p. 95: See Plate XVII; also G. Wickham, 'Contribution de Ben Jonson et de Dekker aux Fêtes du Couronnement de Jacques Ier' in *Les Fêtes de la Renaissance I*, ed. J. Jacquot, Paris, 1956. An extraordinary six-storey tower was presented in the Louvain *Omgang*, of which a picture survives; see nn. 29 and 39 above.

45. *Works*, iv, pp. 292–293. In 1637 he provided the Haberdashers with 'an *Imperial* Fort'. *Ibid.*, p. 313.

46. *Bowers' Dekker*, iii, p. 238.

47. Nichols, *PQE*, i, reprints *The Firste Parte of Churchyarde's Chippes*, London, 1575, in which the whole show is described by the author.

48. *PQE*, i (1572), p. 29.

49. Nichols, *PJI*, ii, reprints Richard Davies, *Chester's Triumph in honour of her Prince*, Chetham Soc., Manchester, 1844, which provides a full description of the show. Munday's pamphlet is in the British Museum (c. 33, d. 5). See also *EP*, i, pp. 229–232.

50. The Argoe appeared in Munday's 'Triumphs of the Golden Fleece' of 1623; this was the water show, the land show being provided by Middleton: see *MSC, III*, pp. 104–105. The Joel was another of Munday's ships, and figured in his 'Metropolis Coronata' of 1615 for the Drapers Company; see *PJI*, iii, pp. 107 *et seq.* The Royal Sovereign was contributed by Heywood in his *Porta Pietatis* of 1638; see *Works*, v, pp. 270f. Webster called his ship (1624) 'the Holy-Lamb'; *Lucas' Webster*, iii, pp. 317–318.

51. J. Ogilby, *The Entertainment of . . . Charles II*, London, 1662, pp. 43 *et seq.*

52. A consort of singers was concealed in a boat under a Dolphin (on which Proteus was mounted) in Leicester's Entertainment for Queen Elizabeth at Kenilworth, 1575; see *PQE*, i (p. 68); also ii, p. 14 for the musical devices in the water-show, Elvetham, 1591. For Munday's very elaborate whale combining music and fireworks see *MSC, III*, pp. 70–78.

For the water-show in honour of Prince Henry in which Burbage made a speech in the character of Amphion on a whale's back, see *EP*, i, pp. 230–233. A similar water-show had greeted Prince Henry in Chester a month earlier; see R. Davies, *Chester's Triumph, ed. cit.*, and *EP*, i, pp. 229–230.

53. For Christian of Denmark's entry see *PJI*, ii, pp. 54–69; also H. Robarts, *The Most royall and Honourable entertainments* 1606, and Stow's *Annales* (ed. 1615), p. 886. For Richard II's Coronation (1377) and his return to London from York in 1392 see *EES*, i, pp. 55 and 69–70.

54. *Works*, iv, pp. 290–291. A fine picture of a pageant cloud-machine survives in the *Omgang de Louvain*, 1594, *ed. cit.*, Plate 11; see nn. 29 and 39 above.

55. *PQE*, i (1575) p. 78.

56. *PJI*, ii, 293.

57. *Bullen's Middleton*, vii, p. 239.

58. Thomas Churchyarde, *A discourse of the Queenes Majesties entertainement in Suffolk & Norffolk*, London, 1578, sig. E3b. A copy of this rare pamphlet is in the Bodleian Library (Tanner 745 (5)).

59. *PQE*, ii, p. 3 *et seq.* A curious and recurrent entry in the accounts of the London City Companies in respect of the Lord Mayor's shows is for digging up areas of paved street and filling them in again; see *MSC, III*.

60. *Lucas' Webster*, iii, p. 317, lines 27 *et seq.* Heywood's 'Londini Speculum', *Works*, iv, p. 310. *Bullen's Middleton*, vii, p. 365 ('The Triumphs of Honour & Virtue').

61. *Bowers' Dekker*, iv, pp. 87 and 94. On this whole subject of costume iconography see *MSC, III*, pp. xxxviii *et seq.*

62. *Works*, v, pp. 272 and 363.

63. *Bullen's Middleton*, vii, pp. 302–304. For Jonson's description of Truth see D. J. Gordon, '*Hymenaei*; Ben Jonson's Masque of Union', in *Journal of the Warburg and Courtauld Institutes*, viii (1945), 138.

64. *Bullen's Middleton*, vii, p. 236 ('The Triumphs of Truth').

65. J. Ogilby, *The Entertainment of . . . Charles II*, 1662, pp. 43 *et seq.*

66. Middleton provides a good example in his Pageant of Several Nations ('Triumphs of Honour and Industry') in which he presents an Irishman, a Frenchman, a Spaniard, a Turk, a Jew, a Dane, a Polander, a Barbarian and a Russian; see *Bullen's Middleton*, vii, pp. 299–302.

67. *Works*, iv, p. 288; cf. the melodious birds of 1624, *Lucas' Webster*, iii, p. 323, lines 243 *et seq.*, and Jupiter on his eagle in 1628, *Bowers' Dekker*, iv, pp. 107–108, and Fig. 12, p. 218 above.

68. Heywood, *Works*, v, pp. 266 and 361. A fine array of birds and beasts was presented on a Flemish stage illustrated in Plate XIII.

69. See E. Welsford, *The Court Masque*, 1927, pp. 116–118, 147 and 148, and especially 159–160; also *EP*, i, pp. 116–123.

70. *PQE*, iii, pp. 58–59.

71. *Ibid.*, ii, p. 127.

72. *Ibid.*, pp. 125–127.

73. See *ES*, iii, pp. 212-213, 402-403 and 463.

74. *ES*, i, p. 148, citing *B.M. MSS. Rutland*, iv, pp. 494 and 508.

75. Le Sieur Henry Humbert, *Combat à la Barrière Faict en cour de Lorraine le 14 Feburier en l'année présente, 1627*, Nancy, 1627. The text is illustrated with engravings by Jacques Callot. On Callot's *Guerra d'Amore* of 1615 and 1616 in Florence, see *CM*, p. 100.

76. *Ibid.*, Sigs. D. iv, and D. iv, b.

77. *Ibid.*, Sig. B. ii, b.

78. *Works*, vii, 232. The two following quotations in the text are taken from the same source, pp. 239-240 respectively. (Spelling modernized.)

79. *Ibid.*, vii, pp. 323 *et seq.*

80. *Guildhall Library MS. 4160*, transcribed and edited by D. S. Bland, *Guildhall Miscellany*, No. 6, February 1956.

81. *Ibid.*, f. 2.

82. See Welsford, *CM.*, pp. 189-191.

83. State Papers, Domestic, James I, vol. 89, no. 15, cited by Bland *op. cit.*, p. 2.

84. *Works*, iv, p. 324; cf. *EES*, i, p. 111 for Jonson's and Dekker's views on their audience for their pageants of 1603, and Jonson, *Works*, viii, pp. 403-404, for the 'Expostulation with Inigo Jones'.

85. *Works*, iv, pp. 279-280.

86. *Ibid.*, v, pp. 372-373; Davenant, *Works*, ii, pp. 301-331; Evans, *English Masques*, pp. 229-245. 'Salmacida Spolia' was the last of the Court Masks and that in the designs for which Inigo Jones completed his experiments in changeable scenery. Davenant's text however presented King and Court with a flattering mirror of themselves which offers no hint of troubles either in Church or State, other than a scenic tempest at the start which is quickly stilled by the appearance of the King and Queen.

87. For the cost of James I's reception see *EES*, i, pp. 289-290; for the Drapers Show of 1639 see *MSC, III*, pp. 128-130.

88. *MSC, III*, pp. 128, 125 and 119 respectively.

89. This practice appears to have been of very early origin. John Leedes, a painter, was instructed by the Merchant Taylors in 1556 to bring in 'a patern' for the Wardens to consider (*MSC, III*, p. 39). The Drapers four years later consult 'a paper drawen' of a pageant to assist in deciding whether to proceed with it. 'Moddells' as well as 'plots' were made in 1603 for James I's entry and for the show of 1609 (*ibid.*, pp. xxxiii & 71). On the general subject of co-operation between poet and painter see Jean Robertson, 'Rapports du poète et de l'artiste' in *Les Fêtes de la Renaissance I*, ed. J. Jacquot, Paris, 1956.

90. See *MSC, III*, pp. 115 *et seq.*

91. *Ibid.*, pp. 117-119; see also *MSC, V*, pp. 4-8. It was usual for the poets and artificers whose tenders were not accepted to receive a small fee in remuneration for their estimates. This varied between as little as £1 and as much as £5; see *MSC, III*, pp. 122-123 and p. 93.

92. *MSC, III*, p. 90.

93. *Ibid.*, pp. 72–78 and 84–85, and pp. 102 and 106.

94. *Ibid.*, p. 165, and *D.N.B.*, sub Munday, A.

95. *Ibid.*, pp. 167 and 177; *J & CS*, iv, pp. 857–858.

96. *Works*, vi, pp. 317–318.

97. Two Pageants by Thomas Heywood, ed. A. M. Clark in *Theatre Miscellany*, Luttrell Soc. 14, Oxford, 1953, p. 45.

98. Davenant, *Works*, ii, p. 327.

Chapter VII, pages 245–275. The Quest for the Image

1. See Welsford, *CM*, pp. 100, 124 *et seq.*, 144, 164 *et seq.* and 176.

2. See *Fêtes de la Renaissance II*, 'Fêtes et cérémonies au temps de Charles Quint', Paris, 1956–60; also *EP*, i, pp. 174–179.

3. See G. R. Kernodle, *From Art to Theatre*, pp. 111–129. The two-way trading-traffic between London and Antwerp, as well as the political traffic between England and the Low Countries, was important enough for rich, resident communities of Dutchmen to settle in London and for similar groups of Englishmen to settle in Holland. The English Merchants in Antwerp contributed a pageant to Philip of Spain's entry into that city in 1549. The Dutch merchants in London contributed a pageant to James I's entry into London in 1603, as did the Italian merchants. These questions will be fully treated in Volume III. For Heywood's remarks on foreign visitors to the Lord Mayor's Show, see Ch. VI, p. 243 above.

4. Campbell, *Scenes and Machines*, pp. 12 *et seq.*; Leclerc, *Origines Italiennes*, pp. 42–43, and 51 *et seq.*

5. *Scenes and Machines*, pp. 14–15; *Origines Italiennes*, pp. 43–46.

6. *Scenes and Machines*, pp. 16–21; *Origines Italiennes*, pp. 51–57.

7. The relevant passages from Book V of the *De Architectura*, relating to the *scena* and to perspective painting are given in English translation by Miss Campbell, *Scenes and Machines*, pp. 16 and 17.

8. See W. G. Keith, 'The Art of Scenic Decoration', in *The Builder*, Vol CVII (1914), p. 46.

9. *Origines Italiennes*, p. 70.

10. *Scenes and Machines*, pp. 52–53; *Origines Italiennes*, pp. 72–73.

11. For Peruzzi's part in the revival of scenic perspective, see Vassari's *The Lives of the Most Eminent Painters*, etc. (trans.: S. Du C. De Vere, 1912–14), Vol. v, p. 69.

12. *Scenes and Machines*, pp. 49 *et seq.*; *Origines Italiennes*, p. 72.

13. See Welsford, *CM*, pp. 85 *et seq.*, and 168.

14. *Scenes and Machines*, p. 53; see also n. 11 above. The description of the landscape curtain for the *Mask of Blackness* is quoted, Ch. I, p. 4 above.

15. *Ibid.*, pp. 84 and 102–103; see also p. 76, n. 2 and *Med. Stage* ii, p. 196.

16. See *MSC, II*, pp. 228 (King's Hall) and pp. 183 and 229 (Queen's).

17. For Magdalen College, Oxford, see *MSC, V*, pp. 48–51; for Christ's and Trinity Cambridge, see *MSC, II*, pp. 153 *et seq.*, and 205.

18. See *Origines Italiennes*, Plates XIV, XV, XXII and pp. 74–83; *Scenes and Machines*, pp. 33–35 and 47, also Plate I and *ES*, iv, pp. 354 and 357.

19. For the labelling of doors see *ES*, iii, p. 40. On mimetic action see T. W. Craik, *The Tudor Interlude*, p. 93 *et seq.*, and *EES*, i, pp. 157 *et seq.*

20. *EDC*, ii, p. 361; also Appendix D, p. 333 above.

21. *Ibid.*, ii, p. 362.

22. The item in the Bursarial accounts reads, '19. februarij dowseo et filio operantibus 8 diebus apud le skrene et theatrum—viijs'. *MSC, II*, p. 185.

23. *Scenes and Machines*, pp. 102–103.

24. Ed. J. Churton Collins, Oxford, 1941.

25. *Origines Italiennes*, Plates XX and XXII and pp. 83–99.

26. *Scenes and Machines*, pp. 29–31 and 61 *et seq.* Pollux, Julii Pollucis, *Onomasticon*, 4°, Basle, 1536.

27. See Leonardo da Vinci's *A Treatise on Painting* (trans. J. F. Rigaud) 1892.

28. *Marci Vitruvii Pollionis viri suae Professionis Peritissimi de Architectura Libri Decum cum notis* PHILANDRI et sexte Frontini. 8vo, Rome 1544; French ed. in fol, 1547. The text of *Il secondo libro di Perspettiva*, ff. 26b–31b, of Serlio's *Architettura* is printed by Chambers in *ES*, iv, pp. 353–365, together with a note on the English edition of 1611 and reproductions of the five woodcuts illustrating the first edition.

29. *Scenes and Machines*, pp. 35–39; *Origines Italiennes*, pp. 74 *et seq.*

30. Anyone who wishes to see this process in action has only to sit in the auditorium of the *Teatro Olimpico* in Vicenza and watch a friend walk up one of the 'streets' behind the arches of the *frons scenæ*.

31. *Scenes and Machines*, pp. 39–41. On the oil lamps still *in situ* in the *Teatro Olimpico*, see *Origines Italiennes*, p. 92.

32. See n. 23 above; also *Scenes and Machines*, pp. 23–24.

33. *Origines Italiennes*, pp. 83 *et seq.*, and especially p. 89; also *Scenes and Machines*, p. 55.

34. For a full bibliography of works devoted to the *Teatro Olimpico* see *Origines Italiennes*, pp. 228–229. See also Leo Schrade, *La Répresentation d'Edipo Tiranno au Teatro Olimpico* (Vicence, 1585), Paris, 1960.

35. *Origines Italiennes*, p. 91. On the disputed question of whether Palladio intended the perspectives to take the form given them by Scamozzi, see G. J. K. Loukanski, *Andrea Palladio, sa vie, son œuvre*, Paris, 1927, pp. 32 *et seq.*

36. *Ibid.*, pp. 88–89 and 95. See T. Buzzi, 'Il Teatro all Antico di Vincenzo Scamozzi in Sabbionetta' in *Dedalo* (1927–28); also 'The theatre of Sabbionetta', in *The Mask*, IX (1923), p. 24.

37. *PQE*, iii. Sig. Ee. 4b; pp. 207–209. *Scenes and Machines*, p. 92.

38. *Scenes and Machines*, pp. 104–105; see also *ES*, iii, pp. 21 and 44.

39. *MSC, III*, p. 39; see also Ch. VI, pp. 239–240 above, especially n. 89.

40. For the progress of the Italian landscape stage in France see S.Wilma Holsboer, *L'histoire de la Mise en Scène dans le Théâtre Français*, 1600–1657, Paris, 1933.

41. Feuillerat, *R.O. Eliz.*, 1908: see Ch. VIII, pp. 282–286 below.

42. See *ES*, iv, pp. 203–205 and 206–207.

43. See Roger Ascham, *The Schoolmaster, ed. cit.*, and *ES*, iv, pp. 191–192; Richard Puttenham, *Arte of English Poesie* (1589), ed. E. Arber, 1869. An early treatise in Latin which shows a close acquaintance with Scaliger's *Poetice* is Richard Wills' *De Re Poetica*, London, 1573; see A. D. S. Fowler's edition for Lutterell Soc., 1958.

44. See n. 24 above.

45. See Welsford, *CM*, pp. 173 *et seq.*

46. *Works*, vii, p. 172.

47. *Ibid.*, vii, p. 171. (Spelling modernized.)

48. 'The Vision of the Twelve Goddesses' is printed by H. A. Evans in his *English Masques*, 1906, pp. 1–16. See also *CM*, pp. 171–173.

49. See J. Lees-Milne, *The Age of Inigo Jones*, 1953, pp. 32–34 and 42. J. Laver (*Drama*, p. 76), suggests that these annotations were made 'at the end of the century', i.e. during Jones' first visit to Italy, but the statement is not supported by any source or authority. Jones' own marginal annotation is dated 'Sundaie ye 23 of September 1623'. See W. G. Keith, 'A theatre Project' in *The Burlington Magazine*, vol. xxxi, p. 65 *et seq.*; also *Scenes and Machines*, pp. 56–57 and 204 *et seq.* Concerning Jones' debt to Giulio Parigi, see Welsford, *CM*, pp. 186–188 and pp. 235–239. Nicoll, *Stuart Masques* (1937), reproduces Parigi's designs for Calypso's Garden, Fig. 44, p. 93, and the Palace of Fame, Fig. 56, p. 103.

50. See *Works*, vii, pp. 203, 243, 265, 321 and 337 respectively; also Ch. VI, pp. 232–234 above and Plate XXI, Frontispiece and Fig. 3.

51. *CM*, pp. 178–188. *Scenes and Machines*, pp. 168–172. See also *The Masque of Queens*, Fac. ed., King's Printers, 1930.

52. *Works*, vii, pp. 463–471. (Spelling modernized.)

53. *Scenes and Machines*, pp. 39 and 60; Nicoll, *op. cit.*, pp. 129–137.

54. For the lighting of the perspectives in the *Teatro Olimpico*, see *Origines Italiennes*, p. 92. On this subject in general see *Oxford Companion to the Theatre*, *sub*. Lighting, Stage. Nicoll, *op. cit.*, reproduces one of the lamps in the *Teatro Olimpico* to scale, Fig. 93, p. 134, and Inigo Jones' 'Throne of Light', Fig. 94, p. 135.

55. *Works*, vii, p. 638. (Spelling modernized.)

56. *Works*, vii, pp. 731–743. The title page for this mask, and for its successor *Chloridia*, carry the rubric,

The Inventors

Ben Jonson   Inigo Jones

The Mask of Augurs (*Works*, vii, pp. 625–647) was printed in Quarto in

1622 in two states, the first anonymous and the second with this inscription.

> '*For the expression of this, I must stand; The invention was divided betwixt* Mr JONES, *and mee. The* SCENE, *which your eye judges, was wholly his, and worthy his place of the Kings* Surveyor, *and* Architect, *full of noble observation of Antiquitie, and high Presentment* . . .'.

Herford and Simpson regard this acknowledgement as an afterthought. For the connection between this rivalry and Jonson's 'Expostulation', which followed *Love's Triumph*, see *Works*, i, pp. 60–62 and pp. 97–98.

57. p. 63.

58. *CM*, pp. 205–207.

59. *Ibid.*, p. 220; see also n. 56 above.

60. See J. Lees Milne, *The Age of Inigo Jones*, pp. 45 *et seq.*

61. E. K. Chambers, *Aurelian Townshend's Poems and Masks*, Oxford, 1912; 'Albions Triumph', p. 57.

62. *Ibid.*, 'Tempe Restored,' p. 99.

63. On Shirley's masks see *CM*, pp. 225 *et seq.* Carew's 'Cœlum Britannicum' is printed by J. W. Ebsworth in *The Poems and Masks of Thomas Carew*, London, 1893, pp. 126–127, from the Quarto of 1634 and by Rhodes Dunlap, *The Poems of Thomas Carew*, 1949, pp. 151–185.

64. Davenant, *Works, ed. cit.*, ii, p. 289. The whole Mask and a commentary are printed, pp. 247–300.

65. *Ibid.*, ii, p. 319; Evans, *English Masques*, p. 233. Settings are reproduced by Nicoll, *op. cit.*, Figs. 78, 79 and 82–83 (pp. 120–125).

Chapter VIII, pages 276–323. Stage Furniture

1. *R.O. Eliz.*, p. 244.

2. *Ibid.*, p. 266. Eleven shillings was spent at the same time 'ffor a barge to cary two fframes to the Court for the Children of windsours plaie'.

3. W. J. Lawrence, *The Physical Conditions of the Elizabethan Playhouse*, 1927; *ES*, iii. Chs. XIX–XXI; Reynolds, *The Staging of Elizabethan Plays*, 1940; *Scenes and Machines*, Chs. VIII and IX; Hotson, *Shakespeare's Wooden 'O'*, 1959, Ch. V, and A. M. Nagler, *Shakespeare's Stage*, 1958, Chs. 4–6; C. W. Hodges, *The Globe Restored*, pp. 52 *et seq.*

    See also R. Hosley, 'The Gallery over the Stage in the Public Playhouse of Shakespeare's Time', *Shakespeare Quarterly*, Vol. VIII (1957), No. 1, pp. 15–31, and A. B. Weiner, 'Elizabethan Interior and Aloft Scenes: A Speculative Essay', *Theatre Survey II* (1961), pp. 15–34.

4. See Ch. IV, n. 83 above.

5. Of the companies which acted regularly in London without inhibition after *The Isle of Dogs* affair of 1597 one was the Lord Chamberlain's, another the Lord Admiral's and the third the Earl of Worcester's. Hunsdon and Howard were members of the Queen's Privy Council; Worcester was sworn in on 29th June 1601. The Earl of Nottingham's warrant for the building of the Fortune (12th January 1599/60), the

undated address of the inhabitants of Finsbury to the Privy Council and the Privy Council's Warrant allowing it (8th April 1600), are all couched in the language of special pleading and suggest second thoughts about an unfortunate decision. The documents are printed by Greg, *Henslowe Papers*, pp. 49–52. The Master of the Revels may well have kept a personal eye on the new building: see *Henslowe's Diary*, i, p. 158 (F. 98b).

6. Feuillerat, *R.O.* (*E & M*), and *R.O. Eliz.* I am indebted to Professor F. P. Wilson for the loan of his personal transcript of the Office of Works Accounts. Extracts quoted in the text above have all been checked. I intend to print these Accounts in full in Volume III.

7. *ES*, i, p. 16, nn. i and 2, citing *R.O. Eliz.*, p. 163 and Holinshed, iii, p. 1315 (from *B.M. MS Harl.*, 293, f. 217), respectively.

8. See *R.O.* (*E & M*), pp. 9 and 189 for this and the preceding quotation; see also pp. 115, 149, 154 and 159. 'Hangings' were taken from the Revels Office in Blackfriars to Westminster in 1549 (*ibid.*, p. 39). For the following quotation see *R.O. Eliz.*, p. 106 (1558/59). See also C. W. Hodges, *op. cit.*, pp. 47–48.

9. In 1564, for 'Edwardes' tragedy', the Revels office provided 'canvas to cover divers townes and howses'; see n. 2 above, and *EES*, i, p. 101.

10. Hall, *Chronicle*, ed. 1809, pp. 722 *et seq.*; see also *EES*, i, p. 220.

11. *R.O. Eliz.*, p. 200.

12. *Ibid.*, p. 338; see also p. 336.

13. *Phillyda & Choryn*, *ibid.*, p. 365. For the 'Rock' made for Leicester's men in 1574 see p. 239; also Ch. VIII, p. 277 above; see also *R.O. Eliz.*, pp. 324, 340, 342–345 and 467, n. 342 (64).

14. *R.O. Eliz.*, p. 365. See also notes 77 and 85 below.

15. In 1579/80, we learn that battlements were railed. 'ffurre poles to make Rayles for the battlementes'. (*R.O. Eliz.*, p. 327.) A Rock for the nine Muses was equipped with a curtain for a Mask in 1564 (*ibid.*, p. 117); see particularly pp. 314–315 above.

16. An item in the Revels Accounts for 1564 reads, 'canvas to cover divers townes and howsses'. In 1571/72 the office provided 'apt howses: made of Canvasse, fframed, ffashioned and paynted'. (*R.O. Eliz.*, pp. 116 and 145). In 1572/73 John Carow was paid for providing, 'Sparres to make frames for the players howses' (*ibid.*, p. 175); four years later 5s. was spent, 'ffor Tymber to make a frame' (*ibid.*, p. 262).

In 1573/74 the painter, William Lizarde put in a bill to the Office for 'Nayles to strayne the Canvas' (*ibid.*, p. 201), and a year later we read of 'vices to Joyne fframes together' (*ibid.*, p. 242). The last item speaks for itself; read in conjunction with the other items listed, it seems to me to be difficult to resist the conclusion that the frames and cloths were assembled in the manner that I have suggested. Readers who remain unconvinced should see n. 18 below.

17. Some frames were reinforced with metal-work. 'Item for Iron woorke for A frame for A seate in A pageant—15/-': 'Item for the woorkmanship of the Seate or Chayer—18/4' 1573/74; *R.O. Eliz.*, p. 227.

18. The Revels Office Accounts groan under travel expenses. There is also frequent evidence of great haste, including meals brought to the workmen at their work; see especially *R.O. Eliz.*, pp. 204 and 301. In 1573/74 John Drawater was paid £1 15s. 4d. 'for Cariage of fframes & painted Clothes for the players howses to hampton Coorte (,) attending the same there till service therwith was past (,) and so returning the same (.) In all (,) with the Carters and Carpenters expences there whiles thay wayted (,) and the Carmens wages & horshier for him selfe—xxxvs iiijd' (*ibid.*, p. 218); see also p. 343 above and p. 343, n. 2 above.

19. In Elizabethan times the Accounts for the year are usually introduced by a list of the plays prepared and presented—first those for the twelve days of Christmas, then those for Shrovetide. For example see *R.O. Eliz.*, p. 336 (1580/81).

Christmas:	St. Stephen's Day	Leicester's 1 City	1 Battlement
	St. John's Day	Sussex's 1 House	1 ,,
	Epiphany	Derby's 1 City	1 ,,
	Twelfth Night	Paul's (children) 1 great city, 1 senate house	
Candlemas:		Sussex' 1 City	1 Battlement
Shrovetide:	Sunday	Chapel (children) 1 city, 1 Palace	
	Tuesday	Leicester's 1 great city	

The city and the battlement were particular to each company and not shared.

20. *R.O. Eliz.*, pp. 349 *et seq.* The only dimensions actually given in the Accounts for a scenic item are those for a pageant car. 'A Chariott of xiiij foote Long & viij foote brode with a Rock upon it & A fowntayne therin' (1572, for a Mask), *ibid.*, p. 157. This accords well enough with the dimensions cited in the text, pp. 288–289, above. They happen to correspond closely in the ratio of length to breadth to my conjectural dimensions for pageant-waggons in Coventry; see Plate XXIX, No. 42 and *EES*, i, pp. 172–174.

21. See note 16 above.

22. See *EES*, i, Plates X and XXVII. The references to such items occur regularly throughout the Accounts. Such are: 'Thomas Leveret the wyerdrawer & his servuntes that attended sundry tymes & wrowght upon sundry propertyes & specially to hang upp the lightes in the hall at xij^{te} tyde—x^s ' *R.O. Eliz.*, 1573, p. 196. 'Wyer to strayne crosse the hall & to hang the braunches with the lightes . . .' and 'Item for vyces & wrestes to draw the wyers tighte wheron the lightes did hang crosse the hall', *ibid.*, 1573/74, pp. 216 and 218. 'Wyer of the greate sorte to hang or to strayne cross the hall at Hampton Coorte' (1574/75, *ibid.*, p. 237), 'Plates for to hange upon Walles to sett v. Candells in' (1579/80, *ibid.*, p. 325), and, 'Lightes of Plate in Braunches xxiiij . . . vj^{li}' (*ibid.*, p. 327). See wages bill for 1578–79.

23. '. . . makinge of Tresselles and placinge of Boordes to stande on to see the Dauncinge and makinge haulpaces for the Qu: ma^{tie} under the Cloth of estate.' *Office of Works* E 351/3218 (1583–84) 'framing and setting up a flower [a floor] in it the grounde window in the haulle for musitions [musicians]', *ibid.*, E 351/3237. On this occasion 'a broad

stage' was 'set up . . . in the middle of the hall'—but the plays and dancing were in the Great Chamber and not in the hall; see also P.R.O., E/401/594/16.

24. *Office of Works*, E 351/3213.

25. *Ibid.*

26. *Office of Works*, E 351/3223.

27. *R.O. Eliz.*, pp. 303 *et seq.*

28. *Ibid.*, p. 327 (1579/80); pp. 240 *et seq.*, p. 203 (1573/74) and p. 175 (1572/73), respectively.

29. *Ibid.*, pp. 120–123; see also *ES*, i, pp. 225–226.

30. *Ibid.*, p. 120, line 15. 'John Colbrande . . . x daies . . . x^{8}'

31. *Office of Works*, E 351/3215. The scaffold under the window was probably part of the provision made for the decoration of the Queen's Balcony in the Accession Tilt of *The Castle of Perfect Beautie*; see Ch. VI, p. 230 above.

    The following works item for 1583/84 at Greenwich (E 351/3219) is also pertinent to the question of the frame and door. '. . . making degrees, p(ar)ticons and dores in the greate Chamb(er) and hall, with Tables, tressells and formes for the plaies there.'

32. See Ch. V, pp. 162–163, and Ch. VIII, p. 301.

33. On the reorganization of the Office, see Chambers, *Notes on the History of the Revels Office under the Tudors*, 1906, and *R.O. Eliz.*, pp. 5 *et seq.* There is a reference to the tacking of canvas to a frame in 1548, *R.O.* (*E & M*), p. 31, and several in the first decade of Elizabeth's reign to canvas for houses or to 'apt houses'; but none to the *making* of frames for houses before the item dated 1572/73: 'John Carow for sparres to make frames for the players howses'. *R.O. Eliz.*, p. 175.

34. See n. 22 above.

35. See n. 8 above.

36. *R.O. Eliz.*, p. 79.

37. *Ibid.*, p. 20; see also pp. 19 and 21. For regulations within the Revels Office regarding the translation of garments, see p. 13.

38. *Ibid.*, p. 93.

39. *Ibid.*, between pp. 16 and 17, transcript of Article 58 of *B.M. MS. Lansdowne*, 83, f. 155, lines 72–75.

40. *R.O.* (*E & M*), pp. 7 and 8; also p. 255, n. 3(6).

41. *Ibid.*, pp. 26 and 266, n. 26(5).

42. See *EES*, i. App. G, pp. 353–354; also T. W. Craik, *The Tudor Interlude*, Chs. II and V.

43. W. W. Greg, *Henslowe Papers*, pp. 3 and 5. Gosson similarly distinguishes between the 'house' and the 'stage': see p. 207 above.

44. *Ibid.*, p. 20; see also Ch. V, n. 25 above. C. W. Hodges, *The Globe Restored* (pp. 44–45) suggests, somewhat hesitantly, that we ought to think of the stage and the tiring-house as separate units. In this I think he is correct.

45. See Ch. V, p. 184, and Ch. VII, n. 31 above.
46. *Henslowe Papers, ed. cit.*, p. 20.
47. See n. 15 and pp. 286–289 above; also *R.O. Eliz.*, p. 270.
48. See Ch. IV, n. 35 above.
49. See *ES*, ii, pp. 413–414.
50. *Ibid.*, ii, p. 411, n. 2. See also *Shakespeare Survey I*, Plate IXB.
51. *Ibid.*, ii, pp. 405–407.
52. *Henslowe's Diary, ed. cit.*, i, p. 4 (F2b).
53. *Ibid.*
54. *Ibid.*, i, p. 6 (F3b); see also *Henslowe Papers*, p. 27.
55. *Henslowe's Diary*, i, pp. 7–10 (Ff 4–5b).
56. *Henslowe Papers*, p. 13.
57. *Ibid.*, pp. 116–118.
58. *Henslowe's Diary*, i, pp. 82–83.
59. *Henslowe Papers*, pp. 119 and 120.
60. *Ibid.*, p. 117.
61. *Ibid.*, pp. 116 and 117.
62. See, for examples, *Henslowe's Diary*, i, pp. 87, 136, 137 and 146.
63. *Ibid.*, i, p. 104.
64. *Ibid.*, i, p. 119.
65. *Ibid.*, i, pp. 182 and 184 respectively.
66. *Henslowe Papers*, p. 118.
67. *Henslowe's Diary*, i, p. 182.
68. The bedstead is listed in the inventory: *Henslowe Papers*, p. 116. See Plate XXVII, No. 38.
69. *Ibid., p.* 118.
70. *Ibid.*, p. 116 (Steeples); p. 117 (Chariot).
71. C. W. Hodges takes a radical line on this point. 'The evidence for hangings has been misunderstood because ... scholars have allowed themselves to believe that the word 'stage' could be read as applying to the facade of the tiring-house'. I agree with him. See *The Globe Restored*, pp. 47 and 48.
72. See *EES*, i. Frontispiece and Plates IX and XXVI.
73. *The Tragedies of George Chapman*, Ed. with Notes, T. M. Parrott, 1910.
74. See *Henslowe Papers*, p. 114, line 22 and note, and *Henslowe's Diary*, ii, pp. 149–167; *ES*, iii, pp. 327–330.
75. *The Scottish History of James the Fourth*, Malone Soc. Reprints, 1921.
76. *Ed. cit.*, Induction.
77. *Ibid.*, I. iii; cf. *R.O. Eliz.*, p. 338 (1580/81). 'Painting of ix titles with compartmentes—xv s.' See Ch. VII, n. 19 above; p. 378, n. 85 below.
78. *Henslowe Papers*, pp. 137 and 142 respectively.

79. Dulwich MS xix, transcribed by Greg and printed, *Henslowe Papers*, pp. 130–132; printed by Hodges, *The Globe Restored*, App. D.

80. See *Henslowe Papers*, pp. 133–135 and 138–142 respectively.

81. See also *R.O. Eliz.*, p. 158, 'A prison for discord—v^s' (1572) and p. 453, n. 157(6). Also p. 327, 'ffurre poles . . . to make the prison for my Lord of Warwickes men'.

82. *Henslowe Papers*, pp. 145–148. Among interludes for comparison see Richard Wever's *Lusty Juventus* and Thomas Ingeland's *Nice Wanton*.

83. See R. Hosely, 'Shakespeare's Use of a Gallery over the Stage', *Shakespeare Survey*, 10 (1957), pp. 77–89; also note 3 above.

84. I got this information from a former pupil, Mr. Richard Hay (now on the staff of Stanford University), the designer and technical director of the Shakespeare Theatre, Ashland, Oregon, when I visited it in 1959 at the invitation of Dr. Margaret Bailey, Head of the Ashland Shakespeare Institute.

85. See *R.O. Eliz.*, p. 338, and note 77, p. 377 above. The nine 'titles' of the Revels Office entry were presumably painted to identify the 'vj small cities' and the 'three battlements' of the same account.

NOTES TO ILLUSTRATIONS

(*Between pages 200 and 201*)

These illustrations are grouped as nearly as possible to correspond with four major aspects of the subject:

1. Plates II–V   Actual and emblematic portrayal of people
2.   VI–XI   Architectural precedent and convention in theatre building
3.   XII–XIX   Stages for Royal Entries
4.   XX–XXXI   Actual and Emblematic devices for the identification of place on the stage.

Group 1 has affinities with Group 4; Group 3 should be studied in relation to both Group 2 and Group 4 as well as in its own right.

The Frontispiece and Plate I should be considered in relation to Group 4. The last picture (Plate XXXII) may be taken as an emblematic illumination of the theme governing Part I of this volume.

FRONTISPIECE

Inigo Jones' setting for the first scene of Sir William Davenant's Mask, *Luminalia* (1638)—Night. The spots on the design are splashes of scenic paint which fell on it when this beautiful landscape was being translated into the 'great cloth' or backcloth used for the Mask.

PLATE I, No. 1

The Water Combat, Elvetham, Hampshire, 1591. The Earl of Hertford entertained the Queen at his home at Elvetham when she was on Progress in 1591. A lake was artificially constructed, being cut in the shape of a crescent moon as a compliment to the Queen.

In this engraving (reproduced from *PQE*, i, facing p. 25, Sig. E), several of the most widely used emblematic scenic devices are illustrated. The Queen herself is shown (left, B) seated on a throne under a canopy. On the extreme right is the 'snail mount' (G). In the centre examples of the Ship (C) and the castle are well depicted. Compare the tritons with those illustrated in Vol. I, Plate XXVIII. For references to this entertainment in the text see pp. 214, 220 and 224–226 above.

PLATE II, No. 2

Thomas Cranmer, Archbishop of Canterbury (b. 1489–d. 1556), the prime architect of the Reformation in England: portrait by G. Flicke, painted 1545. National Portrait Gallery, London.

The most recent biography is J. Ridley's *Thomas Cranmer*, 1962.

PLATE III, No. 3

Thomas Cromwell, 1st Earl of Essex (b. 1485?–d. 1540) who, together with Archbishop Cranmer, launched the attack on the Catholic religious stage in England. Copying German example, he commissioned authors to write plays of violent Protestant polemic and kept a private company of players whose performances were not confined to his own household. Portrait by an unknown artist.

National Portrait Gallery, London.

PLATE IV, Nos. 4 and 5

Emblematic personifications of summer and winter by Giuseppe Arcimboldo: Kunsthistoriches Museum, Vienna. Two similar figurations by the same artist of two of the Four Elements, fire and water, are no less remarkable and are to be seen in the same gallery.

PLATE V, Nos. 6 and 7

No. 6 Emblematic representation of the life and works of Sir Henry Unton (1557?–1596): artist unknown. The detail of the wedding mask in the lower right hand part of the picture, reproduced to larger scale, forms the frontispiece to Volume I of Chambers' *The Elizabethan Stage*, and is also printed by Hodges, *The Globe Restored*, p. 163. See p. 321 above.

No. 7 The Pageants of the London Livery Companies mounted on their barges on the Thames as described by John Tatham in his *Aqua Triumphalis*, the City's entertainment for Catherine of Braganza on her arrival in London, 1662.

This hitherto unknown engraving provides us with pictures of many of the emblematic devices used to identify place in dramatic entertainments, and at a remarkably late date in their development. It includes Thetis on her 'Rock', the 'Tree', the 'Arbour', the 'Ship', various examples of the 'Throne-pavillion', and an assortment of emblematic beasts.

I am indebted to the Huntington Library for permission to reproduce this illustration from their copy of Granger's *Biographical history of England*, London, 1769–74, Vol. 12, p. 30.

PLATE VI, Nos. 8 and 9

No. 8 The triple arched screen of Exeter Cathedral, called La Pulpyte or Pulpitum, surmounted by a gallery of eleven bays, was built in the early fourteenth century in the decorated style. The painted panels in each bay of the gallery arcade were installed in the late seventeenth century. *Cf.* Vol. I, Fig. 12, p. 160: the roodscreen in the Cathedral at Laon with a stage erected in front of it.

No. 9 The Hall of the present Guildhall in Exeter (which together with the Cathedral luckily survived the bombing in the area) was built 1468–70 and remodelled between 1592 and 1594. As the Common Hall of the City, it was used for Council Meetings, for Assize Courts and, when not needed for political and legal purposes, as a hall of recreation—i.e. for stage-plays and other entertainments. Another excellent example still in use is the old town hall at Leicester.

PLATE VII, No. 10

Sketch-plan with elevations of Trinity Hall in Aldersgate Street, reproduced from *Shakespeare Survey*, 6. For the measurements and other details of this hall, see the article accompanying the Plate (C. Prouty, 'An Elizabethan Playhouse', pp. 64–74). See also pp. 185–186 and Fig. 6, pp. 50–51 above.

PLATE VIII, No. 11

Johannes de Witt: Observations on London, c. 1596. Sketch of the Swan Theatre in the common place book of Arend van Buchel in the library of the University of Utrecht. On this drawing see,

K. T. Gaedertz, *Zur Kenntnis der altenglishen Bühne* (1888)

H. B. Wheatley, *On a Contemporary Drawing of the Swan Theatre, 1596*, in N.S.S. Trans., 1887–92, p. 215

and T. F. Ordish, *Early London Theatres*, pp. 264–270.

Also: J. Q. Adams, *Shakespearean Playhouses* pp. 165–181

W. J. Lawrence, *The Physical Conditions of the Elizabethan Playhouse*

E. K. Chambers, *The Elizabethan Stage*, Vol. ii, p. 411

C. W. Hodges, *The Globe Restored*, pp. 94–95

A. M. Nagler, *Shakespeare's Stage*, pp. 9–12.

PLATE IX, No. 12

Theatre for a Tournament in Bologna, 1628. This engraving by G. B. Coriolano is remarkable in illustrating a compromise in the seating arrangements between those normal in the English public theatres (tiered galleries with boxes flanking the lists) and those customary both in banquet chambers and in Italian theatres of neo-classical design (graded scaffolds rising in banks from the 'orchestra' at the back).

This form of auditorium prefigures what, in Italy, was to become the standard design for opera-houses, a form which had already been customary in London for fifty years as the normal means of accommodating large public audiences at stage plays. It strongly suggests moreover that the tiered galleries surrounding circular lists of mediaeval Tournaments at least contributed, by way of architectural precedent, to the design of subsequent regular theatres on the continent as well as in England.

PLATE X, No. 13

The George Inn, Norton St. Philip, Somerset—front, courtyard and upper room—a fine example of the earliest form of monastic hostelry or Inn. This inn, built c. 1223, was originally the guest house of the Carthusian Priory of Hinton, the large upper room being added as a Court room and store for the local wool market. The inn was surrendered into the hands of the Crown at the dissolution of the monastery on 31st March, 1539.

I know of no evidence which associates plays or players with this inn. I have included it among the illustrations to this volume since it has not suffered any serious modification, and can be taken to represent the sort of building described by the word inn, both in London and the provinces, during the Middle Ages and the Tudor era. The contrast between the dimensions of the courtyard and the upper room is striking, the room being almost three times as large as the courtyard. The courtyard moreover is funnel-shaped while the upper room is rectangular. The full length of the room is 90 feet and the width 26 feet.

PLATE XI, No. 14

An open-air theatre in a Flemish village painted on copper, *c.* 1600, by Jan Breughel the Elder (1568–1625).

The small stage is raised about 4 feet 6 inches to 5 feet above the ground on wooden posts and is set against the front or backside of a house, possibly an inn. A single canvas booth set on the stage serves as a tiring-house and the actors' flag, posted in an upper window of the building, advertises the performance proceeding below.

As far as I know the existence of this picture has not been recorded by theatre historians, and I am grateful to the Curator of the M. H. de Young Memorial Museum, San Francisco, where I encountered it, for allowing me to publish it here. The picture was given to the Museum by Mr. and Mrs. Richard S. Rheem.

PLATE XII, Nos. 15 & 16

Pageant Arches representing the City of London and the Garden of Plenty, respectively the first and the fifth show for James I's Entry. The engravings are two of six made by W. Kip from the original designs of the "Joyner and Architect", Stephen Harrison. The device and text of the 'London' Pageant were Ben Jonson's: those for the 'Garden of Plenty' Thomas Dekker's.

The arch of London, which stood in Fenchurch Street, is supported by the figures of Mauritania and Dorica; at the top is Monarchia Britannica with Divine Wisdom at her feet. Flanking them are the Daughters of the City's Genius—to the right, Veneration, Promptitude and Vigilance; to the left, Gladness, Loving Affection and Unanimity. In the central niche below stands the 'City's Genius', flanked by 'The Councell of the City' and 'The Warlike force of the City' and with the recumbent figure of 'Thamesis' beneath them. The costumes of these figures are especially worth studying. A silk cloud screened the skyline prospect of the city from view until the King approached when it was raised by unseen hands—a mechanical device later to be borrowed and put to use by Middleton in his Lord Mayor's Show of 1613 (*Triumphs of Truth*: see pp. 214–215 above). The musicians in the side arches are the City Waits.

The Garden of Plenty—a grafting of the trellis-work arbour to the formal arch—was positioned above or alongside of the Little Conduit. It was "garnished with lesser fruits, and with all sorts of Flowers, made by Art". An image of Fortune crowns the work. Peace and Plenty sit in the upper-stage. Below them Gold and Silver support the World, flanked by Pomona and Ceres. The larger groups represent the Nine Muses (actor's right) and the Seven Liberal Sciences (actor's left). These parts were taken by the boys of St. Paul's. The little stage at the head of the stairs is occupied by Sylvanus and attendant Satyrs who provided pipe-music.

For full descriptions of these and the other arches, see Stephen Harrison, *Arches of Triumph* (see Abbreviations, p. xxiii above), Thomas Dekker's 'The Magnificent Entertainment, *Bowers' Dekker*, ii, pp. 229–309 and Ben Jonson's 'Part of the Kings Entertainment', *Works*, vii, pp. 81–109. Harrison's designs are excellently reproduced by Hodges, *The Globe Restored*; the accompanying notes are sketchy.

PLATE XIII, No. 17

A Flemish three-level pageant stage. This emblematic tableau celebrates the canonization of Ignatius Loyola by Pope Gregory XV in 1628, and is particularly useful in illustrating so many features of theatrical convention on an open stage and at so late a date. The use of the top level for heavenly beings, the placing of hangings across the arcade at middle level, together with the throne and the tree and the artificial animals on the lowest level, all hark directly back to the stage conventions of earlier times.

PLATES XIV and XV, Nos. 18 and 19

The Elector Palatine, Prince Frederick (later King of Bohemia) came to England to marry Elizabeth, eldest daughter of James I, in 1613. Returning to Heidelberg, he and his bride were welcomed with pageantry by the University.

The two engravings reproduced here represent the pageant-theatres prepared by the Faculties of Philosophy (No. 18) and Medicine (No. 19). The former supplies us with a simple adaptation of the 'timber-house' with its embroidered 'hangings' and 'painted cloths'. The 'trees' are simply small cut branches lashed with cord to the posts.

The philosophers appear to have been less well-off than their medical colleagues whose rustic-castle and classical gateway declare a far more liberal use of funds and craftsmen than do the simple globes, flags and pilasters of the timber stage.

The engravings are to be found in the Fairholt Collection in the Library of the Society of Antiquaries: *Beschreibung Der Reiss . . . des Herrn Friedrichen das Fünften . . . mit der Königlichen Princessin Elizabetha . . .*, Heidelberg, 1613, in 4°, pp. 140–141 and 144–145.

PLATE XVI, No. 20

Double pageant-stage erected in Antwerp, 1582, to greet the Duc d'Alençon on his return to the continent after his visit to England as a suitor for the hand of Queen Elizabeth I: from an engraving in *La Joyeuse et Manifique Entrée de Monsieur Francoys . . . en sa très renommée ville d'Anvers*, Antwerp, 1582.

This engraving of a theatre provided by the Chambers of Rhetorick is No. 18 in the volume and is described in detail on page 35 of the text. The pageant of Justice on the main stage is surmounted by a traditional 'glory'. The two prisons below the stage derive with equal clarity from the infernal regions of the mediaeval religious stage.

PLATE XVII, Nos. 21 and 22

Two pageant-theatre versions of the 'Temple of Janus'. No. 21 is that erected for Henry IV of France's Entry into Avignon, 1601: No. 22 is one of Ben Jonson's and Stephen Harrison's arches for James I's Entry into London, 1603. (See note to Plate XII above.) The scale is given in both instances so that it is possible to reconstruct accurate models of both and compare the detail of the one with that of the other.

No. 22 is taken from Harrison's *Arches of Triumph*: No. 21 from *Labyrinthe royal de Hercule Gaulois . . . à l'Entrée triomphante de la Royne en la cité d'Avignon*, Avignon, 1601, in the Fairholt Collection, Library of the Society of Antiquaries. The 'Temple' was the 6th Pageant presented and is described between pages 145–151. For discussion of Jonson's 'temple' see G. Wickham, 'Fêtes du couronnement de Jacques 1er' in *Fêtes de la Renaissance* I, ed. J. Jacquot, Paris, 1956.

PLATE XVIII, No. 23 and XIX, No. 24

Engravings representing two of the pageant-arches erected in 1661 for Charles II's Entry into London at the Restoration: from John Ogilby's

The Relation of His Majesties Entertainment . . ., London, 1661, fol.
(Guildhall Library).

No. 23 depicts the fourth arch. It was placed in Fleet Street and represents 'The Garden of Plenty'. It is especially interesting as a complement to Dekker's and Harrison's arch of the same name of 1603 (Plate XII, No. 16 above), since it enables us to measure accurately the change in popular taste that had occurred within the sixty years separating these two Entries. Where, in the former, fruit and flowers are spread in such profusion over the trellis-work of the arch as almost to smother its architectural shape, in the latter the only remaining suggestion of a garden in the arch is the creeper-moulding entwining its pilasters with formal regularity, and the discreetly placed emblematic paintings and banners.

No. 24. The first arch, which was set up in Leadenhall Street, provides a representation in emblematic terms of the theme of the Entry as a whole—the Triumph of Monarchy over Usurpation. Paintings illustrate the King's return to London, the punishment accorded to regicides and (centre),

> '. . . the King, mounted in calm Motion, USURPATION flying before him, a Figure with many ill-favoured Heads, some bigger, some lesser, and one particularly shooting out of his Shoulder, like CROMWELL'S; Another head upon his Rump, or Tayl; Two Harpies with a Crown chased by an Angel; Hell's Jaws opening.'

PLATES XX, XXI and XXII, Nos. 25–29

Engravings by Jacques Callot of the Combat at Barriers at the Court of Lorraine, Nancy, 1627. The engravings illustrate the printed text by Sieur Henry Humbert, *Combat à la Barrière faict en Cour de Lorraine Le 14 Feburier en l'anée présente, 1627.*

PLATE XX, No. 25

The Great Hall of the Court. The combatants are depicted with their lances at the Barrier: behind them are the triumphal cars in which they made their entries. All of these Entries are illustrated independently, and some of them are reproduced in Plates XXI and XXII. Above the cars and suspended from the roof of the hall is a large cloud, described in the text (Sig. B iib) as being made of blue cloth and capable of opening to reveal a 'glory' of figures representing the planets brightly illuminated with coloured lights. I have another engraving in my own possession which is much larger than those illustrating *Combat à la Barrière* and which shows the hall as seen from one end, looking down towards the cloud machine.

PLATE XXI, No. 26

The Entry of the Lord Chamberlain, M. le Conte de Brionne. The cortège was led by twenty pages. Behind them came the Island of Colchos with the Golden Fleece tied to a tree and guarded by a flame-breathing dragon. Next came Mercury on a Rock in front of his ethereal palace and finally the Lord Chamberlain himself disguised to represent Jason. He is depicted standing on the poop of his ship and surrounded by a private orchestra of Tritons. This entry is described in Humbert's text, Sigs. D iv and D ivb.

PLATE XXII

Three details from two separate entries:

No. 27. Monsieur de Couuonge and M. de Chalabre as Minos and Rhadamante led by Proserpine in a chariot drawn by Cerberus and escorted by thirty devils with smoking torches. The car itself represented hell-mouth, and the whole cortège is said to have frightened the audience. (Sigs. D b and D i.)

Nos. 28 and 29. Pageant cars in the train of the Prince of Lorraine representing the Sun.

No. 28. The Garden of the Hesperides. Venus, Pallas and Juno are to be seen on the upper terrace: fountains play below. These, together with the little bushes, translate the terrace into a garden. The entry is described in the text. Sig. F ii *et seq.*

No. 29. Another pageant car in the same entry: a cave in which Vulcan and the Cyclops are making armour for the Sun. See Fig. 12, p. 218 above: also pp. 231–236.

PLATE XXIII, No. 30

Another version of the rock-mountain and the rock-cave, being a pageant of Mount Parnassus and the cave called vlas-mert for the Duc d'Alençon's Entry into Antwerp, 1582. Discord, Violence and Tyranny, the inhabitants of the desolate mountain, are being driven into the cave by Apollo's rays. The contrast of the leafy shrubs on the grassy mountain with the leafless scrub and barren rock of the cave was a familiar emblematic device: it was used in England in a Disguising for Catherine of Aragon's marriage to Prince Arthur in 1501 (see *EES*, i, p. 224, and pp. 213 and 217 above). For the source of this engraving see note to Plate XVI, No. 20.

PLATES XXIV and XXV, Nos. 31, 32 and 33

Water-colour paintings of pageants for the Lord Mayor's Show, London 1616: *Chrysanaleia, the Golden Fishing,* text by Anthony Munday for the Fishmongers' Company. The text, all the drawings and extracts from the Court Ledgers of the Company were published in 1844 by J. G. Nichols (*Fishmongers Pageant*). These pictures, and the others from the same source printed in this Volume, are taken from the copy in the British Museum.

PLATE XXIV, No. 31

The fourth pageant: A lemon tree with the Five Senses sitting beneath it, and guarded by the Pelican. Cf. Dekker's 'tree' for *London's Tempe,* 1629; Fig. 11, p. 216 above.

No. 32. The fifth pageant: entitled variously 'Sir William Walworth's Bower' and 'Farrington's Tomb'. The shields carried the coats of arms of previous members of the Company who had served as Lord Mayor. Cf. Plates XII, No. 16 and XVIII, No. 23: also pp. 211–213 above.

PLATE XXV, No. 33

Merman and Mermaid of the water-show. There is another drawing of a splendid Dolphin designed to carry Arion. Cf. Dekker's sea chariot, Fig. 5, p. 47 above. In the combat at Barriers at Nancy (see Note to Plate XX) the Sieur de Visoncourt made his entry on a Dolphin of which Callot made an engraving, *op. cit.,* Sig. C iii.

No. 34. An engraving depicting Arion riding on a dolphin, one of the pageant devices for the Duc d'Alençon's Entry into Antwerp, 1582. (See notes to Plates XVI and XXIII above.)

PLATE XXVI

No. 35. Artificial animals of civic pageantry. Water colour drawing of a Leopard, used as a mount for the King of the Moors in the Lord Mayor's Show, London, 1616. (See note to Plates XXIV and XXV: also Plate XIII, No. 17.)

The costumes of the King and his attendants are worth remarking, since they resemble those for the Court Masks of the period much more clearly than is commonly supposed.

No. 36. The Elephant and Castle: engraving of a device in the Antwerp Entry of the Duc d'Alençon. See Notes to Plates XVI and XXIII: also *EES*, i, Plate VI, No. 8.

PLATE XXVII

No. 37. Water colour drawing of an angel on horseback representing 'London's Genius' in the Lord Mayor's Show, London 1616. As in Plate XXVI, No. 35, the costume is worth noticing. Cf. *EES*, i, Plate XXI, No. 30, and Note to Plates XXIV and XXV above.

Nos. 38 and 39. Two versions of the 'Pavillion' or tent. No. 38 might well serve as an illustration to the opening stage-direction of the Plot of the Seven Deadly Sins (see p. 319 above). In fact it is a detail from 'The Dream of the Emperor Constantine', one of the Arezzo frescos by Piero della Francesca. No. 39 is a tent on a battlefield which, with its windows and moulded door, more nearly resembles a small house than a tent in our sense of the word. This panel underlies the painting of Baron Vere of Tilbury by M. J. van Miereveldt in the National Portrait Gallery, London.

PLATES XXVIII and XXIX

Seventeenth century pageant-cars, English and French. Nos. 40 and 41 are water colour drawings of devices in *Chrysanaleia*, the Fishmongers' Show of 1616 in London: No. 42 is an engraving depicting a car used for Henry VI's Entry into Avignon, 1601. (See Notes to Plate XVII, No. 21 and Plates XXIV and XXV.)

No. 40. The ship called 'The Fishmongers' Esperanza, or Hope of London.' It was designed and constructed by Mr. Clay, a Carver in consultation with Anthony Munday. (See *MSC. III*, p. 90.) The Keys of St. Peter decorate the stern. The ship itself was the subject of an allegory almost as elaborate as that of Lydgate's Mumming for the Mercers Company two hundred years earlier. (See *EES*, i, pp. 201–202.)

No. 41. This car formed part of the Walworth pageant illustrated in Plate XXIV, No. 32. Anthony Munday describes it as follows:—

> 'In the highest seate of eminence sits the trumpeting Angell, who that day smote the enemy by Walworth's hand, and laid all his proud presuming in the dust. . . . King Richard [II] sitting in a degree beneath her. . . .'

The 'enemy' was Wat Tyler and his rebels. Beneath the King in the car are Truth, Vertue, Honour, Temperance, Fortitude, Zeal, Equity and Conscience, who between them are beating down the prostrate figures of Treason and Mutiny. At the back of the car sit Justice, Authority,

Law, Vigilance, Peace, Plenty and Discipline. They may be identified by the emblematic hand-properties which they carry.

No. 42. This engraving is particularly useful from a technical standpoint since the exact dimensions are given—14 feet long, 5½ feet wide and 7 feet high. The car carries sixteen people and can thus be used to gain an idea of the dimensions of other pageant cars, notably those of 'Isabella's Triumph', Brussels, 1615. See *EES*, i, Plates XVIII, XIX and XXI.

PLATE XXX

No. 43. Miniature from the *Térence* of Charles VI (early fifteenth century) in the Bibliothèque de l'Arsenal, Paris. It purports to illustrate a theatre in ancient Rome with one of Terence's Plays in performance, but in fact it depicts much more accurately the conditions contemporary with the ones described by Lydgate in his Troy Book and governing his own 'Mummings' or 'Disguisings'. (See *EES*, i, pp. 191 *et seq.*, especially pp. 193–194.)

The trouvère or poet-presenter reads his text from a pulpit in the middle of the hall (here, an arena) while the *joculatores* or jongleurs of his troupe issue masked from a tent behind him and mime the actions appropriate to the ballad which he is reading.

In England the poet-author probably retained his prerogative to serve as Presenter until late in the sixteenth century: the mimes however took over responsibility for presenting the main body of the narrative in dialogue form much earlier. The tent was correspondingly developed into the screen with tiring-house behind it. See Ch. V, p. 164 above.

No. 44. Woodcut on the first page of Horatio Vecchi's *L'Amfiparnasso* printed in Venice, 1597; from the copy in the British Museum. The poet-presenter of No. 43 has here been replaced by the Prologue (alias Chorus). The 'tent' has been extended into the full Serlian 'comic scene' of houses aligned in receding perspective. The audience, far from sitting round the stage, or even on it, has been confined to the area immediately in front of the stage. See Fig. No. 18, p. 254 above.

PLATE XXXI

No. 45. Setting for a Mask by Inigo Jones, probably *Oberon*, 1611. Although the effect aimed at is clearly a picture within the landscape convention of scenic presentation (see Frontispiece), the two units of which it is composed are among the most popular of the emblematic conventions used for identifying place. The 'palace' is here simply set inside the 'rock' or 'mountain'. From the original at Chatsworth House.

PLATE XXXII, No. 46

TRAGICUM THEATRUM; Actorum, & Casuum Tragicorum LON-DINI Publice celebratorum, Quibus Hiberniae Proregi Episcopo Can-tuariensi ac tandem Regi ipsi, Aliisque vita adempta, & ad Anglicanam Metamorphosia via est aperta. Published anonymously by Jodocum Jansonium, Amsterdam, 1649. The engraving is placed between pp. 184 and 185.

Few pictures can be more ironical. The trestle stage, with spectators standing round it and looking down upon it from roofs and windows, might be that of any street theatre in Europe in the sixteenth and seventeenth century (see Vol. I, Plate XXVI, No. 39 and in this Volume, Fig. 10, p. 180 and Plate XI, No. 14). The tiring-house in this instance however is the Banqueting Hall which Inigo Jones built for James I in the Palace of Whitehall, the scene of many of the Court Masks. The scene here proceeding on the stage is not that from a play, but the execution of Charles I. We cannot be certain whether or not Cromwell chose this site deliberately for the act of regicide, but we can at least be sure that the significance of the setting was not wasted on the audience. That is established by the author of *Tragicum Theatrum* in the title he selected for this work.

LIST OF BOOKS AND MSS.

The following list comprises only those books, articles and manuscripts directly referred to in the text and notes of this volume. A classified bibliography will accompany Volume III.

ADAMS, H. H. *English Domestic or Homiletic Tragedy, 1575 to 1642*, Columbia U.P., 1942.

ADAMS, J. C. *The Globe Playhouse—its design and equipment*, Harvard U.P., 1942.

ADAMS, J. Q. *Shakespearean Playhouses: a history of English theatres from the beginnings to the Restoration*, Cambridge, Mass. (1920).

ANGELO, S. 'The Court Festivals of Henry VII', *Bulletin of the John Rylands Library* (Oct. 1960), Vol. 3, No. 1.

ANTIQUARIAN REPERTORY. See GROSE, F.

ASCHAM, Roger. *The Schoolmaster*, ed. E. Arber, English Reprints, 1870.

BACON, N. *Annals of Ipswich*, 1884.

BALE, John. *The Dramatic Writings of John Bale*, ed. J. S. Farmer, 1908.

—— *God's Promises*, ed. J. S. Farmer in Tudor Facsimile Texts, 1908.

—— *Three Laws*, ed. J. S. Farmer in Tudor Facsimile Texts, 1908.

BENTLEY, G. E. *The Jacobean and Caroline Stage*, 5 vols., 1941–56.

BLAND, D. S. 'The Barriers: Guildhall Library MS. 4160', *The Guildhall Miscellany*, No. 6 (Feb. 1956).

BOAS, F. S. *University Drama in the Tudor Age*, 1914.

BOWERS, F. See DEKKER, Thomas.

BUCER, Martin. *De Regno Christi*, London, 1557.

BULLEN, A. H. *The Works of George Peele*, 2 vols., 1888. See also Middleton, Thomas.

CAMPBELL, L. B. *Scenes and Machines on the English Stage during the Renaissance*, 1923: reprint 1961.

—— *Shakespeare's 'Histories'—mirrors of Elizabethan Policy*, 1947.

CARDI, P. N. *Venuta della Serenissima Christina di Loreno*, Florence, 1590.

CHAMBERS, E. K. *Aurelian Townshend's Poems and Masks*, 1912.

—— *The Elizabethan Stage*, 4 vols., 1923.

—— *The Mediaeval Stage*, 2 vols., 1903.

CHAPMAN, George. See PARROTT, T. M.

CHURCHYARDE, Thomas. *A discourse of the Queenes Majesties entertainement in Suffolk & Norffolk*, London, 1578.

CLARK, A. M. 'Two Pageants by Thomas Heywood', *Theatre Miscellany*, for Lutterell Society, No. 14, 1953.

COLLIER, J. P. *Annals of the Stage*, 3 vols., 1831.

CRAIK, T. W. *The Tudor Interlude*, 1958.

DANIEL, Samuel. See Evans, H. A.

DAVENANT, Sir William. *The Works of Sʳ. William Davenant Kᵗ, consisting of those which were formerly printed, and those which he design'd for the press: now published out of the authors original copies*, T. N. for Henry Herringman, London, 1673, fol.

—— *The Dramatic Works*, see Maidment, J.

—— *'Love and Honour' and 'The Siege of Rhodes'*, ed. J. W. Tupper, 1909.

DEKKER, Thomas. *The Dramatic Works*, ed. Fredson Bowers, 4 vols., 1953–61.

DE VERE, S. du C. See Vassari.

DIXON, R. W. *History of the Church of England*, 6 vols., 3rd ed. 1895–1902.

DRYDEN, John. *Essay of Dramatic Poesie*, ed. with introduction and notes by D. Nicol Smith, 1900.

DUNLAP, Rhodes. *The Poems of Thomas Carew*, 1949.

EBSWORTH, J. W. *The Poems and Masks of Thomas Carew*, 1893.

EDWARDES, R. *Damon and Pithias*, Malone Society Reprints, 1957.

ELIZABETH, Princess. See Entries.

ELIZABETH I. See Nichols, J.

ENTRIES, Royal. Princess Elizabeth, Queen of Bohemia. *Beschreibung Der Reiss: Empfahung des Ritterlichen Ordens: Volbringung des Heyraths: und glücklicher Heimfrihung: wie auch der Einfrihrung: gehaltener Ritterspiel und Freudenfests: des Herrn Friedrichen dess Fünften, Pfaltzgraven bey Rhein, mit der Königlichen Princessin Elizabetha, Jacobi des Ersten, Königs in Gruss Britannien, einigen Tochter*, 4° Heidlburg, 1613.

—— Francis, Duc d'Alençon. *La Joyeuse et magnifique Entrée de Monsieur Francoys fils de France, et frère unicque du Roy, par la grace de Dieu, Duc de Brabant, d'Anjou, Alençon, Berri, &c. en sa très renommée ville d'Anvers*. Antwerp, 1582, chez Christophle Plantin.

—— Henry IV of France. *Labyrinthe royal de Hercule Gaulois triomphant sur le suiect des Fortunes, Batailles . . . de . . . Henry IIII Roy de France . . . Représenté à l'Entrée triomphante de la Royne en la cité d'Avignon, Le 19 Novembre l'An MDC*. Avignon, chez Jacques Bramereau (1601).

—— King Charles II. See Ogilby, John and Tatham, John.

—— King Christian IV of Denmark. See Robarts, Henry.

—— King James I. See Harrison, Stephen.

EVANS, H. A. *English Masques*, with an introduction, 1910.

EVEN, Edward van. *L'Omgang de Louvain*, Brussels and Louvain, 1863.

EXECUTION, King Charles I. See Tragicum Theatrum.

FARMER, J. S. See Bale, John.

FERNE, Sir John. *The Blazon of Gentry*, London, 1586.

FEUILLERAT, A. 'Documents relating to the Office of the Revels in the Time of Queen Elizabeth', in *Materialen zur kunde des alteren Englischen Dramas*, ed. W. Bang, vol. XXI, Louvain, 1908.

—— 'Documents relating to the Revels at Court in the Time of King Edward VI and Queen Mary' (The Loseley MSS.) in *Materialen zur kunde des alteren Englischen Dramas*, ed. W. Bang, vol. XLIV, Louvain, 1914.

FOAKES, R. A. and RICKERT, R. T. *Henslowe's Diary*, ed. 1961.

FOAKES, R. A. 'The Significance of Henslowe's Diary' in *Philologica Progensia*, III (1960).

FRANCIS, Duc d'Alençon. See ENTRIES.

FURNIVALL, F. J. *Robert of Brunne's 'Handlyng of Synne'*, ed. for E.E.T.S., 1901.

GAEDERTZ, K. T. *Zur Kenntnis der altenglischen Bühne*, 1888.

GARDINER, H. C. *Mysteries' End: an investigation of the last days of the medieval religious stage*. Yale Studies in English, 1946.

GILDERSLEEVE, V. C. *Government Regulation of the Elizabethan Drama*, N.Y., 1908: reprint, 1961.

GORDON, D. J. '*Hymenaei*; Ben Jonson's Masque of Union', Journal of the Warburg and Courtauld Institute, viii (1945).

GOSSON, Stephen. *The Schoole of Abuse, containing a pleasaunt invective against Poets, Pipers, Plaiers, Jesters and such like Caterpillers of a Commonwelth*, London, 1579. Ed. E. Arber, *English Reprints*, together with *A Short Apologie of the Schoole of Abuse* (1579), 1868.

—— *Playes Confuted in five Actions* (1582), reprinted by W. C. Hazlitt in *English Drama* (q.v.).

GREENE, Robert. *Plays and Poems*, ed. with notes by J. C. Collins, 2 vols., 1905.

—— *The Scottish History of James the Fourth*, Malone Society Reprints, 1921.

—— '*King James the Fourth*', ed. A. Thorndike in *Minor Elizabethan Drama* (*II*)—*Pre-Shakespearean Comedies*, 1910.

GREG, W. W. *Henslowe's Diary*, ed. with commentary in 2 vols., 1904–08.

—— *Henslowe Papers, being documents supplementary to his Diary*, 1907.

GROSE, F. *The Antiquarian Repertory* (ed. for the Society of Antiquaries), 4 vols., London, 1775; 2nd ed., 4 vols., 1807. (Referred to as Ant. Rep.)

GUALTEROTI, R. *Della descrizione del regale apparatu fatto nella città di Firenze, per la venuta, e per le nozze di Christina di Loreno*, Florence, 1589, in fol.

HARRISON, Stephen. *The arches of triumph erected in honour of K. James I . . . 15 March 1603*, London 1604, fol.

HAY, D. *Polydore Vergil, Renaissance historian and man of letters*, 1952.

HAZLITT, W. C. *The English Drama and Stage under the Tudor and Stuart Princes, 1543–1642*, printed for Roxburghe Library, 1869.

HENRY IV, King of France. See ENTRIES.

HENRY VIII, King of England. See LETTERS AND PAPERS; STATUTES OF THE REALM.

HERFORD, C. See JONSON, Ben.

HERMANN, M. *Forschungen sur deutschen Theatergeschicte des Mittelalters und der Renaissance*, 1914.

HEYWOOD, Thomas. *The Dramatic Works*, 5 vols., London, 1874.

HOLDEN, W. P. *Anti-Puritan Satire, 1572–1642*. Yale Studies in English, 1954.

HOLINSHED, R. *Chronicles of England*, London, 1586, fol.

LIST OF BOOKS AND MSS.

HOLSBOER, S. W. *L'Histoire de la Mise en Scène dans le Théâtre Français, 1600–1657*, Paris, 1933.

HOMILIES, Book of. *Certaine Sermons or homilies appointed to be read in Churches, in the time of the late Queen Elizabeth of famous memory, and now thought fit to be reprinted*, 2 vols. in 1, London, 1623.

HORNE, D. H. *The Life and Minor Works of George Peele*, New Haven, 1952.

HOSLEY, R. 'The Gallery over the Stage in the Public Playhouse of Shakespeare's Time', *Shakespeare Quarterly*, Vol. VIII (1957).

—— 'Shakespeare's use of a Gallery over the Stage', *Shakespeare Survey*, 10. (1957).

HOTSON, L. *The Commonwealth and Restoration Stage*, Harvard U.P., 1928.

—— *The First Night of Twelfth Night*, 1954.

—— *Shakespeare's Wooden 'O'*, 1960.

HUMBERT, Le Sieur Henry. *Combat à la Barrière Faict en cour de Lorraine le 14 Feburier en l'anée présente, 1627*, Nancy, 1627.

HUNNINGHER, B. "A Baroque Architect Among Painters and Poets", *Theatre Research*, Vol. III, No. 1 (1961).

JACQUOT, J. *Fêtes de la Renaissance I*, Paris, 1956.

—— *Fêtes de la Renaissance II*, Paris, 1956–60.

JONSON, Ben. *Complete Works*, ed. C. Herford and P. Simpson, 10 vols., 1925–52.

—— *The Mask of Queens*, Fac. ed., King's Printers, 1930.

JOSEPH, B. R. *Elizabethan Acting*, 1951.

KEITH, W. G. 'The Art of Scenic Decoration', *The Builder*, Vol. CVII (1914).

—— 'The Designs for the first Movable Scenery on the English Public Stage', *Burlington Magazine*, Vol. XXV.

—— 'A Theatre Project', *Burlington Magazine*, Vol. XXXI.

KERNODLE, G. R. *From Art to Theatre*, Chicago, 1944.

—— 'The Medieval Pageant Waggons of Louvain', *Theatre Annual*, Vol. x (1952), N.Y.

KNIGHTS, L. C. *Drama and Society in the Age of Ben Jonson*, 1937.

LAMB, J. *Collection of Documents from Corpus Christi College Cambridge*, 1839.

LANIER, W. H. *The First English Actresses*, N.Y., 1930.

LAWRENCE, W. J. *The Physical Conditions of the Elizabethan Playhouse*, 1927.

LECLERC, H. *Les origines italiennes de l'architecture théâtrale moderne*, Paris, 1946.

LEES-MILNE, J. *The Age of Inigo Jones*, 1953.

LEISHMAN, J. B. *Three Parnassus Plays (1598–1601)*, ed. with an introduction and commentary, 1949.

LEONARDO DA VINCI. *A treatise on Painting*, trans. J. F. Rigaud, 1892.

LETTERS & PAPERS. Henry VIII, Domestic, Vol. XII (1537).

LEWIS, C. S. 'English Literature in the sixteenth century, excluding drama', *Oxford History of English Literature*, Vol. III, 1954.

LOGAN, W. H. See MAIDMENT, J.

LOUKANSKI, G. J. K. *Andrea Palladio, sa vie, son œuvre*, Paris, 1927.

LUCAS, F. L. *The Complete Works of John Webster*, 4 vols., ed. 1927.
LYLY, John. *Complete Works*, ed. R. W. Bond, 3 vols., 1902.
—— 'Endimion', ed. A. H. Thorndike in *Minor Elizabethan Drama II—Pre-Shakespearean Comedies*, 1910.

MACHYN, Henry. *The Diary*, ed. for Camden Society by J. G. Nichols, Vol. XLII, 1842.
MAIDMENT, J. & LOGAN, W. H. *The Dramatic Works of Sir William Davenant with Prefatory Memoir and Notes*, 5 vols., 1872–74.
MALONE SOCIETY. *Collections, I, II, III & V* (see p. xxiv above). *Reprints:* 'Damon and Pithias' (see Edwardes, R.); 'Bale's King Johan' (1931); 'James the Fourth' (see Greene, R.).
MARLOWE, Christopher. *The Works*, ed. C. F. Tucker Brooke, 1925.
McKERROW, R. B. 'Booksellers, Printers and the Stationers' Trade', *Shakespeare's England*, (2 vols., 1916), Vol. ii, pp. 212–239.
MIDDLETON, Thomas. *The Works*, ed. A. H. Bullen, 8 vols., 1885–86.
MUNDAY, Anthony. See NICHOLS, J. G.; also Appendix F, pp. 337–338 above.
MUNRO, J. *The London Shakespeare*, 6 vols., 1957.
MURRAY, J. C. *English Dramatic Companies*, 1558–1642, 2 vols., 1910.
MSS. British Museum. *Cotton, Vit. F. V.* Henry Machyn's Diary. See MACHYN, Henry.
—— *Harleian, 525. 2.* The Romance of King Robert of Sicily.
—— *Harleian, 538.* John Stow's Survey of London.
—— *Harleian, 2177.* Inventory of Goods in Trinity Church, Chester.
MSS. Dulwich College. *Muniment 49.* The Hope Contract.
MSS. Hereford, Cathedral Library. *Register of John de Trilleck.*
—— ————, Town Hall. *The Great Black Book.*

NAGLER, A. M. *Shakespeare's Stage*, 1958.
—— 'Theater der Medici', *Maske und Kothurn, IV* (1958), No. 2/3.
NEALE, J. M. *Queen Elizabeth*, 1934.
NICHOL SMITH, D. 'Authors and Patrons' in *Shakespeare's England* (2 vols., 1916), Vol. ii, pp. 182–211.
—— See DRYDEN, John.
NICHOLS, John. *The Progresses and Public Processions of Queen Elizabeth*, 3 vols., 1788.
—— *The Progresses, Processions and Magnificent Festivities of King James the First*, 4 vols., 1828.
NICHOLS, J. G. *The Fishmongers Pageant on Lord Mayor's Day 1616 devised by Anthony Munday*, 1844. fol.
—— See MACHYN, Henry.
NICOLL, A. *Stuart Masques and the Renaissance Stage*, 1937.
NORTHBROOKE, John. *A Treatise wherein Dicing, Dauncing, Vaine playes, or Enterludes ... commonly used on the Sabbath day are reproved by the Authoritie of the word of God and auntient writers*, London, 1577.
NORTON, T. See SACKVILLE, T.

OGILBY, John. *The Relation of his Majesties Entertainment*, London, 1661, fol. (Charles II's Entry).

ORDISH, T. F. *Early London Theatres*, 1894.

OSBORN, J. M. See WHYTHORNE, T.

PALMER, W. J. *Perlustration of Great Yarmouth*, 3 vols., 1872–75.

PARROT, T. M. *The Plays and Poems of George Chapman, edited with Introductions and Notes*, 2 vols., 1910–14.

PARRY, J. H. *The Register of John de Trilleck, Bishop of Hereford (A.D. 1344–1361)*: transcribed and edited with an introduction for the Cantilupe Soc., 1910.

PAVONI, Guiseppe. *Diario descritto da Guiseppe Pavoni Delle Feste celebrata nella solenissima Nozze del Serenissimi Spossi, il Sig: Gran Duchi di Toscanna*, Bologna, 1589.

PEELE, George. See BULLEN, A. H. and HOME, D. H.

PHILANDER. *Marci Vitruvii Pollionis viri Professionis Peritissimi de Architectura Libri Decum cum notis Philandri et sexte Frontini*, Rome, 1544, 8vo. (French ed. in fol., 1547).

POLLARD, A. W. *Shakespeare's Fight with the Pirates and the Problems of the Transmission of his Text*, 1917.

POLLUX, J. *Onomastion*, Basle, 1536, 4o.

PROUTY, C. T. 'An Early Elizabethan Playhouse', *Shakespeare Survey 6* (1953).

PRYNNE, William. *Histrio-Mastix. The Players scourge, or actors tragedie*, London, 1633.

PUTTENHAM, Richard. *Art of English Poesie*, 1589: ed. E. Arber, English Reprints, 1869.

RESPUBLICA. *'Lost' Tudor Plays*, ed. J. S. Farmer for Early English Dramatists Series, 1907.

REYNOLDS, G. F. *The Staging of Elizabethan Plays at the Red Bull Theatre, 1605–1625*, 1940.

RICKERT, R. T. See FOAKES, R. A.

RIDLEY, J. *Thomas Cranmer*, 1962.

RIGAUD, J. F. See LEONARDO DA VINCI.

RINGLER, W. 'The First Phase of the Elizabethan Attack on the Stage, 1558–1579', Huntington Library Quarterly, Vol. V (1942).

ROBARTS, Henry. *The Most royall and Honourable entertainment*, of the famous and renowmed (*sic*) King, *Christiern the fourth*, London, 1606.

ROBERTSON, Jean. 'Rapports du poète et de l'artiste dans les cortèges du Lord Maire'', *Fêtes de la Renaissance I*, ed. J. Jacquot, Paris, 1956.

ROSENFELD, S. *Strolling Players & Drama in the Provinces, 1660–1795*, 1939.

SACKVILLE, T. and NORTON, T. 'Gorborduc', ed. A. H. Thorndike in *Minor Elizabethan Drama—Pre-Shakespearean Tragedies*, n.d.

SALTER, F. M. *Mediaeval Drama in Chester*, 1954.

SCHRADE, L. *La Représentation d'Edipo Tiranno an Teatro Olimpico*, Paris, 1960.

SHAKESPEARE SURVEY. See HOSLEY, R.; PROUTY, C.; and SHAPIRO, I. A.

SHAPIRO, I. A. 'The Bankside Theatres: Early Engravings', *Shakespeare Survey I*, 1948.

SHERGOLD, N. D. *The Staging of the Secular Drama in Spain, 1550–1700*, Ph.D. Thesis, Cambridge, 1953.

SHUTE, Sir John. *First and Chief Grounds of Architecture*, London, 1563.

SIMPSON, P. See JONSON, Ben.

SISSON, J. *Lost Plays of Shakespeare's Age*, 1936.

SOUTHERN, R. *Changeable Scenery*, 1952.

—— *The Mediaeval Theatre in the Round*, 1957.

STATUTES OF THE REALM. 9 vols. in 10, 1810–22.

STEVENS, J. 'Music in Mediaeval Drama', *Proceedings of the Musical Association*, 84th Session, 1957/58.

STOW, John. *The Annales, or generall chronicle of England*, with continuation by Edmond Howes, London, 1615.

—— *The Survey of London*, ed. C. L. Kingsford, 2 vols., 1908.

SYDNEY, Sir Philip. *An Apology for Poetry*, ed. with introduction and notes by J. Churton Collins, 1941.

TATHAM, J. *Aqua Triumphalis* (being the account of London's reception of Catherine of Braganza on the river Thames), London, 1662.

TILLYARD, E. M. *The English Renaissance: fact or fiction?* 1952.

TOWNSHEND, Aurelian. See CHAMBERS, E. K.

TRAGICUM THEATRUM; *Actorum, & Casuum Tragicorum LONDINI Publice celebratorum, Quibus Hiberniae Proregi Episcopo Cantuarensi: ac tandem Regi ipsi, Aliisque vita adempta, & ad Anglicanam Metamorphosia via est aperta.* Published anonymously by Jodocum Jansonium, Amsterdam, 1649.

TYREMAN, L. *The Life and Time of the Reverend John Wesley, M.A.*, 5th ed., 3 vols., 1890.

UNDERDOWN, P. T. 'Religious opposition to the licensing of the Bristol and Birmingham Theatres', *University of Birmingham Historical Journal*, Vol. VI (1958) No. 2.

VAIL MOTTER, T. H. *The School Drama in England*, 1929.

VASSARI, G. *The Lives of the most eminent Painters, Sculptors and Architects*, trans. S. Du C. De Vere, 1912–14.

VECCHI, Horatio. *L'Amfiparnasso*, Venice, 1597.

VENEZKY, A. S. *Pageantry on the Shakespeare Stage*, 1951.

WARTON, Thomas. *A History of English Poetry* (a full reprint—text and notes—of ed. London, 1778–81), London, 1840.

WEBSTER, John. See LUCAS, F. L.

WEINER, A. B. 'Elizabethan Interior and Aloft Scenes: A Speculative Essay' *Theatre Survey II* (1961).

—— *Phillippe de Mézière's description of the FESTUM PRAESENTATIONIS BEATAE MARIAE*, Yale, 1958.

WELSFORD, E. *The Court Masque*, 1927.

—— 'Italian Influence on the English Court Masques', M.L.R. (Oct. 1923).

WHYTHORNE, Thomas. *The Autobiography of Thomas Whythorne*, ed. J. M. Osborn, 1961.

WILLIAMSON, W. 'Notes on the Decline of Provincial Drama in England, 1530–1642', *American Educational Theatre Journal*, Vol. XII (1961).

WILLS, R. *De Re Poetica*, ed. for Lutterell Soc. by A. D. S. Fowler, 1958.

WITHINGTON, R. *English Pageantry: An Historical Outline*, 2 vols., Harvard U. P., 1918–20.

YOUNG, K. '*An Elizabethan Defence of the Stage*', (Wisconsin Shakespeare Studies 103) 1916.

—— 'Phillippe de Mézière's Dramatic office for the presentation of the Virgin', P.M.L.A., Vol. XXVI (1911).

INDEX